PENGUIN BOOKS

A DIARY OF THE LADY

'Made me laugh out loud and stay up so late reading
it that I shot terribly on the first drive' Mrs Moneypenny,
Financial Times

'Surprisingly brilliant' A. A. Gill

'Amusing' *Sunday Telegraph*

'Boisterous and compulsive' Roger Lewis, Books of the Year,
Sunday Express

'Fabulous, wonderfully written and a total hoot' Deborah Ross

'I devoured the whole thing with huge joy. It is a
wonderful book, so brave and so honest and so funny
and so touching. What a heroic struggle like Horatius
keeping the bridge' Jilly Cooper

'It is only when you read this engaging diary that you
realize just how much sweat and fury has gone into dragging
this old Lady on to the dance floor of modern life'
Emma Soames, *British Journalism Review*

'Rachel Johnson edits *The Lady* but doesn't write like one,
thank goodness. Instead, her memoir unwittingly reveals
some unbecoming truths about class, race, sex, media, money
and power. *A Diary of The Lady: My First Year as Editor*
is a mad scramble through the madly scrambling world
that is magazine publishing' Bidisha

'Confidential, hectic and clever' Sheena Joughin,
Times Literary Supplement

'I love stories of pluck among the ruins of print'
Toronto Star

ABOUT THE AUTHOR

Rachel Johnson is married to Ivo Dawnay, has three children, and lives in London and Somerset. Her previous books include *The Mummy Diaries*, *Shire Hell*, and the international bestseller *Notting Hell*, all of which are published by Penguin.

A DIARY OF

The Lady

My First Year *and a half* /as Editor

RACHEL JOHNSON

PENGUIN BOOKS

PENGUIN BOOKS

Published by the Penguin Group

Penguin Books Ltd, 80 Strand, London WC2R ORL, England

Penguin Group (USA) Inc., 375 Hudson Street, New York, New York 10014, USA

Penguin Group (Canada), 90 Eglinton Avenue East, Suite 700, Toronto, Ontario, Canada M4P 2Y3
(a division of Pearson Penguin Canada Inc.)

Penguin Ireland, 25 St Stephen's Green, Dublin 2, Ireland (a division of Penguin Books Ltd)

Penguin Group (Australia), 250 Camberwell Road,
Camberwell, Victoria 3124, Australia (a division of Pearson Australia Group Pty Ltd)

Penguin Books India Pvt Ltd, 11 Community Centre, Panchsheel Park,
New Delhi – 110 017, India

Penguin Group (NZ), 67 Apollo Drive, Rosedale, Auckland 0632, New Zealand
(a division of Pearson New Zealand Ltd)

Penguin Books (South Africa) (Pty) Ltd, 24 Sturdee Avenue, Rosebank, Johannesburg 2196,
South Africa

Penguin Books Ltd, Registered Offices: 80 Strand, London WC2R 0RL, England

www.penguin.com

First published by Fig Tree 2010
Published in Penguin Books with seven new chapters 2011

1

Printed in England by Clays Ltd, St Ives plc

ISBN: 978–0–718–19232–7

www.greenpenguin.co.uk

MIX
Paper from
responsible sources
FSC
www.fsc.org   FSC™ C018179

Penguin Books is committed to a sustainable
future for our business, our readers and our
planet. This book is made from paper certified
by the Forest Stewardship Council.

To all readers of The Lady *— may our tribe increase*

'If you ask me what was more terrifying, putting a helicopter down in a 25m² clearing in the Florida Everglades or running a genteel ladies' magazine in the centre of London, I'd say the latter.'

Ben Budworth, Sunday Express, 12 April 2009

Acknowledgements

I would like to thank everyone in Bedford Street from the bottom of my heart – and, um, most importantly, *in advance*, before they read what follows – for being so sporting. I would like to single out for a gold medal Ben Budworth, who has put in and continues to put in dazzling, Olympian displays of tolerance and forbearance. I would also like to thank the Budworth family as a whole for entrusting the editorship of their beloved ancestral magazine into my hands. On the editorial and production side at Penguin, Jenny Lord and Juliet Annan, respectively my editor and publisher at Fig Tree, have been terrific in getting behind the project and seeing it through in double-quick time, especially the frighteningly efficient and steely Jenny. Sarah Day copy-edited rapidly and sympathetically in between – as one thrilling email told me – 'reading bits out' to her weary family. Penguin's Katherine Stroud and Alex Elam, thank you for all you do on the Dark Side to do with publicity, marketing, rights, etc. – you know – and finally, thanks as ever to my agent, the legendary and laconic Peter Straus.

Cast List

*Cast of main characters at 39/40 Bedford Street,
job description, and dates of service:*

MR BEN BUDWORTH: publisher and chief executive, 2008–
MR ADAM BUDWORTH: barrister and director of *The Lady*, 2008–
MRS JULIA BUDWORTH: matriarch and director of *The Lady*, 2008–
MRS MAUREEN GOODMAN: PA to the publisher, 1996–
MS ARLINE USDEN: eighth editor of *The Lady*, 1993–2009
MS RACHEL JOHNSON: ninth editor of *The Lady*, 2009–
MISS GILLIAN SPICKERNELL: PA to the editor, 2003–
MS LINDSAY FULCHER: assistant editor, 1993–2010
MS CLAIRE WOOD: design consultant, 2008–
MS CHRISSIE TAYLOR: chief sub-editor, 2000–
MS CAROLYN HART: editorial consultant, 2009–
MRS JUDY LAMB: production manager, 1979–
MR NIC BOIZE AKA 'B-CAL': marketing consultant, 2000–
MS JANINA POGORZELSKI: features editor, 1995–
MS EDWINA LANGLEY AKA 'BEENIE': marketing and PR, 2009–
MISS KATH HANLEY: classified ads manager, 1976–
MRS JOAN BISHOP: classified ads administrator, 1976–
MR MATT WARREN AKA 'THE MALE FROM THE MAIL': 2010–
MISS HELEN ROBINSON AKA 'HELS': head of sales 2010–
MRS ROS PAPI: telephonist, 1995–
MR THOMAS BOWLES AKA 'UNCLE TOM': owner of 39/40 Bedford
Street, resident proprietor of *The Lady*, 1959–2008
COCO: office dog 2009–

"THE LADY." 20th April, 1899.

The Lady

6d

Per Post 6½d.

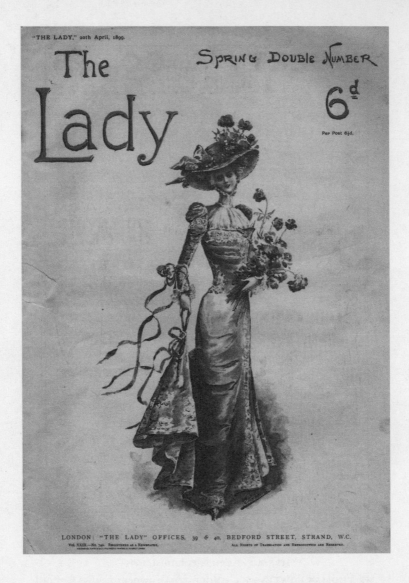

LONDON: "THE LADY" OFFICES, 39 & 40, BEDFORD STREET, STRAND, W.C.

Vol. XXIX.—No. 740. Registered as a Newspaper.   All Rights of Translation and Reproduction are Reserved.

JUNE

9 June 2009

Was working after a light lunch in the raw bar of Daylesford Organic on Westbourne Grove (slogan: 'A taste of the Gloucestershire countryside in Notting Hill'), i.e., was back in bed having an iNap. Those who don't go to offices will be familiar with this posture – stack of pillows behind head, MacBook on duvet, flipping between Word document, Google, the *Daily Mail* website, Facebook and email while labouring to crank out what one hopes will be bestselling novel. Then it came through, the contact that was to change my life.

It was from Penguin. From my publicist, Katherine. My husband makes a hollow noise – like a sheep with croup – when the words 'my publicist' come out of my mouth. He says that is the one position supernumerary to staffing requirements in any Johnson household. But anyway. Here it is:

From: Katherine Stroud
To: Rachel Johnson
Sent: 9 June 2009 15:33
Subject: FW: Rachel Johnson

Hello!

Hope you're very well – see below email re: *The Lady*.

Kx

From: Ben Budworth
To: Katherine Stroud
Sent: 9 June 2009 14:53
Subject: Rachel Johnson

Dear Katherine

Many thanks for agreeing to act as intermediary. As I explained on the telephone, I am the publisher of *The Lady* magazine and would be keen to have a chat with your client Rachel.

I don't however appear to be having much luck finding a telephone number for her.

All my telephone numbers are below.

Many thanks and regards
Ben

Ben Budworth
Publisher/CEO
The Lady magazine
39/40 Bedford Street
London
WC2E 9ER

The Lady?

All I knew about *The Lady* was what all middle-class mothers of a certain age and income bracket knew about *The Lady* – before, that is, the internet took over the world. It was where you got a nanny from. End of. I didn't know it was still in existence. I'd never read it, not even when I'd advertised for help in it, not even when a nice woman called Beverly came all the way from Devon to interview me in my Notting Hill habitat for a dear feature called 'My Favourite Things', which is, as you would expect, about kittens in mittens and parcels tied up with string. (I talked about Agas, Exmoor, Land Rovers, my family and my beloved dog, Coco.) I had never knowingly seen it on a shelf, nor heard anyone mention it, for a decade and a half (Ludo is sixteen, Charlotte Millicent fifteen, Oliver thirteen, and I haven't had so much as an au pair for five years). I thought, in fact, that it was extinct.

But still. Ben Budworth, 'Publisher/CEO', was keen. That meant something. For jobbing freelancers like me there is but one certainty in the digital age. We are like miners under Margaret Thatcher – guaranteed only built-in obsolescence instead of a pension. So we must take what crumbs we can. Despite my current lucrative gig with a many-sectioned Sunday newspaper, not to mention my sundry other commitments (my third novel is supposedly nearing completion and I am about to launch my first, *Notting Hell*, in France), I duly pinged off a precautionary email back to 'my publicist', Katherine, in which I asked whether she'd given Ben my number. She said no. So in an expansive way – as if taking out eggs and plopping them down in different baskets, and chucking irons into various fires – I sent B. Budworth my mobile number.

Now, I gave him my mobile number because I didn't want to talk on the telephone by my bed (where I fully intended to stay until my daughter came home from school), which has a loud buzzing noise on the line. And I didn't want to have to go downstairs to take the call. I was too comfortable where I was. It was then that I remembered.

When I was a thrusting young reporter on the *Financial Times*, spending my working day writing about bond markets and the coupon on the 2013 gilt, I'd left a gripping press conference at the Institution of Mechanical Engineers (or Association of Accounting Actuaries – can't remember) about the reweighting of the Retail Price Index or something, and had been dawdling past an imposing six-storey Georgian building in Bedford Street. It reared

over Covent Garden in a smart livery of pinkish cream and gold
and had the elegant title '*The Lady*' and the claim 'Rebuilt in 1861'
picked out in gold paint on the façade, as if a Merchant Ivory film
set had been plonked and forgotten amid the coffee shops and
burger bars and bland retailers of twentieth-century tat.

As I passed, I'd thought to myself, my goodness, what a mag-
nificence of an edifice. I'd paused in front of a double glass door
saying 'General Enquiries' on one side and 'Classified Ads' on the
other, also picked out in gold on the smart, polished glass. I'd gazed
at the covers of *The Lady* magazine mounted for display inside
glass cases that passers-by passed by without a glance, and read
some of the cover lines. This week was, I noted, a 'You and Your
Health' special:

> What to do about watery eyes?
> Do you have ovarian cancer? The tell-tale signs

... along with:

> Autumn colour
> Tasty treats – moist cakes the grandchildren will love

Enchanted, as if guided by some unseen, gloved hand, I entered.
Within, it looked like an Irish funeral parlour *circa* 1948, with a sad
vase of flowers on a side table to the left, and straight ahead, my
passage was barred by a sort of pub entrance with a wooden
counter containing a flap you had to flip up to pass through. There
was no one in sight. Telephones buzzed, and I heard genteel voices
answer out of shot, as if they had all the time in the world, 'Good
afternoon. *The Lady* magazine.' No one came.

There was a white button on the counter with a bell, and a sign
propped up alongside it, which said, 'Please ring.'

I stood there wondering what to do. An *Alice in Wonderland* moment. I had decided already that this would make an amusing featurette in the Saturday paper, which would allow me to show my range beyond bonds and gilts. I could already see my piece about *The Lady* in the *FT*'s weekend section, the arch headline. I therefore determined to make a general enquiry forthwith.

And so I'd pressed the button. Eventually, a woman wearing a long tweed skirt beneath which – I peered closely to confirm – a pair of greying fluffy slippers peeked out shuffled to the counter, and regarded me with suspicion. With her assistance, I arranged to interview the editor, a woman of indeterminate age called Arline Usden, at a date several weeks hence.

Fast-forward to the appointed day. In my smartest suit, I'd turned up again. As far as I remember (i.e. not very far), another middle-aged woman took notes, for an unspecified reason. I was given a cup of tea on a saucer, shortbread, and – a strange but nonetheless welcome touch, this – a freshly laundered, striped blue and white tea-towel, as if I would need to dry myself off afterwards.

I was absolutely charmed by the whole experience. The piece duly appeared in the Weekend *FT*. All I can remember is a phrase about 'teacups rattling in the Home Counties' because – shock, horror – Arline Usden was shifting the small ads and classifieds from the front to the back of the magazine, and the editorial from the back to the front. Apart from that, my mind is blank. That was the sum total of my previous experience and knowledge of *The Lady*: I once hired a nanny through its pages. And I once interviewed the previous editor.

And now a Ben Budworth was after me. It sounded like a made-up name, very Gilbert and Sullivan. I wondered what he wanted. Whether it was a wind-up. I hadn't – cough – edited a magazine since 1986, and that was a student magazine. But I had been writing for nationals continuously since then, and how hard could doing a weekly be, anyway? So I whizzed off my mobile number.

Please ring, I thought.

10 June 2009

Was in bed iNapping – it was after all mid-afternoon – and my BlackBerry vibrated.

'Ben Budworth here,' came a bouncy public-school voice. 'Thank you for your email. Did you give me a mobile number with one digit wrong on purpose?' He read out my number, one digit awry, in a staccato Alpha-Bravo-Delta voice. I wondered whether he'd ever been in the army. 'I got a builder instead of you. Twice. I had to go back to Penguin. Are you trying to make it difficult for me on purpose?'

'No, no,' I protested, apologizing. When I started out in journalism, I was forced to undergo an expensive, six-month residential training course paid for by my future employers at some outpost of the Westminster Press in Hastings. This was a precondition to my becoming a graduate trainee on the *FT*. In those palmy days of the trade, a stint in the provinces on a local paper, or failing that an accredited training course, was a union requirement before bylined Oxbridge graduates could be wafted on to national newspapers. Despite my six months on the south coast, I have no Pitman shorthand and a scanty recollection of media law, but I am horrified if I get a name or date wrong in print. Giving out a duff mobile number was the sort of thing girls did at discos to losers, and reeked of smugness. I felt very much on the back foot.

'Anyway, I've got you now,' he said. And then he came straight to the point within seconds. 'I'm looking for a new editor for *The Lady* magazine,' he said, a note of pride entering his voice.

At this point, for some reason, previous covers I'd viewed in disbelief, featuring vases of daffodils, kittens and owls, or fishing boats bobbing in Mousehole Harbour, swum into my consciousness. I was a national columnist, for goodness' sake, of many years' standing! A novelist, with two novels already published, and another due in by Christmas – less than six months hence. The proposition could not have been more out of the question, for any number of compelling reasons. I hated wearing tights and heels. During office hours, I prowled Notting Hill in unattractive sweat-pants, dipping into eye-wateringly expensive designer boutiques to try on jeans and picking up 'pan-roasted' salmon and griddled aubergine scattered with pine-nuts and pomegranate seeds for dinner from Ottolenghi, before filing the occasional article.

Never mind that the sum total of my editing experience had been, to date:

1. editing four issues of *Isis*, the Oxford University mag, in the Trinity term of my second year;
2. editing a book called *The Oxford Myth* as a student, which was greeted with a Royal Flush of vicious reviews by notables such as Alan Rusbridger (now editor of the *Guardian*), Joanna Coles (now editor of *Marie Claire* US) and William Boyd (now and then bestselling novelist); and
3. one viewing of *The September Issue* – a documentary about the effort and expense that went into producing one month's edition of US *Vogue* – on DVD.

As a result of the above, I assumed that editing was a piece of cake. No, the last thing I wanted was a . . . day job, something I'd successfully avoided having since 1996!

So I said, 'It's awfully sweet of you to think of me. But it doesn't fit my timeframe. But listen, good luck, why don't you . . .' Then, feeling charitable, I mentioned the name of an ex-*Telegraph* senior editor who had written a book about housework and I thought would fit the bill admirably. How nice of me to plug her for this job, I told myself. She will definitely owe me one.

But Ben didn't seem to pick up the signals at all.

'Never mind all that,' he said. I could hear him Googling the name 'Rachel Simhon', the person who I thought would be just the ticket, as he spoke. 'Just come in and have tea and a nose around. And then decide.'

I put his name into Google too. It came up in a nanosecond. Helicopter pilot, forty-five, who'd been working in Florida. Had also run radio stations. I clicked on a picture and a man with a decided expression, dark buzz-cut hair and sharp little blue eyes clarified on my screen. He looked like a woodland creature from *The Wind in the Willows*, slightly vole-like, but kind. And he sounded nice.

'OK,' I conceded. 'I'll come and have tea next week.' We made a date: '1700 hours,' he said; 'BST,' he added. Then he explained that BST was British Summer Time.

I knew I would cancel it – I mean, why would I spend over an hour getting to Covent Garden, and an hour getting back, not including getting-ready time, just to have tea at an old-lady magazine I had never read and didn't want to edit? But I had to get Ben – I could already picture him wearing a pilot's short-sleeved shirt with epaulettes and in a peaked cap – off the phone.

'Great. We'll get everything squared away then,' he said, as I wondered what he meant.

'Goodbye, sausage,' he chirped.

'Goodbye,' I said.

I was in slight shock.

Did a man just call me 'sausage'? My boss at the Sunday newspaper, a very tall and famously clever woman who has had issues with me since the start, only ever spoke to me in a raised voice, as if I were a very small, unruly, disobedient toddler who has emptied my potty on her desk.

I didn't know then, but Ben had me at 'sausage'.

11 June 2009

Took Coco to Kensington Gardens after I'd dropped Milly at school. Was walking past Round Pond, listening to the geese gabble and watching the Japanese tourists take endless pictures with enormous cameras of squirrels nibbling tiny nuts. George Osborne – the Shadow Chancellor – whizzed by in a neon anorak and a pair of white short shorts, schoolboy knees pumping. 'Good look!' I yelled. He smiled and gave a wave, and pistoned his way past me, fast-tracking no doubt to Number 11. Just then, my BlackBerry started ringing. I fished it out and saw the words 'Els Millsmobile' on the screen.

Accept or decline? Els Millsmobile was Eleanor Mills, the woman who had hired me for the paper. She'd left six months previously in order to edit the Saturday *Times*. That hadn't really gone to plan. And now, it had been announced in the *Guardian* Media section, she was to return to the fold of *The Sunday Times* as a writer and columnist. I had dimly wondered where her new column would go, and it had even flitted across my mind that it might be in place of mine.

However, John Witherow, the handsome, boyish, tennis-playing, virile, etc., editor of *The Sunday Times* had taken me out to lunch not so long ago at Shoreditch House, and had promised not to sack me. That was in February. Ivo, my husband, who is a glass-half-empty person, said that this meant nothing. But I, very much in the glass-half-full camp, sort of hoped that John Witherow's word was his bond, although I knew it was possible – especially in the current climate, with journalists leaving papers in sackfuls – that it was nothing of the kind. But still. We played tennis together. Mixed doubles. No one sacks their tennis partner!

So, feeling confident, I pressed the accept button on my Black-Berry. Might as well get it over with. Nothing worse than uncertainty.

And anyway, I assumed that everything would turn out for the best eventually.

'Hey, babe,' she said, in her confident, upbeat tones. No one gives great phone like Els.

'And hey, *you*,' I said, getting in first. 'I was going to call *you*, hon! Well done on your triumphant return to base. So you're coming back to *The Sunday Times*. Which is great!' I enthused. 'And hey – I hear you're going to write *a column*! Do you know, y'know, where in the paper it's going to go?'

Brief pause.

'Remember you asked me to tell you if I ever, you know, got wind of anything?' Eleanor began. 'Well, babes, I'm just giving you the heads-up, as a friend . . .'

'Oh yes?' I asked, striding on, keeping an eye on Coco, who had darted into the Round Pond by the sign that said 'Dogs Must be Kept on a Lead in this Area' and were forbidden to enter the water, my heart, by now, in my boots. People only used the phrase 'as a friend' as a prelude to delivering a cosh blow that the recipient was unlikely to recover from, even unto their deathbed.

'What I mean is, you might need to put out feelers,' said Els. 'To other papers. You know. Maybe give your chum Will Lewis on the *Telegraph* a bell.'

The sun bounced off the pond and straight into my eyes. I wanted to sit down, but couldn't, as Coco had disappeared. I couldn't call Will Lewis. The last time I'd seen him, it was to resign in order to join *The Sunday Times*. At this brief meeting, he'd predicted (only too accurately) that I'd last two years and then come crawling back, tail down, to the *Telegraph* fold.

'So you're going to write my column?' I asked directly, stopping to drink at a water fountain, my mouth dry, keeping things very light. *The Sunday Times* was my day job. My main source of income. And I was for the chop. If this wasn't the case, why would Els suggest I reverted back to the *Daily Telegraph*, from whence I came?

'Listen, babes, I don't know for sure,' she said, wavering. But of course she did. I knew without any doubt that I was being whacked by *The Sunday Times* by the very tall woman who found me annoying, in order to make way for the shorter one who had been so good as to hire me in the first place.

'Well done, Eleanor,' I managed to say. 'You deserve it.' The weird thing was – I meant it. I really liked Els. It was, as we say, Her Time. She had small girls, while my children were now hitting teenagerdom, so I'd had my time with them, and I would always be super-grateful for that. I did sports days and plays and endless ten-week summer holidays without breaking sweat, let alone my contract. But as I spoke, my golden years of being able to work from home, earning a salary from writing one column a week, passed before my eyes as if I were drowning.

I knew I'd never get a gig like it again. It was all over for people like me. We were, as I said, the miners of the third millennium. Columnists were thick on the ground, fighting for survival as the aftershocks of the digital earthquake just kept coming and coming, and dying in droves. Those that remained would write anything for anyone, and all were after the same golden ticket that I'd just this second lost as I circumnavigated the Round Pond: a well-paid weekly column on a national they could knock off in their pyjamas in a few hours.

I said goodbye to Eleanor, thanking her profusely for having me sacked so she could get my slot in *The Sunday Times*.

Then I dialled Ivo. When one of the children spills their Coke in a restaurant or we miss a train, he goes off the reservation, but when the shit really hits the fan – a child intubated in hospital, either of us getting sacked – he is utterly magnificent.

'Darling, all columns come to an end,' he said. 'You knew it couldn't last for ever.' Then he said in a strategic-toned voice: 'When are you seeing that nutty Ben chap at *The Lady*?'

'I don't know,' I whimpered. 'I sort of put him off.'

'Well, how about this for a scheme? I've got to go to some ghastly thing in a trendy hotel in Covent Garden for Kevin McCloud – you know, the *Grand Designs* bloke off the telly – tonight. Why don't we both go, and see him en route – there's a Tube strike, so we might as well kill two birds with one stone,' he suggested with a trace of swagger, 'and take a minicab.'

On Ivo's instructions, the next call I made was to Ben Budworth. I liked the sound of him. Plus, my only hope, I could see, as I was being dispensed with by the thundering juggernaut of *The Sunday Times*, was to somehow secure the corner office in *The Lady*, the oldest women's weekly magazine in the world (which only survived at all because its readers were too old and scared and digitally excluded to do anything – their shopping, reading, hiring – on the internet), a mag that, if it hadn't been around for 124 years, no one in a million years would even dream of inventing now . . . not *even to give it away.*

By this time I was near the Serpentine Gallery, and walking fast in the direction of the future.

'Hey, Ben,' I said. 'I have to come into Covent Garden tomorrow, so I might pop in and have tea with you after all, if it's convenient.' I made it sound like a favour, but in fact the boot was on t'other foot, though Ben didn't know this yet, and I wanted to keep it from him for as long as possible.

The Lady was in want of an editor.

And I needed a job.

12 June 2009

Having dwelt on Eleanor's call, I screwed up the courage to call my supreme commander, John Witherow, editor of *The Sunday Times*, i.e., one of the biggest cheeses in newspapers, and ask WTF was going on. After all, I only had I was being fired on Eleanor's say-so – maybe she was trying to panic me into resigning? Though I somehow doubted it. Everything she said sounded eminently plausible to me. I got put through not to John but to his secretary. 'Can I come in for ten minutes to see John?' I asked.

A kind note entered her voice when she heard my name, so I knew the rumour was true. I was being cleansed. 'He's very busy this week,' she said. 'Rupert Murdoch's in town.' There is also a Tube strike, so I am calculating as she speaks how long it will take to get a minicab to Wapping if I do get an audience with Witherow and how much it will cost. £30? Then she came back on the line. 'John says can you put whatever it is you want in an email?' she said.

So then I called the tall woman, Susannah Herbert, my section editor, who finds me annoying. I told her everything Eleanor Mills had said during the Round Pond exchange.

'Just wondered, y'know, what's going on,' I said. 'The thing is, if I do have to sell my house and send my children to Holland Park Comprehensive – which is very good, I hear, and I'd be lucky to get them in – it would be nice to know at some point.' I did not say that, in the course of the year, as newspapers tanked and circulation dived and readers went online, and magazines and newspapers cut freelance contracts left, right and centre, I had lost the following gigs.

- a weekly column on the *Evening Standard*;
- a monthly column on *Easy Living*;
- a monthly column on *Esquire*; and
- a monthly column on *She* magazine.

Nor did I spell out that the only remaining regular income I had left – excluding bits and bobs of freelance work (mostly *verboten* by my exclusive *Sunday Times* contract) – was my column . . . *for her.*

To her credit, she rose to the occasion, drew herself up (I imagined) to her full height of nine feet eight inches, and agreed it was outrageous that my contract was being terminated, plus it was appalling that I had heard via the person who is going to replace me. So hey ho. The grim facts of the situation are pretty much as Els Mills outlined.

I had gone from a grand total of twelve columns a month at the beginning of the year to . . . a big fat zero by the middle of 2009. It was awful. I was going from earning more than my husband (a fact he crowed about regularly) to being a *non-laying hen* in the course of a few months!

Well, at least things were clear. There was no possible way, with our spending commitments (with three children in private school, two boarding, about a trillion pounds a term), that I could join the ranks of the so-called 'economically inactive'. I had to act. And FAST.

Later, Ivo and I shared a cab to Covent Garden, en route to the Kevin McCloud thing, via tea at *The Lady*. As we bowled down Chandos Place, I gazed up at the pinky-cream façade of the magazine building, girdled by sash windows. Then I saw that the man I'd viewed online with the buzz-cut dark hair was leaning out of the window, over a box of violent-red geraniums. 'I'll let you in,' Ben called, as Ivo paid the taxi. 'Everyone's gone home.'

We went through a side door, to the left of the main Irish undertaker's entrance that I had penetrated before. Ben opened the heavy, metalled double doors edged in bronze with a small Yale Key. He pushed the right-hand door with a shoulder, stood and held it open for us to pass through, and we stepped back in time sixty years. It was like clapping eyes on my first boarding school back in 1975 – the interior was both strange, yet completely familiar at the same time. The cream and eau-de-nil paintwork inside was as proudly chipped as on my last visit. The same mail sacks with labels for 1st and 2nd Class and Overseas delivery still hung dejectedly in the passageway. The strange felty floor tiles were just as sticky.

It felt like home.

We charged past an ancient cream noticeboard with the words '*Lady* Editorial', '*Lady* Classified' and '*Lady* Advertising' picked out in elegant black paint, and arrows pointing to different parts of the building. 'That sign's completely misleading,' said Ben. He explained that upstairs was where his 'Uncle Tom' lived, in a sprawling nineteen-room apartment fitted out like an old people's home, and pointed down to a scary-looking basement where odd-job men lurked, where the presses that used to print out many thousands of the 'Journal for Gentlewomen', at one time a power in the land of publishing, once thundered.

'Lovely,' I say. The whole place seemed completely bonkers: dusty, tatty, disorganized and impossibly old-fashioned, set in an age of doilies and flag-waving patriotism and jam still for tea, some sunny day.

I was hooked.

I didn't even think about the money. I assumed the money was crap. It was the sense of possibility – there's nothing so genuinely satisfying as the prospect of setting a nice old lady back on her feet – that had me and Ivo tailing after Ben around the warren of the ground floor.

'This way.' There seemed to be many doors and staircases to choose from. We passed stairs that plunged into dank Fred West-style declivities. We weaved past desks piled with papers, a huge open safe with a golden seal on it. Within sat open packets of cereal and bags of Tate & Lyle sugar, Fray Bentos pies, Huntley & Palmers biscuit tins, mugs; all mixed in, it appeared, with lever-arch files and paperwork. It looked like a time capsule of another, safer but shabbier age.

'I like the paintwork,' I said to Ben, running my hand over a panel in cream and pale green. 'When did you last have it done?'

'Very recently,' he replied. 'In time for the Coronation, in 1953.'

Ben showed me and Ivo into a strange mirrored corridor with a side table with a telephone sitting on it, and a room which had Dralon sofas, standard lamps with fringed shades, and a rattan coffee table. There were no windows but there was a depressing mural of a spaniel in front of an Arcadian landscape on one wall. '*The Lady*'s smoking room,' he said, shutting the door. 'I think I'll leave the third floor and the Thora Hird-stroke-Alan Bennett room to another time.'

We went upstairs via a fine central staircase that wound itself up and up to a top-floor flat that Ben, with a wave of his arm, called the Anne Frank annexe. 'My Uncle Tom lives up there,' he said. 'He handed the magazine to me last year.' We processed past several doors marked 'Private', with little keys in the locks, and prim, curtained smoked-glass windows. I learnt later that these were the loos that only the management and editor can use. I also learnt that the editor of *The Lady* has her own private lavatory, tiled in avocado with a peach WC, and every day receives two freshly laundered tea-towels. I hoped that these customs would persist in perpetuity if I was offered the job, which I assumed I would be within the hour.

Ben, the new proprietor, clad in belted black Levis and a checked shirt, pushed open a door, and we entered into a large dark room dominated by a mahogany table covered by a blue baize cloth. As we entered, he swept an invisible speck off the table with his hand (one of his tics, I was to learn – he even keeps a Dyson dustbuster on standby if someone so much as *mentions* a biscuit in there) and asked us to wait. He disappeared through another door then returned. I went to one of the two sash windows, shaded with blinds, and looked down on to Chandos Place. It seemed rude to ask to open the blinds, so we sat down in the dark and a sweet-faced woman in her sixties came in, staggering under the weight of a tea tray – cups, jug, teapot and biccies. 'Thank you, Ros,' said Ben politely. He had, I noticed, impeccable manners. Ros had put the tray in front of me.

'Shall I be mother?' I said.

We sipped our tea and I stared around the room. The chandelier was not lit. Paintings – good paintings of men in waistcoats or in uniform – were dotted sparsely on the walls. Ben pointed out a picture of his great-grandfather Thomas Gibson Bowles with quill pen poised over parchment and told me he'd founded both *The Lady* and *Vanity Fair*, sold *VF* for £20,000 while he was a Member of Parliament, but retained *The Lady* because it was a nice little earner.

'Yes,' I said, nibbling a biscuit. 'Who on earth needs piddling little *Vanity Fair* when they could have *The Lady*?'

We spoke – well, Ben spoke, with huge, sleeves-rolled-up energy and infectious zeal – about *The Lady,* and how, despite the downturn, it remained a great title with a golden future. He revealed that in its heyday back in the seventies it was selling 70,000 copies or so a week, but was now down on its heel ('It lost its way') and bobbing between 25,000 and about 30,000. Uncle Tom – he pointed to the ceiling to denote he was still in residence – had, he explained, 'raped' the old girl for years, failed to invest, and allowed the managers to write their own rolling contracts while starving Editorial of funds, and until only November 2008, when B. Budworth arrived from Florida, basically, the place was run on steam-powered typewriters on a shoestring.

I digested this in silence. He also explained that the magazine was part of publishing history, and well positioned to benefit from the demographic, which is that, soon, everyone in UK will be fed up with *Heat* and *Hello!*, not to mention deeply antique and wearing those cords with buzzers round their necks that ring the social services when they fall over (as in the famous ad picturing a Mrs Hope, outstretched on the lino, who's had a Nasty Fall but knows that Help is Coming).

Ben was most amusing and chatty. As we drank tea, he revealed (he was very indiscreet, thank God, because so am I) that Graydon Carter, the editor of *Vanity Fair*, had written to Uncle Tom Bowles while Uncle Tom was ruling the roost, asking to come and see the old place, for old times' sake.

Ben pointed to the *bergère* chair with a baize board in which Spy drew his original cartoons in a dark corner, and told how Tom Bowles, proprietor of *The Lady*, had written back to the editor of *Vanity Fair*: 'I quite see why you would want to come and see us. But why would we want to see you?'

Then he launched into a seamless spiel I sensed he had delivered many times before. About how he wanted to bring the mag into the modern age. Double the circulation to 65,000 (I gulped) and restore the lustre the title once had, when it graced the shelves as the UK's first and finest women's weekly (a boast that still resided on the cover). Oh yes, and almost halve the average age of the reader from seventy-eight to anyone over forty-five. (I gulped even harder.) He explained how the old editor, Arline Usden, had finally gone in March, that they'd had a mini-relaunch, followed by an interim editor in May (Sarah Kennedy) and that they needed a new one in September. 'So, Rach, will you do it?' he asked me directly.

I tried to look diffident. As if the editorship was neither here nor there. But I felt my pulse quicken.

I still hadn't been formally whacked by my paper, but that was only, I knew, because no one from News International could be bothered to pick up the phone to tell me and confirm what I'd already been told by Eleanor Mills ('the short one') and my commissioning editor, Susannah Herbert ('the tall one').

'Hold on,' I parried, sipping my tea and nibbling a luxury biscuit from the M&S assortment on a plate. Some were wrapped in foil, I noticed. The chocolate was nice and thick.

'Are you offering me the job without seeing anyone else?' I smelt a rat, a big one, that you could see from space. 'Who else have you seen? Tell me!'

An opaque expression crossed Ben's face, and he muttered a couple of names. Then he covered the moment by mentioning a salary that was reasonably attractive given my income had plummeted, but was between a half and a third of what I earned in a good year. But this was June 2009: these were, as we all knew, not good years for journalists, and this was proving to be a particularly crap year money-wise for me.

As I clattered down yet another dusty staircase out into Covent Garden, I graciously told Ben I would think about it.

It was only as the heavy door shut behind me that it dawned on me.

Not only did I totally need the old-lady-mag gig, I really wanted it too.

30 June 2009

Got the call from the paper formally whacking me today. Richard Caseby (the managing editor) concluded the very perfunctory kitten-drowning session by asking me if I wanted, despite my contract being terminated at the end of June, to continue to file my weekly column for the News Review all the way through July and August until mid-September – i.e., work all through the summer so that my replacement, one Miss Eleanor Mills (surprise!) could have the summer off to romp carefree on sunny beaches with her children. I admit at that point my good humour momentarily deserted me. It's impossible to find people to write in July and August and I was buggered if I was going to be a stand-in for my own slot.

'Mmm . . . no thanks,' I told Caseby in a lordly way, as if money was no object. So that's it. As of now, I have no income, three children at private school, two houses to run, a dog to feed, and a summer holiday to get through on tick.

I immediately got on the blower to Ben, and threw my hat back into the ring with a vengeance.

I recanted on my previous position that editing a magazine 'doesn't fit my timeframe'. I am going for the job hell for leather. I have even gone out and bought and read a copy of the magazine for the first time ever. And it is immediately clear to me why no one's buying it apart from those who always have. It's full of random articles, about seasonal flowers and furry animals. It has its charms – if I was stuck in a dentist's waiting room for two hours it would be marginally better than reading nothing – but *The Lady* bears absolutely no relationship, so far as I can tell, to the modern universe, or the news cycle, let alone the third millennium.

In turn, Ben has asked me to come up with my manifesto for change and uplift. So what I immediately did was what I always do. I called Ivo.

'Is there anyone at the National Trust who could help me produce a dummy issue of *The Lady*?' I asked. I've been writing for the nationals since I was in short trousers, but still have no idea, you see, how a photograph or a Word document makes it from my screen on to the printed page. How it fits. How you add headlines, and pictures, and page numbers, picture credits, and make it look glossy and appetizing. Even at *Isis*, I had a designer and teams of pushy freshers to do the *actual work*.

'Sure,' Ivo said. 'I'll call Sue Herdman.' Sue Herdman edits the *National Trust* magazine, which has a circulation of – oh – several million. So within minutes I'd whistled up a professional freelance designer called Caroline de Peyer, who agreed to come to my house the next day. I rubbed my hands. Bingo! I knew it was in the bag.

When Caroline arrived, she quickly mocked up a dummy of *The Lady* while I gazed on with awe. On the inside pages of the PDF, she laid out my 'manifesto', which was basically a list of me dropping every name I could think of and offering them up as potential contributors, from Boris to Paxo via Jilly Cooper and Kirstie Allsopp.

I came up with a list of cover girls and my mission statement for the magazine. This is basically that it must be a portal product for any woman over forty-five who is fed up to the back teeth with staple weekly women's fare: mags in the hairdresser all about Posh, Britney's knickerlessness, Kerry Katona's coke habit or Demi Moore's plastic surgery on her knees. I said *The Lady* had to become a must-read for anyone who thinks that there is more to life than telly, celebrity baby-weight, Hollywood and gossip. I think my dummy – which has a winsome pic of a grinning Dame Cath Kidston of the Floral Oven Gloves on the front – is a winner. On page two ran my pitch:

The Lady is looking younger. She's definitely mislaid her Zimmer. The pastel-hued relaunch of spring 2009 is a small and sprightly step in the right direction. But she still needs someone to turn the clock back a few decades to enhance the title's appeal to vigorous, busy women in middle age as well as those in their twilight years. Someone to establish the revered *Lady* brand once more as a title on crowded shelves; to market the magazine tirelessly via television and radio appearances and authored pieces; and also to commission copy that is going to be picked up, and reprinted in the nationals.

It goes on:

Like a crumbling stately home in need of a new roof, our Lady of Bedford Street needs a facelift. She needs freshness (not in the feminine-hygiene sense, I hasten to add), confidence and humour. *The Lady* will become more hip, less hip replacement.

This was a shameless filch from Emma Soames, who applied the same claim to her *Saga* magazine with spectacular results.

More sunny-side-up, less sunset home. I can even put the fun into funeral, as Dafydd Jones, London's top society photographer, will attend the smartest memorial services and parties across town and bring you exclusive photographs of the *vieillesse dorée* in their finery for a new feature.

My pitch ends:

Under my editorship, we will together lift *The Lady* up to where she belongs, and take the title to these new readers, and give them what they want. *The Lady* can never be a Bitch or a Slut, and she is never going to be that interested in gossip or celebrity news. She will always be fragrant; she will always be *The Lady*.

I fired off the PDFs of the cover and my manifesto, feeling superconfident, with a covering email that said:

Dear Ben

I have pleasure in submitting for your perusal my early thoughts and suggestions to titivate your gracious title.

With all good wishes
Rachel

I didn't in all honesty see how Ben could resist.

After I'd sent it, I went for a walk. As I strode along, thinking about my 'manifesto', I had a wobble. However zippy I made *The Lady*, I still couldn't see why, in all honesty, my friends would buy it when they got the *Telegraph* mag on Saturday and *Style* magazine on Sunday for free with their papers, and the internet all day every day for nothing. Even if I did edit it – even if I did get scoops and interviews and fantastic writers. The problem was, however killer my manifesto, however good my feature ideas, and however bulging my Rolodex, *The Lady* – a hand-held glossy magazine for women of a certain age – was a printed media format, and therefore a product for the second millennium, not the third. And nothing was ever going to change that.

My BlackBerry vibrated. I fished it out of my pocket, hoping for something nice. After all, I had just been fired, and needed cheering up.

It was from someone I didn't know. Who'd found my email address.

From: Jimmy Burke
To: Rachel Johnson
Sent: 1 June 2009 17:57
Subject: Hmmm

I wouldn't usually do this – in fact, I've never done this – but I just feel compelled to let you know that I think it's a real shame that the media is clogged with people like you. Your essays in *The Sunday Times* are simply terrible. Badly structured, dreary and lacking any sense of purpose. No gusto, no insight, nothing but cliché. I can't detect even the faintest whiff of talent. Clearly, your career owes everything to your good fortune in being born to whom you were. And this is why I used the word 'shame': there are genuinely talented writers and journalists out there, and people such as you are keeping them from working, and us from reading them.

I stared at this for a while, thinking, WHY ME? Then I pinged mine back to him, knowing it was a mistake to rise to the fly of one of the green-ink brigade. It contained one word – 'Chippy!' – as if I didn't care. But I did.

Bad day.

THE LADY
23rd DECEMBER 1909
Weekly.—[Yearly subscription, 10s. 10d. post free]

ALL RIGHTS OF TRANSLATION AND REPRODUCTION ARE RESERVED.
Entered at the New York Post-office as second-class Matter.
The Postage to Canada, at the Canadian Magazine Rate.

REGISTERED AT THE G.P.O. as a NEWSPAPER
Vol. LIV, No. 1373.

The Lady

6d

Per Post, 6½d.

Christmas Number

LONDON: "THE LADY" OFFICES, 39 & 40, BEDFORD STREET, STRAND, W.C.

JULY

2 July 2009

Went to *Spectator* party. Now back home feeling even more crushed.

Not only did everyone ask me without fail, 'Is Boris here/coming?' while looking past me, as if my brother and I are joined at hip and communicate telepathically, and it was the usual crush of Piers Morgan and David Cameron and runts who work for the Tories, but A. A. Gill and Rod Liddle, now former colleagues and fellow scribes, teased me about being sacked, and when I asked Rod how he knew, he said, 'Kid, the sackee is always the last to know,' and blew smoke at me. A. A. Gill merely laughed. Then I bumped into Rowan Pelling. Rowan has a column in the *Telegraph*, and used to edit *The Erotic Review*. We stood jammed together holding glasses of champagne, and it emerged that she was in the running to edit *The Lady* too. And so were X and Y and Z.

'Hey, hold on!' I cried, spilling my champagne down my cleavage in shock. 'So have I!'

We stared at each other, then laughed. Then we rapidly established that we were both going to the beauty contest at *The Lady* in Bedford Street on Saturday. I'd been asked to Meet The Budworths (four Budworth sons and their mother), all of whom were directors. When Ben told me about this event, I had naturally assumed this would be my coronation – all that remained was that Ma Budworth and the Budworth boys, all four of them, were going to see if the crown fitted.

Hah! Then Rowan rattled off a list of other hackettes/authors she knew were up for what she called the 'editor's silk crêpe bonnet' too: many of whom I knew. Daisy Waugh. Imo Lycett-Green. Molly Watson, and about a dozen more from the *Standard*, *Mail*, etc. The list went on and on. 'All the candidates are clearly being played off against one another by Ben Budworth, like teen beauty queens in a *Mandy* mag story,' she said.

So I was up against the steely granddaughters of Evelyn Waugh and John Betjeman, two of the greatest and most entertaining men of letters England has ever sired. I would have to run against women I not only knew but had worked with, played tennis with, bitched with and counted as my friends. We gazed at each other in horror. I loved Rowan! And Daisy! And Molly! But I was going to have to grind them under my heel, like cockroaches! And Rowan was clearly thinking the same. So we both agreed. If she got the gig, she would do it as a jobshare with me, and vice versa. 'I'm totally not bothered,' I lied. 'It would be great if you got it!' We parted on the best of terms, thinking that at least we had said the right things and had not committed the cardinal error of being seen to have tried too hard, or actually *cared*.

That night I had a terrible nightmare and woke up with champagne head and heart hammering. I'd dreamt that A. A. Gill and Rod Liddle had danced around me at the *Spectator* party, and instead of being nice to me because I was a contributing editor and sister-of-Boris had jeered and taunted me, 'You've been sacked, you've been sacked.'

Then I remembered. It wasn't a dream at all. It had really happened.

4 July 2009

The day of the beauty contest has dawned. I went by cab to Bedford Street and was then taken through the mirrored corridor and made to sit by a wiry woman with a German Expressionist face and shingled hair in the airless *Lady*'s smoking room amid the rattan furniture, the unforgettable mural of the spaniel at Versailles, and copies of the magazine. I declined tea. The woman who showed me in told me that her name was Maureen and she was a belly dancer. This seemed highly improbable – the fact that she was a belly dancer, that is, not her name being Maureen. Then Ben bounced down to fetch me. He had a swift cigarette on the stoop; 'Only my forty-fifth,' he said. Then I followed him as he ran upstairs, and went back into the 'boardroom' where I'd been before. This time, cafetières of weak coffee took the place of the tea trolley, and I was too nervous even to eat a biscuit.

I settled into a chair at the head of the table, around which sat Mrs Julia Budworth (handsome, grandmotherly), and the four remaining Budworth boys, Adam (barrister, aquiline, floppy dark hair), Ben (as before, cheery and smiling), Richard (lawyer, grey hair and specs) and Willie (Worzel Gummidge). They were all incredibly kind. I particularly liked Mrs Budworth, who had the spirit of the Blitz and a cosy no-nonsense approach but also a definite touch of the Aunt Agathas about her. She was very direct and did not mince words, a sure sign that, sooner or later, as P. G. Wodehouse would say, out would pop the cloven hoof. I felt the interview went like a train. But then I always feel that.

Then I went to Cornwall with my oldest child, Ludo, as he had finished his GCSEs and that is the sort of thing that mothers like me must do. We go to Rock with our teenage sons and wear fleeces on beaches. We do not enter cut-throat contests with friends and fellow freelancers to edit female and frowsty weekly magazines.

15 July 2009

Still, I have heard nothing. No puff of white smoke from Bedford Street. Only news I've had is a snippet from a diary which quotes

Ben, saying, 'I was expecting applicants from *Crochet Today* and *Jam Tomorrow*. It's a hard decision – I wish we could have had them all.'

I text Daisy Waugh. I feel she is the opposition.

'Are you her Ladyship yet?' I asked.

'Yes,' she texted back.

'Well done,' I replied. 'I'd love to write for you.'

I tried to get through the evening – Sue Crewe, the editor of *House & Garden*, came to supper, and I'd made delicious watermelon and feta and red onion thing from the Ottolenghi cookbook – but inside I had died. I felt incredibly sad that I'd failed.

16 July 2009

Daisy texted again. 'Only kidding,' she confessed.

19 July 2009

My triumph – I have been appointed the ninth editor of *The Lady* magazine in 124 years – is announced in a grisly spread in the *Mail on Sunday* with a hideous photograph of me lounging in a frock and Uggs, looking like the lost lovechild of Myra Hindley and Björn Borg. I immediately receive gracious emails from Rowan Pelling, Molly Watson and Imo Lycett-Green. Nothing from Daisy Waugh, who I later learn is convinced I have secured the job via 'foul means'. (I wish I knew what she means – I would have defo used them if I could.) I am off to America with the children to a ranch called Mountain Sky in Montana. I can only afford this because I am writing it up for a picture-spread for lovely Sarah Miller at *Condé Nast Traveller*. Ben is off, he tells me, to Butlins,

Minehead, for the inside of a week, with some mates. 'I am still awaiting my commission from *Condé Nast Traveller*,' he added.

The die is cast. In September I will renounce my existence of shopping and coffee in chi-chi Notting Hill and take up an office job for the first time in fourteen years, a job which I happen never to have done before, and in which I am almost guaranteed to fail (show me a mag where the circulation is rising). And that's not even the catch! No, the catch is – there's a plan to film a fly-on-the-wall reality documentary for Channel 4 as I do it. They – i.e., the crew from an independent production company – are going to come in and start filming a trailer the day I start work, apparently. The company is called Optomen. So here's the deal. I don't just get to screw up, and kill off the first and finest women's weekly mag in the world. I get to screw it all up on national TV!

THE LADY.
16th APRIL, 1914.
Yearly—Yearly subscription in this issue, 32s.

ALL RIGHTS OF TRANSLATION AND REPRODUCTION ARE RESERVED
Entered at the New York Post-Office as second-class matter.
The Portrait of Osborn on the Christmas Magazine, 20th.

REGISTERED AT THE G.P.O. AS A NEWSPAPER
Vol. LIX.—No. 1528.
Per copy 6d.

The Lady

SPRING
Number
6d

LONDON: "THE LADY" OFFICES, 39 & 40, BEDFORD STREET, STRAND, W.C.

SEPTEMBER

1 September 2009

Woke up at 7.30; the curtains were wide open. Something felt wrong. I experienced a feeling of dread as the realization dawned that it was my first day as editor of a national magazine. Average age of reader, seventy-eight. Circulation – around 28,000. My new job? To lower the age of the reader to forty-five plus, despite rapidly ageing national population, and double the circulation, despite the fact that all advertisers and readers have vanished to go online. My chances of succeeding? Vanishingly small.

I got up and put on one of my eight identical West Village dresses then decided it was too clingy. Took it off. Put on my pink tweed Rachel Riley dress, i.e., Carla Bruni meets the Duke of Edinburgh: demure and ladylike *ma non troppo*. As threatened, the crew filming the trailer from Optomen arrived at 8 a.m. As all this went on, Ivo grumpily stomped about with two bags of laundry and left without saying goodbye. We'd had a torrid fight day before in which he said everything I did was done to 'bolster my massive ego'. He has a point there, of course.

'Goodbye, love,' I said, wanting to make nice, as he barged past me while the C4 crew unloaded their gear from taxis and minivans prior to filming me 'getting ready' for work at home.

I waited for him to say, 'Good luck, darling.' It was my first day as editor of *The Lady*, the oldest and finest weekly in the world, the journal for gentlewomen, founded 1885. I stood on the doorstep. He drove off in his battered green VW Passat without a glance.

I threw open the front door to admit the crew, dressed identically in the uniform of ironic seventies rock T-shirts and Diesel jeans. 'Coffee, anyone?' I cried, heading down to the kitchen followed by Mollie (director), Claire (VT), Derek (sound) and George (cameraman). 'We're all caffeined up,' said Mollie. 'But we can film you making a cup of tea for cutaways, can't we, Derek?'

After half an hour of the delightful crew being in my kitchen I was already exhausted by the strain of being interesting and lively and trying not to show my broken nose on my bad (i.e., right) side. They asked me to leaf through a recent issue of the magazine. I do so and find a whole article about cucumbers. I also point to the cover – which has a pretty photograph in pinks of blowsy blooms – and sneer. I say to camera that the cover makes me think that 'someone has died'. The crew snorts with laughter. They clearly want me to knock my own product. The part of me that wants to please is only too happy to oblige them, but this is breaking the first rule of PR (never piss in your own pool). So even though it's the Budworths who have gunned for this documentary to be made, more than me, I cannot see what I am getting out of this filming project apart from adding to my already well-established reputation as a publicity-prone irritant.

We cab into Covent Garden in order to film my 'surprise' arrival at *The Lady*. I have to get out of the cab three times. This means poor Kath in Classified (though I don't remember her name when I see her – have managed to delete the names and faces of everyone I've met on previous visits in my panic) has to come and answer my ring on the bell three times. There is the same sign in the entrance, the same sad vase of flowers hanging limply, and it all feels so mournful that one expects an undertaker to glide out and intone, 'We are deeply sorry for your loss.'

Instead, Ben comes out and we embrace. We are made to do this twice. I was waiting for him to call me 'sausage', but he said, 'We've waited a long time for you.' It sounded like a rehearsed line, but I liked it anyway. At my age, you have to take whatever you can get.

I go up to my new freshly painted in grey-green Farrow & Ball office with its empty shelves and a shiny piney desk. The view from my window overlooking Maiden Lane is of a new office block atop a pub on the ground floor with a beer garden. On the side of the office block there is a blue plaque, saying that J. M. W. Turner once lived there. There is a card from the literary editor, Paul Blezard, in my in tray, welcoming me.

As I struggle to switch on my PC, Gillian Spickernell, my PA, sits outside and answers the telephone in a sweet, calm voice. Vicky Murden, who does letters and the website stuff, sits opposite. In the room beyond, there is Judy Lamb, the production manager, and in the two rooms beyond that overlooking Bedford Street and along Chandos Place – sit the designers, and the picture desk, and round the corner there's a room with three sub-editors and a white-faced Janina Pogorzelski, thirty-seven, the treasured youngest daughter of the former editor, Arline Usden, who has been here her entire working life and whom I have inherited as my features editor and welcome-on-board bonus.

Everyone seems to know what they're doing except me.

During the next two hours, I meet all the staff again and have a session with Claire Wood, the lovely Olive Oyl-lookalike in-house designer. She gives me the deeply alarming low-down re: staff, budgets, outlook, etc. When I get back from lunch there is a note from Gillian on my desk. Gillian is a willowy, balletic woman of around my age with a sweet, toothy smile and long brown hair. She looks like the sort of person who used to wander round university towns as a slip of a girl carrying a violin in a case and wearing a long corduroy skirt and a purple floaty top. She is very graceful and, like many ballerinas, carries herself beautifully and stands in second position.

'Janet called from Ipswich. Returning your call. She's at work till

1.15 p.m.' I go through to where Gillian sits in my outer office, hero-ically dealing with endless readers who ring up to complain. They ring up not just to complain, I sense, but to talk to someone – anyone. Gillian is endlessly patient as they bang on about the trouble they've had finding *The Lady* at WHSmith between *Chat* and *Take a Break*, or ask Gillian how to lay their hands on a back issue from 1973.

'Sorry, Gillian,' I say. 'I don't know anyone called Janet, and I don't know anyone in Ipswich.' There was no surname or number on the message. 'And I haven't rung anyone,' I say, as a parting shot. Then I say, 'BTW, did any mail come for me over the summer?'

I was, after all, announced as the new editor in July, and had been working pro bono for two months, commissioning copy, dreaming up columns, planning a redesign, etc. To this end, I had written in mid-July to the artist David Gentleman asking him to conjure up a figure to incarnate *The Lady*, just as *The New Yorker* has the dandy with the monocle and *Tatler* has the Bystander chap in a frock-coat peering into a spyglass.

'Yes, there was some mail for you,' she says, handing me a few letters from time-wasters. I glance through. 'Are you sure there wasn't any more?' I query. 'I have been expecting, in particular, a letter from the artist David Gentleman.' I don't explain at this point that I was surprised by his lack of response, as his daughter is mar-ried to my younger brother, Jo, and I know him quite well and admire him greatly.

'No, sorry, Rachel,' she replies. 'Nothing at all.'

Then I have a one-on-one with Lindsay, the assistant editor. Lindsay is a handsome woman of a certain age, with shoulder-length white-blonde hair. In the course of our chat, she tells me she wants to be my right-hand woman and will do whatever I like. That she wanted me to get the job. That she had dealt with two editors before me. Then she tells me that the problem with *The Lady* is that the magazine is done and dusted two weeks before publication, and that this is very inconvenient, and that she would prefer any given week's edition to be made ready to go eight weeks before. I stare at her dumbly. Surely the point of a weekly is that you can change things the week before? On *The Spectator*, I would often write something on a Tuesday that appeared in the magazine on Thursday that same week. But at least Lindsay's remark explained why *The Lady* looks as if it has been produced at any random point in time in the last 124 years (this week's edition has features on garden gnomes and woodland walks) and bears no relationship to anything in the modern world. Because it has! As she leaves, she reveals – as if on a need-to-know basis – that she lives in the next-door street to me in Notting Hill and that we both go to the same newsagent. I digest this in silence.

I have lunch with Ben and try to get him to give me 1. gym membership, 2. a car and 3. a sofa for my office. This is, after all, our honeymoon period. He will get fed up with me, only too soon.

The *Daily Mail* rings.

Could I write three hundred words on the mini-skirt, i.e., when should you stop wearing one; and do I agree with the results of the survey that say forty is the outer limit for mini-skirt wearing, commenting on the fact that, ten years ago, the survey said age thirty was. Does that mean women are getting more attractive/glamorous?

I have to get in copy from Charlie Glass – have commissioned a seminal piece I hope about the dos and don'ts of bedding the nanny.

So first I called Charlie re: his copy, then called the *Mail* back re: mini-skirts. You bet I could! Finally – something I know how to do, which is write almost any amount of words on any given subject for a pound a word.

I rattle it off – then the picture desk rings. Can I supply a pic of me in a mini-skirt? 'I'm at work at *The Lady*,' I swanked. 'It's my first day, actually.'

Then, of course, I agree to their request for a photograph of me wearing a mini. I have to leave the building, go to Topshop on the

Strand, buy a mini-skirt, and be photographed wearing it. I stand in the middle of Covent Garden on a sunny summer day wearing a horrid skirt and tight T-shirt as crowds of tourists check me out in dismay.

'Your breasts are . . . majestic,' says the photographer, showing me a picture in the viewfinder on his digital camera. Whenever I put on weight, it goes straight on to my boobs, and I have put on half a stone in America in the summer. I recoil in horror, and spend the rest of the shoot with my arms crossed against my chest.

I leave the office with Mollie, who is directing the trailer, for the Ivy Club, to meet Pat Llewellyn, aka 'the most powerful woman in TV' (according to the *Guardian*). Pat is head of Optomen, the company that hopes to be making the doc for Channel 4. She has made Jamie Oliver, Gordon Ramsay and Valentine Warner, and I sense she is about to unmake me. She is pitching *The Lady* doc with the title 'The Devil Wears Barbour' to the Channel 4 *Bodyshock* man who commissions docs like 'Half-ton Mum' and 'My Daughter Grew Two Heads'.

'So, how was your first day?' she asks, offering me wine. It's lovely in the Ivy Club. I sink back into a sofa and mainline honey-roasted cashews. It feels so modern, after *The Lady*. Leslie Phillips is in. So is John Patten.

'Hardcore,' I say. 'Everyone I met was sectionable,' I joked. Pat glanced at Mollie, who is directing the trailer.

'Did you get her saying that?' she said. 'That line about everyone at *The Lady* being sectionable?'

'No,' admitted Mollie.

'It's a great line,' Pat enthused. I am suffused with relief that I didn't speak it to camera – phew. What a narrow escape. I am already envisaging my new staff watching me bitch them up on national prime-time TV.

'This is just the sort of thing Channel 4 wants,' said Pat, nodding meaningfully to Mollie. 'Get it taped tomorrow, OK?'

2 September 2009

Day two. Woke, and my first thought was: can't believe I have to go to an office . . . again! I went to an office yesterday, done that. Now I want to lie in bed, playing with my novel, drinking coffee, bumping into fellow loafers like my mates Shane Watson and Charlie Glass in the Tea and Coffee Plant in the Portobello Road! I opened the *Mail* and paged through to the mini-skirt and age feature. Predictably, they haven't run the picture of me muttonishly wearing the Topshop outfit so have wasted forty quid.

Belt in on Tube, as an experiment, to Tottenham Court Road. Find the experience of the Central Line in the rain in the rush hour horrid. I got to the office keenly early. No PA, no Lindsay. There was a staff meeting, and I had to make a Gettysburg Address to the troops. In the end, I introduced myself and said nice things about Ben ('He's been a delight and a bunny so far,' I said honestly.) During the staff meeting, I made the editorial staff introduce themselves, say what they did and how long they've been at *The Lady*.

It's beyond belief. Judy (the cosy den mother, production manager, aka Arkala) has been there thirty years. Capable and efficient. Janina (who is obviously bright but very nervy) refuses to disclose how long she's worked here on camera (I think it's about fifteen years . . .). Pretty, but looks awfully pale and won't make eye-contact. She must be freaked about the fact that she is now working for a new boss who hasn't given birth to her, and is being filmed by a TV crew, which is fair enough. Lindsay makes out that she basically puts the magazine out single-handed. 'I do everything really,' she says. I notice the subs and the production manager roll their eyes. Then there's Edwina, the beautiful, slender, dark-haired marketing girl, who arrived, late, with Paul Blezard, the literary editor (Paul Smith suit, red face, loud voice, flowing scarf), as I am in mid-flow of my inaugural address.

'Our readers are modern and connected,' I boomed, 'so I want *The Lady* to be modern and connected! Old folks now are more Mick Jagger than Miss Marple,' and so on. I went on about how no good magazine ever had a relaunch, they just improved, and how I wanted to make 'subtle and arousing' changes, and that a Lady never vamped, let alone revamped. This was mainly not for the benefit of the staff, who all stared at me as if I had arrived from another planet, but for the C4 crew, who filmed the whole McKinsey-esque event, and then buggered off, thank God.

Later, I asked Gillian if she'd found the letter from David Gentleman yet.

'Not so far as I know. Sorry, Rachel,' she said.

Dreary p.m., as I had a crash course in magazine editing. I went through folders of existing copy (inventory – we either have to run it, or spike it, and pay kill fees). There are endless pappy travel features, and a seemingly endless supply of articles about weekend breaks in country-house hotels written by members of staff.

So that's existing copy. As for existing staff, I've no wiggle room whatsoever. As Ben explained, for reasons of employment law, we could not sack anyone.

'Ben, all editors come in as new brooms,' I pleaded. But it was no good.

As Ben explained in words of one syllable, whatever my grand designs to spiff up the mag, I have to make do with what I've got. I can commission whoever I like to write, but in terms of staff, as opposed to freelancers, my hands are tied. And so are Ben's. If I want to get rid of anyone, and replace them, we both have to go through a long-winded process of analysing incompetence and issuing first, second and final warnings that could take months.

So it's going to be absolute agony. Editors are expected to make changes – but I can't make any. But there is one ray of sunshine. I'm smuggling in Carolyn Hart tomorrow. She is a food editor from the weekend bits of the *Telegraph*. I interviewed her in July, and liked her a lot. Not only did I like her, but she had experience of magazines which she would be able to transmit to me. Small, dark, funny, and with a wing down, as her 'partner' had buggered off, leaving her single-mothering three teenagers. For legal reasons, she is going to be called an 'editorial consultant'.

And I have to get a magazine out on this basis. So I looked through folders of copy and what is due to run on 15 September – my first issue. And what I found is – absolute cack about dormice and the ramblers and the magical properties of vinegar. Nothing there. Everyone would buy *The Lady*, and it would be the same old same old even though I'd arrived. I cast about in desperation. I had to do something, get in one piece of the type that you might possibly read in another magazine.

Then I had a brainwave. My father had written a piece for *The Spectator* about his gall-bladder op. *The Spec* hadn't had room for it, but it was bound to be better than what was available in the folders I'd scoured called 'Unused Copy' and 'Quirky Fills', 'Travel', 'Favourite Things', and so on, that I'd been shown. I called him; he whizzed it over; and I liked it. So I dropped in Dada's copy on his emergency gall-bladder operation and made it the cover story, with the line, 'They saved my life'. I also decided to launch a column called 'The Gents', a sort of antidote to 'Femail', in which we courteously give the floor to the gents and allow men to whinge about women, in revenge for all the whingeing women do in print about men. Milly, my daughter, came in for lunch and we went to Covent Garden. She looked beautiful.

Went for coffee with Blez – Paul Blezard, the literary editor. I felt bad because, in my first staff meeting, I had announced that I was dropping the short story. It turns out he had big plans for the short story. He wanted *The Lady* to be known all over the literary world for its short story, and the first thing I did was drop it.

Blez is tall, good-looking, etc., but I have noticed that he pretends he has thought of everything first, and he drops so many names in a booming voice that, according to Ben, 'There are dents in his floor.' J. K. Rowling is Jo, and Alexander McCall Smith is Sandy, and he told me on our first meeting that he has been offered a six-figure sum by both to run the Edinburgh Literary Festival on a full-time basis and is only staying at *The Lady* 'out of loyalty to Ben'. Mmmm.

In the afternoon, I picked up the phone and called various writers, on a massive copy-commissioning jag. I've asked for pieces on divorce, nannies, Agas, puppies, rose-covered cottages, crumbles, rescue ponies, etc. – all the sort of things one longs to read about. I am determined that *The Lady* will be, above all, cosy and *gemütlich*.

Lindsay came in and showed me a list of the freebies the staff had been on and all the advertorial I would have to run as a result. I love a freebie as much as the next man, but this was something else.

The inventory list of copy I have to run or spike is endless, as there seems to have been a total gravy-train when it comes to travel. There are scores of features written by freelance contributors and staff about their trips abroad (known as 'freebies'). In return for free travel, hospitality and sightseeing, the hack is expected to file a slavishly positive piece in order to please the holiday-giver's PR. I had heaps of this slurry to get through and, in theory, run. And I had to run it, in order to fulfil our side of the equation: if your hack has freebie, your paper then is honour-bound to puff her holiday. It's deeply corrupt, but that's how it works. So there were, in the folder called 'Travel Unused', endless 1,200-word pieces about Tunisia, Mexico, India, the US, the Algarve ... And there were even longer and puffier pieces about three-week cruises or press jollies taken by staff members who had then proceeded to file 3,000 words detailing how it was a wrench to leave the comfort of the hotel/ship/Nile paddle-steamer, and how they were too full for pudding.

When I gasped and protested to my publisher – some freelancers and *Lady* staffers went on a jolly a quarter – I was told by Ben that, under previous regimes, travel freebies were used – like MPs' expenses – in lieu of income, and were handed like sweeties as rewards for good behaviour to the various office pets.

3 September 2009

Day three. My birthday. Carolyn arrived. Thank God. Someone who has some magazine experience at last. We went to Caffè Nero, opposite. I took my list of ideas for new columns, and she brought with her the flatplan – basically, the flatplan is a diagram showing the run of empty pages. Editorial pages (the ones I have to fill) are in white. Advertising pages (those the display and classified-ads departments have to fill) are shaded. So what we did was fill them. Empty page one is the cover. Two is an ad. Three is the contents page. Four is a list of contributors. Then five was going to be Mary Killen on her life in a cottage (aka the 'grottage') in Wiltshire. We filled it all in (luckily, there's stacks of classifieds and quizzes and bridge cols. and gubbins at the back), all fifty pages or so until we got to the inside back cover, now 'The Gents', on page ninety.

So, in half an hour, we literally thrashed out the basic shape of the new *Lady*. After we'd played fantasy flatplan, we went over the dream review team – obviously, Nancy Banks-Smith, Lynn Barber, Julie Burchill – all the best writers we could think of.

Then we went back to the office, and we did cover lines (you know, the shouty bits on the *Cosmo* cover saying, 'Your Best Orgasm Ever', etc., only in our case, they read 'Treasure Houses of Great Britain', and 'Alan Titchmarsh's Favourite Things'). Then I read extant copy for the 15 September issue and – this seemed bizarre – chose a cover for that of the twenty-second. I have no idea what should be on the cover on 15 September let alone a week later, but then I discover it is Twiggy's sixtieth birthday and there are free images from the National Portrait Gallery, so that's easy.

I realize that being closeted with Carolyn gives a terrible impression to Lindsay, who has of course claimed that she wants to be my right-hand woman and, as officially my assistant editor, will be feeling left out. So Lindsay called me all day to relay trifles such as the fact that she is writing a list of all the men we can commission to write 'The Gents'. She says she has a hundred names. She is clearly going to try to wrest this plum role (talking to amusing men) from my grasp!

We now have a wishlist of writers, and following on from our coffee morning in Caffè Nero, Carolyn and I kick about names for agony aunt (Debo Devonshire, Georgia Coleridge, India Knight, Drusilla Beyfus), film critic (Jasper Rees, Howard Jacobson, Julie Burchill), TV reviewer (Toby Young, Giles Wood, Alexander Chancellor), and so on. Lots of other thoughts too: Merryn Somerset Webb, the *FT* columnist and editor of *Money Week*, as money honey; 'Change of Life' occasional column; Clementine Hambro to replace Carol Klein as my gardening columnist – Carol writes for the *Guardian*, is ubiquitous, snowy-haired, and I want younger blood.

I have lunch with my friend Nicola Reed at Soho House. She came from Central St Martins, where she's doing a postgrad course, me from Bedford Street. We sat on the roof terrace and froze. Delicious salad. Goat's cheese, beetroot, rye bread, cappuccinos. She is nice to take me out. She had to, I suppose, after I told her it was my birthday. And she is a member, and I'm not.

That afternoon, in desperation, I call David and Sue Gentleman at home to delve further into the mystery of the missing letter.

Sue answered. 'But David replied the next day,' she exclaimed after I falteringly explained why I was calling. 'He can't do it, he's too busy, and it's not his sort of thing, but I am absolutely sure he wrote back, straight away. To *The Lady*.'

At this point the red mist descended. I marched out to Gillian's nook and remained superhumanly calm. 'Are you sure there has been No. Other. Mail. For. Me. Since July?' I demanded.

'Well, there's that,' she said, pointing to a wire basket above a cupboard. She had to take off her shoes and clamber on a chair to hand it down. In among about a dozen letters to me was the very nice, handwritten letter of regret from David Gentleman, dated July, declining my commission. It was marked 'Personal'. It had been opened.

'Why didn't you show this to me?' I howled.

'I thought you'd be too busy,' she said.

Bolted at 5.10 p.m. to get home for birthday tea with the children and Grandma. The boys had made cards, and Milly had bought me some earrings. I love them all more than words can ever describe. They don't like me going to an office, especially Oliver, who sobbed when I kissed him goodnight. But I've been more cheerful the last two days than for any time since he was born. In fact, though I can't yet admit it to anyone, I am rather enjoying myself. I am forty-four.

4 September 2009

Day four. Arrived with latte in hand. Tired. Had to write big piece for *Mail*, had been up until 1.30 a.m. with it in order not to write it in office hours, and didn't sleep.

'Carolyn's not coming in,' said Ben. My heart sank. That's two issues to commission on my own, in about two days, i.e., fifty-odd pages of editorial; otherwise we will have to use the stuff in the folders, all about dormice and garden gnomes and woodland walks. And I still don't understand the magic process whereby people send in rubbish on email and it then appears looking marvellous accompanied by nice photographs and headlines on the right page. Chrissie, the doughty chief sub, who smells encouragingly of cigarettes, explained: the copy arrives and is put in 'Copy In'. Someone – i.e., me – reads it, edits it and shoves it in a folder called 'Copy for Subs'. Then the subs check it and correct it. Then they write headlines and make sure it's the right length and isolate 'pull quotes', i.e., the bits which are dotted about in the middle of the text to break it up. Then they send it to 'Copy for Art'.

The designers then play with it for ages and do layouts and spreads and so on. Then the subs add picture captions, and credits. Once the whole magazine has been laid out, page by page, Judy, who looks and sounds as if she should be running the Girl Guides (Ben calls her 'Matron'), presses a button, and a massive PDF is emailed to our printers. This is what Judy calls 'passing the issue', as if it were a massive gallstone.

I eventually asked Nathan, one of our brilliant designers, to write a bluffer's guide to the magical alchemy that can turn some cobblers sent in by some hack on email from his BlackBerry into a beautifully laid-out glossy page in a nationally distributed magazine. This is what Nathan sent me:

The Lady Production Process

1. Commissioned copy arrives.
2. Copy is subbed for content and/or cut to approximate length.
3. Picture desk sources low-resolution images for layouts, and suitable images are selected.
4. Layouts are created by Design and returned to subs.
5. Picture desk obtains high-resolution images for approved design layouts.
6. Copy is subbed for exact fit and removal of bad line breaks, widows, orphans, etc. (These are printer's terms for the stray single words either at the beginning or end of a paragraph.) Picture captions and credits are added. Final editorial additions, cuts and changes are made.

7.   Final subbed layouts are returned to Design.

8.   Design colour-corrects all images and prepares layouts for print.

9.   A press-ready PDF (portable document format) file of each page is generated for submission to printer.

10.   Production desk sends final layouts to printer via FTP (file transfer protocol) upload.

Additionally, a press-ready PDF of an early version of the cover is sent to the printer early in the week. We then receive a proof for colour matching. This allows us to make accurate colour edits to the cover image. Normally, we go through two or three rounds of colour edits each week, receiving a new proof each time.

I am implicated in stages 1 to 4 of this process, but Nathan left my biggest jobs off the list: I commission the whole magazine, and have to proofread it. Luckily, luckily, Carolyn came in after all, so I didn't have to do all that on my own.

Someone has pinched the bottle of champagne that Ben gave me for my birthday. I left it in my office last night. I must check to see if the card is still preserved. It's awful – now I feel I can't leave anything in my office at all, like spare Topshop tights or my Her Ladyship mug. Tried to think wildly who it could be.

Lindsay? She applied for the job, and didn't get it, so has a motive – but I don't see her sneaking in and whipping it from the bookcase. Janina? Don't think so. She knows – being the daughter of the previous editor – that she is here on sufferance, and she appears more than eager to please. Gillian? Again, no. She has other ways of destabilizing me that are more effective. I may be getting paranoid but it does seem that the people I've been coddling for months she is turning away – I hear her voice saying, 'Sorry, did you say your name was Joan Collins? Rachel's in a meeting,' and not taking a number. But time-wasters who send long articles in on spec about funny things their cat has done and then call up to see if anyone has noticed or is intending to run it (highly unlikely even under the *ancien régime*) she puts straight through.

'It's Marjorie from Snape Maltings. She says she sent in a long piece about the teazel thistle. Says she knows you. Just putting her through.'

'Tell her to go away!' I yell through to the outer office. 'She's lying!'

But she's lovely to deal with. She sends me adorable emails, and always smiles when she says hello.

Rachel,

You've been invited to afternoon tea at Temple Place on 10 Sept, for the launch of a biscuit range TLC.

Do you want to go, so I can let them know?

Thank you.
Gillian

How cosy is that?

PS: The champagne is by no means the only mystery here. There's also a ghost, apparently. When anyone goes down into the Fred West basement where the archive is, they always tell someone, as if otherwise they will be bludgeoned over the head and lie there rotting for weeks. And when I arrived, people would sometimes darkly allude to a dread matter known only as 'the unpleasantness in the ladies on the editorial floor'.

This sounded jolly. I enquired further – there is also a ladies on the ground floor where Classifieds sit – but Judy just shook her head and said that I'd have to talk to Ben. So I trotted into the boardroom.

'Ben. The ladies by my editor's loo. Tell me.'

So Ben told me in full.

'It was about 4.55 p.m. local time on a Thursday, in February 2009,' he began, like a constable reporting an incident on his beat, 'and I was going about my lawful business as publisher and chief executive of *The Lady* magazine, sitting in the boardroom with B-Cal, I think it was (B-Cal is Ben's name for Nic Boize, the pipe-smoking marketing chap, because the last company he worked for was British Caledonian). Anyway, suddenly the door of the boardroom was flung open, and Maureen' (Maureen is Ben's scrawny, belly-dancing PA) 'was silhouetted in the door frame. She was standing there, staring at me with her mouth open. She had a look on her face as if she'd just discovered a number of corpses. She said, "You don't want to be going in there. No. No. No."

'I sat and looked at her, backlit in the door. I assumed there had been a murder.

'I walked towards her, but she barred my path. She just repeated, "No, no, no. Don't."

'"It's OK, Maureen," I said. I was trying to exude calm and clinical tones. Like a pilot over the intercom when all four engines have failed. I had to push past Maureen. She was petrified. I went out and turned right out of the boardroom, and went down the corridor, through all the various doors and fire doors. I could hear Maureen still pleading with me not to go, sounding like a Hollywood starlet being strangled. I saw all the editorial staff in a group at the end, standing silently by the door marked "Ladies".

'I thought I would find a body, so I opened the door of the ladies with some force. A cursory inspection revealed nothing untoward at eye level. As my eye travelled downwards, I became aware of a familiar medieval smell.'

At this point Ben paused, as if it was too much to go on.

'Keep going,' I said, neutrally. But I was thinking – what the *f*ck*? What sort of place had I come to work in? Which of the, er, 'gentlewomen' I had met so far would DO a thing like that? And then I wondered – had he told the Channel 4 crew about this?

'My eye fell on what looked like a small brown puppy,' he said. 'Right in the middle of the floor in the ladies. And someone had trodden in it. And we'd only just put in that loo block; it was installed after the Silver Jubilee,' he recalled, with a misty look. 'Arline and Mum were very proud of it. It had cubicles and washbasins and a sink for washing up . . . '

'Please just finish the story,' I said.

'I told Maureen to fetch a bucket and a scrubbing brush. But Maureen was in shock and couldn't respond to simple instructions and, as it was by now 5 p.m., she was also naturally worried about missing her train back to Eltham,' Ben continued. 'So I had to go to the cleaner's cupboard for a brush and a bucket. There weren't any gloves.' He paused at this detail. 'Everyone else had taken themselves off to as far away as they could get from the incident and had formed a cluster at the other end of the building, like passengers on a sinking ship. Maureen had recovered enough by this stage to act as a special constable at a crime scene, and as news of the incident spread like wildfire throughout the building, and people from other departments came to rubberneck, she moved them on, saying, "There's nothing to see here, go back to your desks," while I cleared it up.

'As I was returning to the boardroom, Arline bustled past, on her way home. I said, "There's been a terrible incident in the ladies in editorial," and she said, "So I hear."

'I said, "I will be making enquiries, but I have my suspects." That was a Thursday. On Sunday night, I was at home and a strange number popped up on my mobile – an 0208 number. I answered it, and Arline's voice was on the end of the line saying, "It wasn't me, it wasn't me."'

'Arline has her own loo anyway, so it couldn't have been. Nice of her to tell you herself though,' I said. 'Did you ever find out who did it?'

'I wanted to, but apparently you can't DNA a turd,' Ben said with a look of infinite regret.

'So we'll never know.'

8 September 2009

My *Daily Mail* piece came out about what it means to be a lady today (in short 'I don't know' expanded over 1,600 words). Usual gurning, smug-looking photo of me. Awful day also because the system went very slow and then crashed, for hours. So I couldn't access email, read copy, commission copy, etc. I'm afraid the iron has entered my soul re: Lindsay, despite her being my neighbour, but I am warming to Janina, who has a dry delivery and a sense of humour. In features meetings she has mentioned Fiona Shaw, Jodie Foster, Rosie O'Donnell, Susie Orbach (twice) and Jeanette Winterson. Lindsay rang me up several times to read out emails I've sent her. I have told her not to. Then I had to send her a second chaser ordering her not to send me attachments. The system is so crap, they take hours to open.

Blez had a hissy fit in front of whole office about the fact that I teased him. He had claimed that he could get *The Lady* half an hour with Michelle when the Obamas were in town, and we simply fell about laughing. As you would.

'I work my nuts off for this magazine,' he roared, going redder, while Ben and I had to choke back our sobs of mirth all over again while he chuntered on about how he'd wrangled PRs in 'getting access to the Obamas', and so on.

Left at five. The boys go back tomorrow, and I want to be with them. Made risotto with home-made stock as a sort of penance. They guzzled it and ate a whole packet of Parmesan.

9 September 2009

Had to show Lindsay the writing was on the wall today. To her credit, she seemed aware, and said, 'I know the axe is hovering over my neck.' I kept the film crew at bay – I didn't want this going out on national TV, and nor did Lindsay. Still, it's incredible how quickly one adjusts. I have already picked my nose and changed from a tracksuit into an M&S black sleeveless shift dress and tights, forgetting that a camera filming the trailer is pointing at me throughout. I didn't disagree with Lindsay, but tried to smile as kindly as I could. She has written twenty-three 'quirky fills' since the beginning of the year, mainly about random nature subjects, and I doubt any of them would be printed anywhere but *The Lady*. Not even in an inflight magazine or contract publishing. I felt awful; didn't know where the conversation was going at all. As she left, she said to the cameras, 'Well, I'll be out of a job by Christmas.' I have also decided that the last thing we need is an in-house, full-time, staff literary editor with a very loud voice who produces one page a week.

When Lindsay had gone, the crew scuttled back in to ask how it went. I sat there. This was agony. I didn't really know Lindsay, or Blez, but I could assess their work rate, read their stuff, and I wasn't happy. But I wasn't happy about being a prize bitch to camera either. 'I think I'm going to have to do a couple of sackings,' I said.

There was a thing in the snidey Ephraim Hardcastle column in the *Mail* about how I 'decided' to be filmed taking over *The Lady*, and was that ladylike?

10 September 2009

Manic day commissioning copy, reading stuff already in, and looking at layouts. I feel bad about changing pics when the design team have already spent hours twiddling, but I find I have an aversion to generic illustrations, so have placed a fatwa on them. We are a weekly mag. Cartoons, yes. Soppy drawings of couples holding hands, fluffy hearts, flowers – God, please, no! Two-thirds of our sales come from the newsstand, one-third from subscriptions. Every week I have to come up with new gimmicks to entice new readers to pick up the blessed mag in Smith's, and heighten 'subscribability'. I must be ruthless.

I had a quick lunch with the youngest Budworth boy, Adam, at EAT (I paid). I told him I was in two minds about the C4 programme – the thing has yet to be commissioned still – and that I had everything to lose. Meanwhile, getting decent copy is like pulling teeth. Justin Webb's piece on America – well, on a little two-bit town somewhere with tumbleweed – is great. Matt d'Ancona's hasn't come in yet. Meanwhile, getting teasing emails from the gorgeous Sarah Kennedy, the interim editor, who has sensibly fled to New York.

Hullo,

If you want the vitamin D piece, I can write it, of course. Also, the recession dining is the only feature going forward that I had commissioned. Apart from: Wicker Baskets I Have Woven and a ten-parter on Funeral Florals.

Tee hee,
sx

Soon it will get to the stage when I will be actively commissioning pieces on raffia and pickling your own Christmas presents.

On the plus side, a man called Barry Fordham, a commercial-property solicitor who I bumped into in Caffè Nero, told me I was 'far too pretty to be the editor of The Lady' (Ha ha! My aching sides) and called me up and asked me to lunch.

Oh yes. During lunch at EAT on the corner, Adam said that The Lady would fold within the year. So, great! I am the rat they have hired to send the sinking ship to the bottom of the deep. I associate myself completely with a brand, become the face of The Lady, shake my tush at Vogue parties (am going to one given by editor Alex Shulman at Burberry tonight, for example) and then I am held responsible for felling the fortunes of the world's oldest and finest women's weekly. Great career move.

The *Vogue* party was fun, though. Took one of my cabs and saw massed phalanx of paps popping flashbulbs at freakishly tall models – Claudia, Stella Tennant, Eva Herzigová. They are freaks of nature (except for Stella, whose face rends my heart, for some reason).

14 September 2009

Walked Coco to Covent Garden. It took exactly fifty minutes. As she followed me in at my heels, everyone fawned over her. 'It's Take Your Dog to Work Day,' I said. Ben rushed in and said she needed a basket. If you gave me *a sofa*, she could lie on that, I pointed out. We had meeting after meeting. Production meeting, then wrote piece for *Evening Standard* on mannies, ably assisted by my ex-manny, now workie guy; then features meeting, in which Janina listed how many people she'd interviewed over the phone, from Stella Rimington to ancient showgirls whose memoirs were coming out.

Jessica Jonzen came in. Jess is a refugee from *The Sunday Times*, and has asked me to give her shifts. The answer is, yes, you bet. Jess was lovely to deal with, very efficient, and calm, and was brilliant at wrangling celebrity interviews, which is key. There's no problem writing them up, it's the getting them that's impossible. Problem is, she wants a lot of money. More than Carolyn. How will that work?

Barry Fordham (the solicitor who tried to pick me up in Caffè Nero) called twice, and emailed. Now he's pretending he's got a story. 'I'm always on for a story,' I said. His condition is this: no coffee, no story.

Lindsay – who has been merrily in charge of travel – was absent for most of the day 'at Grenada Tourist Board lunch'. I gloomily inspected cartoons to replace the 'Lady Laughs' cartoon, spoke to Sarah Langton-Lockton, a woman in her sixties who is keen to do an allotment column, wrote my editor's letter, commissioned copy, ate a Leon superfood salad with chicken at my desk, talked to Ben about La Fulcher, talked to Carolyn about Tamasin Day-Lewis, who sends me emails asking if I have given any thought to her request to write a food column (answer is yes, but Carolyn wants to do it), fielded calls from the increasingly hysterical-sounding woman who claims to be my 'long-standing theatre critic', worried about my novel, thought about my boys, and generally the day flew by. I wonder how many we will sell of my first edition – the one with my father's gall-bladder op in it?

Oh yes, also planned specially exciting Menopause Issue to coincide with World Menopause Day. Jill Shaw Ruddock, married to important hedge funder, Tory donor and supporter of the arts, has written a very positive piece in which she basically says everything is tip-top, life never better, etc., once tiresome periods stop and hairs start sprouting from your chin. So I have decided to go for it, make Dr James Le Fanu, our in-house doctor, do his column on The Change; Sof McVeigh, who writes about home remedies and homeopathy, tackle 'herbs for hot flushes'; and ask writer Charlie Nevin to contribute 'humorous' article about facing the change with Liv O'Hanlon, his imposing herbalist wife of Nordic extraction.

Rushed to Westminster School open day. Afterwards, I proudly mentioned my planned menopause special to Ivo, and how this would bring in advertisers.

At the words 'vaginal dryness', he blenches whiter than Ben. 'You've got 30,000 readers who love the magazine as it is,' he begs. 'Don't drive them away, or you won't get your bonus.' My bonus kicks in if I can raise circulation above 35,000 and keep it there. On current showing, even though my first figures are yet to come in, I'd say my chances of achieving this are zero.

15 September 2009

I have decided that we must redesign. Even though the magazine has been redesigned and relaunched and this has already been PR'd this year, in March. So I interviewed a designer called Jeremy Leslie, which meant I couldn't attend artist Sarah Graham's wedding to dealer Ivor Braka in the House of Lords. (Ivo's excuse for not going, meanwhile, was that he was 'too upset to RSVP'. He openly fancies her like mad.) Claire the Olive Oyl designer agrees we need a fresh, new, modern yet *Lady*-like look. I am desperate to make *The Lady* look like a magazine rather than a Bupa catalogue in a care home crossed with *Boots* magazine, replete with ads for dryness, runny eyes, leaky bottoms, and so on.

I liked Leslie, and told him I'd call him in a while. I have to interview another designer, this one called Stefano, and decide. Then I had to chat up a banker from Fleming's who Ben is trying to borrow serious amounts of money off to beef up editorial. He asks me three big-name writers I'd like to hire. I am a bit stumped. Then I say, Zoë Heller, Joanna Trollope, Jilly Cooper.

I go to two parties: one is design guru Stephen Bayley's at Lutyens in Fleet Street, where I try to commission blokes to write 'The Gents'; William Sitwell, the foodie writer and editor of *Waitrose Food Illustrated*, thinks me being editor of *The Lady* is a hoot, evidently. 'I think you should have a competition!' he interrupts me, shushing me as I am trying to tell a funny anecdote. 'Win a Stannah Stairlift!'

Carolyn has already asked Nick Welch for any old iron – and hurray, he is filing on having been Florence and the Machine's roadie (he is FATM's father, and it's already been in the *Mail*, but do I care? Do I hell). Sir Terence Conran is there, but I bottle out of asking him. Sir Stuart Rose, chief exec. of M&S, is very smooth again, for the second time in a week, and tells me he is looking for a girlfriend. I quite like the old silver fox. I forget to pick up my goodie bag, which includes a pair of M&S pants. I will email Sir Stuart and get him to send me some spares.

As I left, I realized that the cover of the 15 September issue (i.e., my first one as editor), with Dada's NHS piece, is a picture of three nurses in blue scrubs running down a hospital corridor in rubber-soled shoes towards an emergency. So, having complained loudly to all and sundry that *The Lady* looks like a Bupa catalogue, the first one I have had any input in producing looks like a Primary Care Trust annual report. Hope no one notices. File memo to self that must have women over forty on the cover almost every week, as per my manifesto, or it will look as if I have lost my way already.

16 *September* 2009

Walked Coco to and from Covent Garden today, so she, at least, is one happy puppy. Busy busy again, polishing off the 22 September issue, doing cover lines and contributor copy, making sure that the 29 September issue is on track, and there are some things on the back burner for 6 and 13 October. The subs came up with 'Nanny Status' for Charlie Glass's piece – on the dos and don'ts of nanny-bedding – which was v. encouraging. Not a bad headline.

During the day, calls came in bewailing the absence of the short story and the fashion. And my in tray was full of plaintive letters too, about this and that. So I composed a nice letter to Jeffrey Archer asking him to write a short story for *The Lady*, and copied it to Ben. He called up to say I'd referred to the venerable man of letters as Mr instead of Lord Archer.

Meanwhile, I am madly trying to sell ads for the exciting, totally funky menopause issue. According to my contract, if I manage to get any advertising, above a certain unattainable threshold, I can claim a cut. So far on my list to call: Vagisil, Menopace, Menoforce and Astro-glide. I asked Lindsay if she wanted to write something, and her eyes filled with tears. She started talking to me about the change, and I realized I wasn't up for this. 'Well, don't tell me about it,' I said briskly. 'Write about it,' and then snapped my gaze back to my screen.

17 September 2009

Well, going to an office certainly sorts out the problem that dares not speak its name – what on earth does a woman do with her day? No longer do I amble from Tom's Deli to Nicole Farhi to Daylesford wondering what to have for supper and spending the children's inheritance on some sourdough bread and Sicilian tomatoes on the vine, hoping to bump into mates in the Hi Street (what Ivo calls Kensington Park Road, as people wander up and down saying 'Hi' to each other), seeing how my novels *Notting* and *Shire Hell* are doing in the Travel Bookshop, and signing any copies with a flourish of biro.

No, I march from Notting Hill to Covent Garden with my iPod shuffle on, greeting casual acquaintances and passers-by, telling people, 'I'm going to *work* in *my office*,' and being too important to halt on the thoroughfare to pass the time of day.

Frenzied day, again: interviewed second possible designer for the planned relaunch, Italian Stefano Arato, in the p.m. I liked him; a smooth, white-haired, fleshy man. The best thing is, he's in love with the archive. In the Fred West basement, in a special climate-controlled room, swathed in plastic shrouds, lie copies of every issue of *The Lady* ever produced, dating back to the magazine's inception in 1885, i.e., a 'veritable wealth' of a priceless publishing resource, with line drawings, cartoons, articles about knitting foot muffs, cold cream, poultices – you name it, it's there.

'I want to go forward to the past,' I kept saying to Stefano and Ben. I worry Stefano might be a bit too chic and deluxe and cosmopolitan for us, so I kept saying our readers were ancient and out of town, but I'm not sure he believes me.

I had an extraordinary email from Julie Burchill's agent, sending me an attachment of a piece about visiting Diana's grave at Althorp that couldn't have been more precision-engineered to have readers cancelling subs in droves if Swiss watchmakers had written it. It went on about how cruel and callous the Royal Family was, and thick, i.e., wife-beaters in ermine robes, and how Fergie was fat and only a duchess because Prince Andrew 'ejaculated inside her' and how the only attraction of Althorp was the fact that they had 'Diana, dead', and so on and so on. So I sent this back to her agent:

It is a completely brilliant piece, of course, and in its gleeful Turk-at-Christening way, completely unsuitable for *The Lady*. I'd love to run it more than anything, but I can't. Will you tell Julie that I have literally wet dreams at the prospect of her writing for me, and I am desolate I can't use it (she should offer it to *The Sunday Times* magazine; they pay brilliantly, and would love it).

However, here's the thing. Would she like to be my TV critic? My film critic? Or my restaurant critic? She can choose, am fending off hordes of wannabe *Lady* columnists.

Will you get on to her? I am respraying the mag now.

Rachel
(In the Ladygarden)

I have also written begging letters to the brilliant *Guardian* radio reviewer Nancy Banks-Smith, Debo, and so on. I won't give up! I want them. And Lynn Barber, and Posy Simmonds.

Ben has told me to concentrate on editorial after an unfortunate incident involving a potential advertiser for lubricants in the planned menopause issue. Her name was Elizabeth Grant. She had emailed me after I'd written a piece in the *Mail*.

> I read the above article written by you in the *Daily Mail* 30 March, and although I am a previous fan and avid reader of your articles in the national newspapers and magazines, I thought you really excelled yourself with this article, which must have given many women readers a new outlook on what to look forward to and hope for a good future that lies ahead of them. It is the subject of menopause, and one of the side effects which has a most debilitating effect, and that is 'vaginal dryness'. Our company, Harlow Lubricants Ltd, are the UK distributors for Astroglide, which is recognized by women and men worldwide as probably the best personal lubricant in the marketplace. We have at the present time over 460 of the UK's leading gynaecologists recommending Astroglide, as well as the Relate organization and independent sex therapists also flying the flag. Cancer nurses are also on board, as it offers great relief to women who have had radiotherapy treatment for cervical cancer. I could go on extolling the virtues of Astroglide.

As we all could.

After that, I assumed she was in the bag, and all I would need to do was tell her about the menopause special and wait for the advertising to roll in. I also told the advertising people to get on to her. Then I got this, which slightly stopped me in my tracks.

> Good Morning, Rachel,
>
> I am astonished how both you as editor and your advertising department behave towards potential clients.

The saga started on Monday 14 September with a phone call from Bridget in your advertising department saying she had received an email from me saying that I was interested in advertising in *The Lady* magazine regarding a forthcoming issue on vaginal dryness and the menopause. As I had not emailed her, but was interested in the article with a view to advertising, I asked her to email me with both the email I had supposedly sent her, and all the information on the costs, etc., regarding the article, both of which I did not receive.

The next day I received an email from yourself telling me that I wrote to you after you had written an article in the *Daily Mail*, and you suggested that it would be an opportunity to advertise Astroglide in the issue coming out on the menopause in *The Lady* magazine in October.

I responded by asking you to telephone me to discuss the article once again with a view to advertising; you responded by emailing me, telling me you were extremely busy and that I should phone you: 'Hi Elizabeth, Will try but if I unaccountably forget, pls don't hesitate to call me at *The Lady*. It's all a bit busy. Rachel.'

Bridget then telephoned me to tell me that the email I had sent her had been deleted and she was unable to send it to me (surprise surprise) plus no email on costs, etc.

I then received a second email from you saying: 'Elizabeth – sorry, simply frantic – what do you want to discuss? Am on (my office number).'

What on earth did you think I wanted to discuss? It certainly wasn't to pass the time of day. We are also very busy and at times 'frantic' but always make time for customers with a view to future business.

I will not now be interested in advertising in *The Lady* magazine and will inform my MD of the reasons why.

Elizabeth Grant
Harlow Lubricants Ltd

Took Guy the workie to a launch party for war reporter Sam Kiley at Bloomsbury. He wants to be a war reporter. Love Sam, etc., but there's no question – I am not a party girl any more. Now I spend the entire day talking and interacting, I don't want to talk to anyone after 6 p.m. ever again. Sam tells Guy not to be a war reporter 'because it's shit'.

18 September 2009

The correspondence with Julie Burchill proceeded apace.

From: Julie Burchill
To: Rachel Johnson
Sent: 18 September 2009 16:50
Subject: FROM JULIE

Dear Rachel,

Congratulations on your job. I should very much like to become your restaurant critic.

There are three reasons why I feel this might work:

1. I live in Brighton. I'm betting you've got a lot of readers in Sussex, and this will play well against the capital-centric tone of most restaurant columns. I am, of course, more than happy to travel to Londres and beyond, so long as Mr Raven and myself are put up at a decent hotel overnight.

2. You remember the old saw about Jack Sprat and his missus? Mr Raven and I, though compatible in many other arenas, are comically ill-suited in the eating department. I only have to look at food and it disappears; my husband, sadly, has a narrow gullet and the appetite of a supermodel. Often, we will end up temporarily estranged as I persist in stealing food from his plate. The comic possibilities of this are endless.

3. Finally, as you may have noticed, I'm NOT a lady. On paper, it's the last place I should be. But I'm fond of anomalies.

Yours,
Julie

PS How much?

You can get me cheap for a restaurant column (if you decide to have one) – £200, plus bill and small hotel?

HOWARD JACOBSON Is my hero and heartthrob (I dreamt about him last night here in Crete), and if he's onboard, so am I! Failing restaurants, TV good!! xx

From: Rachel Johnson
To: Julie Burchill
Sent: 18 September 2009 19:22
Subject: Re: FROM JULIE

Dear Julie

Thank you very much for this. I love the idea of you being *The Lady*'s restaurant critic, but the fee we can pay is a trifling, canapé *amuse-gueule*-type affair rather than the News Corpulent-type banquet you are used to and, of course, deserve.

We pay a bit more than *The Spec* and the *Guardian*, i.e., £250 a column (the *Indy* is now paying everybody £50 for anything), but then there would be the bill and the hotel bill and *The Lady* would fold, me having bled it dry in the first year.

I shouldn't have asked, because we can't afford you, but I thought it was worth a shot because you would see the comic value above other considerations.

What about telly? I'm shooting for Nancy Banks-Smith for radio, Howard Jacobson film . . . and may decide not to do restos at all.

Go on . . .
Rachel

I do feel Julie B. isn't for us, but I also have to show that I have pulled some big names. And Julie's definitely that. I'll also have to make sure I get Jacobson now. Blezard's copy was tripe this week – it somehow managed to be bland and gushing at the same time – and he whinged about 'how hard' he had to work in Kerala for a week and said he didn't think he should have to take any of it as holiday as he was so busy being run ragged on the press trip. Hah! Told Ben I was, despite all this, having a ball.

20 September 2009

Took Milly to London Fashion Week. It was like taking an angel to heaven. 'This is me, this is my life, this is my world,' she said as we went into the cobbled courtyard of Somerset House and stood behind Erin O'Connor and Jasper Conran at the espresso bar.

'That's Alexandra Shulman, the editor of UK *Vogue*,' I said, when we got into Betty Jackson. Alex was sitting there in a sequinned top, looking bored (how many fashion shows does she have to sit through every year?). Susie Forbes, editor of *Easy Living*, in Breton top and bare brown legs, plopped down next to Alex. I texted Bill Amberg, Susie's husband, who makes beautiful slouchy leather things: 'What's Susie's mobile number? She's sitting right opposite me across the catwalk and I want attention.' Lucinda Chambers came in looking ratty-haired and scatty – Grace Coddington to Alex's Anna Wintour. Then Lisa Armstrong of *The Times*, Hilary Alexander of the *Daily Telegraph*, and Roberta Massy-Birch of *InStyle*, who offered Milly an internship. I told Lisa I would give her daughter work experience if she had Milly into the *Times* fashion department. One can see why everyone hates the middle classes so much – they divvy up the glittering prizes now even before university has already begun, in a sort of members' enclosure to which only the very privileged VIPS ever gain entry.

I leeched on to Hilary Alexander, who helped me and Milly get seats (and champagne) at the Royal Opera House for Nicole Farhi.

'This is Rachel Johnson,' she said in a loud voice. 'She's the new editor of *The Lady*.' She said it with such conviction that the velvet rope dropped and I swept through with my entourage of daughter, together with the first Mrs Rod Liddle, in her gleaming, merry slipstream.

22 September 2009

Jess Jonzen came in to do her first shift from *The Sunday Times*. It was nice to see her, and she brought a new sense of oomph – she's doing a 'Favourite Things' for us. She might turn into one of my favourite things. Janina looked whiter than ever, like an extra from *Corpse Bride*. Had two meetings – straightforward production meeting to go over flatplans for the issues of 29 September and 6 October, and fill holes. Still no sense of how I am doing: the readers are all writing in in droves, mainly five to one against. The post is a daily trauma – I dread opening the letters, the tide of dismay that fills my in tray, but all this is a natural process: we have to flush out the old ones before we bring new ones on board . . . I suppose. Though it would be better, I accept, if we could keep the old ones happy, or at least happier, while hooking some new ones in, but this seems to be a completely impossible brief.

Why did this not occur to me before?

Then at 2 p.m., we had a features meeting in which I asked Lindsay what she'd written since the beginning of the month, and the answer was basically zilch, apart from the 'funny and frank' piece I'd asked her to contribute to the menopause special on 13 October in which she'd described her menses in shattering detail (the words 'chopped liver' swam before my eyes). Then she went, and I got back to my emails. I've worked out that every piece I commission takes at least eight emails. This is how it proceeds, when someone 'pitches' an idea to me anyway:

Someone emails with an idea – I email back saying yes/no. If yes, they email back saying great, how many words? I email back. Then they ask how much (this is usually a bashful aside) and, finally, when do I need it. That's four emails. Then they send the piece. I usually stare at it glumly and forget to acknowledge it. A wounded period of radio silence ensues. Then they email me lightly to ask whether I received their piece. I usually answer this one. A few weeks go by, and they email me to ask when I am going to run it. Then I remember I have it, and try to schedule it. After I finally have run it, they email me to ask who to send their invoice to. And query the fee.

During all this, people keep coming and standing in my door, waiting to tell me things I don't need to know. Or they hover until I look up and then they say, 'Can I ask you a question?' I think that pretty much sums up office life at the moment.

Went to Le Café Anglais for the Portobello Trust dinner. It was huge fun but the evening was totally hijacked/ruined by drunken, tragic, aggressively self-pitying William Cash, who groped everyone and asked me things like, Did I still have a great sex life with Ivo?, and then went on about how our generation was useless and none of us had achieved anything. 'And I include you,' he slurred.

Went home and told Ivo, and he said, 'I hate those Notting Hill people.'

23 September 2009

I spent most of the day worrying about going to the Burberry show and afterparty and not being thin enough and not having waxed my legs or had mani-pedi since before the summer. HELP. Brought Fendi sample dress with cut-out panels into the office to change into, booked blow-dry, then went into a presentation with Fleming Family Bank, someone who used to be head of programming for Sky, and Emma Bridgewater, the painted-china magnate. The bank people wanted to know what I'd done to spiff up editorial before they broke open their cheque book. So I told them that I had 'Florence and the Machine's father', a piece by Michael Cockerell about Mark Thatcher's relationship with his ma, and so on, then remembered that Clemmie Hambro is going to be our gardening writer. So I mentioned at least twice that she was Princess Diana's bridesmaid, while they looked at me blankly, and then said, 'And Clemmie's going to be our *Lady*, er, Garden, er,' and the man from Sky roared with laughter and the ice was broken.

After lunch, Ben said that Emma Bridgewater talked to him for three hours about running her business. 'The good news is I now know all there is to know about running a pottery in the Midlands,' he said.

The Burberry catwalk show was WILD. Held in a marquee in Westminster. I went in with Sarah Sands, deputy editor of the *Standard*, in a state of barely controlled delirium, shrieking, 'There's Anna Wintour! And her entourage, OMG, Gwynnie with

Agyness Deyn and Emma Watson and Twiggy and Matthew Williamson,' and on and on.

Was texting Milly the whole time. I loved the venue, decked out in cream, and just before the lights went down and the music started pumping a voice came over the tannoy saying, 'Please uncross your legs.' Apparently this is because crossed legs means awful ankle-boots and high heels jutting into the middle of the picture and utterly ruining the 'purity' of the shot. I noticed that Anna didn't obey this edict but twined her legs even tighter so they looked like lean, tanned lengths of bony rope. She kept her shades on so no one could see how bored she was by the endless takes and twists on the 'classic trench'.

At the afterparty in Horseferry Road I was rammed up against Twiggy, so I said, 'Oh, hello, I just wanted to say thank you for being our cover girl this week,' and introduced myself. She looked alarmed until I mentioned which publication I was from.

'Oh – oi love *The Loidy*!' she said, moving swiftly on, with David Walliams (bigger and more good-looking in 'real life'). Flirted madly with Stuart Rose, who escorted me to my car.

Note on the Burberry afterparty. The Kooks were apparently playing live, but that passed me by. All I noticed was the music was very loud.

24 September 2009

Passing the issue day. Now I only use words that I have heard Anna Wintour saying in *The September Issue*, like 'Fix it' or 'Out of my way' or 'Make it happen, like, yesterday.'

Janina is getting even whiter of face, quieter of voice. Lindsay is trying desperately to please, which only makes me want to shout at her. Sandi Toksvig appeared suddenly at lunchtime, so I took her to Terroirs. Super-smart and dumpy, blonde hair and green eyes, she talked about documentaries and told me not to do C4. She said the head of docs had called her in, and looked concerned and said, 'We'd love you to do something for us on the difficulties you've had as a lesbian mother.'

She was furious, so said, 'I'd love to, Dawn (or Sue, or Jenni, or whoever, all BBC women are called Sue or Jenni), but there's just one slight hitch. I've never had the slightest difficulty as a lesbian mother. It's been a piece of cake.'

We ate rillettes and salami, and so on, and then Sandy Buckingham the illustrator finally arrived and showed me her work, and I fell slightly out of love with the project (they are proposing a column on Great British Women, words by Sandi with an i, illustrations by Sandy with a y), but I sense our readers will be happy. As Sandy left, she said, 'I've got to go and write jokes for the *News Quiz* now. Gotta go and be hilarious.'

I went through proofs excising words like 'tasty' and 'treat' and 'sweet' and 'light bite', and awful phrases like 'magic moments' or 'treasure trove'. Then I walked home through glorious sunshine thinking how lucky I am to have a job I enjoy and people to love.

That night we went to Toby Young's for supper. 'Who else is coming?' I asked as I glugged my first glass of Sauvignon Blanc.

'Susannah Herbert,' said Toby.

'Ha ha.'

'No, she really is coming,' said Caroline, Toby's wife, looking anxious. I considered leaving, but didn't. Susannah is, of course, the tall editor of the News Review who visibly found me annoying. She arrived, and all was well. No hard feelings – what's the point?

We watched the C4 documentary *When Boris Met Dave*, which I participated in, was directed by John Dower, and produced by Toby. I only did a spot in it because I was told it would be about me and my generation at Oxford, my book and Nigella. But it wasn't; it was about the rivalry between Cameron and my brother. So now people are puzzled, and my brother wounded, that I have popped up out of blue in this doc to pronounce on the Bullingdon, the Oxford Union and his university career. I thought I was being interviewed about *The Oxford Myth*, my book of juvenilia, something else entirely. Burnt fingers. My keenness to participate in the documentary on *The Lady* has dwindled further as a result of all the above.

28 September 2009

At the tennis club yesterday I saw *Sunday Times* supreme commander John Witherow. 'How's Daisy (Waugh)?' was his first question to me after sacking me in July. His second remark was, 'It's grrrreat having Eleanor (Mills) back,' grinning as if someone had given him a puppy.

First, production meeting, then hammering away at keyboard, then lunch with Jess Jonzen and Carolyn. Janina suggested a piece about alien abduction, and used the words 'anal probing' in conference, in front of Ben, for which one has to take hat off to her. I have asked her not to send me emails in the middle of the night/at the weekend. She asked Jess if she is the sort of person who 'has a glass of wine with her lunch'. Lindsay, meanwhile, has mentionitis about J. G. Ballard, whatever that means – God knows, one never ever knows these things in my view – and has stuck up pictures of Ballard and Ted Hughes in what she calls her 'Boyfriend Gallery' on her office wall.

Re: the *Lady* doc. We held a meeting with the lawyers in Bedford Street (more tea and *Family Circle* biscuits) to discuss filming, in case the trailer leads to the doc being 'greenlighted'. Conversation too boring to repeat here. Basically, as all lawyers do, they counselled excessive caution and wittered away about damaging the brand. Ben mustard-keen on doc, of course. I am detecting the feeling that my expensive appointment, coupled with the documentary, are one of the last throws of the dice. Ben arrived from Florida in November 2008, and is running the magazine like a proper business at last. But if it doesn't work, the gamble doesn't pay off and circulation falls, then it's game over. For us all.

As I was leaving at 5.40 p.m., I bumped into Ben and Adam with Uncle Tom, who lives upstairs and who had handed over control of the mag to Ben, with the five directors now being his nephews, and one sister, Julia Budworth. Tom Bowles was rheumy-eyed and had recently, one sensed, reeled out of some Pall Mall club. I said, 'How nice to meet you finally.'

He said, 'Finally?' Obviously no pushover. Talked about 'the rotten magazine'. So then I tried to smooth up to him, with limited success, by telling him I loved the building exactly as it is. He liked me more after that. Then we talked about the Mitfords, and he said that when families started to write about each other, they lost the plot. Help!

29 September 2009

Big surprise. Blez – who went AWOL last week – came back, and has been whacked by Ben. I've been asking for this since I got here, but I had nothing to do with his dismissal in the end. So the literary editor is no longer in the building. Ben told me he took it like a lamb, and handed over his key. I felt very exhilarated. In theory, that saves Ben about fifty grand a year. To pay contributors who can actually write. The page rate – i.e., the cost of producing one page of editorial and buying in images – has gone up to about £300–£400 from about £200, and now the Budworths have mortgaged 38 Bedford St (no. 38 is his mother's property, and includes a mysterious shop on street-level called Vera Trinder that sells 'Stamps & Coins, Albums & Accessories') next to *The Lady* HQ at 39/40 to pay for my editorship and relaunch. So no pressure then.

Now I need to find a literary editor. Or, maybe I don't.

On my way back to Covent Garden from the frozen-yoghurt place, I find marketing man Nic Boize standing on the stoop, puffing on his pipe with Piers, the computer guy. Boize puffs smoke at me and opens a conversation about how we are going to celebrate/ commemorate *The Lady*'s 125th, which falls in February 2010. Had I any thoughts? 'Not so far,' I said. So then he tells me his. Namely, that Ben will dress up as his great-grandpa, Thomas Gibson Bowles, the quill-wielding founder of *The Lady* and *Vanity Fair*. And I will wear full eighteenth-century costume, complete with crinoline and bonnet. And then we will call a photo-opportunity with '*Heat* and *Hello!* and *Tatler*', who will all be dying to come because – 'Wait for the *pièce de résistance*, Rachel' – Boize planned to invite the mayor, my older brother, to swoop by while me and Ben are standing there like lemons in full period fig 'to unveil the plaque' while the flash-bulbs popped.

I gazed at Nic Boize, stunned. At first I thought he was joking. But he clearly thought this was the wheeze of a lifetime, and watched my face for signs of early delight breaking out. I almost choked on my 99 per cent fat-free blackcurrant and gooseberry frozen yoghurt and had to restrain myself from lunging at him. 'Please will you let me into the building,' I ordered Piers. I was broken. Honestly, the man has had three months to come up with a spectacular for the 125th – in fact, he's probably had twenty-five years – and he comes up with a scheme Boris wouldn't touch with a bargepole and guaranteed to send me aka 'Boris's sister' harry bonkers.

30 September 2009

Tried to explain to Janina that the copy on a page that says 'News and Reviews' – a page she writes, which comes after the list of contributors, right at the front of the mag – has to bear some slight resemblance to, er, News and Reviews, rather than random things that people she has interviewed have told her over the telephone. There was a lead item about a 29-year-old in a boy band called Blake who was, she said, interesting because he enjoyed reading history. I said, 'That's not news.' She said, 'He's really well spoken.' I said, 'That's not news.' Then she said, 'He said "gymnasium" rather than "gym".' I said, robotically, 'Still not news.' She finally got the message and went away.

It must be weird for her, and difficult being the daughter of the woman who edited the mag, and now no longer being apple of the editor's eye, no longer the Dauphin in the Court of the Sun King (or whatever. I think a Tudor court is probably a more appropriate analogy). Plus, the fact remains: the eighth editor, though no longer in the building, is still on the masthead as editor-at-large, and is hanging on to her opera, travel and beauty gigs. Meanwhile I only have two in-house editorial staff, one is Lindsay Fulcher, and the other is my predecessor's daughter.

THE LADY
24th APRIL, 1925
Weekly—Yearly subscription, Inland and Canada, 32/-;
Abroad Ordinary Edition, 28/-;
The Foreign Edition, 19/-

THE POWER OF PLAIN-LANGUAGE AND THOUGHT THAT NEVER WILL RELAX;
Entered at the New York Post Office as second-class matter.
The Postage to Canada at the Canadian Magazine Rate.

REGISTERED AT THE G.P.O. AS A NEWSPAPER
VOL. XXXII.—No. 2006.
Postage 2d.

The Lady

SPRING NUMBER   ONE SHILLING

LONDON: "THE LADY" OFFICES, 39 & 40, BEDFORD STREET, STRAND, W.C.2

OCTOBER

1 October 2009

Oh my god, what a day. An item appears on some website saying that Janina is now books editor following Blez's sacking and the 'successful relaunch of *The Lady* under Arline Usden'.

Nigella declines my offer to be Christmas cover girl. I am not doing very well with my PA, Gillian – and know from bitter experience of having nannies and au pairs that it's more my fault than hers. She has managed to deter Sally Muir and Joanna Osborne, whom I've been fluffing for ages so I get first serial rights for their new book on knitted dogs (this is the sort of thing that I get really excited about now). On the Muir/Osborne debacle, they emailed me to say they would be in town on Friday, and could they come to see me to show me proofs of their enchanting knitted dachshunds, etc. Could they ever! I'd been after the knitted pets for *months*!

'Tell them I literally can't wait to see them,' I emailed from my BlackBerry. Gillian, unfortunately, took this to mean I was too busy to fit them in. These snafus are inevitable in the world of instant communications.

'Are you sure?' they asked. After all, my married surname is Dawnay, and this whole event had been brokered by their agent, my sister-in-law Caroline Dawnay, so they were, naturally, puzzled. 'She seemed v. keen before.'

I didn't know any of this until United Agents sent the whole correspondence to me in despair later and we revived the meeting (with the result that a pattern for a knitted reindeer helmet appeared in mid-December, just in time to turn your dog into Rudolf for Christmas).

Then it turned out that it was Gillian who had inadvertently relayed to BookBrunch that Janina would be books editor. 'Why did you say that?' I wailed. 'It's not true. Now the whole publishing industry thinks Janina is my literary editor.'

'Because I didn't know what to say when they asked,' said Gillian, looking upset. We were officially having a bad day by now. 'She did on occasion look after the short story.'

I know it will all come out in the wash, and it's impossible to be cross with someone who kindly books my taxis and is supernaturally pleasant at all times, even to the people who ring up *The Lady* editorial because they've got no one else to call. But I can see an avalanche of books and invitations to Booker dinners and literary prizes cascading on to the teetering piles on Janina's desk, where she has erected walls of press cuttings and books and notebooks to repel intruders or interest.

Later, in Holland Park Avenue, I was loitering in Daunt's when I spotted a man with a crumpled plastic bag at the counter. He withdrew a couple of copies of a fun-sized hardback book and pressed it on to one of the languid youths who mans the till. I craned my head and saw the book was *Seasonal Suicide Notes*, and deduced from the title that the Womble was the author, Roger Lewis. Whom I'd thought of as a possible replacement for the Blez! It seemed too good to be true. Lewis left Daunt's, and turned right and beetled down Holland Park Avenue, like a wind-up troll. I couldn't let him go. So I ran out and caught up with him.

'Stop!' I called. He turned around. 'Are you angry Roger Lewis who lives in Hertfordshire?' I asked. It sounded a bit great-auntish, as if I was asking if he was a Worcestershire Dalrymple. Lewis looked suspicious but admitted, *mutatis mutandis*, that he was. 'I've been trying to get hold of you,' I said, explaining that I edited *The Lady*. He looked amazed and appalled at the same time, but not uninterested.

'You can get me through Short Books. Is this the way to the Orangery?' he went on. 'I'm going to a do given by Michael Winner.'

I quite wanted him to ask me to accompany him, but he didn't. I don't think I've ever met a more unattractive writer in my life, but I liked the way he responded to my offer with the words, 'I never turn down work,' and thought me important enough, despite lack of literary cred, to show off about his Michael Winner invite.

5 *October 2009*

Am shattered. I doubt my ability to do this job properly and the wisdom of shoehorning the putting out of a ninety-page weekly mag into four days. It basically means: no lunches. No chatting on phone. No old life at all. It means eating salad at my desk and sending out a peon for coffee. Luckily, we are hemmed in by fast-food restaurants (the juxtaposition of *The Lady* and TGI Friday's is particularly piquant) and coffee shops. Have decided the EAT latte is streets ahead of Caffè Nero, and the porridge is good too. So Monday was manic (must stop using that awful word from Bangles song), with Carolyn away in Shetland writing about lamb and scallops, and Lindsay off, and Chrissie, chief sub, struck with flu and Judy creaking around, clutching at her stomach (she has had small op, poor love) and sighing.

Meanwhile, Janina has noticed that I have locked her out of 'Copy for Subs' and 'Art' folders after the ding-dong over her mother's cruise copy last week, so she can't get into documents and make edits. On Thursday, she finally admitted after twenty minutes' harsh interrogation (we almost ended up waterboarding her) that she *had* re-edited her mother's piece about having a two-week free cruise on Swan Hellenic, and kept putting back the same 300 words that Carolyn had kept taking out. So we have locked her out, and Lindsay, too, for good measure, as a shot across her bows.

There are daily negotiations between C4, Optomen and the Budworths re: the doc, about access, privacy, and also – they need to appoint a director.

8 October 2009

Mary Killen, who I have hired to write a column about life in the grottage in Wiltshire with Giles Wood, her husband, came into the office today and mungered and clettered, leaving her bags like old tea-cosies everywhere, and spending most of her day with her face buried in a large carry-all, looking for what she calls her 'noseguard' – an alarmingly magnifying round mirror from Boots in which she inspects her face for rogue hairs that might have 'marched out' over-night, and other blemishes. I spent some time gazing at Janina's copy on Dan Cruickshank, then Mary and I rewrote her piece on 'Bossy Women', and then Emma Tucker, editor of the *Times* T2 section, came in to have lunch, and I showed her off – all slim and glamorous with shiny-conker hair from the salon. Vanessa de Lisle, a former Voguette, who is doing some fashion for us, came in to discuss the shooting spread. Penny Smith filed her copy. It's naughty, like she is – I am thinking of calling it 'Bad Penny'. Ludo has broken his wrist, so instead of writing my novel *Winter Games* tomorrow I am on the train to Swindon, to the Great Western Hospital.

9 October 2009

Spent day in Great Western Hospital. When Ludo saw me, he blushed and I cried. I am so glad I came to be with him. Then we sat for four hours, he was anaesthetized, then we sat for another two hours and I went home, shattered, as my BlackBerry buzzed with Avril Groom, another of my newly appointed fashion editors, sending me endless images for her coats copy instead of sending them to the picture desk. Ate toast and then went to sleep even before *Newsnight Review*.

10 October 2009

This came in from a friend in telly:

To: Adam Budworth; Rachel Johnson
Sent: 10 October 2009 17:59
Subject: C4

I don't know if C4 has come up with the TV equivalent of a puff of white smoke but I just thought you both might like to know that the director they want to do it (i.e., the doc on *The Lady*) is the one who made last week's *When Boris Met Dave*. He was their original first choice, and he turned them down, but the project he has been hanging out for has disappeared and he has told them he'd do it. I think he's called John Downer but I've been sampling sloe gin and my memory isn't what it should be.

Does that help?
Xx

So I sent back this:

John Dower is a swine – he tricked me into appearing in that doc! Said it was about my book *The Oxford Myth*, and Nigella, etc., then he Boratted me – first hour on me, my book, etc., then bam – five qus on Boris and Dave. I said, 'Why are you asking me about Cameron and the Bullingdon? . . . Bloody sting operation. I even TOLD Pat that was why I didn't trust C4 docs. Jeez.

Keep the info flowing
xx

11 *October* 2009

Went for a long walk on Richmond Park with Milly and Coco, then to Petersham Nurseries, the fashionably rural outpost of chef (Skye Gyngell's gaff) for eye-bleedingly expensive hummus sandwiches, creamy chicken salad and unexciting carrot cake, while sitting in the rain amidst wheelbarrows and trugs. Then went to see Mama. She's more unwell than usual. Wondering whether to postpone her hip operation. I lay on the floor. I love her so much it hurts. As for the children – now they're getting so big. It's reached the stage when I don't worry about me getting older – that's already happened. I worry about them getting older. My neck, as Oliver told me the other day, looks like Alan Hansen's, and my moustache – as the French call it, a *duvet* – is now, comfortably, a winter-weight tog.

12 *October* 2009

Felt ill. Tummy thing. Tottered in. Production meeting in 'the boardroom' followed by the apparition of Kimberly Quinn in demure Puritan black shift and puff-sleeved white virginal Ralph Lauren (I asked) blouse. Kimberly Quinn was publisher of *The Spectator*, and a legend at getting advertising. She was a pocket rocket. Everyone told me in words of one syllable not to let her cross the threshold, but who cares? I am open to all comers. She came out with a whole load of stuff I wish I'd thought of, and was particularly inspired about reader offers. 'Beatrix Potter boxed sets!' she squeaked. 'If something new comes out, offer them the old one again, like *Emma*, or *Brideshead*! They always hate the new one, so flog 'em the old one they like! Everyone hates change! And if all else fails, sell them Winston Churchill's speeches. Again.' I listened, open-mouthed. Complete genius. She is brilliant at this stuff. No wonder the circulation at *The Spec* climbed into the seventies.

I only came up with one good gimmick in her presence. Every time someone writes in complaining about the axing of 'The Lady Laughs' (as Ben says, it's more likely that Elvis is found on the moon than that someone raises a faint chortle at one of the 'Lady Laughs' cartoons) or the end of 'Readers' Queries' (how to get Vicks® VapoRub® out of candlewick bedspreads, etc.), I will send them a nice letter and – the sucker punch – an old copy of *The Lady*, just to remind them how 'sensationally bland' (and I quote Sathnam Sanghera, the *Financial Times*, 2002) it actually was.

Had just got rid of darling Kimberly when Jill Shaw Ruddock – who wrote us about what a blast the change is – shows up out of the blue and surges into the boardroom in her AllSaints leather shrunken jacket and gives us a PowerPoint lecture about how *The Lady* has to become *The Modern Lady* – for the new woman in you – or something. Ben handles her with aplomb. I feel red mist descending and stand up and tell her I want *The Lady* to be a readable, covetable cross between *The Spectator, Waitrose Food Illustrated* and another title I plucked from the air (could have been *More*). I think she is cross that we bottled out of putting the word 'menopause' on the cover. We put a bucket of apples instead, under the cover line 'Missed Fruitfulness'. WTF did she expect? 'Menopause' is basically the least sexy word in the English language.

By 3 p.m., I hadn't managed to get out of the office yet and slunk into EAT to grab a big soup. Ben joined me. No word yet on C4 and who is going to direct. But it sounds as if it might be John Dower then, the director of *When Boris Met Dave*, as my friend in telly forewarned.

The funny thing is, I do hope it's Dower – even though he tricked me. The devil you know, etc. Plus he gave the distinct impression that he had a brain and might know who Debo, Duchess of Devonshire, and the Mitfords and so forth are, as Mollie, who directed the trailer, certainly didn't. I liked him.

13 October 2009

Had to get up early. Breakfast award ceremony, or to give the epochal press backslapper it's full title, the Editorial Intelligence Commentariat Awards 'Champagne Breakfast', where I had to give away a gong to the Best Diary. It went to the 'Londoner's Diary'. Exhausting to have to network at 8 a.m. It didn't help that I had left behind the organizer-supplied notes about the three contenders for this prestigious award and had to riff. Ivo (known by Ben as 'Hopalong', as he has crocked his knee) came into lunch with Ben (known by Ivo as 'Dover' for the obvious smutty reason) to talk about their respective aims. Much chortling about Nic Boize and his cunning plans to have me in crinoline come the 125th anniversary in February. My position is that if anyone so much as mentions a bustle and a bonnet again I will auto-defenestrate them into Bedford Street. I slogged through the afternoon and then walked home through the dry park, passing Peter Snow in the parade-ground bit. It's sad when men who used to be so hugely energetic get old and bowed. Be me soon.

I had to break the news to Janina that I didn't really need her to come into my office to tell me every time she'd changed a comma in her copy (she showed me a change from a comma to a semicolon in the proof; am not kidding), nor did I need to know by telephone if Lindsay had placed some copy in 'Copy In'. In fact, I intimated, if they did persist in telling me, I would never get anything done at all and would go completely mad. I tried to appear reasonably threatening (again, channelling Anna Wintour in *The September Issue*).

Dada called and asked me to lunch at the Garrick, reminding me that, when he didn't answer a couple of messages yesterday, I'd had nightmares about him.

14 October 2009

The day of the *Tatler* 300th anniversary party dawns! I get into the office and am told that I have to do a Titchmarsh show on the north-south divide. North-south divide? Why me? I kick up an arsy stink. Saying I don't have to do daytime telly and it's naff and demeaning, and so on. Ben basically gives me my marching orders to the sofa, rattling off audience figures (1.3 million watch Titchmarsh). I am wrong, in other words. Daytime is our only hope.

So I rattle through the copy for the 27 October issue and look at the 3 November copy and forward-plan covers and make calls and then strip off my sweaty jogging clothes and put on a frock for my public (West Village navy with green collar). Then lovely, clean-smelling EcoLogic car arrives, and Coco and I hop in and zoom to White City where, for the first time ever, I have my own dressing room in readiness for Titchmarsh exposure. I switch on plasma and lie on the sofa sipping a Costa latte and watching *Dial M for Murder*. It is a wrench to have to go into Make-Up, where Martin Shaw is worrying about his hair and Heather Smalls from M People is warming up her voice and making noises like a Moog synthesizer, and Lynda Bellingham, fresh from being dumped from *Strictly*, is adjusting her cleavage. Then we are on for the regulation two minutes where I say nothing of note but kiss Alan Titchmarsh's pancake face at least eight times. I feel deeply ashamed of myself for doing it. Then home to Milly, and Sam Kiley comes for a drink prior to the party and I ask him, 'Why am I doing the C4 *Lady* doc, why why?' And Sam says, 'Because you're vain.'

The *Tatler* party is something. Lancaster House. Beautiful boys dressed up as Bystanderish footmen, with glasses of champagne. Tables of macaroons, pyramids of cake and champagne, delicious risotto, huge rooms, so no being pressed into a corner being sprayed with salmon-flecked canapé breath.

I love it, but the next day people complain it was déclassé and say there was 'no one there'. My brother Jo and Dada were there; enough for me. Nick Coleridge gave a speech. Catherine Ostler, who is super-smart and doesn't need to blow her own trumpet, didn't. I liked talking to two immensely tall men: Henry Wyndham and Harry Worcester. And I also liked being photographed with them in the photo booth. Told Andrew 'Radio' Roberts I'd enjoyed his piece about diary-writing (like having children, a bid for immortality). Ivo had to drag me away.

15 October 2009

Felt champagned all day.

Lots in the papers about Edwina Langley, our gorgeous in-house PR (Ivo comes in just to look at her) – reason being, she was at the theatre with the Queen. She had to actually *stand up* at the New London Theatre in order for the Queen and Dook to *squeeze past*. I had given this story to the *Tel*, but they'd buried it at the bottom of the 'Mandrake' column and then, lo! the *Standard* splashed with it. Edwina was adamant about not having her name in the press. Then I understood. The Queen had gone incognito to the theatre because she wanted to avoid any song and dance about Brenda (*Private Eye*'s name for Her Majesty the Queen) going up west. And then *The Lady* had rumbled her. Should I apologize in my ed's letter about breaching Her Majesty's privacy?

I shouldn't really mention this here as Edwina was so fiercely protective of Her Majesty ('I really didn't want to betray the Queen's privacy and was v. reluctant to talk to any journos who rang up about it . . . so it wasn't so much I just wanted to keep my name out of it, but also, equally, I didn't want to mention it at all,' she explained to me later). Oh well. What are diaries for, if not revealing the private affairs of the monarch, I ask you?

I had to eat a huge carb-loaded lunch at Leon to sop up the *Tatler* alcohol. I found out that the documentary, finally, has been green-lighted by C4, and John Dower is to direct. Liza Campbell, author of *Title Deeds*, artist, etc., came in the afternoon and we chattered away like old friends as she drank sweet tea and ate an egg sandwich and told me about her life: car-boot sales to make money, sings in a choir. She's funny and clever and beautiful (it meanly crossed my mind to wonder whether she'd had trout pout done). Ben was panting after her like a hound, but I could see she was hotter for barrister Adam, who arrived in dashing black chalkstripe, eating a Mars bar, bringing the wind from the High Court straight into the boardroom.

That evening I headed for Soho House for Emma Soames's sixtieth. I propped up the bar with Sue Crewe and Nicky Haslam, post-morteming the *Tatler* party. Nicky said the venue was too big and you lost people. But then Kim Fletcher said it had everything. I agreed. I was quoted declaring it 'obviously, the party of the year' in the *Standard* (*quelle* suck-up I am!), alongside pic of self grinning and Dada looking very drunk with mouth wide open.

Here, at Emma's do, Michael Howard, former Tory leader, very sternly told me that I had to tell Dada to *stop* trying to be an MP. I said, 'Why?' Howard said, 'He's too old.' I said, 'In what other country would sixty-something be considered too old?' It was depressing. And ironic (Soames as editor-at-large of Saga has become unofficial czar for oldies). Why should I discourage him from doing something he wants to (in the parlance, 'follow his dream') when all he has ever done, as Mama has, is encourage me?

19 October 2009

Still trying to wrangle terms with Pat Llewellyn, MD of Optomen, re: the bleeding doc. Philippa Walker, i.e., Mrs Alan Yentob – to whom I told whole *When Boris Met Dave* saga, etc., angling it most favourably to me – said I was on a 'hiding to nothing' agreeing to be on TV, which is moderately amusing, when you consider she is documentary filmmaker herself.

I got to work within fifty minutes, picked up skinny latte from David at EAT, and strode confidently in, saying hello to Kath and Joan downstairs in Classifieds. It's always so cosy to see them. Chaired the production meeting in the boardroom. Janina's ideas all left me cold, which was awful. Am longing for her to come up with something that appeals. 'I'm trying to get excited about Lulu/ Leslie Caron/Jack Dee,' I said. But I couldn't.

Then she said, 'Tattoos,' in the same sibilant way she'd said, 'Aliens,' and gone on to talk about anal probing and abductions.

'Edinburgh Tattoo: yes; tramp stamp: no,' I said. She meant the latter.

At the moment, the magazine is costing between 6k and 8k to produce, i.e., about 2.5k more than it used to when it was commissioned in-house. I think Ben is cool; however, he says that the Maggie cover has tanked somewhat. Did not go down at all well with core readership, who think Mark Thatcher is a spoilt waste of space and a mummy's boy. Won't get figures till six weeks after the cover has been out – which means the end of the month . . .

I had lunch with Susannah Herbert, to show all is forgiven. She dropped Max Hastings' name four times. Total mentionitis. On the way back, I told Ben that I'd decided about the doc. Channel 4 definitely wants it, but now it's our turn to make up our minds. I said to Ben that a one-hour one-off was high risk. So if they wanted to do it over 3x60 minutes, fine; otherwise, *nein*. I made a persuasive case. The story could unfold; they would have to show texture and context. Otherwise, the family risked 'spunking up against the wall' (to use Ben's immortal phrase) 125 years of publishing history on 48 minutes of TV (one hour minus 12 minutes of ad breaks).

Production meeting. Chrissie (who has been off for two weeks) banged on about everyone getting behind and wants copy in about six months before publication. We are chasing an interview with Liz Hurley. Jess (looking very pretty) said Liz Hurley had requested copies of the mag. Ben said a man on a bike (i.e., B. Budworth) would courier them round, although he wondered whether a penny-farthing would go down better. After the meeting, we went back to the doc, and I said again: doing a one-hour thing will do us no credit, make me look like self-publicizing bitch and insult our readers. However, a three-parter will be able to take it slowly and let things unfurl more organically, like a young fern in springtime.

20 October 2009

Clover Stroud came in, blonde with big gardener's hands. Liked her. She has a mother in a coma aged seventy. I commissioned her to write three pieces and agreed to try her out as agony aunt.

Have now told at least three people they can be agony aunt.

21 October 2009

The top people from Optomen came in. Becky Clarke (blonde, perky, Northern) and Pat (small and dark, Welsh). Adam and I told them in words of one syllable that it was a three-parter or nothing. They shook their heads and said they'd tried to get it away as a three-parter, that C4 didn't want a three-parter, it was a *Cutting Edge* or nothing. It would be a 'leap of faith' on our part, and unless we trusted them, we shouldn't do it. So then we spread our legs and begged for it, basically. I do think that if they are true to their word (OK, telly people will sell their own grandmothers downriver) then we should be fine and, on balance, the benefit just outweighs the risk. But then, it's not my family company I'm gambling centuries of unblemished respectability on for the dubious joys of being taken down on national television.

There is a Frank Johnson memorial party in the evening. A panorama of hacks drinking champagne at Christie's. I enjoyed talking to McHackie, Sarah Sands, Veronica Wadley, Mike White, Tim Razzall and Jane Bonham Carter, Norman Lamont, Amabel Lindsay, Nicky Haslam – of course (I asked Nicky if he had a picture of himself in Master of Foxhounds rig, as we were thinking of ditching our Kate Middleton cover in favour of one of him, and his eyes glazed in a way that revealed how excited he was by the prospect of camply appearing on cover of Our *Lady* and whipped out his BlackBerry to ensure that his tame PA would email the image first thing) – Christopher Simon Sykes, Virginia Fraser, Clemmie Fraser, Rachel Billington … the list is endless. When I got home Ivo asked me who was there, and I said it would be quicker and easier to tell him who wasn't there.

22 *October* 2009

Well, we've all rolled over now and let Pat and Becky tickle our tummies. The Budworths have finally agreed terms with Optomen. So it's going to be on C4. That little Becky is impossible to say no to. The Nicky Haslam in jodhpurs image is divine but not a cover. Must remember it's not my magazine, my new baby; it belongs to the Budworths. They are the ones who are paying my salary and for the children's education and buying it, and not my smart London journalist writer friends.

Lunch with Ben in Terroirs; he is adorable and lovable, like the Andrex puppy. I have realized what was at stake: *The Lady* needed an editor, but, even more, Ben wants a wife. I must find him one – it's clearly part of my job description. I have discovered that Janina hasn't taken a single day off this year. When I asked her to, she said she couldn't, because 'something would happen while I was gone.' Stefano, who has been appointed design consultant for the relaunch, came in to show me his cover designs – I love them: colourful, playful, modern, witty. Ben will hate them, because the old clunky masthead with 'The' enfolded into 'Lady' on a white strip (to stand out on the shelf) will have to go. The cartoonist Zebedee Helm came in and I have commissioned him to do a cartoon every week. Stefano will email him images from the archive. It will all be fantastic, so long as Ben agrees to the new cover look. In the end, we run with a pap shot of Kate Middleton, and cover lines like 'Playing the Field, *The Lady*'s guide to country pursuits'. Inside, there are pieces about Norman Tebbit, who pretends that Cherie is in his sights when he's shooting; cooking wild game; and a fashion spread with a Holland & Holland jacket costing £1,000. Well, Ben did say he wanted it to be more country, less town. This issue is very gamey. I hope it does well on the newsstand. Jessica Fellowes posts this on her blog in celebration:

Tuesday 27 October 2009
The Lady

Possibly the poshest publication of all, *The Lady* has recently undergone a revamp with Rachel Johnson (sister of Boris) at the helm. For almost a thousand years, *The Lady* has been the place for posh people to find their staff. Occasionally they'd also book a villa in Tuscany or Provence through the small ads too. The rest of the pages were basically ignored, except possibly for the occasional person who ordered a pair of fleece-lined slippers or a walk-in bath. Now it's rather glossy and groovy, with top contributors – including your very own posh self. See my article on dos and don'ts for townies in the country this week. And my piece on posh foodies next week. OK, yah?

Vol. CVIII. No. 2899. 15th December 1938

The Lady

4ᵈ

LAST-
MINUTE
PRESENTS

Evening Gown by HEIM
Photo by DORVYNE

15th December 1938

NOVEMBER

8 November 2009

Half-term. I came in on Wednesday after a break with the children and raced into the office to see the Rosamund Pike edition being laid out and subbed. Looks good. Ding-dong over the Remembrance Sunday poppy on the cover. Claire had put an artsy, silky, blowsy one which I'd peeped at on my BlackBerry (which has since died, losing three hundred telephone numbers). Ben asks to restore the red paper and green plastic British Legion poppy one. I agree. It is a design classic and cannot be bettered, and I don't want it to look as if *The Lady* thinks it's not good enough for herself.

I have reconfigured the office. Major dramas. I have moved Vicky from my antechamber and brought in Carolyn, and removed Janina to what is called the 'cab's office' with Lindsay. So Carolyn is in, and Janina out, of main enfilade of rooms. The plan is: me; then outside me a room containing Gillian and Carolyn; then Judy the production manager and Rachel Chapman, the advertising production co-ordinator, who is now known as Little Rachel; and then a couple of big rooms with art, pictures and subs; and on another part of the same floor, through many doors and across landings, will sit Lindsay and Janina.

Janina totally freaked.

'Most journalists would be pleased to be given their own office,' I told her.

So Carolyn now sits where Vicky was and Janina has gone into the cab office with Lindsay, to the evident displeasure of both.

Ooh – this just in. *The Lady* really is SHRN. That's So Hot Right Now.

From: Lady Antonia Fraser Pinter
To: Rachel Johnson
Cc: editors@lady.co.uk
Sent: Sunday 8 November 2009 15:51
Subject: *The Lady* Killer?

Dear Rachel, I just had your French publisher – my close friend Laure de Gramont – to lunch and she brought me the wonderful edition of THE LADY with Clemmie on the cover. I read it all, as a result: amazing and enjoyable. I just had an idea that you would like a crime slot, i.e., a weekly review of a crime novel. I used to review crime for the short-lived *London News*, and I have of course written seven Jemima Shore crime novels. I thought it could be called THE LADY KILLER. Ladies read lots and lots of crime fiction (hence the leading genre on PLR [Public Lending Right]) so I thought it might be a good idea.

Ignore if inappropriate or too soon or too late. In any case, it's a deeply enjoyable periodical.

Love Antonia

Of course, the fact that she wants a column is not entirely unrelated to the fact that her newest, dewiest daughter-in-law is now *The Lady* gardener. I showed my mother on my (new) BlackBerry and she commented, 'That's the first time to my knowledge that Antonia has ever asked for anything.' The beautiful, talented, etc. Tamasin Day-Lewis is also pushing and asking if I have had 'any further thoughts' about her doing something 'regularly', but I am afraid the door is not open at 39/40 Bedford Street but firmly closed. I can't give away more prime real estate! They will have to pay me if they want to contribute. Meanwhile, strange presents from people have started to arrive, as well as ratty letters, and everyone seems to want to write for *The Lady*, as if it has become height of camp granny chic. I can't help being worried that things are going well. This is ominous. The last time I said that to myself was in 1998, and no sooner had the words formed in my mind than Ivo and I were both sacked from our *Sunday Telegraph* gigs by Dominic Lawson and had to decamp from Washington DC after only fifteen months. I had to spend the next two years on my own with three children under five in Belgium, living in a gloomy villa in the suburbs of Brussels surrounded by conifers. So scratch that.

Things are no more rubbish than usual. But then the first proper, audited circulation figures have yet to come in . . .

9 *November* 2009

After a hiatus, the telly people are back. It's all been very confusing, but now they are filming not the teaser/trailer, but the actual fly-on-the-wall documentary for Channel 4. The doc has been commissioned, so this is for real. So it is – bizarrely – the first day of actual filming. Am very relieved I do not work in telly. It's a total pain in the arse.

I found the crew setting up lights, etc., in my office, consisting of director John Dower in full Tour de France rig (he bicycles), plus a pretty dark-haired cameraman who looks about fifteen called Wesley, who wears Topman jeans and V-neck T-shirts. Gave them half an hour, during which they tried to get me to dish on all my staff. Dower (director of the aforementioned *When Boris Met Dave*, and an award-winning doc called *Thriller in Manila* about the prize fight between Muhammad Ali and Joe Frazier) asked me who I was going to sack.

'Piss off, John,' I groaned. It's no secret that Ben has hired me to be his attack dog. And I've already said to camera that I'm going to have to 'do a couple of sackings'. But I'm not going to spell it out. Name people. Jeez.

Ben has already warned there would be redundancies – he'd already summoned up the prospect of the P45 at the weekly Thursday meeting he's introduced. It's called the 'Strategy and Development' meeting. His PA Maureen sends round an email about it catch-lined 'Stat. (sic) & Dev'. We all sit in the boardroom, around the blue baize table. Janina lurks by the door. I usually sit at the head of the table. Classifieds, marketing, PR, distribution – all attend. Ben chairs. During the meeting Ben tells us we have to come in earlier and work later, or invites someone from the sales or marketing or distribution side to say what they do, which is to sell, market and distribute the title, so far as I can tell. We all listen respectfully. It's all getting very Power-Point. Ben has even bought a whiteboard. After the meeting, he goes over the blue baize with his dustbuster, to remove crumbs and hairs.

But back to this morning. The 10 a.m. production meeting is enlivened by Coco pushing her muzzle into Judy's crotch (she shrieked) shortly after I'd wigged chief sub Chrissie about a massive typo. Ben said something I didn't follow about a teddy bear and Mrs Budworth, and then it was Chrissie's turn to shriek while everyone covered their faces with their hands.

'What teddy bear?' I asked.

'You're not to worry about the teddy bear,' he said darkly. 'It's all under control.'

In my experience, when men say, 'It's all under control,' it never is, and there is something nasty and woodshed-sounding about the teddy bear.

11 a.m. Hugh St Clair comes in with the mood board – soft furnishings, swatches, and so on, for my office-redecoration project. My office is grim and bare, and I have persuaded Ben it needs to be cosy and elegant. Luckily, Hugh St Clair is a firm believer in 'pretty power' when it comes to office environments, and has brought mouthwatering wares. I picked out a Cole and Son wallpaper with hummingbirds against a duck-egg background and orange velvet to cover the sofa or *chaise longue* that I have demanded. Want it now!

1 p.m. Clemmie comes in for lunch and squeals with joy when she sees herself on the cover in the window of *The Lady*.

2 p.m. Brother Leo, who is easily most successful yet modest sibling to date in that he has actually made money by selling a company he created himself, Sustainable Finance, to PriceWaterhouseCoopers, joins me and Clemmie for coffee at Wahaca. They bond. They both have daughters called Ruby, the same age.

2.30 p.m. Late features meeting. Janina – who I can't fault for industry or application – pitches her NASA idea about the Old Harrovian astronaut for the nth week running. I slump back in my chair in the boardroom and roll my eyes – remembering too late that the cameras are also rolling. Pretty blonde Vicky – who does our letters page and coordinates editorial for the website – is very bushy-tailed and keen to write, which is good. Am keen to encourage youthful talent! I get her to write a piece about keeping chickens – again, it's SHRN (So Hot Right Now).

4 p.m. Stefano comes in to talk about the redesign of the mag. I want him to strip it down to its elegant nineteenth-century origins, when people actually bought *The Lady* for its editorial, and the title was celebrated for its illustrations by well-known artists rather than for stairlifts/sprigged cotton nightgowns with four-way stretch/jolly-hockey-sticks ads for under-matrons to pair boys' socks at prep schools. He sits in my boudoir and reveals his new cover design on his huge silver MacBook. I love it – it's elegant and refined, with a double frame of violet and another colour each week – yellow, or pink, for example – and 'The Lady' in a font dating from 1885. It is modern and funky as well as being timeless, but I can see that Ben doesn't think it looks enough like the *Boots* magazine for our current readers, average age seventy-eight. He says the redesign isn't developed enough yet for him to 'piss away the family business on'. He may have a point there. I tell him it's a work in progress and tell Stefano to keep going. If we're going to make *The Lady* more hip than hip-replacement and as successful as *Saga*, we have to change the way it looks as well as how it reads.

7.30 p.m. Walk home via Tesco to get food and Ivo shouts at me when I am making supper at 8 p.m.

10 *November 2009*

Worked like an indentured slave from 8.30 a.m. until 7 p.m., when I got in a cab to go to the *Evening Standard* Influentials party to celebrate publication of the list of 1,000 London Influentials. Boris was number 1 most influential and I was, I think, bottom, at number 1,000. But much, much worse: am not included in the Meeja section, but in frisky, bubbly, blonde, fun-loving 'Most Invited' category, which makes me think: I must get out less. Andrew Roberts – the well-known historian, diarist and name-dropper – arrived and said, 'I can't stay here, I have to go and see Kissinger,' i.e., someone much more influential. Suzy Menkes, the fashion writer from the *International Herald Tribune* and living legend, is present, with her hair arranged in a dark Nanki-Poo coil on the top of her head. She saw me and demanded, 'Where's Christopher?', i.e., Bailey, the Burberry designer. I was carrying the Remembrance Day edition of the mag with Rosamund Pike and the British Legion poppy on the cover throughout, in the hope of being photographed for product-placement purposes.

I have found out that our menopause special – with apples on the front and the cover line 'Missed Fruitfulness', my brilliant (though I say so) reworking of Keats – tanked. Only 27,000 copies, I fear – way short of my bonus-triggering weekly sale of 35,000 copies a week, let alone the 80,000 figure that Adam on occasion mentions. When he first let slip that he thought I should aim for a circulation of 80,000 in my first year – i.e., almost trebling circulation during a savage print-media recession – I looked around for the men in white coats, but none came.

11 November 2009

Masses of Remembrance Day action in Trafalgar Square. Stephen Fry, inevitably, in the thick of it, probably tweeting during the two minutes' silence. Watched Oliver play rugby against Colet Court. It was nice pretending for one afternoon that life was back to normal, that I was a jobbing freelancer and didn't have on my plate the mountainous challenge of trebling circulation of a magazine that people had forgotten existed, or face the sack for failing to do so. So had lovely time standing in my wellies eating cake and egg sandwiches, and chatting up other Dragon School mummies at post-match tea. Having said that, it was still to some degree *work*. Becoming editor means that every time I meet anyone, I either have to 1. listen to their pitch for a column about their life in a thatched cottage in a Hampshire village keeping saddleback pigs and growing their own veg, or 2. try to get them to write something. Often the only way to get out of 1. is to offer them 2. Ergo, line between work and play has become fatally blurred. At various prep-school touchlines this term I have so far signed up fellow Dragon mums Lady Helen Taylor and models Saffron Aldridge and India Hicks to be three forthcoming cover girls, deals struck between cries of 'Come on The Dragon!' and 'Well tackled, darling!'

Our sons are in the same dorm; frankly, they can all take one for the team.

I have just received an email from Janina asking if we want to interview Joan Ruddock MP. I desperately want to give her a fair crack of the whip, but I felt my heart sink somewhat. I said it didn't do it for me. So she said she was chasing Jane Asher. 'That's more like it. Think Cotswold cottages, crumbles, puppies, rambling roses, bonfires, cupcakes, pink-cheeked children in red mittens, at all times,' I instructed. There is no room in the magazine, sadly, for

the kind of searing reportage I mentally file under the category
'Clitorectomy in the Congo'.

Found out later we have already interviewed Jane Asher this year.

12 *November* 2009

Speccie lunch at Claridges. Sat between Sebastian Shakespeare (my
ex-boyfriend from Oxford, editor of 'Londoner's Diary') and *Observer* columnist and scourge of New Labour Andrew Rawnsley,
but only by dint of leaping up when two comparative dullards in
suits sat on either side of me, one an ill-favoured MP and the other
from the sponsors (dread word), Threadneedle. 'I must go and
tell the "Londoner's Diary" something,' I said. I had blissful two-
hour flirt with Rawnsley. Boris made hog-stamping speech in
which he said that MPs had taken the bullet for the bankers.
Mandelson in glistening good form, saying that he and Boris had
something in common: '1. Brussels, and 2. the desire to undermine
Cameron at every opportunity.' Everyone roared as they slugged
claret. Mandy caressed boyish *Speccie* editor Fraser Nelson's hair in
front of assembled gathering, i.e., the entire Westminster Village,
at one point.

Back in the office, the issue had been passed and the *Mail* was
on the phone. Would I write a piece about which frontbencher I
fancied? This was apropos Miriam Gross writing a *Spectator* 'Diary'
in which she argued that women secretly found Brown attractive.
I was only too happy to oblige, for my usual fee. And sent them
this:

I agree with Miriam. I think Gordon Brown is appealing in a primi-
tive, Cro-Magnon way – like a bull mastodon with a secret sorrow.
He is big yet vulnerable (the wonky eye, the working jaw) and has

that brooding quality which hints at profundity rather than the usual hidden shallows of most public figures. His tortured jowls tell me he thinks deeply about credit swaps, etc., but is much too masculine and modest to copy a mere flibbertigibbet like me into his innermost thoughts. He would prefer to battle on, saving the world alone. Unlike Bill Clinton, Brown doesn't just say he feels our pain, he looks as if he is actually in the grip of a violent gastroenteric upset most of the time. I can't help finding that terribly attractive. I long to rush to his side, clutching a tube of Tums.

Having said that, if pushed to choose, I would go diplomatically for either Dave or George. Brown is dark and rumpled and harassed-looking, which has the curious effect of making David Cameron look extra smooth and pink, and George about twelve. But both are nice and tall with great hair and seem to like women and know how to talk to them, which always helps . . .

And so on. The *Mail*, which always commissions three times as much copy as it can use, never ran it.

Butch Stewart, the owner of Beaches, Sandals, and so on, the richest man in the Caribbean, and a good friend, cancelled coming in for tea, but totally came through on ads. Apparently he's booked about £10k worth. So a course of ads for Sandals (a resort for couples where 'all you need is love') and Beaches (for families) will be appearing in *The Lady* – a mag currently read by the over-75s. Result! Especially for us!

I went into the boardroom to ask something. Ben was on the phone: 'No, Mum. We are not going to run a half-page picture of the teddy bear.'

I raised my eyebrows. He is refusing to explain and just says it is a hangover from the previous regime and that I 'don't need to do anything'.

It all sounds very sinister.

13 *November 2009*

Called Debo, the Dowager Duchess of Devonshire, and invited myself up to Chatsworth, where I intend to go down on bended knee to ask her to be a columnist. She sounded very charmed when I called. I do think she's marvellous. She asked for a sample question over the telephone. So I came up with: A grandmother writes in despair to ask, 'What is to be done if grandchildren arrive for lunch and persist in eating with their mouths open?'

'Oh,' she cried, happily. 'Beat them! You must beat them!' She then complained about my father's dirty tricks during the Heywood Hill bookshop's recent P. G. Wodehouse competition. Different persons of differing note, i.e., Debo, my father, Daphne Guinness, members of posherati, had to nominate PGW's funniest line, and everyone had to vote online. She told me that a friend had warned her, 'Give up, Debo. As soon as a Johnson wants to win, it's all over.' I was tempted to repeat Ann Leslie's line about Johnsons, which is that they are 'like Hungarians – they enter a revolving door behind you but always come out in front' – but thought better of it.

14 *November 2009*

Drove to Tisbury for *Harper's Bazaar* travel editor, the superluscious Catherine Fairweather's birthday dins in the Beckford Arms. Sat next to the photographer Don McCullin, who is married to Catherine. Susie Forbes, the towering Nordic editor of *Easy Living*, told me *The Lady* would fold whatever. 'No one cares, no one's going to read it, it's all over,' the Long Blonde told me helpfully. 'Just get what you can out of it.'

16 November 2009

Got home, ate supper, and as we were watching *Curb* (Your Enthusiasm) felt ill. Will pass over volcanic details. Two days in bed.

18 November 2009

Huge hoo-ha over Christmas party. Between them, the office (without my input) has managed to invite pretty much every single maddening time-waster who has ever filed for publication a 2,000-word article about cucumbers and the magical properties of horse chestnuts (usually downloaded from the internet) to our staff, Christmas, three-course, sit-down lunch at Browns in St Martin's Lane.

I cover my eyes with horror. All invitees – and there appear to be hundreds of them – will now naturally assume they are part of my new-look, going-forward modernizing team! I don't care whose fault it is. Or that lots of perfectly nice people are coming. It's a disaster. I am furious. Between the three of them, they've invited every single living person who has ever published a piece in *The Lady* over the past forty years rather than 1. the regulars who have written weekly for yonks and 2. my new roster of columnists, none of whom has ever so much been offered a Kettle Chip at Bedford Street.

Massive inquest ensues. I march into the boardroom saying, 'This is so cocked up!' I tell Ben it's not normal to ask mere contributors to a lunch, only regulars and columnists. Mere occasional contributors count themselves lucky to be offered a glass of warm white wine once a year, if that. I keep making this point, and keep trying to explain the distinction between a generic Christmas knees-up for hundreds and a sit-down lunch. He tore a strip off

Gillian for the guest-list crisis and then summoned down Maureen and Lindsay for interrogation in the boardroom. Under conditions that would not have shamed the Spanish Inquisition, it was my PA Gillian who rather magnificently fought back, a mole against a lawnmower.

I have borrowed black sparkly sleeveless frock from Moschino embroidered with safety-pins for the *Spectator* readers' dinner, an annual ordeal in a marquee on the Embankment (black tie). Talked to ex-*Spec* editors Charles Moore and Alexander Chancellor, who are civilized and amusing. Andrew Neil – editor-in-chief, telly personage, etc. – told me I talked too much (coming from him!). I retreated to a knot of hacks, i.e., Fraser Nelson, Dylan Jones (editor of *GQ*), Toby Young and the event's star attraction, magician David Blaine. I murmured to Blaine, I couldn't help myself, 'You're hot,' and he stared at me meltingly, like a spaniel on Night Nurse, as he did card tricks for us. Neil kept shouting, 'She's still talking!' No one was talking to *The Spectator* Readers, needless to say. Neil's hair was looking particularly ginger and bristly and well thatched. Dinner was the usual nightmare. Superficial conversations with eight readers who all wanted to know what it was like being Boris's little sister.

19 November 2009

Camilla Long, the super-foxy, geek-spectacled, blonde *Sunday Times* interviewer, came in, to inspect my new premises; Avril Groom came in, to talk fashion; Lady Antonia came in, to be crime critic. Coco nosed up to her. 'This is the office bitch,' I told her.

'One of many, I expect,' she flung back. We had delicious picnicky lunch of terrine and cornichons, and so on, in Terroirs. She held back on the bread. 'I don't do wheat,' she said, like a Notting Hill yummy mummy, but managed to put away three large glasses of house white. I do like Antonia. She is dry as sawdust and super-smart and has kept her sensuous Marianne Faithfulness as she approaches her ninth decade. I love the way she always introduces my husband, Ivo (Dawnay; communications director for the National Trust), to people as 'Ivor Gurney' (sensitive war poet).

Went to Rigby & Peller for a crash course in corsetry as it's their seventieth anniversary. The whole thing was filmed by the crew from Channel 4. With hindsight, taking C4 to my bra-fitting might have been a mistake. I was thrilled to be told that I was not, as I thought, 36C, but a somewhat breathtaking 32E, and my excite-ment got the better of me. Having asked the fitter if R&P visually assessed Her Majesty (the company is corsetiere to the Queen) and received the correct answer, 'We treat all our customers exactly the same, Ma'am,' I forgot the cameras were there and emerged from my curtained cubicle in a padded balconette in a colour called 'smoke' and couldn't resist cheeping, 'Hello, boys!'

'That was really nice,' John said, perking up for the first time since filming started. 'Can you do that again?'

Then I rushed back to the office, where the entire staff of thirty or forty was in the boardroom and had to give a short address about the future of *The Lady*. I told them my line about trying to keep older readers and bringing in new ones. I did not reference the fact that we are in perfect shitstorm of negative conditions, in which old readers think I have done the equivalent of dressing the Queen in hotpants on Remembrance Sunday and krumping her down the Mall because I have got rid of the theatre review/short story/endless interviews with bearded actors, and are dying in droves. The cold facts remain. Women my age are used to getting their content free with weekend papers; younger readers think *The Lady* is for old people or where you get a nanny; and readers as yet unborn will have no use for the written word at all.

When I went into the subs' room they were checking a half-page with a picture of a blue teddy on it. It was made out of felt stitched together, and very sweet. The teddy had – as teddies do – eyes made of glass buttons. 'Reader Alert!' shouted the accompanying text. 'In July *The Lady* ran a picture of this teddy in a feature on knitted toys. *The Lady* would like to warn readers that the teddy featured has dangerous buttons that small children could pull off and swallow. Please be very careful.'

I studied all this carefully. At last. This was the teddy bear they were all trying to keep from me.

'Did we run the pattern for this teddy?' I asked.

'No,' said Chrissie. 'Just used this picture as an illustration for some feature about crafty careers or the rage for knit-your-own presents or something. I can't remember now offhand.'

'So, why, in that case, are we running this massive consumer alert then?' I asked. Chrissie sighed, deeply. 'I think you'd better take it up with Ben,' she said, without meeting my gaze. 'This is on publisher's orders.'

I made mental note to do so as a matter of urgency, then filed 1,000 words on brassieres.

20 November 2009

Went up to Chesterfield with director John Dower and cameraman Wesley formally to ask Debo, Dowager Duchess of Devonshire, to be the agony aunt for *The Lady*. As we tucked into our first-class seats on the 9.55 a.m. from St Pancras to Chesterfield, who walked in and sat down a few rows ahead of us but Nick Clegg. So we are alone in the compartment, apart from the Leader of the Lib Dems. He kissed me hello and then, when he opened his mouth to speak an awful croak came out, instead of the voice of compassionate Middle England. 'I'm very fluey, I'm afraid,' he said. At which point I thought – revenge at last.

It's a long story, and in a previous millennium now, but here's why: in 1999 we both went to a New Year's Eve millennium party at the British Embassy in Paris. It was lovely and much enjoyed by all but, unfortunately (for Clegg), I then wrote up a garish account of this revel in the *FT*. In my account I implied that a guest by the name of 'Nick' had stayed out all night. There was more than one Nick at the party, but Miriam González Durántez – Nick Clegg's then fiancée – assumed this was Nick Clegg and called off their engagement. I had to crawl on my belly to apologize formally to her. This was when we all lived in Brussels, a lifetime ago. All I can tell you is that Miriam is one hell of a woman. And Nick a lucky man. And this was the first time I'd seen him since I'd almost ruined his life with her. 'Lovely to see you, I do hope you don't give me your nasty flu,' I said, sitting out of range of germs.

We chatted the whole way, and as I hopped off he gave me his mobile number and was so charming – and water-under-bridgey – that I almost came across. To the Lib Dems, I mean.

We picked up a taxi and drove to Chatsworth, where the land-scaped water meadows lay, reflecting the blue sky like silvered mirrors, and hikers hiked across footpaths, and the golden-stoned façade with about thirty-six windows gazed proudly towards the spire of Edensor and the high hills of the Peak District. I've only been once, and I found it overdone – too much gilt, too rich, too ornate. The Dowager Duchess seems very happy slumming it in the eight-bedroomed vicarage with her devoted butler, Henry, and darling factotum, Helen.

I handed over the flowers to 'Her Grace', as everyone refers to her (as I predicted, coals to Newcastle: the vicarage is bursting with blooms from her cutting garden, including white, spindly roses which she showed me with a true countrywoman's pride). I complimented her on the brilliant, billiard-table-green paint in the hall, and gazed about. Predictably, all is perfection: smell of flowers and log fires; dogs padding around; Norman Parkinson photos of Debo and children draped about Chatsworth; in the study-dining room, where work on her memoir is underway, a huge full-length photo of Nancy *en valeur* in a long gown, very sweet expression, with dimples and thoughtful eyes. A round table had been set for two.

Butler Henry served pheasant casserole, three veg, garlicky *pommes dauphinoise*, then the most marvellous tangy blackcurrant crumble. She refused to be filmed during lunch, when she talked about Eton being full of Asians and Hong Kong Chinese, as well as family. She is living history. After lunch we did a little interview. I asked her the sample agony-aunt question again – 'What does one do if one's grandchildren eat with their mouths open?'

'You bash them,' she pealed. 'You bash them, and then you put something huge and uncomfortable in their mouths.' I noticed she didn't exactly sign up on the spot to the offer of doing a weekly col., but I was so enchanted I didn't press it. After the fireside chat for the cameras, she put on wellies – she wore very unfashionable short green ones lined with downy fluff which she swore by – and went out to the henhouse. She also wore a lurid high-visibility jacket. She says she gets most of her clothes at 'game fairs'. She still looks marvellous.

The greatest thrill of all came at the end. When I needed to go to the loo she showed me into her *own bathroom*, a sunny, light, big, carpeted room upstairs. White monogrammed linen napkins had been spread out to hide her toiletries; her hanging cupboards were concealed by curtains of white toile. When I came down I gazed into her very blue eyes, sticky with macular degeneration, and held her hands to say goodbye and thank you. 'Can you see faces?' I asked, having made a great effort with my own toilette and maquillage for the excursion, worn my trusty pink-tweed shift dress, etc.

'No, not at all,' she told me. 'Yours looks like a sponge.'

When I pressed my suit upon departure, she sort of agreed to be an agony aunt, but is quite slippery about being nailed down until after her memoir, *Wait For Me*, is finished.

22 November 2009

Lunch at Al/Boris's with many children, and siblings. Marina in India on Bar Council trip. I am late because of rain, filthy traffic, roadworks. 'Every day in every way London is getting better and better all the time,' Boris intones, as he does whenever anyone complains about roadworks or the Tube. Delicious roast beef, *pommes boulangère*, roast potatoes, roast parsnips, boiled carrots, so every sort of root vegetable really. Champagne, good wine, all the cousins on form. We walk down Regents Canal. 'Good job, Mr Johnson,' everyone says respectfully. This time a year ago, they used to shout, 'Oi, Boris.'

25 November 2009

Joan Collins, the superglam seventy-something, came in for tea. I had invited her after I'd received an email from a mutual friend claiming she was 'throbbing' to write for us. She was wearing a curious grey woollen beret that looked like a mushroom. She never removed it, but kept patting the beret so it rustled, as if it were packed with tissue paper. She also kept combing out her hair extensions/wig. Having said all that, she looked fantastic, even alongside Percy, her husband-cum-business manager, forty-four. They arrived hot from the accountant in a very ill temper. At first they seemed unaware C4 was in doing the doc and would be filming them (even though I had very correctly forewarned them in writing). They made as if to leave soon after they'd been ushered into the boudoir, faces dark at the sight of Dower and Wesley.

'But I emailed Percy,' I wailed. He then started checking his BlackBerry and found the email from me warning them in advance about the filming. 'Did I show you this?' Percy asked Joan. She glanced down. 'Yes,' she admitted. So I took them through and showed Joan to the subs and the layout teams, and they took it all in their stride. I showed her the cover and asked her what she thought. She peered at it. 'Not bad,' she said in a flat voice. Then we went through to the boardroom for a slap-up tea of cake out of a packet from Tesco in Bedford Street brought in by Ros, our telephonist. Joan spooned sugar into her tea and laid about the walnut cake as if she hadn't eaten for weeks. 'This is absolutely delicious – where is it from?' asked Joan, and sent the crew packing. 'I will not be filmed eating!' she said. Her make-up was at least an inch thick, and she kept reapplying Clinique pancake and lipstick.

Then we chatted about what she could do, and I dropped Debo's name furiously and soon she was on her knees virtually begging to write for free.

'I had to chip her make-up off the teacup before I could wash it,' said Ros after.

'The teacup's now for sale on eBay,' added Ben.

I allowed the reader alert about the killer teddy-bear buttons to run, once: but apparently Mrs Budworth is in a complete tizzy about it, and wants us to run it – big – three more times, which is utter madness. I will put my foot down.

Have set-to with Lindsay about work-rate and send her stinker email. She sends me one back simply saying, 'We need to talk.'

26 November 2009

I get up at 6 a.m. to do Nick Ferrari show in a deserted LBC studio in Leicester Square. He kicks off by referring to my organ as '*Lady* Magazine'. I hold up a warning hand. 'Steady on, you're making it sound like *Nuts* or *Razzle*,' I interrupted. 'It's *The Lady*.' Coco is in attendance, and he talks about how his dog has just died and keeps stroking her intensely and telling her what a good girl she is.

Emma Soames, editor-at-large of super-successful *Saga*, comes in, and I take her to lunch at Terroirs. The canteen. She tells me lots of good things, and how we should go fortnightly. That sounds very good to me. Ben joins, and he dismisses her suggestion out of hand. She is very friendly and sparky – I do like her – especially after she tells me that *The Lady* will not be the first thing I edit, but is kind of *starter-mag* for self. I fear she is being too kind. Unless things pick up *a lot*, there won't be a *Lady* to edit this time next year, let alone any sort of second act for me.

30 November 2009

Usual manic Monday, in which I feel ill and grumpy. We have to publish five issues this month, because of the Christmas holiday: we have to sub, lay out, and so on, all the issues up to the Christmas double issue and the 5 January issue, and do all this before 23 December, when the office closes for two weeks. On top of this, Stefano wants to launch the new design for the Christmas double issue. So do I. I find an email from Claire Wood, the designer, which she sent on Friday when I was 'working from home' telling him there's no way they can do the redesign before 2010. I stared at this. Why not? It's not as if there's ever a good time to have a baby. She took my point. 'But this redesign for the Christmas edition is a stonking 15-pounder, delivered without drugs,' she observed.

Vol. CXV.—No. 2967. 1st January, 1942.

The Lady

4^d

KNITTED WOOL
JUMPER WITH
BECOMING
DIAGONAL
STRIPES

□

DIRECTIONS ON
BACK COVER

1st January, 1942

DECEMBER

1 December 2009

Phoebs (Fiona Mates, wife of ITN's James Mates, a great friend) came in for lunch and we went to Terroirs. They know me by name by now. '*Bonjour*, Rachel,' they say pleasantly as they see me hoving into sight with a fragrant guest, ready to eat the pork and pistachio terrine, the rillettes, etc. The most delicious boy behind the bar – tall and dark with a shortish beard – told us he would sneak us the recipe for the pork and pistachio terrine. Tried to look like a MILF.

After lunch, endless meetings: first, PR chap James Herring. Ben is trying to get me on TV to put the word out about the new-look *Lady*, and is splashing out on PR firms, one called Primal PR and now this new one, called Taylor Herring, not counting, of course, our in-house marketing PRs and 'consultants' Edwina, Nic Boize and Nicola Borton. My mouth gaped in dismay at the prospect.

'But I'm already over-exposed,' I whined.

'As Rachel Johnson you are, as editor of *The Lady*, you're not,' he flashed back. Point there.

But I still gazed at them stonily as they outlined plans to have my bum superglued to sofas on all available mumsy daytime chat shows and channels.

Called Mrs Budworth to tell her the good news that we have run the reader alert of the teddy bear as a quarter page. Then I took a deep breath to deliver the bad news. 'I'm not running the reader alert about the teddy again, Mrs Budworth,' I said. 'Our readers are sensible people. We can't assume they're imbeciles. They know about glass eyes on soft toys. I've run the thing once, and that's it. They don't need to be told four times in words of one syllable that small children can choke on buttons.'

'Yes they do!' pealed Mrs Budworth. 'I will not rest until we run the warning again. You say once is enough? Tish! What if someone didn't buy a copy of *The Lady* that week? And then they missed the warning? All over the country, small children could be pulling the buttons off that teddy and choking to death, and it would be All Our Fault! How can you sleep at night?'

'Mrs Budworth,' I said, 'my decision is final. We have already run a large item on the killer buttons on the teddy. That's quite enough. We have made our point. The editor's decision is final.'

'Not on *The Lady* it's not!' she told me in tones of decided crispness, reminding me that while I merely edit the magazine, her family owns it, and has done for a century and a quarter.

2 December 2009

I got a panic call from Lady Helen Taylor as I was walking in the rain from Embankment Tube via Pret a Manger on the Strand to the office. It was about my cover interview with her. She's already seen the photos – we did a shoot at the Timothy Taylor gallery – and now she wants to see the piece. I soothe her and say the piece is basically me saying how beautiful she is, interspersed with slack-jawed admiration of her husband's Mayfair gallery (sadly true).

Stefano came in, suited and swathed in cashmere and, having agreed on the cover-design format, we cracked on with the inside.

I worked out that endless pages are wasted on profitless and depressing special offers for pen-lights, *Lady* tea-towels (mysteri-ously known as 'glass cloths'), calendars, snuggly leisure socks, and so on. I need more editorial pages – at least four more, to launch our crack team of reviewers in January 2010, and to include an actual review on the spread called 'News and Reviews'. I announced to Ben that my last remaining child at home – Charlotte Millicent – is going to boarding school in September because I am so busy doing two events a night and twelve-hour days.

'Good,' he says.

Julia Budworth calls. I am worried we are going to have to row about the killer buttons on the teddy again, but she gets to the point, and announces that Debo doesn't know what an agony aunt is, and is worried. 'The Mitford family has had so much agony,' she bulldozes, while I weakly try to explain what an agony aunt means, and readers writing in with questions. Mrs B. suggests Debo files a country diary instead.

'Lovely, Julia,' I say (thinking, 'Not a bad idea'). 'Will you call her or will I?'

There is a silence. 'I'm not going to call her,' she sighed. 'I can't take it. Whenever I do, the Prince of Wales is there for tea, and Henry, the butler, says, "Her Grace is with His Royal Highness the Prince of Wales. She says could she possibly call you back in five minutes?" It's slightly lowering.'

Lesley White from *The Sunday Times* is in all day writing a magazine piece. I stay relentlessly on message and say things like, 'Being a lady is not about blood and breeding but behaviour,' and that we have to 'search for the lady inside ourselves' until I feel like getting drunk, going cougar and falling out of a taxi knickerless with a toyboy after a long night in Mahiki. At the end of the long session with Lesley, I crack.

'Do you think you're going to make it work?' she asks, smiling as her pen hovers over her notebook.

'Listen, Lesley,' I reply. 'We are in a perfect shitstorm of economic crapness.' I presumed that Lesley wouldn't quote me exactly, but would come up with some elegant formulation instead. 'The women's weekly market is down 14 per cent year on year. I really don't know.'

3 December 2009

Stefano back in after lunch. We carry on working on the redesign of the columns, features and regulars – such as food, house and home, beauty, health. We go through images that Wendy – the archive editor – has scanned in from the archive to doll up the inside pages (all the mags dating back to 1885 reside in cellophane in the Fred West basement – the staff are frightened to go down there alone and always tell someone they're going, in case they never come back).

We pick a *soigné* line drawing of a man twirling a ballgowned lady on the dancefloor for 'The Gents', and wonder whether a picture of a terrier stealing a roast chicken from a table would do for Mary Killen's column about the grottage, called 'Week In'. We find line drawings of a woman doing callisthenics for our medical page, and a glamorous nightclubby scene for the Penny Smith column underneath Mary Killen, called 'Week Out'. Then we get the two Helen Taylor covers up side by side, as an experiment. On one side we have Helen in the old-*Lady* format with the white rectangle at the top and 'The Lady' in its clunky navy script. On the other is Helen in the new format, all glowing, three-dimensional vibrancy with 'The Lady' given proper spacing, rather than as now with 'The' crouching above the 'L', with everything framed in a two-tone border so all the colours pop.

It is thrilling. I do hope that Ben is behind the redesign. To get him behind it, I said, 'This is the sort of magazine that chicks will read – this'll totally bring in the chicks,' I repeated.

'I was hoping that you were going to bring in the chicks anyway,' he said. Which gave me pause. I always knew that his mission was not merely to find an editor for *The Lady*. It was to find himself a wife, too. That's why he treated a succession of twenty-one women journalists to a fish lunch in the Forge restaurant in what is now known as the 'I have a bream' series of dates.

Any time I bring a girlfriend in, he insists on having her brought through to the boardroom so he can inspect her, and Googles her quickly when she's gone. When I brought (Lady) Liza Campbell, who is a sultry blonde daughter of Cawdor Castle, for example, he was very excited, until he discovered she had two teenage children, one called Storm and the other Atticus.

4 December 2009

Today is the office Christmas lunch in Browns on St Martin's Lane. Everyone is quite dolled up. Merry atmosphere. I regret having had hissy fit about it. It was, I see now, very ungenerous of me. I showed a telling lack of seasonal good cheer to all men.

We mill about with champagne while a band plays, then we all sit down. I am next to Ben, and opposite Mrs Budworth. At one point, as the starters are being cleared away, Mrs Budworth seemed to launch herself for no reason at James Le Fanu, and suddenly snapped across our round table for ten in his direction, 'Were you laughing at me? I'm sorry you find me funny,' and he looked beatific (he is used to it, luckily, as is South London GP). Ben went into rapid-reaction-force mode and doused the flames expertly. Ben made a nice speech from a podium to which I could not reply, as I had completely lost my voice by this stage and was anyway on the verge of total breakdown.

There were lots of contributors from the *ancien régime*, including a man who wrote a 16,000-word piece on garden mazes. At the adjoining table, I noticed that Lindsay was placed next to Janina. On another table (we must have been around a hundred in all), Mary Killen was between our fashion writer Vanessa de Lisle and the bearded man called Keith who supplies the Ladygram. The Ladygram is a word puzzle at the back of the mag beloved by all our readers. I get tons of letters saying things like, 'Whatever you do, please keep the Lady-gram.' So I went over and told him with honesty, 'You are the only thing in the magazine that remains popular with the readers.'

The lunch was very good, and it was held in a vast banqueting hall upstairs. There were not one but two camera crews on hand to capture every festive moment. I drove home with two of my top columnists, Clemmie Fraser and Sof McVeigh, who had appeared on the seating plan, thanks to Ben's bellydancing PA Maureen, as 'Clemmie Fisher' and 'Soy McVeigh', to their unconfined delight.

As I left with Clemmie, and Sof, the band – comprising lawyer friends of Adam's in reduced circumstances – played on. As we baled out it felt a tiny bit like disembarking from the *Titanic*.

7 December 2009

Had to go to a Bentley lunch thing, so nipped in for a blow-dry at Mirror Mirror, the hairdresser on Chandos Place (slogan: 'A better-looking you or your money back') before heading off to West Halkin Street.

The lunch was at the Mosimann club, with Julia Marozzi, the über-skinny, glam PR who used to work with me on the *FT* (and more recently introduced me to the miracle of J Brand jeans), Prof. Wendy Dagworthy the fashion designer, ex-*Daily Mail* deputy Christina Appleyard, etc. We stood around in the Bentley room – all curved twenties gleaming sheening luxury – with champagne. Christina Appleyard revealed that she had been to lunch with Ben in the Forge, i.e., had participated in the long 'I have a bream' series of lunches and had been scoped out as a possible editor. 'But you're a former deputy editor of the *Mail*,' I pointed out. 'Why would you . . .' And trailed off in case I put my foot in it.

There followed a long presentation of Bentley products, i.e., cufflinks, skis, Dinky toys. Tried to look keen. Thank God delicious bangbang chicken appeared in crispy baskets, followed soon after by sea bass, followed by crumble, followed by *le chef* himself, who had forgotten he gave me lunch back in June and when I reminded him did manage to remember who I was and said, with pride, 'We had your brother in the other day.'

I rushed back to the office for a features conference. I have sent an email round in which I asked Carolyn, Lindsay, Janina, Jess, etc., to come 'armed with suggestions' for our Christmas cover – which hangs around for two weeks, i.e., it is a double issue. Janina's picks were Madonna and Heidi Klum. Ben exploded. 'How could you have an old tart like Madge on the cover over Christmas? Our observant readers would be outraged,' he ranted. 'You can't have Madge when our readers want the Blessed Madonna and Holy Infant! I still have nightmares about that ghastly coffee-table book she did' – Ben was clearly too traumatized to mention the title, *SEX*, published in 1992 – 'with the aluminium cover.'

I suggest Judi Dench and the Queen, with sense of *déjà vu*. We would indeed look like *Majesty* magazine. Not the forward-thinking vibrant image we are trying so hard to project. Then I suggest a series of women all called Kirstie/y, i.e., Kirsty Young, Kirstie Allsopp, Kirstie Alley, Kirsty Wark. When I run out of Kirsties I put up Judy Finnigan. Then we workshopped ideas for cover girls upcoming – Jane Asher, Darcey Bussell. Then Jess piped up, 'Don't forget we have a bid in for Julie Andrews.' So in the unlikely event we get a cover interview with Mary Poppins in time, we have pencilled in Darcey Bussell with her daughters in sparkly fairy costumes with wings for the Christmas cover. Which left us with finding a fallback cover image of Jane Asher. Even pouring from a coffee pot in a fifties-kitsch kitchen, she looked just a little bit pale and thin and bloodless, as redheads sometimes do. She didn't convey lush carnality and caramel like Nigella.

I felt the feats meeting had a poisonous atmosphere. No one made an effort. I was mean to Lindsay. I was horrid to Janina. Even the C4 crew seemed dejected by the prospect of casting the Christmas cover.

Everyone slunk out of the boardroom, but Ben and I stayed, because the cover meeting bled into the next meeting, which was with, I know now, the Chief Exec. of Aga and the Aga 'brand ambassador' writer Laura James. However, I'd forgotten all about it – who, where, why? So when they appeared – Ros bearing trays of cake and teapots – I hadn't a clue. Nor did Laura give us the Chief Exec.'s. name, which was William McGrath (as I discovered far too late). I couldn't introduce him as CEO of Aga, because I didn't know his name or job title. So Ben was unsighted and the whole meeting was total shambles. Ben didn't know who they were, and started talking, for some reason, about internet porn. Eventually, the penny dropped my end, and I managed to steer the conversation towards an Aga cookery course for *Lady* readers. It was all my fault. As Ben pointed out later, if only he'd known, he could have had us 'lining up a nationwide programme of mutually lucrative events'. I went in to see him after they'd gone and grovelled.

8 December 2009

This morning I swung into damage-limitation mode. To William McGrath, CEO of Aga, I wrote:

Dear William (if I may)

It was lovely to have you and Laura, Brand Ambassador, into tea yesterday afternoon. Thank you very much for the magnificent Aga-themed gifts.

I do think that we could both do well out of a reader event – maybe we should consider doing something nationwide?

Thank you for being so sporting about the general level of chaos and ignorance – we were so honoured to have the Chief Executive in our midst, and I failed to give Ben Budworth (my publisher and CEO, whom you met) a proper brief, as our features meeting ran into tea – we are having problems trying to find a fitting subject for our Christmas cover.

Best
Rachel

To Laura, I wrote:

Am so sorry abt fucking shambolic visit yesterday our end. A features meeting ran into tea which meant I couldn't brief Ben Budworth properly and I panicked and forgot McGrath's name – and then Ben clearly panicked and started ranting about internet porn. You must have thought we were deeply unprofessional. It's not usually like that.

Will you apologize? Have sent McGrath, who was so nice and came laden with gifts, an email, but he hasn't replied.

God I'm sorry
Rxx

Got this back from Laura:

Hi Rachel,

I'm laughing so hard I can barely type! I was on the phone to William a few minutes ago, and all he could talk about was *The Lady*. He read me your email and was positively delighted with it.

I promise tea with you both was the highlight of our day yesterday and we had a lovely time. I smiled all the way home on the train and

I'm sure people thought me quite mad. William is very keen to be involved with the magazine as much as possible next year and I promise it was all down to our visit. I thought the best bit was when Ben – who I thought was divine – started talking about chamber pots.

As for me, I've almost got over being filmed with wet hair, no make-up and an ancient jersey!

Lots of love
Laura

I sent it all to Ben with a covering note saying, 'Just ignore bit abt internet porn.' Then when I was packing to go tonight, I asked him if he had a big sack to put all my stuff into, and he said, 'Yes, I do have a big sack,' much in the same way as he enjoys talk of 'squeezing in a small one from behind', and so on.

Following lunch with Mrs Appleyard, I have asked Ben if I can see an unpurged list of the twenty or so other women he interviewed for the job of Ladyship in the 'I have a bream' series. 'Did you just scope them out to be the next Mrs Budworth, or were you really looking for an editor?'

'I'm not a dog on heat the whole time,' he remonstrated mildly.

We had a good meeting this morning with someone called Corky, yet another of Ben's hires on the PR and marketing side. Corky has roadtested the new Stefano arty covers at WHSmith in Gatwick. Of the twenty-five people tested ('We couldn't get airside,' she said. 'Problem with the passes') more than 50 per cent of people questioned preferred the new covers. Total result! We all celebrated with a chocolate biscuit in the boardroom. Only thing is, now Ben has given the thumbs-up to the cover redesign we just have to get on with the inside even faster. We can't raise expectations of a, er, visual feast that we can't deliver. And we have to have a cracking cover every time. 'If you haven't got your new dress, full make-up on and fuck-me shoes, there's no point in going out,' said Stefano. 'As no one will pick you up.'

Just before I left, Jess rang up. We've got the only print interview with Dame Julie Andrews, anywhere. She's not doing any other newspapers: no *Daily Mail*, no *Hello!*, no *Telegraph* – only *The Lady*! I squealed with joy and, it has to be admitted, disbelief.

We only have to give her picture approval, copy approval and agree not to syndicate it, which is absolutely fine. For a cover story and exclusive with Dame Julie for our relaunch issue, I would be more than happy if she wanted to write the interview and edit and distribute the whole magazine herself.

I went off to *Today* presenter Justin Webb's diabetes party at the House of St Barnabas, lugging Ivo's birthday pressies, blocks of A4 paper, a small teapot and a traditional fruitcake I'd been sent from the Fabulous Fruitcake Company from a nice lady who signs herself 'Samantha Wickham aka Mrs Fruitcake'. Every day, as well as several mainly green-inked letters, I get care packages and strange parcels. From now on, I will itemize each freebie, letter, book, etc., as it arrives in a proper log.

9 December 2009

Ben v. perked up by our Dame Julie triumph. Claire the Olive Oyl designer is singing, 'The hills are alive,' every time I pass. I don't want to risk it, so am keeping at bay John Dower and Wesley the cameraman (who now wears plunging V-neck sweaters without a shirt and is so boyband pretty that the subs have rechristened him Weslife) at bay. They are already churning with fury that they can't film us interviewing Tracey Emin about needlecraft.

Janina entered my office in Battersea Dogs Home mode, i.e., with pleading, red-rimmed eyes. She's found out I have appointed a new opera reviewer as I go about dismantling her mother's empire brick by brick. So while Arline Usden remains for the time being on the masthead as 'editor-at-large' I have appointed Kate Shapland beauty editor and now Penny Smith of the *GMTV* sofa as opera critic, while Lindsay has taken on travel.

'Is it true someone else will be writing opera?' she asked with admirable directness.

'Yes it is,' I said, gently.

'Can I ask when?'

'Next year.' Then she asked me to let her mother (she refers to her as Arline, as if she was no relation to her at all) know in writing, which of course I did.

10 December 2009

Got in late. Dower the director was waiting for a cab en route to see Arline Usden, who lives in East Sheen. He has snagged an interview with the previous editor for the doc! 'She's been gagged from saying anything negative about the magazine,' he said dolefully.

'Bad luck,' I said. I have a joke with Dower that whenever anyone says anything positive, i.e., Debo saying she likes *The Lady* or whatever, or someone saying they enjoy reading it – any compliment really – I turn to the camera and say, 'You won't be using that then.' All they want is friction, drama, confrontation, or in the dread TV word, 'jeopardy'. So they went off to East Sheen.

I had lunch with Carolyn in one of those unchanged, Formica-tabled, Italian cafés serving chicken escalopes and omelette and chips. Polished off the remains of today's freebie – Whoopie Pies from Harrods in strange flavours, i.e., pistachio and peanut – for pud. The C4 crew came in with their tails down. They'd heard that Percy Gibson, the fifth Mr Joan Collins, is refusing to sign the release form, and that Joan Collins's agent is asking for a £20,000 fee for Miss Collins to appear in the documentary, and meanwhile, Arline's interview was disappointingly unexplosive (the main scoop was that she said that Gillian, my PA and her former PA, and her daughter Janina were 'brilliant writers'). Oh yes, and apparently, A. Usden said I only got the job because I was, and I quote, 'connected to someone famous', and moaned that I had contacts and a budget to pay for writers and images, and that she never did. Which is not entirely untrue.

So Dower and Weslife were glum, and am not so chirpy myself. Though the mag is no longer sensationally bland, and has some articles that even men might read on the loo, advertising is dire. There is none for our showcase Christmas redesigned edition on 22 December apart from a few pages of prepared meals-on-wheels, walk-in baths, stairlifts, incontinence pads and special offers for slipper socks and pen-lights.

So I rang my chum Julia Marozzi at Bentley, who'd just had me to the Mosimann lunch. I offered her a free page so she could show off the new Bentley Mulsanne (retailing at £200,000) to our readers. I also contacted Justin Cooke Burberry but he, inexplicably, didn't leap at my offer of a free spread in the new super-soar-away *Lady*.

It's a bit worrying when you can't even *give* away ads in a national magazine. And you can't put women on the cover without getting some earache. Apparently Rosamund Pike was spitting about the fact that she was on the cover last month (we used a library image that had been cleared for release). And when Lady Helen Taylor was on the cover, she said that friends called her to titter, 'I'm standing in the middle of Waitrose laughing at the fact that you're on the cover of – hee hee – *The LADY*!' One day, I told Helen, you'll be showing off about that shoot. One day *soon*. I am *very* proud of the magazine and hate it when people slag it off.

In the middle of this, Daisy Prince, who writes for *Vanity Fair*, came in for tea looking blonde and lush, and I appointed her my

New York correspondent on the spot. Now I have a Paris correspondent, a New York correspondent, a Royal correspondent, a top team of book reviewers, a spiffy new design, and writers queuing up to contribute.

All that's missing is readers and advertisers.

11 December 2009

Tore around buying flowers and shortbread (from Poundland in Portobello – awfully good) and tidying up in readiness for the arrival of a dozen French journalists (my novel *Notting Hell* is being published in Paris under the title *Le Diable Vit à Notting Hill*). Then I get a text. They are held up by an illegal immigrant on the Eurostar. When they finally arrive, I have eaten all the shortbread and drunk six cups of coffee. In a frenzy I march them around the communal garden pointing out various offending £8 million mansions while they smoke furiously. Then I bootmarch them down Elgin Crescent, pointing out the old family flat at number 61, where me and my brothers lived with my mother. 'This is where I lived since 1978,' I said. 'This is old Notting Hill, when poor people actually lived here. Now it's a ghetto – *comme Srebrenica* – for the super-rich, super-models and international celebrities.' I waited for the woman from *L'Express*, who had a naughty face, to take note. I showed them the Grocer on Elgin ('Eet is like Dean & Deluca,' one said), and Couverture and Garbstore, owned by James Dyson's daughter, and we pressed our noses against the window of new bookshop, Lutyens & Rubinstein. Robina Rose, a neighbour in her fifties who's been here even longer than me, sailed by on a sit-up-and-beg bike, and I made her give a short speech about old Notting Hill and new Notting Hill, old money, new money, or in my case, no money. Then we walked to Jade Jagger's new shop on All Saints Road. Mick's daughter was sitting at a round desk at the back, not front of house, tapping into a laptop, looking haughty. I approached and told her who I was and asked if I could bring in the hackettes. 'I'm off then,' she said, gathering her things, and tossing her head, snootily taking herself downstairs as if to avoid contamination.

Late Friday night, younger brother Jo was selected as a parliamentary prospective candidate for Orpington (Con, of course). I am thrilled for him. It went to five ballots. As I've always said, he's the one to watch. Called the mayor, and before I could say anything, he said, 'Have you heard the bad news about Jo?'

13 December 2009

Weekend in Wiltshire. Today, Sunday, my eye fell on my own name as I was reading the News Review section of *The Sunday Times*. Had been laughing heartily at Roger Lewis's (author of *Seasonal Suicide Notes*) diary extracts about living in poverty, his disappointing children and being Welsh.

> Things You See When You Haven't Got a Gun (2): Boris's sister, Rachel Johnson, came running out of the hairdressers and chased me along Holland Park Avenue. 'Get back, lady, unless you like the taste of mace,' I was ready to say.
>
> 'Are you mad Roger from Hertfordshire?' she asked in a non-hostile way. Indeed, she was almost hearty.
>
> 'There's more than one category mistake in that sentence,' I ventured, ripe for a philosophy debate. But I don't think Rachel wanted to go into that side of it.

I think what Roger is saying oh so subtly is that I am a person that he would like to cleanse from the streets, like in *Taxi Driver*.

It's slightly startling to discover that one has a strong negative impression on people one meets. I had stupidly assumed he had fallen prey to my charms.

14 December 2009

Today is my interview with Dame Julie Andrews. At the Langham Hotel. Her suite. All morning, am very nervous. I keep leaving my desk to see if anyone has sent any food to Carolyn. As she is our food writer, she gets tons of goodies – there was a red-letter day last week when Bighams (posh foodies) sent us a box of canapés, including pigs in blankets and devils on horseback. I get odder offerings. I open a box that has arrived for me from a lady (all our readers are, by definition, ladies) called Clarissa. In it are the following: two teabags of Twining herbal tea, 'blended to recover'; a blow-up globe; bookmarks of famous explorers; some wrapping paper; a face-pack; DVDs; and a bar of Lindt 70 per cent chocolate. I eat the chocolate as I read the letter. 'I made these short fun films about famous people for my own children,' she wrote, and suggested that I wrap presents, put on a face-pack and eat chocolate while the children watched the improving DVDs about explorers. It's sweet, but I don't think so. It upsets me that people have to try so hard to sell anything to anyone or to get a mention.

The taxi arrives. I get in with Weslife and the Nagra – a broadcast-quality recorder I have borrowed from the BBC. I am wearing a fur Russian hat, which has a dribble of candlewax on it from having been left on the table of Mary Killen's grottage during supper at the weekend in Wiltshire. Also in black coat and a black dress. Earlier in the day, lots of people have pointed out the candlewax (it does admittedly look disgusting): 'You've spilt yoghurt on your hat.' Weslife films as I sit there chewing my nails, and he asks me, as is his wont, the same question over and over again in different locations.

In the taxi: 'So, is this a big deal for *Lady* readers?' In the hotel: 'So, is this a big deal for *Lady* readers?' I keep repeating that Julie is one heck of a cover story and that our readers love her, etc. I am shown up to her suite, and Weslife is sent packing. I get hotter and hotter. Am bright red in the face and glugging water when DJA arrives. I have been sitting in a large hotel room for hours, it seems. When she floats in, long legs scissoring in black slacks, loose shirt, white scarf – my mouth goes dry. I cannot speak I am so excited. This has never happened before in my whole life. She is adorable, and spending an hour with her is like sixty minutes of heaven. I think it goes brilliantly.

When I listen back to the interview on the tape, I am appalled by how unprofessional, wet and thick I sound. Also, Julie Andrews has given stock answers to most of my questions, although she does reveal to me that she is thinking of taking out US citizenship.

I think maybe we won't podcast it after all. Afterwards I meet with her manager, Steve Sauer (by name), in another part of the suite – I think she has whole floor reserved – to talk about cover images. He has sent us some, three in all; the problem is – we don't like them. He is tall and wisecracking and very Hollywood. In his turn, he doesn't like the vintage cover Stefano has picked out for him to approve either. So, we wrangle. He wants to see the copy I write. 'Well, I'll send it over, but there won't be time for argument, we go to bed tomorrow,' I tell him importantly.

'Do we?' he asks, in a rather nice, twinkling way.

I find Weslife outside the hotel. He wasn't allowed to wait in the lobby, and has been standing on the pavement in the rain for ninety minutes. As I climb into the Addison Lee mini-van, he points the camera at me and asks, 'So, was that a big deal for *Lady* readers?'

I groan out loud. He says, 'Did you know you've got some yoghurt on your hat?'

15 December 2009

Stay home till 11 a.m. to write up the interview; appalling luvvie gush. Then race into office with Coco. Get call from Stefano. We have a big problem. The picture of Andrews makes her look as if she's dead, he says. I know, I say. As if she'd been made up for an open-casket viewing. I call her Hollywood agent, my new best friend Steve Sauer, in a panic, to see if we can run with any other images. Before I get to plead, he opens with, 'Hey there. Good morning. Have you called to ask me out on a date?' In order to avoid running the Mexican Day of the Dead style portrait, I on the spur of the moment invite him to come to the film producer Gerry Fox's Christmas party. After all, the tills will definitely not be alive if we run it.

As soon as I put the phone down, Stefano comes over, v. excited. He *has* used the open-casket image supplied by Dame Julie A.'s people to promote the O2 show, after all. It works because he has run the chinoiserie wallpaper from the Belvoir Castle spread on Emma, Duchess of Rutland, behind it, and it looks fabulous. I laugh. We have Christmas cover, and I have a date with agent-to-the-stars Steve Sauer.

Just before I leave, I nip into the boardroom, where Ben is sitting with little blonde Becky from Optomen, John Dower and his brother Adam. They are talking about filming in the Budworth house, Deerbolts Hall, in Suffolk. The Budworths seem unkeen. Either for the crew to go to their house, or to talk to their mother. Mrs Budworth, the matriarch, is also a director of *The Lady*.

'So you want to snoop around the stately,' I say unhelpfully. Turns out Deerbolts hasn't been in the family very long. Lord knows what Mrs Budworth would have to say. We talk about the title of the doc and how it started off being 'The Devil Wears Barbour'. I suggest we call it 'Coming Inside *The Lady*' instead.

16 December 2009

Rattling through the massive festive double issue plus the relaunch is testing us all. Claire is keeping calm. Stefano has pretty much moved in – we have only a few days to go before the new design goes live. He's been working round the clock, has even redesigned the classified pages at the back, and it's looking good. Nic Boize/B-Cal the pipe-smoking in-house PR chap wants to run a flap of the old masthead over the new cover so people recognize the magazine in the newsagents, so there is much flapping about flaps as well as Ben's *double entendres*. But there's so much to do – not just the Christmas double relaunch edition, there are also the issues for 5 and 12 January to do, and everyone's ill.

In the in tray: an outfit called 'Cami Confidential' has sent me a hot-pink-lace post-mastectomy collection vest top.

17 December 2009

We pass the Christmas double issue (i.e., send it all off to be printed, one page at a time) as if we are passing a grapefruit-sized gallstone. Then we feel hugely relieved. The new design looks wonderful, old but up-to-date at same time, elegant but accessible. Stefano has wrought wonders, and the design and subs team have been quite magnificent. Chrissie and the subs team start work on the 5 January issue immediately.

18 December 2009

Did some Christmas shopping in the morning and then continued work on the issue for 5 January, which we have to 'pass' – still can't get over that word – before the office closes for Christmas on 23 December.

It's unreal! We all need a holiday.

21 December 2009

Walked in wearing black tracksuit bottoms that had trailed through the mud of three London parks – Kensington Gardens, Hyde Park and Green Park, and then through the slush in Trafalgar Square. The climate-change camp has gone. But there's always something new in its place. Last week the square became a huge canteen with farmers giving away produce such as wonky carrots or outsized sprouts that they can't sell to the supermarkets. So there is such a thing as a free lunch. It was organized by a freegan called Tristram to call attention to food waste. You couldn't make it up.

I love what the cops call 'T. Square'; there's something going on every day: Stephen Fry reading the lesson in between tweets; the bloody Gormley daily exhibitionist on the plinth; the Christmas carols; the bring-our-boys-home services; the skateboarders and rollerbladers; the ever-changing *va-et-vient* out of the National Portrait Gallery; this week, the Norway spruce tree with grid lines of white lights ... the square has become the stage-set for the whole of London, providing free entertainment on a daily basis (must stop that – sound like stooge of City Hall).

As I enter the Irish funeral parlour lobby in Bedford Street, I notice someone has draped tinsel around every computer, and that little robins squat on desks, and signs saying 'Happy Christmas' in slopey writing that look as if they date from before the First World War hang over the flimsy wooden partitions. Kath and Joan in Classifieds are virtually wearing reindeer antlers, and carolling. There is also tinsel twined around the banisters. Upstairs, there are lots of cards from staff on my desk. Sweet.

I walked in covered in mud and muck, and Gillian said, 'You're doing ITN at lunchtime, do you want one of your cars?' Aaargh! ITN! I'd thought I was having a down day. But no. I had to go and have my hair done in Mirror, Mirror and buy yet another whole new outfit in Topshop on the Strand.

22 December 2009

Went Christmas shopping again. Trying to pass the 5 January issue, which is going to have Bahamas-based island beauty (have lapsed into fluent glossy-speak) India Hicks on cover, barefoot, looking bronzed and inviting. Ben spends most of his time nipping off to Sloane Square on his motorbike to buy toys for his nephews and nieces. 'Just off to load the sleigh,' he says.

A festive mood is definitely abroad in the office. Gillian has bagged up all the swag we've been sent during the year – Jo Malone bath oils, Martin Miller Gin, etc. – and doled it out. There is a Christmas cake slowly eroding by the kettle – people keep digging in with teaspoons, as if it's a Stilton.

As I'd rather had the pick of the beauty stuff already, I made a great show of declining my own unearned portion of the goodies. I spent most of the afternoon trying to buy a particular sort of very thick-rimmed brown porcelain espresso cup from Italy online and ended up finding them on a US website and clicking to buy, a split second after seeing that the P&P alone was $50.

The in tray (and logged in the 'gifts' file): Christmas-pudding-flavoured biscuits; travel guide to Angola (as *Lady* readers would really want to go to a war zone). Michael Winner has also sent Janina a Christmas card with quotes of how wonderful he is from Sir Roger Moore, Sir Michael Caine and John Cleese.

23 December 2009

Last day of *The Lady* year. Office closes later, reopens 4 January.

In the morning I had to do a dreaded *Sunday Times* photoshoot for the pictures to accompany the Lesley White magazine piece about me taking over *The Lady*. Zipped into Bedford Street to send some emails, cleared my desk for 'festive period', saw Carolyn, said 'Happy Christmas' to Lindsay, and Janina, went upstairs, and Adam was uncorking bottle of white with a broad grin. 'We've just had our Chambers lunch,' he slurred. 'Drink?'

'Where's Ben?' I said, declining. It's not the same when Ben isn't here. There's no one to scrap with.

'He said he might come in if the drizzle stopped,' said Adam. Then I pushed off to J Sheekey before *La Bohème*, at the Royal Opera House. It all felt very decadent. I gurgled oysters soaked in lemon and shallots and smiled at Ivo. Then I said, 'I'm so lucky, this is the absolutely perfect job for me. I don't want to do another one now.'

Then I had a terrible flashback of something that Carolyn had said after the Christmas lunch, during which I couldn't speak, because of laryngitis. Mrs Budworth the Matriarch had said something ominous. I'd asked Carolyn to try to remember exactly what Mrs B. had said. 'I think she said there was money until September,' she said. 'But that she could pull the plug at pretty much any time.'

So as it's end of December, that gives me nine months to turn her Ladyship around. Three months to get circulation staying above 30,000 (if it hits 35,000 and stays there – ha ha – I get a bonus). As I write, the *Guardian* is laying off dozens of journalists, the *Observer* has only narrowly escaped closure, there is blood all over the carpets at Condé Nast. So what chance do I have?

When I got home, I spotted that a flier from the cake woman had been sticking out from the pen-tidy on my desk during the shoot. So I'd been posing for the *Sunday Times* mag the whole time in front of a postcard saying 'Real Fruitcake'. A perfect end to my first four months at the helm.

January

5 January 2010

Twelve days out of the office, and now back to a flapdown. No one knew I wasn't in on 4 January. Some of the wrong pieces are being laid out, with the wrong pictures, in the wrong places, i.e., instead of ex-BBC 4 radio producer Olivia Seligman's treatise on *The Archers*, complete with Vanessa Whitburn quotes (Whitburn is the editor of *The Archers*), the subs were laying out an extract from Charles Collingwood's autobiography about playing smoothie Ambridge rotter Brian Aldridge and Aldridge's long affair with Siobhan and their lovechild Ruairi.

So I tried to remain calm. The truth is, they do the lion's share of the work, not me. And they never complain. However, people are still ill, or cut off in snow, so God knows how we are going to put out and distribute the mag. According to the *Evening Standard*, an 'extreme weather event' is on its way. Our friend, Milly's godfather, novelist Henry Porter, has just rung to say that the M4 is shut, so I'm unlikely to get Ludo back to school at Marlborough tomorrow. Just now, someone on *The World Tonight* said that Gatwick, Luton and Liverpool airports are all closed, and has just interviewed someone who is cut off somewhere in Lincolnshire. The presenter asked, 'Have you had a problem with grit theft before in Market Rasen?' Honestly, it's all about the weather at the moment. When I worked on *The World Tonight* it was all about the rise of China and 'Who cares for the carers?' and was so intergalactically worthy that Ivo rechristened the programme 'The World Tosleep'.

Over the Christmas holiday, between cooking and washing up and shopping and wrapping, I'd tried desperately to clear mental space to think about the direction of the magazine. I'd been too busy before, cranking it out week after week.

Who is it for? Would I buy it? Who is it aimed at? What is its audience? But these are questions to which I still cannot give very clear answers, which is a problem. It's a magazine that – were I not editing it – I would definitely flick through, and so would most of my friends, if it was lying around. But we wouldn't, necessarily, *buy* it. I think the mag's miles better than it was. For a start, it looks like a magazine, which helps, and it's well written. My columnists are among the best around. Above all, *The Lady* is unlike anything else in lots of ways: it's simply not trashy, and follows a different agenda. We do masses on the secret life of the lady's maid, and we are planning a five-parter on old-school nannies that will be endlessly reassuring. My reckoning is, if I can come up with features that will make it a must-read for people who have *staff*, just as *Country Life* is a must-read for people who have country piles, or wish they did, we'd be on to something. Am worrying about this pretty much all the time. And I'm not sure I'm on the right track; I'm losing old readers (I should add that Ben keeps insisting I call them 'established' rather than 'old' readers) faster than bringing new ones on board.

Over New Year on Exmoor, a friend of Ivo's called Lady Henrietta Rous told him the magazine was too *Spectator*-ish and upmarket. 'The only people who read *The Lady* are the lower orders,' she told him earnestly. Aaaggh! What if she's right? Then the twinkling charm of Clemmie Hambro and Mary Killen will be falling on stony ground.

On the plus side . . . Coco's column, launched in the Christmas issue, is a surprise success. Joan from Classifieds now sends Coco emails in the voice of her dog, Meesha, which I have to answer. Coco is also getting lots of letters and emails starting with the salutation, 'Woof woof' and ending, 'Tailwags'. Have had a slightly less pliable response from within the office: an anonymous email from someone who called himself (or herself) Office Plank saying that I am a flea-bitten old bitch. This forcefully reminds me that I have only been in the saddle for a few months, my champagne got nicked and not everyone necessarily likes me.

It is very cold in Bedford Street. There is no central heating, only radiators, so rooms are either hammam-temperature or freezing. Uncle Tom Bowles is haunting the central staircase in his pyjamas, over which he has layered his outdoor clothes.

Edwina, the beauty in the marketing department, is cross – she wanted to pen the Coco column, and is pitching to interview Joanna Lumley. Am all in favour of youthful ambition; I want her to write; but I know just the chap I want to interview Joanna Lumley.

Roger Lewis – the writer who wants to shoot me – is clearly the right man for the job.

6 January 2010

Text from Dada. 'See Rowan Pelling in the Tel!!' it says. I am en route to the boardroom to see Ben and have a fight about the Penny Smith cover (he wants an image of presenter Penny Smith wearing a depressing blue dress with a ruffle front that looks funereal; I want her in a sparkly sequinned jacket). So I surged into boardroom and, as I got the row underway, I plucked the *Telegraph* from his table, opened it to the comment pages and speed-read Rowan's piece as we ding-donged.

Then I almost threw up.

It was entitled – 'So the G-spot doesn't exist after all? Thank God for that!' I searched for my name, and quickly came to it, in the first and longest gobbet of Rowan's notebook. She says she has always thought that the G-spot was invented solely to terrorize women, and admitted in the public prints that she didn't have one. 'The next day I ran into Rachel Johnson, now the exuberant editor of *The Lady*, whose opinion had also been sought and who admitted to no such deficiency. Johnson was aghast at my lack of G-ness, a particularly poor show in the then editor of an erotic mag.'

I didn't have the heart to fight Ben after my internal genitalia had been publicly discussed in a national newspaper.

I wrote a letter to Roger Lewis. In it I said I was sorry that my brief meeting with him had sent his trigger finger into spasm, but did he want to interview Joanna Lumley for us? I told him we paid terribly badly and had only a very few readers left, mainly in care homes. I thought that would appeal to him.

Rosie Boycott – Boris's food czar is one of her many hats – came to supper. She looks incredible. I won't even say 'for her age', because I have decided to try to ban any reference to female age in *The Lady*, unless it is the hook, i.e., 'Dame Jennifer Jenkins at ninety'. I told her about my daily walks through Trafalgar Square, and warbled about the fourth plinth being, in a sense, redundant – the whole square serves as a plinth anyway, with a different protest or installation, or service or whatnot, or climate-change protesters or hardwood trees there daily. I said that a year in the life of Trafalgar Square could be a good book and graciously allowed her to steal my idea and offer it up to Boris as a tidbit.

7 January 2010

Roger Lewis called twice in ten minutes. He has received my card and said he loved it and has agreed to interview Joanna Lumley, so long as I pay his return train fare to Wales, or wherever it is he lurks. I told him there was a catch. 'You have to go with an aston-ishingly beautiful twenty-four-year-old called Edwina,' I teased, expecting him to start panting like a hound.

'No, all that's over,' he said. 'Not for years now.'

So then I said that she was like something out of the Mick Jagger song: 'She'd make a dead man . . .' I started.

'No,' he cut me off. 'Not a sausage.'

We had a long talk which I concluded with, 'Well, I'm glad we're such good friends now.'

Kate Shapland, who writes our beauty page, came in to discuss selling beauty advertising and noticed that her beauty notebook, with luscious references to luxury products from Guerlain and Dr Hauschka, and so on, was placed adjacent to a quarter-page ad from Tena with the words 'TENA *Pants* Discreet in NEW cotton-like material', and a photograph of a woman pulling up her trousers over her bottom. She screamed and covered her face.

The in tray:

- free sample of Replens MD, the leading vaginal moisturizing gel. 'Clinical studies have shown that best results are achieved from regular use, three applications a week, preferably in the morning. It means you can be flirty and fabulous for ever!' the accompanying leaflet puffed. Have left it prominently on my desk to frighten Ben.
- an assortment of Sarah Smith vibrant floral 'flower-power scourers, cleaning cloths to add a splash of colour and make my household cleaning fun and easy to help remove stubborn stains'. Like the Tena pants, the cloths claim to be 'ultra absorbent'.

11 January 2010

Discover there is a kindly message from Jeremy on the answering machine that I haven't listened to. 'Hello. It's Jeremy (modest, dactylic pause) Paxman here. Just to say that I think *The Lady*'s looking really rather good. Much better. There are articles that I could theoretically imagine reading. Maybe. Anyway. Well done.'

Also one from writer David Jenkins, Alex Shulman's inamorato, saying, 'Just thought I'd pass on that everyone keeps saying what a good job you're doing. Gratters, old bean.'

Now I'm getting plaudits, I fear I should be even more worried. It must mean the mag is destined for the plughole even sooner than Mrs Budworth intimated. And tomorrow we get the figures for how the Christmas-relaunch Julie Andrews cover has done, so fear really grips.

Had a session of acupuncture with a lovely creature called Annee de Mamiel at Home House. She asked me lots of questions, i.e., how often I opened my bowels and whether I had well-formed stools. I answered positively. Then she stuck needles into my legs and arms and said that my right side was blocked. And that my skin was dry because there was no 'energetic activity in my womb'.

I felt very spaced out afterwards and had to eat the entire presentation box of Betty's of Harrogate's box of white champagne truffles which were sitting on my desk when I arrived.

12 *January* 2010

The circulation numbers for the 22 December issue have come in. We sold 32,000 copies. That's a 20 per cent increase week on week and year on year. 'But I thought we were looking for something nearer 40,000,' I said, when Ben unveiled the numbers. This is what I had been told a double Christmas issue cover would sell in the good old days.

Ben bridled. He went on about how we are a publication bucking the trend in a recession that has hit print media hardest of all. So I am to think that 32,000 is good news. We're up a bit, and everyone else is down. Have asked Ben to send over the figures so I can see the trend. Adam emailed, saying that Graydon and Anna Carter (editor of *Vanity Fair* and wife) just luuurve *The Lady* and read it every week and want to come in and have tea.

So we will roll out the Joan Collins memorial walnut cake again.

Hugh St Clair is slowly transforming my office. The wallpaper looks delicious and uplifting. He has covered two *bergère* chairs with his own fabric, and hung twelve or so *Lady* covers in identical silver frames (chosen by me). And now my *chaise longue* has arrived. Joan (fluffy slippers) and Kath (longest-serving member of staff, at thirty-four years) – both marvellous – stood around and laughed at it. It is upholstered in orange velveteen (it seemed a good idea at the time) and is not a *chaise longue* but a doll-sized *chaise courte*. Even my abbreviated limbs dangle off the end. Ben came in – after all, he has paid for the new wallpaper, the framing of *Lady* covers, the furniture. 'Those are the worst-framed and hung pictures I've ever seen,' he said, then shuddered at the bottle of Replens on my desk. 'And what the hell is that?' pointing at the fun-sized Tango-hued piece.

'It's the *chaise courte*,' I said, sitting on the doll-like item and hoping it wouldn't break.

'The *chaise* shit more like,' he said, before disappearing for his forty-fifth Silk Cut of the day.

Went into the boardroom to find Ben, Edwina and Nic Boize (B-Cal) working up ten key points I have to make in the BBC *Brekker* interview tomorrow morning.

'Which celebrities would we never have in *The Lady*?' Ben asked. Before I could answer, he spun into an anecdote about being a witness to the crash that left Heather Mills legless. 'I was proceeding down Kensington Gore on the A track and saw a DPG Hunter pack of two diplomatic policemen on separate bikes,' he explained. He always talks like this, because he flies helicopters and has been in the army. 'And Mills stepped out into the street. The claret was running down the pavement,' he said. 'It was all her fault! The sirens were blaring and everything. I felt sorry for the police bikers. I mean, it was all right for *her* – she went on to marry Paul McCartney, but the one who hit her was in bits and was probably invalided out of the service.' I think at one point Ben even said he was one of the 'lucky few' who've ever seen 'Heather Mills's other leg'.

13 January 2010

Car arrived at 7.55 a.m., to convey me to TV Centre and on to the BBC *Breakfast* set, where I am booked to appear on the sofa at ten to nine. I arrived at the same time as Kevin McCloud, who is immediately ushered to a swanky dressing room with his name on the door. I am shooed into Make-Up, don't get my own dressing room. 'This has got to last till a party tonight, so lay it on thick,' I urged. Did my spot, which came on after what seemed like interminable package followed by live interview with a man who had had hiccups for two years and was on to tell the nation all about it. My first question from Sian and Bill of the Sofa was – Was I taking *The Lady* upmarket and/or in search of younger readers?

'No,' I gushed, mindful of what Lady Henrietta Rous had said over the festive period, i.e., our readers were all from the *lower orders*. 'It's all about age, not attitude.' What I meant was, of course, attitude not age, as Ben reminded me the second I came off air. The only time the interview came alive was when they asked if it was true that there was a dog on the staff. 'Yes,' I pealed. 'She writes her own column!'

Next, a car arrived to take me to the Cath Kidston shoot and interview at a riverside 'dream house' in Chiswick in lee of Fuller's Brewery. The air by the Thames was a heady mix of hops, mash and riparian vapours.

I apologized for my heavy pancake as soon as I'd got through the security gates and into the dream-home interior, filled with light and colour and art. Cath looked at me carefully. 'I want even more make-up, and for you to Photoshop me too,' she said. 'Just Photoshop away, won't you?'

She was heavenly, the house was heavenly, it was all heavenly. Stepdaughter Jess's bedroom was a poem of white bunks and pretty colour, as was the study, bedroom, sitting room, hall. Modern art mingled with film posters, i.e., still from original of *St Trinian's* with gymslipped schoolgirls brandishing hockey sticks from the windows of the school train. Whenever I asked who did anything, she airily replied, 'All on the cheap,' or 'It's white lino,' or 'Shepherd's Bush market stall'. I can spend thousands on something and it still looks cheap and nasty. Kidston spends a few pee, and makes it look like *World of Interiors*.

I rushed back before the crew from *Madame Figaro* arrived, which they did promptly at 2.30 p.m. Did interview and photoshoot in the snow in the communal garden while little children called things like Romilly and Lilac romped around with puppies and mummies. It was like something out of the Boden catalogue, with a slight Ingmar Bergman feeling, with the light very grey and the ground very white and the stucco looking almost dirty against it all, and the bare branches etched against the snow and the stucco like filigree. The round topiary bushes by the playground had bonnets of snow and looked just like Christmas puddings in *Beano*.

Later, I went to the opening of the Ruddock Medieval Europe and Medieval/Renaissance galleries at the V&A. Jill Shaw Ruddock made an adorable speech which mentioned the Middle Ages but, thankfully, not the menopause. I was chatted up by David Willetts. He wanted to talk to me because I sit on this quango, called 'The Family Commission', I think.

'It's not merely that the old are getting younger, but the young are getting older,' I pronounced, as if addressing a studio audience on *Question Time*. I saw his eyes gleam behind his specs. 'That's mine. I've copyrighted it,' I said. It was cold in the galleries, but the mojitos were good and I recognized the chilli-caramel roasted nuts – they were Ottolenghi and about £25 a kilo.

14 *January 2010*

Want *The Lady* to profit from the blanket publicity surrounding Lady Antonia's book, *Must You Go?*, about her affair and marriage to Harold Pinter. I have rejigged things so our reviewer Susan Hill interviews our reviewer Antonia for what I hope will be a cover story with welly. After all, it's not often that a *Lady* columnist is headline news.

Then I have to go to a meeting upstairs about our coverage for the mag's anniversary, which falls on 16 February, by which time *The Lady* will have been in continuous publication for 125 years. I have the idea that we will come up with a list of 125 Ladies of Today to mark the occasion, plus lots of other stuff. I can't believe the pressure never lets up. Stop the train – I want to get off. The sales of the 22 December Julie Andrews issue have collapsed to 31,700 after Sainsbury's sent back 700 unsold copies.

15 *January 2010*

Susan Hill called to say that whenever she asked Antonia any questions about Daniel (Harold's son), Vivien (his first wife), or the children's reactions to the loss of family life, she merely replied, 'Pass.'

'You're both my writers, and you're friends,' I told her. 'You're not Lynn Barber, and *The Lady*'s not the *Mail*. Just have fun with it.'

16 *January 2010*

Car arrived (I seem to be writing those words too frequently) to take me to Broadcasting House to record *Loose Ends* 'as live' at 11 a.m. Clive Anderson was hosting, Emma Freud guest interviewing.

There were three luvvies and a hack on. The actress Emilia Fox talked about *Silent Witness* and pathology and dead bodies, interrupted by Paul Whitehouse, who has a sort of comedic Tourette's. John Hurt talked in a husky voice, interrupted by Paul Whitehouse and his own hacking cough about his hoodlum picture, called '44-inch Chest', I think.

Emma Freud – astonishing huge violet eyes, skinny legs, glossy hair – and I had already compared breast cup sizes in the Green Room over filthy BBC coffee. She says she is DD, sometimes E. 'Same,' I said. 'Snap!' I was pathetically trying to get her to like me. Then, when we were recording, she went for me rather, as I would, to be fair, if I had the grim task of interviewing me.

She opened the interview about me trying to put the ooh la la into *The Lady* by mentioning the full-page Stannah Stairlifts ad, her eyes goggling at the very idea. 'I'm grateful for all our advertisers,' I responded stoutly. Next up came the Charles Glass piece. 'I think you're referring to the fiasco known as humping the help,' I confirmed. Then she had a go about me writing endless columns about myself and Notting Hill neighbours and said I was an outcast in our hood. At this point I sort of collapsed like a pricked inflatable and just rambled on about *The Lady* and broadcast an apology to all those I have serially offended. I should have snapped back, 'You clearly regard both me and my readers as equally incontinent,' and pointed out that she and our Notting Hill neighbours are not exactly huddled masses in need of urgent international aid – the news from Haiti gets more awful by the minute – but live in vast mansions staffed by tiny Filipinos. But, as ever, it didn't occur to me at the time.

Repaired to the pub, where beige platters of re-formed meats and pastry in the shape of sausage rolls, mini-pasties and spring rolls awaited us. I sat in between Whitehouse and Freud in the pub and had a lovely time, as Whitehouse did impressions and made up a special face for me (eyebrows raised in mock surprise combined with cheeky grin). He asked me what I was doing later. 'I'm playing tennis in a tournament,' I (rep)lied. 'In the rain, wearing a shortie skimpy white tennis dress and no bra.'

He nodded approvingly. 'Thong?'

'I haven't decided,' etc., etc. We went on like this. Jumped into taxi.

'Don't forget to text me a picture when you're on court,' said Whitehouse.

On the way home, I became New Best Friends with Freud and talked about fathers, cancer, blended families, schools, children, men. 'No man has fancied me for years,' she said sympathetically.

'Me neither,' I said. Whether true or not, I wouldn't have dreamt of replying otherwise, as we were now in the throes of bonding over both loving the same Topshop blue velvet jacket. We parted on the best of terms. I made her pay for the taxi. When I got home, I felt incredibly depressed by the experience. Emma Freud had actually used the phrase 'social pariah' of me on BBC Radio Four and it would be broadcast to the nation at 6.15 p.m. How did I get here?

18 January 2010

Monday's always good for post. Today's in tray:

- Rescue® Remedy chewing gum: 'Feeling a little frantic at work or worried about something in your personal life?' Cue Rescue® Chewing Gum.
- a batch of aromatherapy oils from Annee, my facial acupuncturist.
- copy of 'Veteran's World' January newsletter.
- a leaflet from Phoenix-Diamonds. Real memorial diamonds created from the ashes or hair of your partner, loved one or

pet: 'They possess the exact same characteristics as mined gems without the social stigma of blood, sweat and tears of conflict diamonds.'

- a CD of Barry Manilow's *Greatest Love Songs of All Time* with quote from Manilow saying, 'I think this is the most beautiful album I've made.'

Have approached Nigella again and Kirsty Young to do covers. Both turned me down like a bedspread. But later saw freshly single Trinny Woodall at dinner looking skinny and utterly ravishing at financier Peter Soros's Notting Hill mansion ('house' simply doesn't do it justice). She told me she has been busy 'archiving' her wardrobe and had spent three days on coats. This week was dresses. And that she had taken a decision not to buy any more clothes for a year. I asked her to be a cover girl. I can already see the long piece all about the skinny clotheshorse and the joys of not shopping in the mag! I dropped the names of my cover girls Lady Helen, India Hicks, et al. She seemed keen, and pretended to send me an email on her Black-Berry so I would have hers – but it never arrived so, presumably, she'd rather kill herself than be on the cover of *The Lady*.

19 January 2010

Family Commission meeting all morning then lunch at Ivy with Sarah Baxter – editor of the *Sunday Times* magazine – whom I adore. Extraordinary Nordic catlike blue eyes. George Weidenfeld – Antonia's long-standing publisher – tottered past. I detained him. 'I'm Rachel Johnson, you published my first book,' I said. He was with George Walden, the former MP. He looked totally blank. I forgot – I should have said something about him, not me, i.e., 'I'm editor of *The Lady*, and we just ran a big interview with you by Candida Crewe to celebrate all your achievements.' No one wants to hear about you – they only want to hear you talking about them. I must remember that. Email from reader to the editor has come in:

Dear Madam

The Lady has always seemed to me unselfconscious and polite, with a lucid prose style which I hope will not become elliptic, hurried and gossipy, like most other magazines.

The best thing about *The Lady*, apart from its useful update, was the concise biographical gems on historical figures . I remember particularly ones on Handel, William of Orange and the astronomer Herschel and his sister. Yes, I know one can get it all on Google, but that is not the same as sitting down in comfort with *The Lady*. I have not missed the 'Handy Hints' page with its wartime requests as to what to do with scraps of left-over soap or how to remove quite simple stains, nor do I miss the fashion, which seemed a little matronly to me, although it was infinitely preferable to the ugly shooting gear which appeared in an October issue. I had always thought *The Lady* was concerned about the preservation of birds rather than with the glorification of killing them. I have always imagined *The Lady* to be as much a town magazine as a country one, and although I have always lived in or near the country, I rather dislike the somewhat sentimental ersatz paeans of praise to Agas, etc.

However, the real reason that I will not be renewing my subscription is the fact that you have chosen that simpering adultress [sic] Lady Antonia Fraser as your book reviewer. She has never shown any remorse for the misery she caused Vivien Merchant and her son, and I can't help thinking that she and the social-climbing, 'poor man's Samuel Beckett' writer Harold Pinter rather deserved each other. I have not been influenced by the Robert Harris article in Culture in this. It is what I have always felt.

Ouch!

I wrote back saying that we are none of us without sin and that I had no doubt that Antonia was aware of hers. I thought 'simpering adultress' was rather good. Bad news.

The India Hicks cover tanked – we're down to 27,000. I don't know what to do. Hix Nix Hicks Pix! Maybe it's a lesson that our USP is that we're old and unsexy, and we should just hang in there. Next two covers are women around eighty – Honor Blackman and Antonia Fraser – so maybe they will do better. On the other hand, it could have been the snow. As Ben pointed out, there was an 'extreme weather event nationwide', so little old ladies in rural areas were probably struggling to make it into their post offices. Probably.

20 January 2010

To Annabel's for a small party for Graydon Carter. I went with Adam Budworth, a friend of the Carters, in a cab. Coco was banned from entry. It was my first time in Annabel's. The champagne wasn't quite chilled enough. Someone present who must remain nameless revealed that at dinner with Sam and Dave Cameron on Monday (this was of course private, but I can't resist wanting to spread it abroad), Graydon had struck the table senatorially and announced, 'You know what my favourite magazine is in the whole world?' 'Tell us, Graydon,' they all begged. After all, he is the most powerful man in the glossies. '*The Lady*!' I imagined Graydon and Anna lying in bed chuckling over our ads for walk-in baths and sheltered accommodation and couldn't help wondering – *why?* I think I know. It's our way with classified ads, those genteel feelers for little couples who can cook and drive and polish antique furniture and prestige cars that reassuringly speak of a more elegant age, where people can be cared for and looked after.

21 January 2010

Graydon and Anna flaked and cancelled coming in for tea. So Ben's plan to fill an envelope with £20,000 – the sum his great-grandfather sold *VF* for in the 1900s – and slide it across the blue baize table-cloth and offer to buy back *Vanity Fair* cannot, now, be executed. Relief in the boudoir. Weslife is going to doorstep Graydon at the Dorchester and try to get him to repeat his line about his favourite magazine being *The Lady* to camera. This ploy was unveiled in the boardroom, where we all sat in a PR meeting. When I heard this with the PR company Taylor Herring, Edwina, B-Cal and Co. I have to say it made me wince. A very uncool idea.

22 January 2010

Total disaster. Nic Boize was instructed to brief the *Press Gazette* about our soar-away circulation and bumper Christmas edition. The result that appeared online was this:

> *The Lady*, one of the country's oldest magazines, is looking to triple is weekly sales from the 15,000 it sold before Christmas to in excess of 45,000 by the end of the year.
>
> The 124-year-old title, which was originally launched as a 'jour-nal for gentlewomen' and famed for its classified ads for domestic staff, underwent a full-colour relaunch in March last year.
>
> It then appointed Rachel Johnson, sister of London mayor and *Telegraph* columnist Boris Johnson, as its new editor. She joined the magazine in September.
>
> However, the new direction of the magazine, which first launched

in 1885, may have alienated some established readers, as sales fell to an unaccredited 15,937 by mid-December.

The last Audit Bureau of Circulations figure for *The Lady* shows that in the first six months of last year the £1.50 magazine was selling 28,721 copies on average each week.

(In September 2009, to herald my arrival, Ben introduced a price rise of 30p from £1.50 to £1.80, just to make my job even easier . . .)

I called Ben en route to Berkshire for a meeting and tried to explain the significance of this. I said the *Press Gazette* was a primary source that all media hacks would read, and it was a story of career-ending import unless it was corrected, and fast. 'No one reads *PR Week*,' Ben retorted. I said it didn't matter whose fault it was – what had happened was same as if the *Grocer* had reported that sales over Christmas at Tesco had halved when in fact they had gone up. And the magazine in question was called *Press Gazette*, not *PR Week*. So B-Cal got on the blower and it was all sorted – turns out that somehow, the figures for our newsstand sales had been mistaken as our total sales . . .

So then I called the *Press Gazette* from the car, gave a cheery quote about how I was thrilled about the circulation increase (I begin every press statement I make with the words 'I was/am thrilled'), and the story was corrected. But still. Ben has brought in high-profile (sic) editor, relaunched twice in a year, and the net result is a story in the trade press to the effect that I have finished off *The Lady* and the readers hate me. Result!

24 January 2010

Sunday Times magazine do a six-page spread, '*The Lady* and the Revamp'. Ben is unimpressed and gives it a 75 per cent rating. I am amazed it is so nice, and say so, explaining that even if the journalist had been vicious, the piece would still be bloody great. 'In fact, I'm about to write to Lesley White thanking her,' I say. 'She could have gone on about stairlifts, and incontinence pads, and she didn't. She made us look like a player.' Pictures are hideous, as usual.

Roy Greenslade has put something up on his *Guardian* blog saying I am a risky choice and asking readers to comment. I feel horribly over-exposed. I am fed up with reading about me. What on earth do other people think? My mother does not mention it when I go to her flat for tea and I see a copy of the *Sunday Times* mag on a side table. I really mind what she thinks but don't say anything. Her silence makes me wonder whether the Budworths were right and I am wrong after all. But then I reminded myself – it's still 5,000 words of free publicity, and not even the Budworths can argue with that.

Later she calls and tells me she enjoyed the piece and hadn't mentioned it because she hadn't had time to read it before.

25 January 2010

A genial PR man called Julian comes in and takes me on a personal tour of historic Rules restaurant, which is next door. If I play my cards right, I will be given a swipe-card for the tradesmen's entrance and can go straight up to the panelled bar with murals taken from the Savoy Hotel, antlers' heads from estates in Scotland, framed letters from Graham Greene (who set a scene from *The End of the Affair* here) and extracts describing Princess Margaret from James Lees-Milne's diary in the Betjeman room upstairs.

One drawback – no teas or coffees are served at Rules, just good, plain-cooked game and fish and scotch, i.e., manfayre.

Back in the office, Gillian told me that Emma Tennant kept ringing and had made Gillian send a copy of *The Lady* by bike to her in Notting Hill, even though she hasn't written anything but simply wants to see Stephanie Cross's review of her book about

Princess Margaret. She will be punished. I screech, 'By bike! By bike,' in fury at the cheek of it. We don't have money to waste on biking free copies of the magazine to readers simply because they call up and try it on!

This just in from Emma Tennant:

Dear Rachel

Just to say I'm most impressed by the new *Lady* – it reminds me of my life at *Queen* magazine when it had just got started by Jocelyn Stevens and Mark Boxer. It's quirky, clever and goes into any topic it feels like – I think it's going to do very well, and congratulations again.

All best
Emma

So all is forgiven.
In the in tray:

- a Simnel cake.
- a National Trust Plant and Garden Notebook.
- a letter from the people who run Safe Haven for Donkeys in the Holy Land (Julie Burchill had asked that her fee go to them – she is turning into living saint).
- a letter on Basildon Bond from a woman who said she's advertised herself as a carer in Kent in the Sits. Wanted columns of *The Lady*. 'Before I did so I rang the classified dept for a chat; would it be worth advertising, etc., and what would be my chances of successfully gaining employment.' I wondered where this was going. 'I had nothing but perverts ringing me up. I can tell you it was *extremely* [her itals] disturbing and upsetting. I did not expect this at all because of the prestigious nature of

your publication.' Then she went on about our care of duty and how we'd failed her. I am most surprised. So, perverts read the mag, so Lady Henrietta Rous – who told me only the lower orders did – has been proved deliciously wrong.

Tomorrow I have to go through the slush pile of unsolicited submissions to *The Lady*. The fun literally never stops.

26 January 2010

Figures came in. The Penny Smith 12 January cover of the *GMTV* presenter in sequins has ... worked! We are up to 32,000 plus. I am worried that the uplift is down to my bottom on the BBC *Breakfast* sofa, plus outings on *Loose Ends* and *Steve Wright in the Afternoon* on Radio 2.

In the in tray:

- a book called *Have a Nicer Day* by a man called Rickard Fuchs: 'The best-selling guide to achieving a better life from the multimillion-selling doctor-stand-up-comedian-author'. Inside the book he's written 'Have a Nicer Day' and signed his name. Felt better immediately.

I started going through the slush pile, pieces still being considered for publication. The first one I came to in the folder was 'Solving Stonehenge's Secrets' by a man called Ron Toft (I'm sure he's one of the many freelancers who came to our Christmas lunch).

The next was a 1,163-word piece with photographs on 'Cobnuts and Filberts – fresh green hazelnuts', entitled 'Nuts, Whole Hazelnuts', which I opened eagerly and was thrilled to see that the author's intro began, 'In his famous poem "To Autumn" John Keats noted it was the season for nature to "plump the hazel shells with a sweet kernel". Then I saw that they were in a special folder called 'Accepted for Publication by Lindsay A. Fulcher'. Now, can't wait to see the ones that have been *turned down*.

In the features meeting I announced that we are henceforth to call random, old-*Lady*-type articles about nature subjects 'cobnuts' in honour of this last submission.

27 January 2010

The newest Big Idea for the 125th anniversary edition on 16 February from the marketing team upstairs is a specially designed rose. I got this from the head of press and promotions:

Introducing the new Lady *rose created by David Austin*
(the top rose producer in the UK).

The Lady's *Blush*

Ausoscar
Alba Hybrid

A particularly beautiful semi-double variety whose flowers start as elegant pointed buds and develop into open rounded cups. The colour is a pure soft pink, the inner petals often having quite a prominent creamy white strip up the middle and a creamy white eye in the centre. Perfect for all types of borders.

The *Lady*'s Blush is a new rose that has been created by David Austin to celebrate the 125th anniversary of
The Lady – England's longest-running weekly magazine for women.

Is it just me or is that description of *The Lady*'s Blush not pure filth?

29 January 2010

The Lady literary lunch. Guest speakers – Ben Fogle, Gyles Brandreth, Juliet Nicolson (sister of Adam, daughter of Nigel, granddaughter of Vita and Harold). All spoke brilliantly – Gyles terribly mad and funny, full of quotes and pep, with mad swivelling eyebrows and curious dead-straight lashes such as you sometimes see on pigs. Talked about Oscar Wilde and how he was reburied in Père Lachaise cemetery. 'How do you get to be buried there?' I mused. 'You buy a flat right next door like me,' he bragged in a nice way. Am so old now that all I talk to people about is their funeral and burial arrangements. Ben Fogle was ridiculously handsome and had the most beautiful hands I have ever seen on a man. Juliet spoke very well and illuminated to all how important *The Lady* was as a historical resource, with its ads for Victory Toupées ('impossible to detect') and Epilastic corsets. Sat between Ben and Gyles and talked about diaries. Gyles has published his – *Something Sensational to Read on the Train* (a quote from *The Imp. of being Earn.*) – and then he smirked, 'Only good girls keep diaries, bad girls don't have time.'

John Dower asked for a show of hands from the room – a sea of sparkly suits and white hair, one pretty black woman, about five men, including a diarist – of how many approved of my changes. It was like *Any Questions*. About half the hands went up. My favourite part of the whole day was being handbagged by a reader who was quivering with rage and said, 'You've changed everything!' and complained about everything, even how easy the crossword was, as Dower filmed every foam-flecked word.

My second favourite part of the day was when the events manager, Andrew Kaye (this was after Brandreth had made a break for the border after his speech, saying he had to hotfoot it to Loughborough to address some double-glazing salesmen), came over to Ben Fogle like a puppy and said, 'Well, I hope *you're* stopping for sweet,' with a pleading look.

The Lady 10d

A WEEKLY NEWSPAPER, 5th MAY, 1966

PERSONALITIES IN FASHION

ISLE OF MAN

February

1 February 2010

Was reading the *Mail* idly over breakfast and my eye fell on my own name.

Since no one in public life ever seems able to say sorry for anything these days, Rachel Johnson, editor of *The Lady*, has stepped into the breach and refreshingly apologized to readers for changing the 124-year-old magazine. At *The Lady*'s literary lunch at the Institute of Directors, Rachel, 45, announced: 'Tony Blair might be answering to God, country and Sir John Chilcot. But I have a harder task in that I have to address you, our loyal *Lady* fans. I put my hand up and admit that mistakes were made. To my great regret, readers were lost and I'm sincerely sorry for this.'

Let's hope her elder brother, London mayor Boris, is big enough to say the same if the need arises . . . '

It went on. Annoyingly, they have added a whole year to my age!

At 6 p.m. I cabbed to the premiere of *A Single Man*, where there was a parade of slebs on a black carpet at the Curzon cinema. Hurley twirling in front of paps and massed flashbulbs in sleeveless dress. In February! Sat glumly through the film, wincing at the endless scenes of men snogging and choosing impeccably laundered shirts and performing elaborate toilettes. Tom Ford made a little speech introducing Colin Firth and Nicholas Hoult, and so on, to the stage, and revealed he had shot the whole movie in just twenty-one days.

Meanwhile John Dower and the crew from Optomen have been in the building for five months in order to make a 48-minute doc. I must remember to tease them. Over dinner, I told Colin Firth that he would defo be nominated for an Oscar, because the entire movie was about displacement activity (he prepares meticulously for a suicide he never carries out) and delayed gratification and as such was in the same mould as *Brief Encounter* and *Lost in Translation*, two of my top movies of all time. Firth looked very unimpressed with these aperçus.

I sat between A. A. Gill at Harry's Bar (for the dinner for Tom Ford, given by Graydon Carter) and Graydon. Made the mistake of telling A. A. Gill that I was being filmed for a docusoap. Then I made the mistake of telling Gill that the same guy who did *When Boris Met Dave* was directing. 'That was awful, awful,' he grinned happily. 'But the documentary about you and *The Lady* –' he stabbed at his endive and artichoke starter '– that will be *suicidally shit.*'

2 February 2010

The figures came in, and we're still keeping our heads above water, at around 31,000. Which is like the weather – not bad for the time of year.

After Harry's Bar, a blank. At 10 a.m., I went into Ben's office to hear the progress sales (i.e., the estimated rather than the net figure, which we calculate after returns) of how the cover after Penny Smith – Honor Blackman – had done. Still above 30,000. But not, I think it can be agreed, close to the crazed, skyrocketing figures the Budworth boys have in mind.

4 February 2010

Today's in tray:

- brownies baked by Helene, who plays Despina in *Cosi Fan Tutte*, courtesy of the PR at the Royal Opera House.
- a whole box of Lovedean Granola from Lucy O'Donnell, which I have also already eaten.
- a letter from John Springs offering himself as cartoonist.
- one horrid, unsigned four-page letter written entirely IN CAPITALS from a woman who attended the Fogle/Brandreth/Nicolson lit. lunch headed, 'Points of Dissappointment [sic] shared by many': 'Why not ask for a show of hands of who doesn't like the new *Lady*?' it asked. It said that those who were interviewed and said nice things had been bribed with a free lunch, that she and others – readers of forty years' standing – would be cancelling their SOs (standing orders), and ended after complaining about the Bucks Fizz, the Antonia Fraser cover and the lack of flunkies to meet and greet at the Institute of Directors. 'Such a great shame for *The Lady* magazine to have changed so much and in many eyes not for the better.'
- also a short letter marked 'Personal'. 'A little note to say how much I enjoyed your literary lunch. Your hard work organizing it was very much appreciated. [I should admit all I did was turn up, make eyes at Ben Fogle and eat a delicious lunch.] I am a lady GP from the Cheshunt area.'

8 February 2010

Went to work this morning and, when I let myself into the building, I felt gloom settle on me for the first time since I started.

There doesn't seem to be much uplift in advertising. Circulation is where it was when I arrived (the 1 September issue sold 31,164). This morning I received a letter that said, 'It is so refreshing to pick up a magazine that isn't littered with ads,' as if this were an aesthetic decision on our part – no nasty advertising for the new-look *Lady*!

Janina is lobbying me every time one of her interviews with ageing hoofers and Hollywood has-beens is held out or cut; she has just spent an age poring over the flatplan for the 23 March issue and sent me an email complaining that the William Blacker interview about Romania – for which I have commissioned portraits from Laura Carew, and copy from Stephanie Cross, late of the *Guardian*, is over three pages. 'Linda Hamilton has been reduced to two pages, and she's beautiful and all the quotes are new. Could she be back to three please?'

Meanwhile, the subs have discovered that Lindsay has put a piece of mind-blowing dullness called 'Arbours' into our Spring Gardening issue, a piece that was considered too tedious to have run even last year, when the mag was full of long pieces about small furry creatures, as I can prove. Have just received this from a long-standing contributor:

Dear Ms Johnson

I am a freelance journalist and former regular contributor to *The Lady*. You have three commissioned articles of mine (dormice, endangered mammals and Stonehenge) which, it would seem, are now unlikely to be used. I am advised that if this IS the case, I should ask for a 50 per cent kill fee. I look forward to hearing from you.

Of course *The Lady* is a work in progress: I have to bring Debo on board, probably get rid of 'The Gents' (our readers will never accept the name), reintroduce the short story and banish our rather fizzy serial written by Susan Hill's daughter Jessica Ruston to the website, as it leaves our readers cold. For my part, I've relaunched and overseen the redesign, I've sat on daytime sofas and exposed myself to radioactive amounts of self-publicity.

And now I think, 'Mmm, what next?' I sort of know what will make a good feature – Paul Johnson on the passing of the lady's maid – and what won't, as some strange alteration in my news sense has occurred. If someone offers me an interview with a Hollywood actress in panto with a memoir to promote, I groan out loud. But if someone tells me about a woman called Patsy who is a textile designer in her eighties who lives in a cottage in the New Forest and who has designed tea-towels for the National Trust that have become collectors' items, I feel a warm glow inside.

But still – the future is incredibly opaque. When I write a book, I know what the last line is going to be, and I sort of push the boulder uphill towards it. I have no idea what the last line of this diary is going to be. There are three in-house PRs and two PR companies working on *The Lady*. But I still can't help wondering, 'What's the plan?' So I said to John Dower, every time I see Ben or Adam, I can't help thinking, 'What's the plan?'

'*You* are the plan,' he answered.

Me? ME? If he's right, then we're well and truly fucked.

9 *February* 2010

Today's in tray:

- two more Simnel cakes.
- one handmade gemstone necklace with river pearls and intricately faceted amethyst drops and crocheted with purple thread made by destitute Jaipuri women for a jeweller in Killin, Scotland, and a nice letter saying, 'We know that if you were

to feature our website in *The Lady* it would really help our business, which in turn would help needy people, particularly women and children in India. A stamped addressed envelope is enclosed to return the necklace.' The envelope isn't stamped.

- a letter from a reader in Cambridgeshire – v. shaky handwriting – saying, 'Dear Editor, I really love the new *Lady* (altho' I rather liked the stuffy old one as well) ... The lovely Dr Le Fanu has cured my mystery bladder problem – Halleluja! God Protect Him! My GP most interested in the relevant literature he sent me.'
- three cellophane-wrapped packages of Fiona Sciolti 'botanical chocolates' and a letter explaining how, for Fiona, handcrafting each chocolate is a labour of love, and commanding me, 'Prepare to Indulge.'

The 125th-anniversary issue is being subbed and laid out, and Lindsay and Mrs Budworth are gently steaming to each other telephonically about the fact that I am holding out the 2,000-word piece about Lewis Carroll's tenuous links with *The Lady* magazine from our gala collectors' issue.

On which subject – Stefano Arata's cover design for the anniversary special has come in this morning, and while it's pretty, it's very ungrabby. Just a profile of the woman from a vintage *Lady* cover, like a black medallion, and some trellis-like flowers in the background. Have set Claire on to making it look as if it is 2010 as well as 1885.

10 February 2010

Massive kerfuffle between our design team, and lots of tears before bedtime as we try to pass the anniversary edition for 16 February.

Claire, Stefano, Tammy at each other's throats. Too many cooks, I think. Not sure the plan to have Stefano overseeing the cover is going to work, as he calls Claire's designs 'disgusting' to her face, tells Tammy that her choice of pictures is naff, and has on occasion reduced them both to silent sobs. As they are both very calm and level-headed, I can see I am going to have to step in with the water-cannon.

Today's in tray:

- a very nice letter from someone in East Langdon, Kent, saying that she has advertised her apartment on the Italian-French Riviera in the magazine for years and that she is always inundated with enquiries – 'All our guests, without exception, have been delightful and many return as regular guests' – and calling the magazine 'a treat and a tonic'. When nice letters come in I hardly know where to look.
- a letter from Dartford, Kent, from someone who wants Gillian to spend an entire day looking for a back issue from 1937 and enclosing an air-freshener in the shape of a cat and ending, 'All the best for 2010. Another air-freshener enclosed, I guess you can use it.' *Another* air-freshener?

The cover has ended up with the black profile and, inside the profile, the cover line, 'Who is today's lady?', in the hope that the readers will open the magazine to discover in a frenzy of excitement just who is on our list of 125 Ladies of Today.

11 *February 2010*

On editorial front: have asked Alexander Chancellor to do telly for us, and Dafydd Jones wants to provide a photo essay showcasing the country's *vieillesse dorée*. Ben wants us to run a slot for widows/dowagers/divorcees called 'Back on the Market'.

On doc front: the film crew is finally going to interview Julia Budworth. At Deerbolts Hall. I tell them not to mention Buttons the Killer Teddy. Then Mrs Budworth actually manifested in Bedford Street. I was in the boudoir and got a call from Ben. 'Can you shoot your chuff in here for a sec to meet Mum,' he said, very formally. I walked in.

'You're a very rude girl,' she said in a wig-lifting voice, holding out a hand for me to shake.

'Am I, Julia?' I said weakly.

'I wrote to you last week. Did you reply? No. So rude!' I told her I hadn't got her letter. 'I posted it on Thursday,' she insisted. 'First class!' I told her I hadn't received it.

'Ask Gillian,' I said to Ben. 'She opens all my letters.'

'It had "Personal" on the envelope!' said Mrs Budworth.

'Even the personal ones,' I said.

'Gillian, has any mail arrived for Rach from Mrs B.?' Ben enquired. She denied it had; good girl. Then he shook his head, to convey Gillian's message to the boardroom.

'Well, I definitely sent it,' said Mrs B. with finality, as if between us we had conspired to be rude. We have arranged to have lunch, in Terroirs.

When I got back to my office, Debo telephoned, just as I was on the other line to ebookers, i.e., a call centre in India, trying to change a return flight to New York (Ivo had complained about me going for six nights and had told me I would 'feel guilty' if I went for that long). So I had Delhi on one line, a duchess on the other. I told her that Julia B. had made one of her papal visits. 'And how was she?' Debo asked, mischief in voice. I told her that it would have been possible to distinguish Mrs B. with a grievance quite easily from a ray of sunshine. Then I talked about Debo doing a cover, and she said she had a new photo of herself in a long Hartnell taffeta skirt that we could use. She said everyone there was at sixes and sevens because of the exhibition at Chatsworth. 'It's not about

Chatsworth, it's about me and my life,' she said. 'It's been absolute *purdah*.' Then she explained that 'purdah' was a pet phrase and hybrid malapropism for 'murder' and 'purgatory'. Then she talked about her first cousin, Ben's ma, Julia Budworth. 'She's rather sharply right wing,' she said fondly. 'It makes one rather good value, don't you think?'

Stefano came in, and we spent hours trying to come up with a cover for the 125th gala special, an afternoon which left Claire shaking and in tears and Tammy quivering with rage. He has been a brilliant designer, but all good things have to come to an end. More to the point: Claire came into my office and announced that if Stefano remained to oversee covers, she would go. He did the redesign but wants to stay on and make sure the covers remain true to his vision. But this isn't working. The atmosphere is terrible.

Claire has told me she can't take it any more. So I will have to tell Stefano, regretfully, his services are no longer required.

12 *February* 2010

The 125th issue has – unbelievably – struck a chord. Our list of 125 Ladies of Today is running on PA and the *Telegraph*, and passim. So, am pleased. I had an idea; it carried the issue; and people seem to have noticed. It's not like this every week, that's for sure. Received a corrective letter from Callander, Perthshire (on A4), in case I was beginning to rest on my laurels.

Dear Madam,

Many years ago, I first started taking *The Lady* for the Ladygram but found many of the articles interesting. Since the relaunch, however, the Ladygram and puzzles are the only intelligent offering. Can I, I ask myself, afford to pay £1.80 just for the Ladygram? I am very saddened that a good magazine has been reduced to pathetic offerings designed for the flighty unthinking in our midst. Tackling up-to-date topics seriously rather than insulting the readership with such rubbish would have been far more acceptable – etc.

Never mind. There is a whole page of coverage in the *Indy* on p. 3. Pictures of three ladies – the Queen, Tracey Emin, Jacqueline Gold – and a piece which starts, 'When Boris Johnson's sister Rachel assumed the editorship of *The Lady* promising to double the tiny circulation of the venerable publication, she knew that the shock waves from her cultural revolution would get the teacups rattling in the parlours of the nation's gentlefolk . . .' It goes on to reference my own 'quinoa-eating, Range Rover-driving Notting Hill set'. Tsk! How dare the *Indy* mention our tiny circulation? Talk about pot and kettle!

Meanwhile, Kelvin MacKenzie (old mate of Ben's from his radio days) is in. He's taking tea in the boardroom as I write. We have two – actually three – possible covers this week: Joanna Trollope, Alan Titchmarsh, or a still life of some secateurs and cut hyacinths on a trug (very old *Lady*), as it is the hardy annual Spring Garden-ing issue. We are going to ask him to pick it, then tell him how it does.

Kelvin has just left. He marched into my office shouting, 'Luv a duck, you don't need to publish a magazine, this place is old fash-ion, innit! What year is it! You should close *The Lady* down and open a museum, charge everyone to come and look at this. You could all sit here doing nuffink and folks would pay good money just to look at yer.'

I agreed that entering the Bedford Street premises is like slip-ping through a tear in the space-time continuum and is stuck in the fifties (i.e., 1850s) and we are all indeed preserved in aspic. Then I took him through to Claire and she got up the three covers on the Mac. He picked the Titchmarsh cover and told us we had to have more pieces about women in their fifties whose Viagra-fuelled husbands had left them. 'It's the marital equivalent of the government boiler-scrappage scheme,' I said. 'Let's call it "Goat Alert".' He liked 'Goat Alert', then said that just because our readers were old ladies, we didn't have to have an old-lady mentality but, like *The Spectator*, had to grab readers with our attitude instead. Ben plugged his 'Back on the Market' idea.

MacKenzie had lots of other ideas, but he spoke so loudly and fast and mugged for the camera so much that I just allowed his genius and expertise gathered from years of editing the *Sun* to wash feebly over me like a neap tide, in the hope that, eventually, like a migraine, he'd go away, which eventually he did.

15 February 2010

Tammy, the picture editor, has resigned. 'It was nothing to do with Stefano,' she said (citing a better offer at picture agency Corbis).

I whinged all day to Ben about the weekend. He'd twisted my arm to go to review a place called Barnsdale Lodge, a hotel on a reservoir and an A road in Rutland, a low-lying, benighted county with howling Siberian winds. The Edward Faulks family came too. I took the children on Friday night and Ivo met us there on Saturday morning. We had a perfectly nice time biking and lounging around watching the Six Nations Rugby and eating cream teas, but at the end of the weekend I was appalled. After listening to all that PR guff from the Rutland Tourist Board, buying lunch in the 'Rutland Pub of the Year' for everyone, including the manager of Barnsdale, I had to *pay the hotel bill!* That wasn't the deal AT ALL. They'd only knocked off a hundred quid as a press discount.

So I laid the hotel bill (a not unreasonable £451, not including lunch at the Horse & Jockey, Rutland Water) on Ben's desk to await arrival. When I saw him I whined, 'I gave up a weekend to go to stay in a hotel by the A606 in the freezing cold, listen to the hotel manager talk about his eco-development holiday-cottages scheme for the whole weekend, then I had to pay the bill,' I bleated. 'And write the piece.' Ben crumbled. I do love him sometimes. He had just told me that his family name 'many moons ago' was Dutton de Budworth and as a result that his army nickname was Mutton Spudworth, and I had screamed with laughter.

Ben carried the bill himself into Geoffrey, who sits in a cubby hole beyond the boardroom, and asked him to deal with it. Geoffrey does the traumatic *Lady* accounts.

16 February 2010

Was reading the *Guardian* and, as one does, had moved swiftly on to jolly features section G2 and found this on page 3:

Passnotes 2,729: *The Lady*

Age: Is that a question you'd ask a lady? I'll whisper it . . . 125 this year.
Speak up, I'm 93, and a little deaf. Exactly the sort of reader *The Lady* no longer wants, I'm afraid.
Don't be so insulting, young man. I've been reading *The Lady* since I was knee-high to an Irish wolfhound. My mother read it, too. Used it to recruit my nanny, governess, all our domestic staff. I remember Mr McCrindle, the butler, saying . . . Madam, we haven't got time for this. *The Lady* is now a whizzy, happening publication edited by Rachel Johnson, printed in full colour, and seeking to double its circulation by connecting the venerable magazine to the modern world.

Was thrilled! *The Lady* has been Passnoted! And the *Guardian* Passnotes column is totally cookin'! Yesterday, Passnotes was on the Brits. And the day after, Greggs. Yes. Greggs! That's how hot we are.

Greggs is also rebranding. Just like us. Greggs hopes to become 'the Skoda of pies', and kit out its stores in southern England with soft lighting, dark-wood fittings and decorously displayed baked goods. As today's haul included a large – and when I say large, I mean the size of my head large – handmade, hot-cross bun from Betty's (with label 'a spiced Easter speciality'), we very much do seem to have much in common with Greggs, with our dark-wood fittings and endless cakes. At least Betty's of Harrogate didn't send another Simnel cake garnished with marzipan balls to represent the Apostles or whatever.

I don't think even Coco can manage any more marzipan balls.

18 February 2010

Lunch at Hix, swish new Mark Hix vehicle for purveying seasonal English fayre, like elvers, sea kale and pennywort, at New York prices. Little blonde Becky Clarke and Pat Llewellyn from Optomen were taking me. When I nipped down to loo I found Blur bassist, the lush-locked Alex James, sheltering from the rain with his four tiny children in the basement. I do like a posh lunch. We ate green salads (£8 – oof, not that I was paying) and I have to say they were absolutely wonderful – green chlorophylly crunch, dressed with an oil none of us could identify. As we tanked up on white wine, Becky and Pat revealed they've seen rushes (translation: literally hundreds of unedited hours of footage) and are concerned the documentary was too 'soft'. Translation: this means John has gone native and has produced a film in which we come across as *identifiably human.*

'You're OK,' John told me on the telephone, before lunch. 'We only go for you in a couple of places.' Translation: you don't screw up too badly. I know, because I've been told, that people who make documentaries do endless 'decoy' filming, for hours and hours, just waiting till you come a cropper, say something awful, shout, cry, break down in tears, swear, wet your pants, i.e., they wait for some kind of gotcha moment, when they can exhale with relief, because they've got a result. The thing will be aired, and viewers will sit on their sofas agog at how awful you are, which seems to be the underlying principle of most TV programming.

We carried on drinking a lot of white wine. Then John Dower called before pudding. He was on his way back into London from Deerbolts Hall, the Budworth pile in Suffolk. He said the interview with Mrs B. 'had gone very well' and that the matriarch was 'sharp as a tack'. I could have told him that. Saved him the trip to Suffolk.

He also said that when he'd brought up the subject of Buttons, the Killer Teddy, Ben had panicked and made a guillotine motion with his hand. He'd ordered, 'Don't answer any questions about the blue teddy, Mum, they're only trying to make you look stupid!' So, sadly, Buttons has hit the cutting-room floor.

I felt woozy all afternoon and was unable to finish the second book I have to read before doing *Late Review* on BBC2, for which I have to fly to Glasgow tomorrow – Natasha Walter's *Living Dolls*, in which she deplores the Return of Sexism, porn, Asda bras for eight-year-olds, and so on. Also have to read 500 pages of Late Period Amis in the shape of *The Pregnant Widow* and watch a three-part documentary on feminism by Vanessa Engle, by Friday.

Meanwhile, just to make life even easier, Ivo is in hospital having a knee operation. He will not be able to walk – or even hobble like Hopalong – when he exits, and all the children are lying around at home calling me on my mobile when I'm at work, to ask me things like 'Have you moved my iPod/mobile charger?' and 'Why aren't there any Coco Pops?' in aggrieved tones.

I feel very stressed suddenly. It could be reading all these books which explain how little I earn and how much housework I do compared with men, and those surveys reported in the *Mail* that say that marriages wouldn't crumble to dust so fast if men did their share of sock-picking-up and dishwasher-loading.

Also, this week's crash course in whither feminism – in which it has become painfully clear that women are still expected to supply geisha services to men, women have failed to capitalize on the She-decade of the seventies, and women have only succeeded in lumbering themselves with another job on top of the one they've already got – didn't help much either.

23 February 2010

Reader's Digest has gone down with the loss of over half a million souls. I mean, *sheesh*. If a world-famous mass-market monthly with a loyal circulation of 500,000 plus who want to Increase their Word Power, chortle over Humour in Uniform and discover all there is to know about John's Thalamus (three historic *Reader's Digest* columns) can't survive in today's market, *there is precious little hope for us.*

A bearded C4 photographer came in to take stills for the doc. They kept making Ben and me pose like man and wife in front of the portrait of the founder, Thomas Gibson Bowles (a gloomy oil showing the moustachioed proprietor with quill in one hand, cigarette in the other), which is in the equally gloomy boardroom. I felt like the Queen, with Ben at my elbow standing in for the Duke of Edinburgh. As a result, I am scowling and frowning in all the pictures.

The in tray:

- a proposal from a Bexley-based freelancer for an article on other things that happened on Guy Fawkes night entitled

'Remember, Remember the Fifth of November' with an outline specifying some notable events that happened on this date in other years: the polishing of the Cullinan diamond, the appointment of the British Censor of Films (1912), the Discovery of the Body of Tutankhamun, and the Hither Green rail crash (1967). Proposed length: 1,350 words.

• a sweet letter from a reader (on pink writing paper printed with roses) in Lowestoft, which enclosed a cutting of an interview with Ben Budworth in the *Eastern Daily Press*. My correspondent revealed she had been a devoted reader of *The Lady* for forty years and explained that she had started reading the magazine after answering a catering advert. 'This opened a new life for me after my family left the nest,' she wrote. 'My husband didn't return from World War Two so I was on my own, with a living to earn.' Some of these letters are really touching. Then I read on – and it turned out my Lowestoft correspondent had been on the staff of Deerbolts Hall, Budworth Towers! And the letter was about Mrs Budworth, whose husband had been killed in a private plane crash in Suffolk when Ben was ten! 'The Lady of the house was very kind to me,' she recalls. 'She was pleased with my work.' And she even remembered cooking for the oldest son's twenty-first birthday: 'I cooked two geese and a pancake feast soaked in Grand Marnier.' The letter ends, 'I had a wonderful life, all due to *The Lady*.'

Honestly, I could cry. I picked up the telephone on my desk and called this lady – an Eva O'Reilly who turned out to be ninety-six, to thank her for her lovely letter.

I raced to the Burberry catwalk show for London Fashion Week, held in a marquee adjoining Tate Britain. As I got out of the cab I could see that a weapons-grade goatfuck was underway outside. There was a heaving melee of buyers, photographers, bloggers, models, slebs, men in high heels and yellow suits, editors, liggers, all pushing to get past the velvet rope.

'Take a STEP back,' the heavies kept shouting. Inside, I spotted Anna Wintour in cherry-tweed twinset and brown boots, her tawny bob swinging. As soon as the show started, she put on sunglasses. Why does she do this? Beautiful show, loud music, thin girls who don't look as if they've given up anything for Lent; they never took up a single thing to start with. As I now know, having studied reviews in the fashion press, it was a *military-themed* show. I had a nice chat with Sam Cam, who looked lustrously beautiful and said nice things about *The Lady*. She has a wonderful dewiness about her, long-lashed eyes and sheeny hair. When she first turned up at St Mary Abbots CofE primary with Nancy aged four in tow, someone pointed to her – a drooling daddy, no doubt – and drawled, 'So . . . who does that gorgeous Iranian au pair belong to?'

Then on to Duff Cooper Award party (it's a literary history prize) sponsored by Pol Roger at the French Embassy. It's always very grand. The embassy – on Millionaire's Row, i.e., Kensington Palace Gardens – has been redone since I went to the same party last year, and the year before that, back till year dot. Now the residence looks like a cross between an advertising-industry crashpad in Soho and the Palais de Versailles, so is eloquent of a nation in deep cultural confusion. Ancient poets sitting on sofas, drinking Pol Roger, with faces like mountain ranges seen from a plane – deep, snaking runnels and craggy outcrops. I had always believed, until this moment, anyway, the line that people never felt old, they just looked old. What is clear, however, from the line-up at the Duff Cooper (one ancient past editor of *The Times*, my old tutor from Oxford, etc.) is that this lot were clearly feeling jolly old too. Artemis Cooper, daughter of Duff, granddaughter of Diana, made a lovely speech. I was sneaking out before *l'Ambassadeur*, emblazoned with discreet *Légion d'Honneur* rosettes, embarked on his traditional interminable speech in honour of the winner.

I was creeping past a sofa on which sat distinguished men of letters Paul Johnson and David Pryce-Jones, man-about-town Claus von Bulow, etc. Paul Johnson audibly hissed the words 'Stupid girl!' as I passed.

Dinner with Lady Helen Taylor and art dealer and gallerist hubby Tim. It was just the six of us, the Taylors plus a very *soigné* pair – one a hedge funder, the other the half-French CEO of Sisley. The Sisley CEO looked about eighteen, but was thirty-four. Her husband looked about fifteen, but was forty-three. So the pair were a walking advertisement for their product. I stared at them in wonder and when I got home ordered all her 'plant-based' miracle products on the spot, especially after she'd told me my exciting bottle of Crème de la Mer (despite all the guff about 'the broth of the sea', etc.) that had appeared by magic in my in tray was 'too rich' for my skin and how the magic Crème de la Mer formula 'was way out of date'.

25 February 2010

Went to lovely Annee in Home House for my third session of acupuncture. She took my pulse on both hands. 'Your yin pulse is very slow,' she said, with a look of concern. 'And your lung function is weak. Have you been constipated?' Basically, she explained that the yin side is your female side and mine was 'struggling' and I needed to 'release my chakras', and so on. So I told Annee, blinking away hot tears of self-pity, about managing half-term on my own in the February sleet, the fact that Ivo had had an operation (he still hasn't left the house after ten days; am beginning to doubt he ever will) and that at the end of half-term I had to fly to Glasgow to appear live on *Late Review* show with Toby Young, who was funnier than me, then fly back and have people for lunch.

As I whinged on, I felt terribly sorry for myself. She told me my skin was very dry and that I needed a facial. I need more than a facial! It's such a fallacy that me time and self-pampering solve anything. They only add to the sense of panic and urgency.

What I need is more MONEY and more HELP and more TIME.

Two small bottles have arrived in a large box. Carolyn Hart – hardened food editor of many years' standing in Fleet Street – saw them and sighed, 'In the winter it's pies with annoying names, like Higgidy Pies. But after Christmas, it's like a cuckoo, the arrival of the first bottle of garlic vinaigrette. It's the start of *the salad-dressing season.*'

The in tray:

- a letter from a reader in South View, Ilkley, cancelling her subscription and explaining – at length – her decision. After naming and shaming several columnists, she concluded, 'The decisive reminder to drop you was the current issue showing Alan Titchmarsh on the front page – I can't stand him.'

- a letter from a reader in Somerset who had sent in an article about the Forest of Dean in May 2007 which had been accepted for publication by Arline Usden, and enclosing a photocopied note from the then editor to that effect, and asking me to 'clarify the situation'.

I have finally gone through the unsolicited folder containing the most recent submissions, and was enthralled to find the following gems:

1. a piece of 1,000 words entitled 'Ottawa, Tulips and Dutch Royal Family', about the sixty-fifth anniversary of Princess Juliana's gift of 100,000 tulip bulbs to Ottawa, submitted by a freelancer who has contributed to a variety of print and online publications such as *The Stage*, *The Pink Paper* and *Out in the City*.

2.   a proposal for a piece about Anna Korda, a film dialogue coach who worked on the Bond films and with Marlon Brando, Sean Connery, etc., submitted by someone who once published an article in *The Lady* about an 'ex-Bluebell living in Rome'.

3.   a sweet letter enclosing a piece about hip-replacement surgery which starts, 'I know that since you took over as Editor you are planning on rejuvenating the image of *The Lady* – so an article on hip replacements might seem totally out of order!' The piece – titled 'Hip, Hop, Ouch' – was surprisingly readable.

4.   a piece from a reader in Mottram St Andrew about the duties (empty slops, blacken grates, etc.) of servants between 1914 and 1938, written by her late husband's grandmother. In the submission, she points out that servants were not exclusive to grand establishments. The author cites as evidence her late husband's grandmother's house, which was 'a large house in Warrington owned by a solicitor'.

5.   a pitch for a 900-word article called 'Turning the Tide' which tells how a reader in Huntingdon 'turned his life round after a life-shattering experience'. The reader has written for *Waterways World* and *Good Woodworking*. I read the piece – it was a cockle-warming tale about a woman whose partner had died and who, in the absence of a partner, had bought a narrowboat instead.

6.   an article (SAE enclosed) about the Mayan calendar.

7.   a proposal for a nature column about a different mammal, bird or insect each week with a specimen column entitled 'A glimpse of . . . the Hazel Dormouse' enclosed, length: 928 words.

8.   a piece sent in from KwaZulu-Natal about a memorial to the fallen horses of the Boer War which starts, 'They died in their thousands, far from their homelands, for a war they neither understood nor cared about.'

Part of me wishes I could commission them all, because each and every one would reassure antique readers (never forget – the average age of our readers is seventy-eight, so whenever I commission anything my rule of thumb is partly 'What would Mrs Budworth think?') that nothing has changed on the Ladyship. But I can't. I have taught myself that when I read pitches, and emails, and written submissions, or take calls from freelancers, that I must imagine myself running the piece in that week's issue, and dropping something else to make way for it. Just as I have trained myself not to say yes to an event unless I'd be really looking forward to it if it was tomorrow.

As a result, I bin almost everything, and 100 per cent of the short-story submissions (which are almost always about ghosts at Windsor Castle anyway).

26 February 2010

Friday. My shirking from home day. Ivo still crippled after knee op. I finished *Must You Go?* – Antonia Fraser's memoir of her marriage to Harold Pinter, as I am interviewing her Ladyship tonight in front of a paying audience at Waterstones, Notting Hill. Over brekker my eye fell on a snippet in the *Mail*. It ran: 'Two women in Waterstones are standing in front of a poster: "Antonia Fraser in conversation with Rachel Johnson about her new book, *Must You Go?*" the poster says. "Friday 26 at 7pm. Tickets £3, redeemable against cover price of book." One woman is heard telling the other loudly, "Well, I'm certainly not going."'

I met the writer Gilbert Adair at Kitchen & Pantry on Elgin Crescent, to ask if he would be our film reviewer. He explained that going to a screening and writing up the review takes two working days and that the first thing a film critic does when he is sent details of a new film is to see how long it is, and that anything over 100 minutes was to be avoided. He didn't seem very keen.

I rushed home to put on my new silk Bree Van der Kamp-style

blouse, bought specially from West Village for tonight's event. White wine was flowing in the Green Room – i.e., a back office at Waterstones. Antonia was resplendent in a sort of black and white zebra coat with a red lining. The first thing I did was tell her she looked beautiful, which she did. Then she told me she had an idea for a column: a woman of distinction and mystery (a mysterious look crossed her distinguished face as she said this) described an item of clothing she has kept for years and why. 'Like this Jean Muir coat,' she said, gesturing to the zebra. 'I've had it half my life, and it's still going strong.' Having just had an inconclusive conversation with G. Adair about a culture column, I am struck with what I regard as inspiration. 'What a good idea,' I said. 'We should call it "This Old Thing".'

When we go on to the shop floor, the events manager tells us the mics are broken. So we sit on raised office chairs as if facing Magnus Magnusson. 'Hello to all my descendants,' smiled Antonia. The crowd included two of her six children – Natasha and Benjie – and one grandchild.

I launched my cheeky first salvo: there'd been some family reaction to the fact that Sir Hugh Fraser MP, Antonia's first husband, to whom she was married until she had her midlife *coup de foudre*, got shortish shrift in the book. 'So, Antonia,' I asked sweetly, 'what first attracted you to the rich, internationally renowned playwright Harold Pinter?' She either didn't pick up or totally ignored the implication and replied that when she first met Harold he was rude and disruptive and he'd told her that he was rude and disruptive pretty much all the time. 'So I can't say I wasn't warned,' she said, with her superb smile.

She revealed that Harold was a non-observing Jew. 'He made his Bar Mitzvah, but only to pick up the money,' she said. 'He said that he needed it to buy a copy of *Ulysses*. But I'm not sure I believed him.'

During questions, she was asked by a wild-haired man at the back if Harold had contacted her 'from the other side'. She appeared to ponder this for ages, and then said that one day she knew she had to go to his grave. So she took a cab to the cemetery, in Kensal Green, and when she got there she found a languid youth contemplating Harold's unmarked grave. She engaged him in conversation, and he told her he was an aspiring playwright who had come to pay his respects to Pinter. 'He was from Hackney,' she concluded, shortly before revealing that Harold voted Lib Dem.

PS. Harold's grave is now marked. I had this from Antonia: 'In lines from the top it reads:

HAROLD PINTER
PLAYWRIGHT
NOBEL LAUREATE
BELOVED HUSBAND
OF
ANTONIA FRASER
October 10 1930–Christmas Eve 2008

'He typed out everything himself in 1992 except, clearly, the terminal date and "Nobel Laureate", which I added on the grounds that, if you've got it, flaunt it. It was such a relief that he wrote "Playwright", which he also had on his passport, so when people made other helpful suggestions I was able to rebut them. They ranged from "Poet" to "Polemicist".'

27 February 2010

John Dower and Weslife came to do a final and rather unexpected last interview with me at home in Notting Hill, to provide a final scene for the doc. As it was Saturday, Ivo was in bed upstairs reading papers and drinking tea, a ritual he can extend to Sunday night if necessary. I was in jeans and T-shirt. They've come because, apparently, Channel 4 think the doc is still too tame. So poor John Dower is having to recut to provide a posh *EastEnders*, complete with shriekings, firings, sackings, and all into one 48-minute episode rather than muck-spread over twenty-five years.

'It's got to be all blood on the carpet,' said John, dolefully. He is a real filmmaker and doesn't like being told what to do, how to cut, etc. As a result of this ding-dong – John says he has made an intelligent, nuanced documentary, where the main characters are multi-dimensional, etc. – the viewing of the edit has been cancelled in order to give Optomen more time to make the doc embarrassing and buttock-clenchingly awful for the principals concerned, i.e., me and Ben.

The Lady 12p

A WEEKLY NEWSPAPER, 20th MARCH, 1975

6 pages about
BEAUTY
hair—
skincare—
slimming

on offer
King's Pattern silver-plated cutlery

MARCH

1 March 2010

Joan – the lady on Classifieds who wears the fluffy slippers, who has plastered her office walls with studio portraits of her collie called Meesha – is having a birthday celebration.

AS KATH MENTIONED AT THE END OF LAST WEEKS SUPERB
STRAT & DEV MEETING IT'S MY 50th (five hail Marys for that one)
[said Joan]

FEEL FREE TO POP DOWN TO CLASSIFIED FOR HALF A LAGER
AND A ROLLMOP ANY TIME FROM 12PM
LOOK FORWARD TO SEEING YOU LUV JOAN X.

I realized the invitation was not so much for me, but for Coco, to whom Joan is devoted and brings in doggie treats. I sent her an email saying that Coco would be sorry to miss the herring and stout but I was thinking, 'Fifty? She looks at least sixty!'

Made me feel very old as my big Five Oh is in six years and seven months.

2 March 2010

The sales team here is henceforth led by tall blonde glamazon Helen Robinson, Ben's newest hire. Hels – as she is known – wants us to find sponsorship for our various columns. So I have emailed all our regulars asking them to come up with ideas for corporate sponsorship.

> Dear much-appreciated columnists [I whizzed round], As a revenue-raising *Lady*-saving exercise, can you all come up with suggestions as to who if anyone might be prepared to sponsor your cols., as Martin Miller Gin does the letters page? i.e., Mary Killen, who writes about life in her Wiltshire grottage – Rescue® Remedies; Clemmie, our gardening writer – some seed company; Sarah, who writes about her allotment – sheds; James Le Fanu – indigestion; Penny, weekly diarist – Moët et Chandon/Beecham's Resolve, etc. etc.?

Mary has emailed back her list for possibles – includes Eggleston Hall, the finishing school, Sheepdrove Organics, Norland Nannies and Aga.

Sarah Langton-Lockton has come up with Wyvale (garden centres); Gabriel Ash (upmarket greenhouses); Hunter wellies.

Penny Smith, the *GMTV* presenter, opera critic and diarist, says, 'I have a feeling I might not be able to do anything which was sponsored . . . being a news bunny and everything.'

I have decided that I am going to approach Elizabeth Grant of Astroglide to see if she wants to sponsor my ed's letter and, if she doesn't, I feel confident Replens will.

I have discovered that Joan of Classifieds is not fifty but seventy. She looks marvellous for her age. Like many of the fantastic characters here, she is both past retirement age and has worked here almost all her life. You gotta hand it to the Budworths. They are old-school, paternalistic employers of the first water. Once people come into the cream-and-eau de nil HQ of Bedford Street (a sort of pauper's Fortnum & Mason), they never leave. I'll probably be wheeled out of here in my bath chair. Or so I hope, anyway.

My lunch guest today was Mrs Budworth. 'This is a terrible

restaurant,' she said to me when I arrived in Terroirs. She had suggested lunch; I had booked it. And I was paying. Not even Ben. 'It's terribly noisy!'

She clearly wasn't happy, so I beckoned to the waiter. 'Can we move downstairs?' I asked. There are leather booths and a bar on the lower-ground floor; it's not quite so rackety. An odd look crossed his face.

'You should know that the associate editor of *The Sunday Times* is downstairs,' he said. I peered and saw Eleanor Mills, the journalist who'd been given my column by John Witherow/Susannah Herbert, resplendent in a grey wraparound dress. This was rather eagle-eyed of him, I must say. It was where I'd taken Els for lunch (actually, she paid, as I'd given her instant quotes for her piece which I had suggested to Sarah Baxter on the key topic of 'Sleeping Your Way to the Top'). I greeted my old *Sunday Times* chum warmly and we were soon ensconced at Mills's table downstairs and she was happily at ours in the window.

Then Mrs Budworth dived under the table and did a cavity search of her capacious handbag. After rootling she withdrew a long, handwritten list of complaints that covered both sides of the A4. Then she swept aside cutlery, napkin, glass, etc., as I gazed on aghast.

'Let's start with My List,' Mrs Budworth said in a determined voice, as she laid it flat on the table. I went pale. I thought we were going to have a lovely ladies' lunch!

Her list ranged widely from the photograph we had chosen of Nancy Mitford ('Such unfortunate legs,' Mrs B. said. 'Why on earth didn't you cut her off at the petticoat?') to a typo on the '*Lady* and the Royals' piece in our collectors' 125th edition.

After having lumbered me with two large coffee-table books about Suffolk painters and ordered me to review them ('They only came out in early 2009'), Mrs B. asked me if she could write a column about rural life.

'I regard myself as a complete country mouse!' she said. I blenched and grabbed a waiter's sleeve. 'Get me a drink!' I ordered. I definitely needed a tissue-restorer. 'Yes, madam,' he said, handing me a wine list. 'You choose,' I said, thrusting it back.

The list was followed by complaints about Tom, chat about Arline, discussion of Ben's management style, of which I only said complimentary things – i.e., he was perfect for the job and very nice – we did have a lovely lunch. Apart from the filming at Deerbolts Hall, Earl Stonham, Stowmarket, Suffolk, for the documentary – when Ben had headed her off when asked about Buttons – she revealed she hadn't spoken to her son since Christmas, when they had a fight because he wouldn't do what she said he had to do at *The Lady* and put the magazine, and the other directors' interests first, and hers second.

I agreed it must be annoying for her that she couldn't have free rein at *The Lady* but she still had to hold out the olive branch.

'What would you feel if you heard he'd been knocked off his bike?' I said, knocking back my white Burgundy. 'He's your SON.'

'He hasn't said sorry yet,' she said, gathering her things and stuffing the list back into her handbag. 'The word is "sorry".'

I left the office early as it was the tenth birthday party for Mumsnet, hosted by Google in Victoria. The dress code was 'Boden', so I rushed home to put on a cheeky gingham blouse and skinny jeans. We arrived – as one does – shortly after the Prime Minister, as the motorcade double-parked in Victoria Street alerted us. There were two officers in yellow hazard jackets on the door. We went upstairs to the Google canteen (we were taken there by a runner who Reception referred to as 'a Googler'). A huge cake, home-made biscuits decorated with icing and hundreds and thousands, Moët champagne, lots of media, Johnnie Boden, Justin and Sarah Webb, Kathy Lette, thousands of female journalists, Labour ministers, etc.

Justine Roberts, the founder of Mumsnet, made a funny speech about how the Mumsnetters had bullied Brown over Biscuitgate (when he refused to reveal what his favourite biscuit was). Gordon Brown paid tribute to his wife Sarah and referred to himself as Mr Sarah Brown. Then Sarah Brown spoke in broad mockney paying tribute to Mumsnet and her DH (that's Mumsnet for 'Darling Husband').

3 March 2010

Went over to Claire to check a headline, and she was working away at a pattern of interlocking 'L's on her Mac screen instead of the Joan Collins cover. I recognized the pattern – it was the same pattern of 'L's that adorns the *Lady* carrier bags that we give away in Gatwick as part of the global promotional drive for the mag. She was playing with a red banner that went diagonally over one corner. 'AS SEEN ON TV,' it read. 'Why are you putting "AS SEEN ON TV" on the bags?' I asked.

I thought, not even Ben would regard the forthcoming *Cutting Edge* documentary, in the same strand as 'My Daughter Grew Two Heads' and 'Half-ton Mum' and 'The Man Who Turned into a Tree', as a *selling point* to potential readers.

'Ben said to,' she said, clicking the banner into green to see if it worked better. 'Because of *Corrie* and the documentary, he says.'

Corrie! Oh yes. What's happening here is that *The Lady* is being flashed up on a forthcoming episode of *Coronation Street*. In honour of this, we have had to mock up a cover image of *The Lady* with Joanna Lumley on it, so when this screen-flash happens the newsstand edition and the one on telly seamlessly match. We have failed to secure an interview with Joanna Lumley to accompany the cover image, but Ben is undeterred by this tiny detail. His thinking is, when viewers see the magazine on the small screen, they will all rush out and buy *The Lady*, and we must encourage them in this subliminal impulse, by sticking 'AS SEEN ON TV' on carrier bags at Gatwick Airport.

Upon further investigation, I find out that the way the magazine features in *Corrie* is that someone finds an escort by dint of putting an ad in *The Lady*. And the escort is none other than housewife's favourite – Nigel Havers.

Ben is full of expectation of soaring circulation when 1. the documentary and 2. the product placement of *The Lady* on *Corrie* explodes on to an unsuspecting and wondering world.

I began to get it. It's another of Ben's stunts, and it might just come off.

Big news! Having delayed the doc (because C4 wants John Dower to make it more moronic than it already is), *Cutting Edge* has now re-instated it for 9 p.m. on 18 March, as another doc has 'fallen through' for legal reasons and they need to fill a hole. With the '*Lady* & the Re-vamp' doc. That's in, like, *two weeks*. Got this from little blonde Becky.

> We have just heard from Channel 4 that they are now putting the *Lady* doc back in the schedule for tx [transmission] on 18 March. We were really hoping for more time but it's a good slot and it means we'll be very current!
>
> The cut is being worked on and we hope it will be in good shape for you to view next week. We'd like to invite you in to try and work something out.
>
> Just so you know, C4 publicity will want to release a rough cut or some clips to print press this week. It means we'll get mentions in the listings, which we want. We will be able to get later cuts out to reviewers nearer the time.

Oh Jesus.

I have told Ben I am not doing publicity for Optomen/Channel 4. That's *their* job.

Got back from watching Oliver play football against the Oratory outside Reading. Ivo drove, so I could catnap. The publicity stills from Channel 4 arrived – but I couldn't open them until I got home. They are beyond hideous – dark, slightly out of focus, I look like I'm auditioning for a role in the Baader-Meinhof gang. And married to Ben.

So I pinged off frantic email to Becky.

Becky! Have you seen the stills? Ben and I . . . *ugh* . . . we look like a pair of warring married undertakers on non-speaks in a funeral home.

The Welsh writer Roger Lewis's interview with Sharon Osbourne has landed. He has called it 'Secret Bud of Pleasure' in honour of a sticky and intimate passage in her novel about a pushy mother who wants her daughters to be 'bigger than Oprah'. He clearly had a lovely time with Sharon, whom he describes as 'bang tidy' after extensive renovations both to her exterior and interior.

I emailed congratulating him on a brill piece and for inserting an allusion to the clitoris both in the headline and in his piece.

'Oh, is that what it is? I had no idea,' he said in his email back. 'In any case, I always thought a Clitoris was something you kept in a cage and fed on Trill.'

I marched into the boardroom and found Ben listening to Dire Straits loudly on his iTunes. 'Good news,' he said. 'The 125 cover sold 33,800. A few could come back, of course. And some more good news. We made an actual profit last month. A small one, but a profit.'

4 March 2010

It was sunny for literally the first time in four months, but still freezing bloody cold. I was walking down the Portobello at 8 a.m. and I heard one trader say to another, 'Turned out nice again today,' in chirpy Cockney tones that couldn't fail to cheer. When I got to the office I swanked to Ben about the Mumsnet party. 'Why didn't we think of Mumsnet?' he said, as if he blamed me personally for this failure of spark. Then he told me about his website wheezes to rival Mumsnet's popularity and reach.

1. www.sitonmyfacebook.com for people who were fed up with Facebook and wanted casual sex.
2. www.unpcworld.com for people who used internet porn on their computers at work but don't want the guys from the IT dept to find out when they examine the hard drive. 'A number of Budworths and Blezard were among the first to sign up,' Ben said.

The Channel 4 team finally finished today. This involved me doing various so-called 'pick-up' interviews out of sequence about Arline and Lindsay. I had to pretend they were recorded not now, but months ago in November and December last year, when I was hissy-fitting about Arline still being listed as 'editor-at-large' on the masthead, and before we knew Lindsay was leaving, and also of course before the Stefano redesign.

So they filmed me in the boardroom wearing my Bree Van de Kamp silk ruffle-sleeved shirt. They handed me old copies of *The Lady*, with the old-style covers, such as one with a white-haired lady stroking a kitten on her lap, so that I could publicly mock them.

I did this for a bit, and during a change in the lighting I started reading an interesting article about bowel cancer. I was gripped. I cried, 'I take it all back.' The presentation of the piece was – like everything about the magazine then – shatteringly dowdy, but I had to admit that that actual article was useful. But of course they won't use that bit – me being nice about *The Lady* of bygone years when it was edited by Arline – because it shows me being reasonably human, and giving credit where due.

But the truth is, I could see why the readers loved it as it was at that moment. It was reassuring, and informative. It was not remotely concerned with being on trend. There was, I can see now with hindsight, something so old-fashionedly dull and kind about *The Lady* magazine from around the Coronation until about November 2009 that it was almost magnificent.

At the Strat. & Dev. meeting at 4 p.m. Lindsay read out an elegant and dignified speech about having had a marvellously rich eighteen years at *The Lady*. She named the highlights, such as going to interview Norma Major, and attending HRH The Queen Mother's funeral, not to mention endless travel.

At 6 p.m. I was filmed leaving *The Lady*, to provide an ending for the doc. As my get-up was a black anorak and horrid leggings, I didn't want to be beamed into the nation's living rooms in this chav outfit. So I borrowed freelance journalist Viv Groskop's coat. She'd come in to chat (am continually surprised by the keenness of freelancers, so I've asked her to interview Mumsnet's Justine Roberts, and Boden's founder, Johnnie Boden).

I had to repeat the 'leaving *The Lady*' money-shot of me exiting the glass, gold-embossed double doors on to Bedford Street three times with different expressions. As I did so, Ben and Viv (who was waiting for me to give her back the coat) were joined by a small crowd of onlookers who had gathered to laugh and point.

5 March 2010

Email from a freelancer:

Hello Rachel.

I've recently been to Buckingham Palace to interview HRH The Princess Royal about her interest in lighthouses, which you may

already be aware of. [ed's note: can he be serious?] I interviewed
her on behalf of a private-circulation magazine issued to a group
of UK lighthouse enthusiasts called the Association of Lighthouse
Keepers. [ed's note: no kidding!] The interview duly appeared in
their quarterly journal as an A3-sized 'Royal Supplement'. It caused
much favourable comment from everyone who read it, [ed's note:
I'm taking this on trust] and it has been suggested to me that with a
bit of a rewrite to take out all the technical 'jargon' that cropped up,
it would be of interest to a much wider audience [ed's note: again,
I am taking this on trust]. Her interest in lighthouses is fairly well
known in the media – mainly because of her alleged fondness for
'lighthouse-bagging' (a term she hates) but in our conversation she
was particularly chatty, open and honest about other aspects of her
enthusiasm that are not so well known.

I am nonplussed. On the one hand, our readers love the Royals,
as they do Labradors on sofas and home-made autumn chutney in
larders. But a whole interview about Princess Anne's interest in
lighthouses? Not so much, I suspect.

I shove the email in a folder in which I put all pitches and pro-
posals and invitations to speak I can't quite face confronting that
second and hope, in time, will go away.

The in tray:

- a proposal for a 'Diary from a Provincial Lady' from a reader
  in Hampshire called Dinny who would like me to give her –
  surprise! – a regular column. She sends some sample cols.: on
  playing the organ, and gardening, and a survey carried out by the
  UK Bee Farmers Association. The survey was on bee keepers,
  surprisingly enough, and discovered that 10 per cent of bee keepers were dead, 20 per cent were called John, 30 per cent had

beards, and 75 per cent were 'getting on a bit'. She adds, 'And 100 per cent were sartorially challenged. It seems I am married to a stereotype.' I will send Dinny a nice letter. It's really sad, but we don't have space! *The Lady* already has more columns – what with Mary Killen, Penny Smith, Clemmie, Dr James, Sarah L-L, etc. – than the Parthenon, and my dearest wish – to have Debo on board as agony aunt – remains unfulfilled!

- a letter from an Oxford reader complaining about Joan Collins's appearance on the cover: 'Are you trying to give us angina?' and the Penny Smith col. I get a lot of complaints about the Penny Smith column. Readers don't like her, because she is very pretty and frisky and funny.

- a letter from a 99-year-old reader, a Miss Fluck in Skipton, saying she is cancelling because her business partner has died. She conveyed her sadness at the end of a long tradition this represented, a tradition which started when her grandfather returned from Manchester Cotton Exchange on Friday afternoons bringing a copy which had to be kept in a 'mint state until Sunday p.m., when Mother would ask for quiet from the children and recline on the settee. This must have been ninety years ago.'

8 March 2010

First thing, went to a sort of media screening place with a cappuccino bar in reception – soooo Soho – to view the rough cut of the documentary, which is being voiced for the moment, until they find an actor, by John Dower.

Ben arrived mob-handed with a TV lawyer, James Herring from one of his PR companies and brother Adam. John Dower was there. I thought he'd be shitting himself, but he was very cool. '*The Lady* and the Revamp' had some laugh-out-loud moments but mainly I watched through my hands. To see oneself prat about and witter on is, truly, the theatre of embarrassment. I stared at myself. At the beginning I was pink and blonde and plump. By the end, raddled and sunken and grey-faced.

When the credits rolled, in order to foreclose any nitpicking from the Budworth side, John Dower strategically reminded Ben that he'd joked on film about filling a paddling pool with custard and getting me and Arline, Janina and Lindsay to strip off and wrestle in it. Also that he had suggested bricking them into the cab office where they both work, which Lindsay referred to as the 'gulag' in the film. And he also just mentioned that Ben had also said, 'Rach is my ho now.'

And, he concluded with meaning, Dower hadn't included any of those bits in the final cut!

There was a moment when I appear to say that Lindsay was on the 'deathlist' which made me wince. How could I? And a worse moment when I let rip (under duress – the Budworths were less than impressed by my *Sunday Times* magazine coup) and said that '*The Lady* is a piddling little magazine that no one cares about or buys . . . sorry . . . I didn't mean that.'

Ooh yes, and they announced they want Richard E. Grant to voice it. Withnail himself! Swoon.

The in tray:

- a letter from Mrs B., thanking me and running through a few items she hadn't had time to bend my ear about during our lunch at Terroirs. She enclosed a cutting from 1974 written about *The Lady* by Philip Howard of *The Times* on the occasion of the *Lady*'s ninetieth birthday, describing the mag as a 'rock of decorum in the shifting sands of permissiveness and unLadylike behaviour'. I feel there is an underlying message here for me somewhere . . .

- an unsolicited article called 'The Art of Being Polite' about the importance of 'Ps&Qs'.
- a letter from a linguist in Switzerland who served in the WRNS cracking the Enigma Code offering us the text of her talk, entitled 'A Very Personal Pre-dinner talk about Bletchley'. (I add these to my pile of pitches about Bletchley, amazing mazes and modern manners, which I receive on a daily basis.)
- a letter from a reader in Henley offering several ideas, including one called 'Trust me, I'm a witch' about her 'career as a suburban witch'.

Ben said he thought he'd buy *Reader's Digest*. I was appalled. What was he thinking? 'If it makes sound biz sense and you have the money, fine,' I managed to say. 'If your ambition is merely to be seen as a player in publishing, not fine.' I spoke with feeling, as last week we did not have enough money to pay the contributors. This is not the first time we have had cashflow problems, and I sense it will not be the last. Ben explained later that he would buy *RD* minus pension obligations with money raised from mortgaging property and it all made perfect sense.

John wanted A. A. Gill, the TV critic of *The Sunday Times*, to get a copy of the documentary and review it. Said the 'ritual kicking' by A. A. Gill was 'a rite of passage'. I emailed Gill asking for his address and reminding him of the last time we'd intersected.

I loved sitting next to you at dinner, especially when you told me my nose was too big and I was too hideous to appear on TV and that the *Lady* doc was going to be suicidally shit soooooo

where shd the producer send it so you can have your wild hunches confirmed?

Got this back:

Down the toilet obviously

Sent from my BlackBerry® wireless device

When I said this was chippy he flashed this:

Do stop sounding like menstral sloan [sic]

Sent from my BlackBerry® wireless device

10 March 2010

Predictably, the number-one story running on the *Guardian* Media website is that *The Lady* is considering making a bid for *Reader's Digest*. Words fail me. I don't think we have enough dosh to pay the printers this week. But Ben is all fired up, bushy-tailed, seems utterly serious.

The in tray:

- a copy of *Fashion in the Time of Jane Austen* published by the Shire Library (the bliss!) with a note saying, 'I'm confident you will find the book of interest', which indeed it would be if my world was rocked by line drawings of an early-nineteenth-century redingote of cream silk trimmed with swansdown, a development I certainly don't rule out at this stage.
- an invitation to lunch with the Prime Warden of the Goldsmiths' Company Rupert Hambro at Goldsmiths' Hall on 5 May.
- a copy of a book by Lady Ashcombe called *Behind Castle Walls – at Sudeley Past and Present* with a picture of the author standing on manicured green lawns in front of a massive honey-stoned, crenellated, herbaceous-bordered Poshtershire pile. Lady A.'s people have been in touch, i.e., like several million others,

she has demanded a column. I flipped through and read an amusing-ish anecdote about a mix-up one morning relating to a paying visitor to the castle who some peon thought was the plumber, and was called upon to attend to an unpleasant and ongoing situation in the children's bathroom.

OMG! There is stuff in the *Radio Times* on the doc. They call it outrageous, shocking, sad and brutal in turn, and the reviewer ends, 'Compulsive viewing.' Oh. My. God. I have banished the doc from my mind already – so horrified by what I saw of myself on screen, screeching, 'Deathlist!', rolling my eyes when Janina speaks, and going on about sackings as if I edited the *Sun*, not some genteel, cosy women's weekly that still has a place in the nation's heart. The doc goes out on Thursday next week, and in it I look and act as if I'm a cross between Kelvin MacKenzie and Tina Brown instead of a middle-aged mother of three trying to revitalize an old and dusty women's magazine with only plentiful tea-towels at her disposal.

I have to face up to reality – I am going to be a figure of utter ridicule and hatred in only a week's time.

Meanwhile, I have been quietly fuming about Adrian Gill calling me names. On the other hand, after the doc comes out, I might well look back on 'menstral sloan' (sic – Gill is dyslexic as well as rude) as one of the nicest things ever said about me.

11 March 2010

Lindsay is leaving tomorrow, so I took her out for coffee. We sat in Caffè Nero and I complimented her on her Thane of Cawdorish approach to her retirement (nothing in her life became her like the leaving, etc.).

She sipped herbal tea and, to her eternal credit, said only nice things of all her colleagues. Lindsay asked me how I got on with

Mrs B. and told me that I was lucky Mrs B. didn't try to make me run floral-tribute covers instead of my forty-something ladies. 'She always used to try to make previous editors have pictures of vases of violets,' Lindsay told me, as I goggled in disbelief. Really, every day here is Wonderlandish – three impossible things happen before teatime.

Gillian is proving worth her weight in gold and now seamlessly tells time-wasters who want to know whether I'm going to run their piece on dry-stone walling to send an email to Vicky instead. And never fails to offer me a cup of tea with a smile.

The in tray:

- two letters to Coco, whose column has already attracted two offers of sponsorship, one from Pet Protect and one from Porkinson's Bangers. One of the letters is written as if it were by another dog and is signed 'Many tailwags from the Borders'. One is from Leyburn, North Yorkshire, enclosing a parish magazine containing the collected works of Polly, a cocker spaniel. I read it and decided it was much better than 'Coco's Corner' (the only reliably popular thing in the mag apart from the Ladygram). I must raise my game.
- an email from Becky Clarke:

    Sent: 12 March 2010 19:23
    Subject: C4 trails

    We've just seen the trails. They will start running this weekend, I think. They are v. lively! X

Oh yes, heard today from a source who has insisted on remaining nameless that Arline was putting it about that she wanted me to get a terminal illness and *The Lady* to fold.

Crikey. This is probably just malicious gossip – although I'd want me to die too, I'm sure, if I were her.

15 *March* 2010

'Three cancellations already this morning,' said Ben.

He puts it down to the fact that C4 has started 'trailing' the documentary on *The Lady* that's going out this Thursday, i.e., in three days. I was sitting quietly in the playroom yesterday watching *Glee*, and the trailer actually CAME ON. I had the horrible experience of seeing me on screen, telling Ben to 'grow a pair of balls' and stropping about saying that I wanted to sack people. Milly was sitting next to me. 'Lame,' she commented. Frankly, this documentary will see off the remaining readers in their seventies and may fail to bring new ones on board and could be a kamikaze mission after all . . .

The in tray:

- an invitation to the Society of Botanical Artists Silver Jubilee Exhibition.
- a huge presentation box of Tian Hu Shan Pure Tea in exotic, fragrant flavours.
- Rococo Easter mini-eggs in a box.

Lindsay has left the building. When I came in this morning, she'd left a picture of Lady Gaga on my keyboard and she'd written a speech bubble coming out of her mouth saying, 'Put me on the cover and *The Lady* will fly off the shelves.'

16 *March* 2010

Circulation figures are only just peeking above 30,000 again, according to Nic Boize/B-Cal. This was for the Joan Collins cover. She is a big star. And we can't get above 30,000. I am in despair.

What do our readers want? Luckily, an email from a reader arrived to tell me: a 'nice landscape scene' or 'some flowers on the cover'.

I called brand expert Peter York, co-author of *The Sloane Ranger Handbook*, for his advice. Basically, he said we had to be 'naice', with our pinkies out. We were the anti-nasty, anti-trash magazine for gentlefolk, he said, a print publication with a 'functional base' (translation: we are read only by either employers or staff).

'But we have to keep the brand going with the editorial,' I said. We agreed that *The Lady* was a micro-trend magazine which would always venerate the Royal Family and would endeavour to remain reasonably reassuring in a world full of uncertainties. I wittered on until we both had to go – me because Radio 2 had just arrived to ask me the difference between being a lady today and being a lady in the age of Vera Lynn, him to give a speech.

Our brand analysis was inconclusive. Being 'naice' is not going to butter many parsnips.

The in tray:

- a letter thanking me for speaking at the Wellbeing of Women lunch at Fortnum's last week and a voucher for a complimentary facial.
- a letter from a Wimbledon reader expressing approval at my changes, and so on, leading to a huge BUT: 'However, I do have one huge complaint. For some years now you have offered lovely nightwear during the summer and winter months. Quite frankly, a nightie length of 42 inches on me would not cover my nether regions once I was in bed . . . surely you could offer a few of the short-sleeved nightdresses in a longer length? I personally take a length of 54 inches, but would settle for 50 inches.' I carry it out to Gillian. 'This one's about a woman who wants the nightie company that advertises with us to produce a short-sleeve one in 54 inches. It's your lucky day.'

- a letter addressed to Arline Usden pitching a 700-word article about having your own supply of truffles, accompanied by a selection of photographs of the tuber.
- a copy of a new publication by a group called Christians Aware called 'Food, Festivals and Faith'.
- a press release from an outfit called ToDryFor promoting a new collection of designer tea-towels.

With perfect timing, just as I was opening this last item, Viktor (the *Lady*'s Bolivian housekeeper, who emerges from the Fred West basement every morning to rod radiators, hang pictures, sprinkle rat poison behind biscuit-harbouring safes and fridges, etc.) came into my office and handed me a freshly laundered pair of blue and white tea-towels. Everyone else gets one; only the editor gets two. If there's one thing I don't need, it's more tea-towels.

Trailers for the doc are now running on a loop on Channel 4.

Ben is in full overdrive and has put up a huge banner on the website saying, 'Channel 4 Viewers Click Here', which directs them to a special offer: five issues of *The Lady* for £5! He has also increased bandwidth or something to the *Lady* website in expectation of millions of hits following transmission on Thursday night.

17 March 2010

An email arrived from my pet webstalker Jimmy Burke, which I reproduce in full.

Ms Johnson,

I have just learnt that your brother has been confirmed as Conservative PPC for Orpington. I wonder whether dreams of political office have started to occupy your idle moments too?

If so, I beseech you to resist. I know the temptation must be tremendous, and I'm sure you know the perfect people to provide the parachute, but think of the country.

After all, if you can commit such egregious crimes against journalism with a few bashes of a keyboard, imagine the damage that could be done if you were entrusted with something that actually mattered!

Regards,
Jimmy

A call came in. Gillian said in a tentative voice, 'Rachel, I've got Deborah, uh, Duchess of Devonshire on the line. Shall I put her through?'

'Oh all right then,' I said. 'Put her on.'

Debo is ninety at the end of the month, and the papers are full of her. She has tentatively agreed to be a cover girl for us. First we talk about the lovely party *Tatler* and Penguin have just given her for the reissue of Nancy's novel *Wigs on the Green* at Claridge's.

Then she moved in for the kill. 'You were so very kindly talking about me doing a cover for *The Lady*,' she began, then paused. 'To bore you further . . .'

Her timing was wonderful. I shouted with laughter. '"To bore you further" is what my children say to me when we are talking about arrangements,' she said. Then she explained that she felt very over-egged at mo what with Stoker, her son and heir the current Duke, saying the aristocracy was finito in an interview with Camilla Long, an interview he gave to publicize both the reopening of Chatsworth and her ninetieth-birthday exhibition. So we agree to delay the cover till her book – *Wait For Me* – was out in October. 'There's a marvellous picture of me in a long taffeta skirt, you see,' she said. 'That can be your cover.'

We parted fondly then I remembered – she's star of the documentary on Thursday! So I called back and got her PA, Helen Marchant. 'We've already pinned a large sign to the TV to remind Her Grace to watch,' she said.

Ben bounced in to tell me – it's Wednesday – that he's briefed all the diaries about the programme and leaked embarrassing things about me before the doc is aired tomorrow. This doesn't sound good. 'Such as?' I asked.

'Oh, that having you as editor has been like having a new puppy,' he said, terribly pleased with this. 'Everyone loves the puppy very much but it does leave messes about the place for others to clear up.' Somewhere else he described me as a 'firework' that you lit and you weren't always sure whether or where it would go off.

Janina has been asked – not by me – to compile a list of all the writers, and so forth, who have contributed so far under my editorship. There are sixty-three names on the list. Ben was talking about this and sounding pleased over lunch. I should have smelt rat. When I go upstairs to the marketing nerve centre – i.e., the room that B-Cal shares with Piers the computer guy – B-Cal was working on a genius wheeze, which was to put something on the website saying '63 Reasons to Read *The Lady*' followed by a list of every Tom, Dick and Harry from Toby Young to Kimberly Quinn who has contributed a piece over the past six months. 'I don't think that it's right to project the magazine on the basis of one person who has written one article for us back in 2009,' I said.

18 March 2010

Doomsday.

We had a 'celebration' day-of-transmission lunch with Becky and the legal chap from Optomen in Scott's in Mount Street.

When the wine waiter came along Ben ordered a bottle of white wine and announced that he intended to spend the next forty-eight hours in the pub. Janina sent me emails every five minutes.

Poor John Kercher (the father of Meredith, the student Foxy Knoxy was convicted of slaughtering) keeps sending in story ideas via email. It turns out he is an old-time contributor to *The Lady*. Slightly stunned and unclear as to how to exploit this, I ask him to file a diary. Obviously, my motives are not driven snow. I hope he will be moved to write about his daughter. One has to be ruthless. History of the Hampton Court Maze – no. But a tender fatherly account of losing his daughter in a brutal sex game – hold the front page!

It's low of me, I know, but I am in the business of selling magazines, despite the 'Journal for Gentlewomen' tag round *The Lady*'s neck.

I don't watch the doc going out as I am at a 'small kitchen supper for locals, very casual', i.e., a sit-down catered dinner on our communal garden for about thirty given by the divinely beautiful artist and mother of six, my neighbour Nicola Reed. When I switch on my iPhone at 10.15 there are seventy-six new emails and a bundle of texts. And twenty-seven voicemails. I haven't listened to them yet.

19 March 2010

Had sleepless night worrying about having been portrayed as a hatchet-wielding Rottweiler on nationwide TV. Also made fatal mistake of going online at midnight and putting the words 'Rachel Johnson' into Twitter and Google. OMG.

Apparently I am a 'talentless whore' and 'look like Boris in drag'. Some females tweet they have girlcrushes on me. There are whole threads on Mumsnet devoted to trashing me and analysing my wallpaper. Feel incredibly exposed. As for this morning's papers . . .

In the *Guardian*, Nancy Banks-Smith wrote crushingly funny piece correctly linking *The Lady* to P. G. Wodehouse's Milady's

Boudoir. Banks-Smith compared me first to Aunt Dahlia and then my management style to Boudicca (at one point I say, 'Ben's a dear boy, but he hasn't wielded the hatchet enough'). When it got to the bits with Paul Blezard – the doc made it look as though I sacked him in my first meeting, when I didn't – Banks-Smith wrote, 'The literary editor was slaughtered on the spot.'

The Times reviewer was good on the *Lady* readers. 'The old-guard readers emitted the *joie de vivre* of a funeral parlour: one was so steely as she described Rachel's "silly" changes that you suspected her extensive ornament collection might become a murder weapon.' The *Times* review ended with my Ratner moment and quoted me: '"In the real world this is a piddling magazine that no one cares about or buys," she shrieked, before ducking half an octave for, "Sorry, I didn't mean that . . ." (Come now, Rachel, stay real . . .)'

Felt very odd this morning. Have had masses of reaction, but the truth is I only really care about what the people in Bedford Street think. Last night at 2 a.m. I sent an email to Janina saying I hoped she and her mum were OK, and there were no hard feelings on my part, and let's all push forward to the sunlit uplands of 40,000 a week.

But she hasn't answered. I want her to be OK.

Gillian has lost no time in passing on the horrified reaction of appalled readers to the doc who have written in their droves to editors@lady.co.uk – our generic email address for anyone who wants to contact Editorial. We have had thousands of them. My inbox brims with both bile and a sort of stunned approval.

Interesting documentary – absolutely aghast at Rachel's comments relating to the *Sun Times* article – stairlifts & incontinence pads. Rachel might need incontinence pads herself one day.

Outraged by RJ's comments!!!! I'm over sixty, buy the magazine from time to time. Rachel's comments were ageist. Even if you use incontinence pads, you can still think, you still have feelings, you're not sub-human. She should be sacked on the spot. What she said is illegal. Who does she think she is?

I love the bit about what I said being 'illegal'. People actually want me to go to prison for saying stuff.

We've all been supportive to Boris up to now but Rachel's attitude to people is appalling, has probably alienated viewers. I am forty-nine & I feel alienated by her comments. I always enjoyed the magazine hitherto. Dreadful to previous editor who has done her best over the years, she was treated like a criminal, dreadful treatment. There used to be an innocence to *The Lady* magazine & if I wanted to read about Jane Fonda's great sex I'd buy *Marie Claire*. Sharon Osbourne is not *Lady* material, nor is Joan Collins.

One man wrote in saying that my ideas for modernizing *The Lady* were feeble and what we needed was a 'pet page that could be about that new pet cleaner that just came on the market and the London Zoo – a different animal each week, and have a plant and exotic plant page'.

One of Gillian's emails that morning started thus – as if this was her comment rather than a reader's – which rather put me off my stroke at first:

Ben & Rachel,

absolutely disgraceful, I was cringing . . . to behave so abominably – Rachel's attitude to mag & people who'd worked there for years. To humiliate them like that . . . What does she think of herself? – crude, obnoxious, ungallant. To talk about Arline & her daughter publicly is disgraceful. Dumbfounded. Silly questions to Duchess of Devonshire –

a wasted opportunity. Arrogance of calling the shots! No humility or I'll
tread softly approach . . . if it's so piffling, why does Rachel want to work
here? No comfortable feeling at end. I've always liked the covers –
much better than Kelly McGillis, say. It was a wonderful opportunity
which has been wasted. Everything is brash & common now & Rachel
Johnson has spoilt it all. All my friends found Rachel utterly obnoxious.

But it turns out she is merely conveying the comments of a
'Mrs. R., buys it from shop, been on a *Lady* holiday. Lives in Cotswold village, Burford.'

Still, I regret several things. *Je regrette beaucoup*. One, telling
Ben to grow a pair of balls. As David Sexton said in the *Standard*,
'She was not in awe of her boss. It's one thing to observe "You live
in a bubble," another actually to issue him the straightforward
command, when he wouldn't do what she wanted: "Grow a pair of
balls!" Few men hear that whispered softly in their daydreams.'

He went on.

By the end, *The Lady*'s circulation had gone up a bit. Will Johnson
stay at the helm? She is now writing a diary of her time on the
magazine. If it's anything like as entertaining as this larger-than-life
documentary, it'll be well worth reading and a lot bloodier than
anything to be found in Wodehouse.

I also regret my hobnail-booted manner with Paul Blezard and
the rest of the staff, who appear to flinch whenever I enter a room.

22 March 2010

Spent thirty-six hours in Paris, where *Le Diable Vit à Notting Hell*
(*Notting Hell*) has reached almost the top of the fiction bestseller

list. It is number two. I am here to prop it up by whizzing past
bookshops and doing interviews for France Info, France Inter,
etc., *in French*. The weather is balmy and sunny, and after doing
promo I went to the Beaubourg, where I stared intensely at Lucian
Freud's paintings of walls in Holland Park, Irishmen in W11 and
benefit inspectors in his studio in Notting Hill, and felt in two
places at once. In the evening, I met Charlie Glass – the author of
our celebrated 'humping the help' feature – for a drink before I
hopped on the Eurostar. In the bar, my mobile rang. It said '*The
Lady*' on the screen. Ben. His voice didn't sound quite right. 'Can
you keep a secret?' he asked me.

'Of course I can,' I answered, downing my ice-cold Stella Artois
in excitement and hurling a handful of peanuts down my throat.

'Well, B-Cal – you know, Nic Boize – came down a while ago.
Obviously, not all the sales figures are in yet. It's still only Monday,
and the week doesn't close till 10 p.m., but it looks . . . very . . .
like . . .' He started speaking slowly, as if on horse tranquillizer.

'Spit it out, old boy,' I said, thinking, '35,000 if we're lucky.'

'Boize said he'd never seen anything like it, wasn't sure whether
to believe it, but . . .'

'WHAT!' I screamed.

'54,000,' Ben said, sounding delighted.

I repeated the number several times, and said in a loud voice,
'Incredible, incredible,' while gesturing to Charlie Glass to pop up to
the bar and order me another Stella. And – feeling like pushing the
boat out – some more peanuts. This was a cause for celebration.

'It's all been worth it,' I said to Ben. I told Charlie immediately,
then called Ivo from the taxi en route to the Gare du Nord, to share
the good news.

It's not often – ever – that I can say I've had a top-three bestseller
and almost doubled the circulation of a magazine in one week. So
I am going to say it tonight (am sitting on Eurostar with laptop)
because the chances are I'll never have the chance to say it again.

I am thrilled, and proud, and happy. For the first time since I can remember. And all I know is this – it'll be back to square one tomorrow, the book will be sinking down the charts and the doc will be forgotten, so I'm going to enjoy this while it lasts, and milk it for all it is worth.

23 March 2010

I don't know if I have the fortitude to record what happened today.

It started with me surging into the boardroom latte in hand, on a high after posting record figures. Ben's face fell when he saw me. 'Come in, come in,' he said, lifting his bottom off his chair as if going into a *schuss* down an easy blue run. He does that when I enter a room. Still. Even after I said he had to grow a pair of balls on national TV. He has lovely manners. Then he dished the bad news immediately.

''Fraid B-Cal got it wrong,' he said. 'It's not 54,000 after all.' I sank down into a Chippendale chair and placed my Caffè Nero paper cup carefully on the blue baize covering the boardroom heirloom table. 'Go on,' I said, cursing B-Cal privately.

I had been really, really happy last night, thinking I'd turned it around and all the flak around the doc was worth it because I had doubled the circulation, and now, of course, I find out it was a mirage. 'He misunderstood the EPOS (electronic point of sale) figures,' Ben went on. 'It's probably still north of 40,000, mind, and we sold out in Sainsbury's.'

Apparently, the best B-Cal can come up with, based on progress-of-sale gross estimates, is that we will sell, as a result of the doc, between 38,000 and 45,000. Now, between 38k and 45k is quite a wide margin – as Ben said, B-Cal would have quite a good career as an ERNIE-style random-number generator – but it's a lot better than 27,000, which is where I was when I started. Oh well. We fight on. We fight to win.

Gillian and I decided what we would do with the literally hundreds of letters and emails and telephone messages we've had in this week was this. Bundle them up into folders and get a workie to come in and answer them all.

All was going OK until Ben ordered me to join him for lunch at Leon on the Strand. I pottered into the boardroom clutching my wallet and Leon loyalty card, and he started saying something and I started saying something, then he suddenly snapped.

'This has got to stop. No interruptions! I need to have a hearing on discipline with you. No. More. *Interrupting!*' He almost roared.

I studied his face to see if he was joking. He is quite a student of management theory and sometimes talks about being a follower of the 'sandwich method' of dealing with staff, whereby you squeeze in something unpleasant between two nice things, in a sort of shit toastie. I still can't decide but, not unnaturally, he is fed up with people telling him I walked all over him in the doc.

The moment passed, and we trotted to Leon and had a nice lunch, during which he warned me that there was a rearguard action underway to make out I had completely sunk the magazine. He intimated that dark forces were plotting to have Ms Usden and Ms Fulcher reinstated in Bedford Street in a moving ceremony, while I am ushered out of the building via a back exit on to Maiden Lane. It appears to be being orchestrated by none other than Mrs B.

As a result, she has soared in my estimation. She simply can't forgive me for not loving and venerating the magazine as it was when her father ran it, and before I got my hands on it. And she is acting – as no one else will – to save it from moral ruin.

But I think Ben will stand by me. I'm his hire. He picked me out of a line-up of twenty-two others, after all (having said that, I have subsequently learnt that I was blackballed by at least one director-brother, but Ben ignored this). On the way back to the office he insisted that he walked the street side of the pavement. He always does this, as if worried that a brougham is going to career out of control at any point and come crashing into us, and if it did, the gentleman should take the impact.

After lunch I was getting back to work, thinking things were back to normal – phew – when I heard a commotion in the subs room. I heard chairs being pushed back, and nervous laughter. I heard Gillian falter, 'Yes, she is,' and then with a roaring sound Mrs Budworth entered my office, encased in a navy twinset. 'You wretched girl, I'm going to MURDER you,' she said in a loud voice. She stood four-square in the middle of my office, almost shaking.

'What were you thinking of? Why aren't you jumping out of the window at the sight of me?' she bellowed. Her gaze was trained on my Maiden Lane window. Outside, on the other side of the street, towards the modern building above the horrid pub saying that J. M. W. Turner was born there.

I sat down, having politely risen to my feet at her unannounced entrance.

'How. Could. You. Say that awful, awful thing you said, about how we were a piddling magazine no one cared about, or read? You MONSTER,' she said, settling down in one of my dainty chairs.

'I did take it back immediately,' I reminded her. In the next breath. My mouth had gone very dry. It sounded pretty feeble.

'But too LATE! TOO LATE!' she said in a raised voice. 'It is what everyone will remember. And it has been picked up. I read it in *The Times*, and the *Telegraph*.' She looked towards my window again, as if I was expected to auto-defenestrate on the spot.

She went on handbagging me. I tried to explain that the crew were here for six months, and filmed for 400 hours, and had caught me red-handed in one unguarded remark, but there was no placating her.

'You've done yourself no favours, I'm afraid. As for us . . .' She made it quite clear that if *The Lady*'s nineteenth-century pre-eminence, its circulation figures of 70,000, even 80,000, were never regained under my watch, it would be All My Fault, and that I had brought a horrible taint of modern nastiness to the magazine that was heretofore sugar and spice and all things nice.

I tried to steer her away from my Ratner remark and said I really regretted saying it, which I did, still do, and would do anything to take it back, but I can't. Then I said that I wouldn't mind in the least if the directors – i.e., her, Ben, Adam, Willy and Richard – wanted to sack me. I said it. 'Why don't you sack me if that's how you all feel,' I said, looking her straight in the eye.

She dropped her gaze. 'It's all right for you,' she said. 'You've got your career ahead of you, or you *used to*!'

At this point we both burst out laughing.

Eventually, I offered Mrs B. three pots of Lovedean cranberry and almond granola as a peace offering (have a whole crate of Lovedean and a whole crate of Dorset cereals that won't fit in my in tray) and steered her out of my office. 'Consider yourself murdered, dear,' she said as she left, tipping the mini-pots of granola into her huge black handbag.

I felt shattered after that but I knew it wasn't over yet.

Mrs B. had said – *inter alia* – that the Duchess was also 'incandescent'. So I called Edensor vicarage. Some flunkey told me Her Grace was in the garden. An hour later, she called back. 'Hello,' she said in a flat voice.

'Debo,' I began, feeling dreadful. 'I called to apologize. I'm so sorry that my remark about "piddling little magazine" caused such upset.' And then the Dowager Duchess let me have it too, along much the same lines as my previous handbagger, Mrs B. She asked me if I was considering my position.

'How could you sack that nice literary editor who'd been working for the magazine for forty years?' she asked. 'How could you say that awful lie about "piddling magazine"?'

Now, of course, the facts are these: Debo's father, David Mitford, was general manager here from 1911 to 1914 and took it so seriously that, according to legend, he spent his time ratting in the basement with his pet mongoose. And Blez had been working here for only two months, and was sacked by Ben for going AWOL and having his copy sent back nine times by Sarah Kennedy, the interim editor, but I just didn't have the heart to defend myself, or my big mouth, any more. I felt really, really sad that I had let them both down and had allowed the daylight of modern-day documentary broadcasting in on what they both clearly consider to be the magic of *The Lady*.

25 March 2010

After the ordeal of the Mrs Budworth ambush, I have been feeling unaccustomedly shaky. I went in to Ben and gave him my Diana look (from beneath lowered eyelids). 'Come and see Uncle Ben, sit on Uncle Ben's knee,' he said. Like me, you can never keep Ben down for long. He's a cork too. 'Do we have to put you on suicide watch? Take away your shoelaces?'

Then of course I protested that I was fine. He then asked me if I was going to resign. I said no. We passed the issue for 30 March, and tomorrow I go to New York with Milly, for her super-sweet sixteenth birthday, and nothing's going to ruin it. Ha ha.

I have got Gillian to photocopy a catholic selection of both horrified and approving letters to the office since the broadcast and send them to Mrs B. and the Duchess of D.

The in tray:

- a letter from a man from HM Prison Brixton called Peter Wayne congratulating me on my 'Herculean effort revivifying *The Lady*' and offering his services as a contributor to 'The Gents' or, failing that, a true-life account of how the Duke of

Devonshire (Debo's late husband) saved him from arrest in Hatchards and came 'rising to my rescue like a superannuated Sir Lancelot'.

There are so many letters and emails after doc, of which below is a classic example.

From: Gillian Spickernell
Sent: 25 March 2010 11:38
Subject: reader call

Mrs Betty Ruggles from London SE1 rang:

Sharon Osbourne appalling, the likes of her! As for Penny Smith! I don't want to know about her silly little antics during the week! I'm not a subscriber, buy it when I want something to read. Been buying it sixty years. How on earth could you put Sharon Osbourne on the cover?! I saw the last 20 mins of documentary & can't imagine what advice the Duchess of Devonshire will give if she's to be an agony aunt.

Luckily, as I was leaving Bedford Street yesterday, staggering under weight of muesli, granola, Rachel's yoghurt, etc., that I had been sent by PRs following my appearance in the 'What I Ate Yesterday' slot in *The Times*, a girl plucked my sleeve. 'Hello,' she said. She had black hair, Alice band, white face, red crimson lipstick, and was working the shorts-over-woolly tights look. 'I loved you in the programme. If you ever want an intern, someone who would work for free . . .'

'As it happens, I do,' I said. 'What are you doing next week?' She is called Agnes Frimston.

It's as if there is an unwritten rule that dictates everyone at *The Lady* has to have a name from a Barbara Pym novel.

26 March 2010

Well, Ben had a meltdown at last. It had, in fairness, been brewing for weeks.

The trigger was the interview (over the phone) with me in *Campaign* magazine, the house journal of marketing and advertising. The piece started – and I paraphrase, as I am catching up with this diary in the business centre of the Plaza Hotel, Central Park South, New York:

> *The Lady* has had more publicity in the last six months than in its whole 125-year-long history. And it's all down to Rachel Johnson. Before the arrival of new editor Rachel Johnson, the only time one would expect to hear of *The Lady* was on *Have I Got News For You*'s niche slot sniggeringly poking fun at ultra-obscure publications like 'Ukrainian Goatkeepers Weekly' or 'Tractor Part Monthly'.

Ugh.

I didn't know the piece had come out, so it sat between us on the blue baize table as he went on. I was trying to leave the office to make my transatlantic flight, for springtime and my daughter's super-sweet sixteen in New York. Because it sure as hell wasn't springtime in Bedford Street.

Then Ben let me have it. Said I'd used the magazine and abused the magazine for my own fell, self-serving purposes. That I had trashed the magazine publicly (the 'piddling little magazine' comment will, I suspect, haunt me for a while). It was all about me, me, me, and when I gave interviews I never suggested that I was standing on the shoulders of giants, never referred adequately to the illustrious 125-year history of the organ, nor made it clear enough that there were a multitude of departments slaving away night and day to put the magazine out there. He was most outraged to read my answer to the question, 'What is the PR strategy?' – 'I am the marketing strategy.'

To sum up, it was all a bit www.racheljohnson.com and not enough www.lady.co.uk for his liking.

I didn't interrupt, because I worried that if I did, in order to say, 'But Ben, you hired me to make a splash, and to get everyone talking about the magazine. What matters in PR is not so much what people are saying but the volume of sound. We can't control and dictate exactly what other media outlets are going to choose to run with and emphasize, but the important thing is that they are paying attention. In that sense, I have executed your strategy of hiring a high-profile editor and revamping the editorial and creating buzz . . . To The Letter.'

Instead, I sat there staring at the blue baize while he told me exactly what he thought of me, wondering whether I should go back on my previous answer and chuck in the towel, i.e., resign – and at least I would make my flight. I tried not to look at my watch – I had to be at the Virgin Atlantic check-in in less than two hours, and hadn't even packed or picked up Milly, fifteen and three-quarters, yet. Finally, he looked exhausted and said, 'Sorry. I had to get that off my chest.'

While Milly and I were on the Heathrow Express he rang to see if I was all right. Which was a relief. Of course I was all right. I did think the documentary, and the reaction to it, were very hard on him. John and Becky made him out to be a flippy-floppy public-school boy, me the alpha-blonde ball-breaking new broom. It was a caricature. I haven't exactly emerged unscathed either.

But he was definitely the one who took it for the team.

27 March 2010

In New York. Got an email (one of many) from Janina. 'Mrs Budworth called for you.' I forgot to say. Janina has dyed her hair blonde. Several pitches have arrived by email:

- 'I enclose two articles on the theme of petsitting,' writes one aspirant contributor. 'I do have several more of this ilk!'
- a wonderful piece written by a lady in Earley, Reading, on an old typewriter on the end of the war in 1945, with lines such as, 'One thing we have missed lately has been the great friendly noise of our bombers going out on their heavy raids.'
- one called 'tea-time traveller' about how to find proper tea in a proper teapot in the UK (pics available on request).
- a letter on the same lines (these things always come in pairs) saying, 'I enclose a 930-word article with suggested illustrations on the subject of cricket teas.
- a letter saying, 'I enclose a 700-word articule [sic] with suggested illustrations on the subject of pillboxes.'

The
Lady

A WEEKLY NEWSPAPER   6 to 12 SEPTEMBER 1988

extra 8-page
Needlecraft Supplement
featuring
The Lady Originals —
knitted styles of the
Thirties in high
fashion today, like our
Covergirl's Bolero —
plus some
pretty embroideries

Reader Holiday Offer
to Austria

The Canal
    Bridgeman

CLASSIFIED ADVERTISEMENTS
Situations Vacant; Businesses;
Residential Property for Sale;
Hotels and Guest Houses;

APRIL

1 April 2010

The *Mail on Sunday* has begged me to participate in a piece in which I grow potatoes for charity and see how I get on compared with other 'celebrities'.

I declined.

They emailed again saying how incredibly keen they were, and listed the other 'celebrities' who had leapt at the chance of some free self-publicity. They mentioned that they would donate £500 to charity if I just chatted about my green fingers for a few minutes over the telephone. 'You don't even have to do a photoshoot.' As I can give the money to the Parkinson's Disease Society, which is a noble and worthy cause I have a personal interest in (my mother has Parkinson's), I obliged. They agreed to send a sack of peat to the *Lady* office, and some seedlings.

The piece duly appeared in the *Mail on Sunday* with a huge picture of Anthea Turner crouching over a grow-bag, flicky hair, gardening gauntlets and huge smile all in place.

It's the great gardening trend of the year! At garden centres all over Britain, potato-growing kits are being snapped up by families eager to experience the taste of their own fresh spuds [I read in amazement].

But the big mystery is: how many potatoes can you get from one grow-sack? The *Mail on Sunday* has asked seven very different personalities – from politician Vince Cable and Radio 4 inquisitor

John Humphrys. [My name is unaccountably not listed.] We have equipped each of them with a grow-sack, compost and five Vales Emerald seed potatoes and given them ten weeks to produce the best possible crop. The delicious and heavy-yielding variety Vales Emerald is popular as a salad potato. The winner, who will be chosen by BBC *Gardeners' World* presenter Toby Buckland, will pick up £5,000 for a charity of his or her choice. Here our contestants tell of their expectations . . .

If my as-yet-unborn potatoes win, then the *Mail* will give £5,000 to Parkinson's, so whatever it takes, my spuds have got to be bigger than Anthea Turner's, even if it means sending Gillian to the Tesco Metro on Bedford Street for a packet of Finest.

6 April 2010

A huge grow-bag of peat has arrived. Which is lovely. There's only one snag. The bag containing five seed potatoes and the trowel has disappeared. I can't imagine who would bother to steal a bag containing seedlings. So I am going to lose! To Anthea Turner.

7 April 2010

It is the middle of the Easter holidays so we have lined up three covers in advance. This should enable me to get out of Bedford Street. They are, in this order: Liz Hurley looking toothsome in tweed lying on a bale – cover line 'A Role in the Hay'; Tracey Emin; and Johnnie Boden. I had just landed in Palermo airport when my iPhone told me I had a message. It was Ben.

He has had major wobble over the Tracey Emin interview.

I was half-expecting this as, when I went to the 'beauty contest'

in Bedford Street back last summer, the one little tip Ben gave me
before I went in front of the board, i.e., Ben, Adam, Richard and
Willy Budworth and their ma, was that his mother, Mrs B., absolutely loathed Tracey Emin. So I duly announced during my
coronation that *The Lady* would have no truck with the mouthy
baggage, her rumpled and unsavoury bed, her abortions and her
Tampax. 'We would not be touching her with a mile-long bargepole!' I added for good measure.

Needless to say, months later, Tim Willis, ex-*Sunday Times* style
editor, has secured a major interview with her, written it up
superbly and I fully intend to run it in *The Lady*.

In the course of this, Emin talked about possibly voting Tory, her
childlessness and riffs – and this was the bit that gave Ben pause –
about how needlework, through the ages, since the Bayeux Tapestry
until the present day, has been a brilliant displacement activity for
women who – unless their idle fidgeting fingers were otherwise
occupied – would be masturbating instead.

So Ben now wants to circumcise this interview and remove all
allusions to needles and wanking – a private pleasure he for some
reason (he is Old Harrovian) refers to as 'bean-flicking'.

I said this would be OK had I not put out this fire once already,
to whit, I had gone into the office on Maundy Thursday, and I had
warned the reader in my editor's letter that the interview was
strong meat. Carolyn had even suggested that we run a cover line
saying 'Emin Uncensored'.

The argument is, you either move forward, or you don't. You
either run stuff that's going to move the goalposts a bit, or you just
carry on providing the same old pabulum of cobnuts and cucumbers. If you try to keep all the old readers happy while enticing new
ones in, you risk losing *all* your readers.

So as we navigated Palermo airport and tried to find the Sciacca
road, Ben said, 'Having read a lot of the letters from the old guard,
I can't stop worrying. I can't sleep at night. We've got this tricky

business going, where we don't want to alienate the old readers before we get your new ones on board.'

So he wants to cut the interview, remove all the nasty bits about body parts, and shove it online. Then he gave it away. 'I can't imagine what Mum would say, you see, if she read about . . .' and mentioned bean- (or was it bead?) flicking again.

I knew it! The whole cover interview will have to be pulled – all because Ben is frightened that Mrs Budworth will have the vapours. I felt my blood freeze in my veins. Then I took a deep breath. Was I being reasonable with the old family mag's doughty readers? Forget Mrs B. – would the Tracey Emin remarks about masturbation pass the what-would-Debo-think test?

No, they wouldn't.

So I told Ben to go ahead and circumcise the worst bits of the interview. After all, it's his magazine – it's their family money. Not mine.

Next up I foresee a problem with the Boden cover. I adore Johnnie more than life itself and have known him since we were both in our twenties, but Claire hadn't got a clue who he was and his PR people have so far failed to come up with a picture of him that will fly off the shelves, apart from one of him grinning as he clutches Sprout, his terrier, which has already appeared elsewhere. And I edit a magazine called The Lady. Not The Bloke.

8 April 2010

In Sicily. More emails from Janina.

Sometimes people become convinced that 'underneath', I am boiling with suppressed emotion. As Janina put it, 'You could do a Malcolm Lowry with your volcano.' It makes me want to reassure them that underneath that icy exterior, an even more glacial interior can be discovered.

Janina has found out that we are giving an interview to the

Media *Guardian* next week and has sent me an 800-word briefing note, plus points to make and topics to avoid. Meanwhile, I have whinged to Ivo in the Michelin two-starred Rocco Forte restaurant of the Verdura Hotel (we have escaped for three days with the children) about Emin, Janina, etc. He was very sound.

'Darling, it sounds as if Ben is right. Maybe sometimes you have to accept that your readers don't want to read about wanking, they'd much prefer a nice piece about embroidery. Now can we stop talking about *The Lady*? This isn't a romantic dinner at all.'

13 April 2010

Back from Sicily and in office.

Ben needed persuading, as I predicted, to run Johnnie Boden on the cover with my suggested cover lines, 'Ginger Tailor Soldier Spy' and 'Jolly Boden Weather'. My keenness to run with the Boden cover is given fair wind by the fact that the other cover possibility is Jenny Agutter and the pictures make my heart sink very slightly. They look somewhat *sludgy*. They make you realize why editors put photos of fifteen-year-old, six-foot Ukrainian honey-limbed models with eyes like infinity pools on their covers, not sixty-something actresses. It's not fair, it's not right, but it's how it is.

And as I said to Ben over lunch (in which we mainly talked about problems to do with staff), if we were going to survive having people on the front of the magazine every week, i.e., fifty-one contenders for the cover each year (Christmas is a double issue), we would need to diversify. We would have to have the occasional man. I explained that Johnnie was a seriously good egg, best of British, etc., poster boy to launch our England Special on 20 April. Then I added my clincher. 'And Johnnie's holding a terrier,' I said as I crammed my face full of fried eggs on toast with chorizo in Terroirs.

'Last time we had a terrier on the cover – it was a cover with a terrier sitting in front of an Aga with the cover line "Aga Louts" – it sold really well.'

The in tray:

- baby brioches with delicious crisp sugary topping from an outfit called Napket Snob Food.
- tons of letters and pitches and bags of cancellations from readers who say I have despoiled their homes by putting Tracey Emin on the cover. I have had to draft a statement for the PR people:

> I stand foursquare behind my decision to put Emin on the cover. She may not be a dab hand at hospital corners as far as bed-making goes, but Tracey Emin, RA, has reminded a male-centric world that so-called traditional housewifely skills such as needle-work and quilting are in fact an art form, and always have been.

- one upset reader called Patricia writes, 'If I wanted trash there is plenty of choice . . . words fail me. What is wrong with a beautiful picture of the countryside or animals or buildings?'
- one from a reader saying she liked the documentary and has taken out a sub which ends, 'Oh, by the way, I'm pleased you've kept the office dog, Coco, on staff!'
- a pitch for a piece about Harris Tweed: 'No longer scratchy boys' jackets that never wear out'.

But my favourite was from a lady who has been invited to a Garden Party at Buckingham Palace in July. She pointed out that as a forty-year-old mother of two boys, getting shipshape for Her Majesty will cost upwards of £600, and that to add to her woes, she is not a svelte size 16 but a size 28, and wonders (I don't see the link but there we go) whether I will do an issue on Social Etiquette to help her out? 'For me this is a once-in-a-lifetime event and I wouldn't want anything to go wrong.'

14 April 2010

As predicted, the Tracey Emin cover has exploded in our faces – like her cleavage erupting from her Vivienne Westwood dress. The lead story in 'Londoner's Diary' is titled 'It's all getting a bit racy now at *The Lady*'. There are pictures of me grinning and tossing blonde hair smugly. Picture of Tracey Emin doing her sideways gurn. 'When RJ took over as editor of *The Lady* she promised to drag it kicking and screaming into the twenty-first century, but it seems that some subjects are still off-limits . . .' etc. Long exegesis explaining the difference between our two versions of the Emin interview, one in the mag minus bean-flicking, one online complete with bean-flicking, and how lily-livered I am.

I went into the subs first thing Wednesday morning and they were poring over it. 'It's back to the bad old days,' said Lindsay Pine, who is second-in-command to Chrissie, 'When no unpleasant subjects could ever appear in the magazine.'

'Not that masturbation is unpleasant,' I added.

Am waiting for Ben to come in to post-mortem the *Standard* and talk about the lines to take tomorrow, when the Media *Guardian* come in at 10 a.m. to interview us both.

I am also waiting for him to decide whether to remove his mother's executive powers and kick her off the board. Blimey, it's like a daily soap opera. Where are the cameras now?

It's like Wisteria Lane, only with less Botox.

15 April 2010

Media *Guardian* in all morning to interview me – i.e., persuade me to put foot in mouth.

'Are you serious about this job? How long are you going to stay?

What's it like editing a magazine when the family is breathing down your neck all the time? How do you get on with Mrs Budworth?', etc.

I parried and puffed. I said I loved the job, which was true. I said that I understood the family's sensitivities and desire to see *The Lady* remain the repository of all things nice and remain sensationally bland. I did admit that it was hard not to run a taste test on articles like the T. Emin masturbation piece without worrying, 'What will Mrs Budworth think?' I liked the girl who came, Emine Saner, *very* much. She was a beautiful Turk (almost but not quite an oxymoron, American cheese, and am allowed to say this as am proud of my own Turkish blood). Afterwards, I warned Ben she'd talked a lot about the Emin interview. Whenever Ben mentioned bean-flicking, he made a circular movement with his right hand, like a chauffeur rubbing a speck of guano off the bonnet of a car with a moistened forefinger. This was very very disconcerting.

Later Joan shuffled in to pet Coco wearing a new pair of the fluffiest, whitest slippers I've ever seen, as if she had attached a pair of newborn spring lambs to her tootsies, and handed me today's post.

The in tray:

- a registered delivery of two new short stories, one called 'Waiting' and one called 'A Twist in the Tale'.
- an A5 postcard from Harold Pinter's only son, Daniel. In this lengthy postcard he accuses his stepmother, Lady Antonia Fraser, of a number of things and says she is aptly named the Lady Killer (as she reviews crime for us) because she is the Lady Who Kills. The postcard is big and crammed like an artwork with the tiniest writing imaginable and is still legible. 'If Lady A. is the Lady who kills, then who(m), I wonder, is the Lady who gets killed?' etc., etc.
- a letter from a lady called Rae Muddle (am not making it up) who writes from Bognor Regis saying, 'You poor girl! What a

lot you have had to put up with! I think you deserve a medal tolerating an editor-at-large and everyone hovering over you!'

Feel like having it copied round all the Budworths.

16 April 2010

Janina has finally agreed to take some holiday. I forgot to say that, yesterday, a chap came into my office to see me about something. Ben came in after he'd been in the office for under an hour.

After he'd gone Ben lunged towards my AC unit and switched it on. 'It's much too hot in here,' he complained. 'That poor bloke from the *Mail* was sweating like a rapist.'

I have decided to soothe ruffled Debo feathers by organizing a *Festschrift* for her birthday with everyone from Prince Charles downwards.

The in tray:

- a beachbag from Cabbages and Roses.
- glorious Michael Van Clarke conditioner, shampoo, and comb called '3 More Inches'.
- a tray of rocky-road brownies – YES! Big, big TICK!
- an invitation to Hogarthian Rout at Sir John Soane Museum from Rufus and Sally Albemarle saying dress code was periwigs and that sedan chairs would be at 11 p.m.

An excited email from Clemmie Hambro:

Hiya . . .

Sat next to Tim Bell at lunch today and so decided to ask him what *The Lady*'s new marketing strategy was . . . he could only come up with an aged naked calendar, and getting people to write about shagging the nanny. I said you'd already tried that and everyone got a bit upset!!

21 April 2010

Everyone keeps asking me how *The Lady* is doing. Wellll . . . Since they ask.

After the doc, we topped 40k (the Sharon Osbourne cover, thanks to C4), and then the next week we were down to 36,000 (cover girl Joanna Lumley, after a few onscreen flashes in *Corrie*). But now we are back down to 31k, 32k, and yesterday Ben was in despair.

I think the problem is as follows:

1. Even if they want to, no one can find us in the newsstands. Newsagents buy two copies, and they get lost amid *Bella* and *Chat* and *Women's Weekly*. People will go into one newsagents and look, and they might even ask, but after that they will give up. As this email suggests:

   > It is little wonder your circulation is down. I can't find a copy anywhere! My local shop always had one and now it doesn't get that from the wholesaler and my local supermarket never has any copies. How can you boost your circulation if the magazine can't be bought?

2. If they do by some miracle find a copy of the mag (Ben will hate me saying this – he hisses, 'We're in most supermarkets, including Sainsbury's and Tesco, every Waitrose, and in 11,000 newsagents') and read it, the ads tell them they are in the wrong place. Even in the Johnnie Boden, bloke-on-cover, fresh-as-a-daisy issue we've just published on 20 April, there is a walk-in shower ad opposite my ed's letter, and then nothing till Tena Pants and Age Concern

on page 40 except for a few ads for comfy shoes and nighties (sorry, 'Night-Time Luxury'). We don't have many ads, and the ads we do have remind the reader that we are a rapidly ageing population and that we are all going to die, very soon.

3. People still don't want to shell out for the editorial. They are prepared to spend £1.80 to see if their ad looks nice, or to look for a job, but the engine of *The Lady* is still in the back, like a Citroën Deux Chevaux.

4. People are incredibly vain and age-conscious and still associate *The Lady* with their grandma. Or their nan. They feel it's not for them. No one wants their advanced age reflected back at them.

So Ben gave me a short but heartfelt lecture as I stood in the board-room staring at the graph which showed our circulation falling off a cliff. 'I just feel very conscious about not losing any more of our old readers at a point when we don't have enough new readers to guarantee our survival,' he explained. This was the lecture no new editor wants to hear. Don't lose any of our old readers while you bring new ones on board – *or else*. 'That's why I wanted to tread carefully re: Tracey Emin' – Carolyn told me that when he used the word 'masturbation' he couldn't look her in the eye and blushed deeply – 'and your little forays into matters political. The three pillars of *The Lady* over the last fifty years have been: No Sex. No Celebrity. No Politics.'

'Have they?' I snapped. 'Well, in that case, why did you want a new editor, why did you want to update the editorial, and if that really is our mission statement in 2010, that doesn't leave us an awful lot to write about, especially in the run-up to a general election.'

He told me that I clearly hadn't read 'past interviews' with him in which he'd spelt out the magazine's 'mission statement', and explained the three pillars, etc., in words of one syllable. 'Where?' I asked. 'I haven't seen any of these supposed interviews.'

'Well, the interview in *Suffolk Life*, for a start,' he replied.

I said that, strangely enough, I didn't read *Suffolk Life*. 'Well,

you don't know what you've missed then. It is a mass-market circulation magazine . . . in Suffolk, anyway.'

We are getting on very badly at mo. One of the reasons is – the
numbers haven't *stayed up*. His strategy of getting a high-profile
editrice on board, getting masses of publicity, getting us on telly,
was all very successful. But it hasn't turned the magazine around.
It has not been the Viagra he expected, the circulation-boosting
little blue pill. And we are miles from selling the magic 45,000 copies
a week, the critical threshold for advertisers. Below 45,000 we have
no chance of snagging decent ads that don't just remind readers of
their own mortality. So the magazine continues to lose money.
Meanwhile, Uncle Tom – upstairs in abject luxury in his huge
apartments in the Anne Frank annexe – won't allow him to sell the
magazine. Even though – before, that is, Ben arrived hotfoot from
the crocodile-infested Everglades – he'd been planning to 'slit the
old girl's throat'. ('Slit the old girl's throat' is Uncle Tom's phrase,
delivered with lip-smacking relish.)

If Ben sells up, his chances of inheriting the family silver in the
shape of the Covent Garden property portfolio would go down
Swanee. So he's stuck. It's a pig in a poke. Poor Ben. When he
could be training pilots for Bristow Helicopters in Titusville, Florida. Or as he calls it, 'Hepatitusville', or 'Shitesville'.

I could see the despair in his eyes as he talked. As he went on,
I took the *Daily Telegraph* off the table underneath the gloomy
portrait of the founder and leant over the blue baize to read it. As
he passed me to get something from the table, he smacked me on
the bottom, with a rolled-up copy of a 2008 *Lady* which had an oil
painting of a bunch of lilacs on the cover.

After this I returned to the boudoir, pausing only to ask Ros the
receptionist how my potatoes are doing (I had to get the *Mail on
Sunday* to deliver a replacement bag of seedlings). I haven't been
to see them once, but Viktor has chitted them in and is under strict
instructions to water them every day. They have sprouted lustily.

I know this because the *Lady* potatoes are his pride and joy, Viktor's screensaver on his mobile phone.

22 April 2010

Mrs Budworth has sent me a photocopied letter from a cancer patient in a hospice that she has received about me and the Channel 4 doc.

> A hateful performance by a not-nice person who degraded long and faithful staff who kept the magazine going for years – was this so she could storm in and wreck it? [the reader/viewer wrote]
>
> Until you stamp out her penchant for pushing herself into every issue [ed's note: that's weird, have ditched my own byline pic] most people will continue to detest the present magazine – not the changes *per se* but this brash, common tendency to stamp on everyone because she has a vulgarly-monied background [ed's note: I wish – the Johnsons have never had a bean].

Mrs B. has slipped in a note ordering me to 'Reply personally.'
Sir Tim Bell, marketing guru, has had further thoughts. This from Clemmie:

> Hi Rachey. Another thing SIR TIM asked was, are you interviewing all three leaders??
>
> Also a special subscrip. offer for grandmothers to give *The Lady* to granddaughters or daughters . . .
>
> Just passing on the PEARLS!!!
>
> C xxxx

Just made a pilgrimage up to Mumsnet Towers to interview Justine Roberts. Or should I say, I sat there eating a delicious beetroot and ginger cupcake with lemon icing while Viv Groskop interviewed her. As I left I signed the visitor's book. There were only two names, feminist writer Natasha Walter, whose new tome I have just read, and PM's wife Sarah Brown. There was a space to leave comments, and I noted Mrs Brown had said, 'Thanks for the lovely biscuits!' and drawn some kisses. So I signed my name and left a crawly comment about cupcakes, suck-up that I am.

The travel-copy nightmare will never end. Before I got here Arline sent tons of freelancers and office pets on little trips as rewards, and the copy is still sitting on the system at *The Lady*. This is a typical email from a PR:

> I am contacting you from Axis Travel Marketing, we represent
> Cancun CVB in the UK.
>
> We did a press trip last year in July and had the participation of
> Lindsay Fulcher. I wanted to get in touch, to introduce our selves
> [sic] and also too [sic] see if you could give me an idea as to when
> the article is being published. I am preparing a report for my client
> so any news will be much appreciated.

The truth is, I could publish travel articles that are sitting in the 'Travel' folder from now for a whole year and still not run out.

24 April 2010

Have to go on *Newsnight* election 2010 special. Well, I don't have to, but I've been asked, and Jeremy Paxman is presenting, and the others are going to the musical *Hair!*, so I thought, 'Why not?', and said yes.

In Make-Up, Theresa May sat having pancake applied and, in

reply to a question about lipstick (Did she want some? If so in which colour?) replied, 'Pinky-browns.'

I made small talk about having been in Orpington to canvass for brother Jo earlier in the day. As a result, I know absolutely nothing about the Conservative manifesto, entitled 'An Invitation to Join the Government', a navy hardback, but all there is to know about free swimming for the over-60s in Biggin Hill. Theresa May clearly didn't want to be my new best friend (I am regarded as off-message by high-horsed Tories) so I shut up and closed my eyes while they made me camera-ready.

Then Harriet Harman came in, so I was sandwiched between Theresa May and Harriet Harperson, who – like Cherie Blair – is very pretty 'in real life'. Both MPs were wearing black slacks, little jackets and chunky jewellery and have had blow-dries. I haven't washed my hair for ten days. I looked at my neck anxiously in the mirror as the make-up professional eradicated the shadows under my eyes and my sun blemishes with Laura Mercier concealer. I felt a terrible pounding headache start. I asked the make-up woman for aspirin, but as a techie with an earpiece confirmed, the BBC is not allowed to give it out to guests. When I ask, Harriet Harman piped up, 'I've got a headache too.' Which made me like her. At least someone was talking to me.

Then it all started going pear-shaped.

I was brought on to the set with two comedians off the TV (Rufus Hound, Ed Byrne). I was placed to the left of them but – ho ho! – *to the right* of no less a personage than Nick Griffin, of the BNP. The symbolism of the placement did not elude me. When it was our turn we chattered on to Paxo about the election campaign and the debates. I said that up until the telly debates, the election campaign was like the Oxford *v.* Cambridge boat race, i.e., Labour and Conservatives battling it out to be head of the river every year. 'Then the Cleggasm happened,' I repeated (it was an inspirational coinage that came to me in Make-Up).

The studio went into shock. One of the comedians asked if I wanted a multiple Cleggasm. Paxo's eyebrows hit the ceiling. I pressed on. 'So it started like the boat race and then turned into the Henley Regatta, only it's still a festival event dominated by white, public-school middle-class males,' I concluded.

'Well, I don't think that Gordon Brown would agree with that,' said Paxo, who pointed out later that my analogy was not apposite as the Henley Regatta always pitted two boats against each other in a two-horse race. And Gordon Brown was not privately educated.

Still. Simon Hughes for the Lib Dems laughed heartily. Harman and May sat stony-faced.

When I got home from doing *Newsnight* with two comedians, and Nick Griffin, someone had already tweeted it and the Cleggasm was on YouTube. I know this because I was idiotic enough to check (the first rule of life – never self-Google).

'You were shite,' texted a friend who used to produce *Question Time* and who prepped Cameron for his second and third telly debates.

26 April 2010

Felt shattered.

Media *Guardian* interview out today, replete with pic of self lounging on orange *chaise longue* in boudoir. I was wearing a careful outfit of Hennes matelot top, Topshop blue-velvet smoking jacket, J Brand jeans and hemp trainers, to convey the message that *The Lady* editor is moving with the times.

I gave it the once-over. Immediately detected that Emine Saner, the creamy Turkish blonde interviewer, has been judicious and fair. Her piece was a jolly romp with the headline 'They may want someone lower key'. I paused over the pull-quote from me, 'I can't speculate as to whether *Lady* readers have masturbated but my wild guess is they might have done.' The *Guardian* cites our new soar-away figures (40,000 post doc, settled back to 35,000 and heading south) and quotes the publisher saying that *The Lady* is past the worrying point, i.e., we are not, in Lesley White's peerless phrase, merely wasting our time putting dancing shoes on a corpse. The piece was much nicer than I would have been about me.

I sent Ben a text saying I was having brekker in the Wolseley with adman Robin Wight, but added jokingly that I would be 'in for my spanking later'. At the Wolseley, I devoured eggs Benedict and a whole pot of coffee, and an order of crispy bacon on the side, while adman Wight told me it was all hopeless until we completely refreshed our advertising, and we should get in Kimberly Quinn, who is feted and famed for her ability to get luxury ads in *The Spec*.

'I'd love to get in Kimberly, she is advertising gold,' I replied. 'She's already come in, in fact. But if we got in Kimberly, 1. Ben would be out of a job and 2. we'd have to pay her salary.'

'Put her on commission then,' said Robin. To sum up, he said that until we get some high-end advertisers in, we were dead in the water. Given how many ads we do continue to have for walk-in baths, he's not far wrong there.

Then I went into Covent Garden.

Ben was furious about the Media *Guardian* interview. Just as he was furious about the *Sunday Times* interview, the *Campaign* interview and the Channel 4 documentary, and all the free publicity we've got – brackets, thanks to me, close brackets.

'We've got to get away from the jolly-japes, bedroom-farce type of article that keeps being written,' he raged. I couldn't think what he meant, then remembered there is a bit in the piece where I show Viktor the Bolivian housekeeper's cupboard full of loo rolls and Vim, etc., and tell Emine Saner that I like to push Ben inside it, that runs:

Pointing to an understairs cupboard in the corridor, she says: 'Sometimes I ask Ben to get something from the back, he goes in

and then I shut him in!' What japes! I'd like to see John Witherow
do that to Rupert Murdoch.

'This piece is nonsense,' he fumed, as he reread it in front of me,
'right up until the bit about the history of the cherry tomato.' He
did some counting under his breath, like a pre-schooler in literacy
hour. 'There are at least *six lies* in the piece,' he ranted. Leaving
aside Ben's decision to call inaccuracies 'lies', I could only spot one.
(Uncle Tom's flat is not sixteen-bedroom, it's sixteen-room . . . for
now. He is gradually annexing more rooms, in a sort of Anschluss
of our office space. He's taken the Thora Hird room upstairs, where
I used to disappear for power-naps, and now he has his sights on
several more rooms on the marketing/advertising floor. When
asked why, he explained that his friends didn't like tramping all the
way up to the top floor. So we are all being squeezed into the editorial and ground floors as a result, like rabbits in hutches.)

At all this, I felt a twinge of despair.

Then Ben told me that Mrs Budworth has called a board meeting in May to demand my resignation.

He also showed me a letter that Mrs B. had written in reply to a
reader who complained about the documentary. Mrs B. had copied
her reply to Ben. Her letter said, 'If I had my way, I'd have shown
Rachel Johnson the door straight away!'

'Nice,' I said, and handed the letter back. She has always given
me the impression that she regarded my entrance into Bedford
Street as about as innocent as a fox prowling around a hen coop.

When I trotted back to the boudoir, Gillian forwarded me an
email from a happy reader/viewer.

Dear *Lady* Magazine

On Thursday March 18th I watched a television documentary about
the new magazine. I approached this with a completely open mind

since my mother has been a loyal fan for many years and I have enjoyed her passing me her older copies. For her birthday one year I sent for *Lady* binders and receiving the magazine was a special moment in her week, especially since my father died in 2003. The *Lady* she loved was uplifting, interesting and interestingly quirky in a positive way.

At 49, I suspected that I was probably part of the new audience you might be targeting. I didn't tell Mum about it since she was already disappointed with the cynical tone of the new magazine and its attempts to be fashionable by upturning traditional values. My sister also watched. It soon became clear that the older ladies who spoke on the programme were the object of ridicule so my decision stood not to phone Mum, and I didn't. My sister did try and found an engaged tone so went back to the programme.

If only we had kept phoning her that evening. For she was lying alone on her kitchen floor having had an ischaemic stroke that lunchtime. She lay there all that night, unable to move or contact anyone. Her oven was on with her lunch in it. The following lunchtime her friend found her. Mum had been there for 24 hours and was in a very serious condition so I travelled in the ambulance with her to hospital in Bournemouth and phoned the family.

The irony for me is that, for part of that time, her loyalty to your magazine was being ridiculed on that programme with bickering, silly arguments and brazen rudeness. There was no acknowledgement to all the loyal readers who have kept the magazine going. They are not eccentric old ladies but decent people who have worked hard, treated others with respect and know far more about life than we do. They also know how to treat others with dignity and respect.

Mum is still in hospital with dysphasia and dyspraxia so she finds it very difficult to speak or express herself. She is learning to write with her left hand, having had beautiful handwriting and taught many children to read and write herself. She nursed my dad through cancer for three year without complaining until he died and still didn't complain. I am upset that, with the power you have, you feel it necessary to force radical change that verges on bullying. I am studying writing and I am interested in many kinds of magazines but I shall probably not be buying this one. Mum had just cancelled her subscription when she was taken ill. It just seemed very ironic that she was lying so ill and so alone whilst this programme was aired with all its bickering and docu-drama overtone.

Jane Dey

You couldn't Make It Up.

I have pushed it on to Becky and Pat at Optomen, so they feel guilty too.

27 April 2010

When I went into Ben's office the next day, there was a note on his desk. I read it upside-down. There were about ten points scrawled in felt tip on the back of an envelope.

'Sack the editor' was number four.

When he saw me reading it, Ben explained that, last week, he was summoned to the Royal Overseas League to have dinner in an empty dining room with his trustee, Jonathan Lawley. This was on the fiat of Mrs B. The trustee went through Mrs Budworth's agenda item by item.

'I see,' I said.

Nice email has arrived from Gillian.

Miss Lynn Barry from Northampton called. Been buying *The Lady* from her post office for 40 years, now 61 years old. Thinks the way Rachel has turned it around is nothing short of fantastic. Absolutely brilliant! Miss Barry did Barbara Cartland's hair for years & years. She loves the way Rachel is highlighting charities as well, such as the Dogs' Trust.

According to Ben, Mrs B. is planning a boardroom putsch to oust me *and* Ben, and install Adam as publisher and presumably editor in May.

Meanwhile, the fact that Jo (standing as PCC in Orpington) has been using the office to telecanvass has leaked.

This is lead story in the 'Londoner's Diary' tonight.

Tories find *The Lady* is for turning

How will the Tories beat the forces of Cleggmania? Simple – engage the services of *The Lady*. The mayor's younger brother, Jo Johnson, a prospective Tory candidate in Orpington (Tory majority: 4,947), is using the offices of *The Lady* magazine, edited by his sister, Rachel Johnson, to telephone-canvass for votes in order to see off the Lib-Dem threat.

'As you may know, a few of you attended a telephone canvassing held at *The Lady* on behalf of Jo Johnson,' says an email from Einy Shah, a member of Johnson's campaign team, sent to party workers. 'On Tuesday May 4 and Wednesday May 5 we will be giving one last plea to call the Cs (definite Conservatives) and Ps (Probable Conservatives) to get out to vote. Cleggmania briefly hit Orpington but we need to call our voters and tell them to stick to the blue corner ... we'll be relentlessly campaigning ... we need as many boots on the ground as possible. We need all the help we can get and would really appreciate one last push to get Jo elected in Orpington.'

It is certainly another sign of Rachel Johnson's pioneering approach to editorial duties. In a recent Channel 4 documentary she described her new offices as 'a cross between an undertaker's and a lunatic asylum' and said there were far too many fusty old members of staff there by dint of the hereditary principle. 'Ben's a dear boy, but he hasn't wielded the hatchet enough,' she said of her publisher boss, Ben Budworth.

Some of *The Lady*'s more traditional staff might be shocked to learn their organ has now been hijacked by 'dark forces' to serve the Conservative Party cause. The magazine has never been overtly political in its 125-year history. Staff were so confused as to how to operate a newly installed hand dryer they had to have their freshly laundered towels restored while they were given tuition on how to use the baffling contraption.

I slunk in to see Ben to receive another spanking for this. But for some reason he had taken this one on the chin, despite reminders that, when I got here, *The Lady* was a Jacques Tati version of goings-on in the Tudor court, with mothers passing on titles to daughters, falling down staircases, resident ghosts, and so on.

I asked Ben whether he wanted, following the *Standard* story, Jo to cancel his planned telecanvassing session. To his credit he said no and insisted that bro Jo should come in as planned. 'The crusade for common sense and the return of the Conservative regime must continue unheeded,' he said, rubbing his hands. I'd forgotten how 'sharply right wing', as Debo puts it, the Budworths were/are.

It also crossed my mind that the reason he wasn't furious was because he'd leaked it himself ... like he did the Dyson driers and the Emin masturbation.

Frankly, Ben leaks so much he should really be wearing a pair of Tena pants at all times.

28 April 2010

The Channel 4 'Lady and the Revamp' doc was repeated on Monday, so there's another spate of online comment, emails, and so on.

I've only just caught up with this programme, and was mesmerized by Ms Johnson's mercurial tits. She came out of Rigby & Peller with both of them pointing in the same direction (natch – you get what you pay for at the great R&P), and then we saw her chairing an editorial meeting with the two of them slumped under her sweater like two tired puppies that were no longer talking to each other. Most distressing.

. . . blogs someone called Waldo.

The in tray:

- a letter asking me to consider a 'Poetry Page' enclosing a Kiplingesque cutting from the *Sunday Post* of 1970 which begins, 'If you would like to see a better Britain, a country worthy of its daily bread . . .'
- a letter from a reader called Cyril Bracegirdle who wants to write a column about antiques. He is kosher: he's written a book called *A First Book of Antiques* and *Collecting Railway Antiques*.
- Madame Arcati, a media blogger whose name for *The Lady* is the 'old cunties' weekly', has also blogged again:

    Astrologer Eric Francis foretold on Madame Arcati that masturbation holds the liberating key to better relationships in the

future. A sign that he must be on the right lines comes from
Rachel Johnson in the *Guardian* today, invited for the ump-
teenth time to talk about her once-genteel magazine *The Lady*:
'I can't speculate as to whether *Lady* readers have masturbated,'
she says, 'but my wild guess is they might have done.' I wonder
if the magazine's stately owner Mrs Budworth has given the
matter any thought.

There are small mercies. Thank God Mrs B. is offline at Deerbolts Hall, Suffolk, and only communicates by letter first, and
telephone, second, and by loud hunting cries, third.

Someone has hacked into the website and replaced the biog-
raphies of our fragrant *Lady* bloggers – Meredith Ogilvie-Thompson,
Tania Kindersley, Jane Alexander, Lucy Denyer – with spammed
ads for female Viagra and date-rape drugs.

John Kercher's diary has come in. It's all about his holiday, and
each paragraph begins with the word 'Then'. I stare at it glumly.

I can't make Janina deal with it, or even Lindsay, because they're
not here.

29 April 2010

Emma Freud has refused to be our cover girl to accompany her
eulogy piece on Clement. Quite correctly. You can't be on the
cover of *The Lady* because your dad has died. So we are stuck.
Until, that is, Judy hacked into Janina's computer and found all
manner of goodies, among which was an email from *goddess* Olivia
Williams, the slight and wounded star of Robert Harris's movie
Ghost, in her inbox. Hurray! Hallelujah! Janina saves the day.

30 April 2010

Mrs Budworth rang to complain about the Camilla cover, which has HRH The Duchess of Cornwall in a pink hat adorned with pink roses. She asked to speak to Judy (Ros our receptionist is like GCHQ when it comes to telephone traffic, as all calls to *The Lady* come through her). 'She has a moustache like a sergeant major!' she told Judy, and then added a complaint about a wrinkle on HRH's upper lip. 'What on earth was Rachel thinking?'

When I got in, I stared at the cover and could see no trace of upper-lip down or what the French call 'a duvet' at all, not even the wispiest of summer-weight togs.

It is *Marie Celeste* on Fridays, which is why I try to work from home Fridays. Today when I went in there was no Janina, as she is still on holiday. No Claire the designer. No Carolyn (on some foodie jaunt to Helsinki). No Jess, as she only comes in on Mondays, and is having a baby in September.

Meanwhile, Chrissie chief sub is screaming for more help and earlier layouts from the design team. Tammy the picture editor has left for her new job at Corbis, and her replacement, Tamasan, also known as Tammy, has arrived and she doesn't work Fridays. So Tammy is the new Tammy. This from Chrissie:

> Judy has just emailed me the bones of her chat with you re: getting Tammy Myers (i.e., old Tammy) back in as picture editor on Fridays when Tamasan (new Tammy) is off (forwarded here to you). I want to concur with what she says and add my view.

> We really need to be able to send the magazine to press on Wednesdays in future. This means keeping up the momentum that we have attained this last week. The only way to achieve this is for Subs to

get layouts by Thursday and Friday. The only way they can do this is
if copy and PICTURES are in. Copy is now usually here in good time,
but PICTURES are a hold-up. We very much need to have a Picture
Editor in on Fridays not only to get pics but to chase up caption and
credits information so it is ready for Subs.

The person who needs no training to do this properly is Tammy
Myers, so it would seem like very good sense to get her in on Friday
in place of the extra person coming in during the week.

I went in to Ben and said that it was no good, I couldn't do editorial single-handed as I did this week, and also the design team
needed an extra pair of hands at the Mac on Fridays. I mentioned
the chap from the *Mail* again.

He repeated what he said before, which was that there 'was no
budget'.

I understand Ben's reluctance to spend money on a picture editor and the new chap from the *Mail*, but still. I can't help fizzing
with fury. After all, unless there's actually a good product, there
won't be anything worth PRing, period.

The **Lady**

THE VERY SPECIAL
WEEKLY MAGAZINE

60ᵖ

25 to 31
MAY 1993

**ROYAL
CHELSEA**
Preview of
the Chelsea
Flower Show

**HOLIDAY
OFFER:**
Gertrude
Jekyll's
gardens

TEA FOR TWO
Talking to
Thora Hird

**CHESHIRE
GARDENS**
A paradise
for plants

JOBS AND HOLIDAYS
CLASSIFIED ADVERTISEMENTS
Job vacancies at home and
abroad, holiday cottages,
hotels and guest houses,
bungalows to let and for sale

MAY

3 May 2010

Roger Lewis has asked me to canvass for him so he can become Oxford Professor of Poetry despite the fact that he hates the stuff. So he copies me in whenever there is a little snippet/interview. Someone called Duncan Fallowell has asked me to set up a Facebook group to help promote Lewis's campaign. This is beyond my level of social-networking competence. Today, this from the Welsh troll:

> Dear Rachel,
>
> I was watching a DVD of an old black & white John Betjeman documentary – and in the voiceover he said something you might like to put on the masthead:
>
> 'I shan't get up yet. Not now I've got this new number of *The Lady*.'
>
> Amicalement,
>
> Roger

5 May 2010

Up at 6 a.m. to go to the Strathmore Hotel in Queen's Gate Gardens to do a live *'emission'* (do love that word) for Radio France. As *Le Diable Vit à Notting Hill* is still miraculously on the bestseller list in Paris; and as the publishers are flogging it on basis that it's a richly comic satire on the Notting Hill Tories and bankers, etc., I feel duty-bound to turn up. But it's in French. Have sort of mugged up on basic words – like *banquiers gras* (fat cats) and *chefs de fil* (party leaders) but still, it's a car crash. We all sit around a table in front of mics, in the middle of a large function room in the hotel. With the overexcited presenter are me, Jon Henley from the *Guardian* and a lot of gabbling Frenchmen. To one side of the room, there's a sort of mixing desk, and lots of people on computers, and producers, plus people standing around openly talking throughout the broadcast. It couldn't be worse. It's 7 a.m., noisy, I have an audience of attractive dark Europeans. I have to fill the airwaves for forty-five minutes and I don't really speak more than restaurant French.

I whisper this to John. He says, 'Don't worry,' and claps me on the arm: 'You'll be *fiiiiine!*'

I feel better for a second, until he tells me he lived in Paris for ten years and is married to a Frog. Whenever I open my mouth to utter in the tongue the people in the hotel seem to be laughing, silently. It is very distracting. I was so drained and depleted afterwards that I had to stop at a café on Pall Mall at 8.30 a.m. to eat a full English breakfast to recover.

Lunch with Rupert Hambro at Goldsmiths' Hall in the City. Once you accept something, you sort of have to go. Lots of very old men in very elegant suits approached me holding drinks and said, 'Ha ha ha – so you want to know all about us, do you?' I didn't. But they then proceeded to tell me all about silversmithing and palladium. I sat next to a retired man called David Peake, a former head of Kleinwort's, who told me he was ashamed to say he was a banker and that when he was head man at Kleinwort's, he was paid (or he paid himself) about the same as a junior trader at Goldman Sachs. The lunch was enlivened by a delicious 2006 Meursault, but otherwise unproductive, even though I got a guided tour of the assay office, and was frisked upon leaving.

6 May 2010

Election Day. Brother Jo is standing for election in Orpington. The subs have put up a gallery of pix of Boris culled from newspapers – Al with Indian dancers, Al on bike, Al rumpling hair at City Hall – and now they've pinned a little Photo-Me-sized pic of Jo to the wall too. Which is tactful.

The prospective parliamentary candidate came in last night for his final telecanvassing session. His 'Get the Vote Out Script' is on my desk when I arrive. It includes the line 'Every vote is crucial and we really need your vote.'

The in tray:

- a letter about God from mad reader.
- a furious letter from a reader in Blackpool saying she'd written in a couple of weeks ago enclosing an SAE asking for the address of someone who dispatched olive oil by mail order and that she has been 'disappointed not to have heard back' from me about it. 'I sent letter to Office Dog Coco,' the letter ended.

Ben came in. I am trying to get him to spend some money on editorial rather than expensive PR accounts, so I showed him some snippet in the *Standard* 'Diary' about me (an item that Taylor Herring copied round as if they'd placed it) and said, 'And for this you are paying a PR company five grand a month?'

Then he told me I was a slut and to fuck off.

Newsweek has gone down. Sheesh. First *Reader's Digest*. Next *Newsweek*. Titans of the newsstand! If they can't make it, what hope for us?

Carers Week is now following me on Twitter. And ooh – so is *Dementia* UK. I now have 500 followers (to India Knight's 15,000 – go figure).

Had an email from a contributor:

> I was wondering if you've been able to find a slot for the piece I sent
> you on Helen Bertram, the new chairman of the Beatrix Potter
> Society. Could you let me know when you've got a mo, please?

Judy, having hacked into Janina's email, has found that she has
set up a Google alert so that whenever my name comes up on the
web, she gets the link. What a brill idea! I immediately set up a
Google alert for myself. However, I find out very quickly that there
is a champion hurdler of the same name in the US, so I am getting
real-time updates of her achievements in track and field – and
ominously little about anything here at *The Lady*.

7 May 2010

Up all night as Jo elected in Orpington with historic victory,
trebling Tory majority, and delivering modest speech as he was
declared MP. We all went down to sit in Bromley Civic Centre as
the long hours passed. The first thing the returning officer did was
hand him a brown manila envelope saying 'Rules and Regulations
for MPs, Important and Confidential'.

I am so proud of him.

Following the crash course in assay and silversmithing, this
gold-plated invite has arrived from a PR:

> I am hosting a small media dinner with Carol Marlow, MD of P&O
> Cruises, and Peter Shanks, MD of Princess Cruises and president of
> Cunard Line, on Tuesday 15 June at 6.30 p.m. at the Groucho Club.
> Whilst it will be very informal [the email went on] topics will
> include cruise marketing, the changing face of cruising, attracting

new-to-cruise customers, Azura launch, looking ahead to Cunard's
Queen Elizabeth, launch of Adonia and fly/cruises for P&O Cruises,
business projections, cruising and the environment, 2011 launch
and world cruises.

The fun literally never stops!

Google has alerted me to the fact that Edwina, our twenty-
something beauty in marketing, has given a long and considered
press interview to a journalism website about the future of *The
Lady*. Well. I've always thought that she would make a cheaper,
younger, and much slimmer and more sensible replacement for
me in the boudoir, and now I have proof.

Meanwhile, good news. Apparently Debo has finished her book.
If she wasn't furious with me, I'd call her up and try to bend her to
my will again and ask her to be my agony aunt, but I don't dare.
I think that she has been turned against me by Mrs B. They are
cousins, after all. I have proof. The Dowager Duchess has declined
my unbeatable offer to address readers at our next literary lunch at
the Institute of Directors in October, on the grounds that she is
'ridiculously booked up'.

This makes me want to sob uncontrollably. I mean, apart from
Jilly Cooper and the Queen, Debo is one of the few women that I
utterly and completely revere, and her rejection cuts me to the
quick.

8 May 2010

Drove to Pershore to stay with Nick Coleridge, the MD of Condé
Nast, and Georgia, his wife, who is a friend from school and university. Absolute heaven, very relaxed. I don't have house envy (though
the place is late-Georgian perfection, light, and airy, and even better, he has a splendid young Russian 'cook-general' couple to make

beds, delicious meals, drive, etc.). No, I have organizational envy. Let me count the ways, as Nick is very methodical and would doubtless approve of this.

1. He has copies of every single one of his stable of magazines leatherbound in zinging boiled-sweet colours, i.e., *Vogue*, *Tatler*, *Interiors*, *House & Garden*, ranked together in tall white fitted bookcases.

2. He has twenty-seven bespoke vellum Florentine photograph albums filled with amusing pictures of clever friends that he is still friends with many decades down the line, complete with hand-inked names and captions.

3. He has an entire breakfront bookcase filled with his own works in their various foreign and domestic, hardback and paperback editions.

4. He took photographs during lunch and swimming and walks that Georgia revealed would be stuck in and annotated within a few days, if not hours.

I know people bang on about how wonderful and marvellous, etc., women are when they manage to get children to school *and* go to work, but really.

I DON'T KNOW HOW HE DOES IT.

9 May 2010

Gaaahd! Must learn to control myself. I will go down in history – if at all – not merely as Boris's sister, but also as mistress of the unhelpful remark after my performance at Bromley Civic Centre. Jo wisely ran his whole campaign under the radar, declined press interviews, refused to have *Times* sketchwriters follow him round, and confined media to the *Bromley Advertiser*, etc. At the count, we'd been sitting for hours with not so much as a beaker of tea, and the exit polls were predicting a hung parliament and the Tory total was inching up, but not nearly high enough to claim victory, and I tweeted, 'It's all gone tits up. Call for Boris.' At around 4.27 a.m. I was bored. And had got rather merry at the Café Anglais earlier – much earlier – in the evening.

Then I went back to watching Dimbles TV. When I looked at my iPhone twenty minutes later I had about a hundred new messages, as for some reason scores upon scores of people had decided to follow me on Twitter, which prompted Twitter to tell my iPhone this via messages. Then I got a text from Jenni Russell, the *Guardian* and *Sunday Times* columnist: 'Is your tweet giving you problems?'

Eh?

Help. I looked at my Twitter account (only a few hundred measly followers) and saw that India (who has billions) had retweeted it, i.e., sent it to all her followers, and then *Guardian* editor Alan Rusbridger retweeted it, and it went into the *Guardian* website's live election blog and then . . .

That morning, it was a headline in the *Sunday Mirror*. Page lead. 'IT'S ALL GONE T*TS UP. CALL FOR BORIS,' it screamed in twenty-point headline. 'Johnson sister in Twitter swipe.'

In the piece – tagged 'Exclusive' – Vincent Moss, the political editor, wrote, 'The despairing sister of the Mayor Boris Johnson, Rachel, took a swipe at the Tory leader to Twitter saying . . . etc.'

Oh Jesus. What a galumphing fool I am, verily the Fergie of the Johnson family. Luckily, we are in hung parliament, so people so enraptured by wall-to-wall constitutional coverage from Westminster and Downing Street and Lib-Dem HQ as Clegg flip-flops between Brown and Cameron that very few have pointed out that I have been 1. disloyal (I am always presumed to be good Tory gel, simply because I have two openly Tory siblings, an assumption that always makes me want to join the Socialist Workers' Party) and 2. inappropriate (the editor of *The Lady* should not have strong opinions, let alone voice them). Apart from Sarah Sands, the minxy deputy on the *Standard*, who invites me to expand my 140 characters into 1,200 words for tomorrow's paper. I decline. She is very artful about persuading writers to write the one piece that will do them most damage, and I have to side-step my natural urge to jump in with hobnailed boots when she comes calling.

The second rule of life is clearly: Don't tweet.

On the plus side, Dave Shelton, who is in charge of distribution, has done a micro-survey in his West Sussex rural locale. We are now selling six out of eight copies in Sweets 'n' Things in Lancing, and two out of three in Wick News, Littlehampton, which is, respectively, two copies and one copy more than the same week last year.

Wahay!

10 May 2010

Gordon Brown has resigned. Or announced he will by the time of conference in the autumn. William Hill has posted odds on Jo Johnson being PM by 2010 as 13–1, so maybe I am overestimating the impact of my tweet (which is still being repeated *passim*, with result that now have 1,000 followers on Twitter).

Meanwhile, as the Tories and Lib Dems and defeated Labour parties try to form a government, I have important pitches to consider:

- would you be interested in a 1,000-word feature entitled 'Founding Mothers' asking two female vicars about the realities of life working in the Church of England and their hopes and aspirations for the future of the institution?
- a letter from a lady in Blackburn, Lancashire, which begins, 'Dear Rachel Johnson, I wonder if you would consider a series of articles on Margate? I enclose three, and have a further five in the pipeline.'

- another letter: 'I am a staff nurse and started to write poems to cheer people up at work; they seem to like them and I would enjoy seeing them in print. I also write short stories, but have not had anything published yet.'

BLESS!

I have also received six typed letters, obviously all from the same nutbag, about the Camilla cover, all equally poisonous. Goodness, some people do use bad words!

Janina came in today, but is off again now for a week.

11 May 2010

As I write, there is no new PM, Jo is an MP, the country is glued to the TV, and here at *The Lady*, I have been invited to various important events. An email just in:

> I have just spoken with your PA and sorry to hear you have yet to receive your invitation to our very special Designer Hat-Making Tea Party at The Gore Hotel, hosted by celebrity milliner Katherine Elizabeth and presenter and interior designer Linda Barker, in aid of The Eve Appeal's Make Time For Tea campaign.

Party Pieces (the Middleton family firm) is now following me on Twitter and oh, yes! Paul Blezard is, according to the *Indy*, writing a *roman à clef* called 'Saving Grace' about 'a balls-to-the-wall lady editor' who comes in to try to relaunch ailing, old cunties' weekly and sacks all and sundry.

As it's Tuesday, the figures came in. We're up to well over 32,000 again, so Ben is being v. nice to me, so it's all good. Or at least, better.

A woman called Denise came in to interview me for a newspaper with a readership of 800,000 that prints out of Dubai. It's called the *Khaleej Times*. I've never heard of it. How does everyone do it? Why are we only bobbing above 30k? She was a clever woman in her fifties. She queried my cover choices, such as Camilla PB and Tracey Emin, and then admitted she hadn't read *The Lady* since she was in her twenties and her chums were training to be nannies. 'What did you think of it?' I asked. 'Then?'

'Dunno,' she said. 'Never read it. It was just something benign in the ether.' A rather good description of its nebulous charms.

What I ended up saying to the lady from the *Khaleej Times* was this – what I love about working here is, almost above all, the classified ads. I could burble on for hours about how proud I am that we are a trusted global *entrepôt* for domestic staff, and in our glossy pages (and online) we provide a forum where those who employ and those who seek employment in a domestic setting can profitably meet.

In our 'Situations & Appointments' column this week, for example, there was a long, long ad – must have cost hundreds to place – in search of a live-in couple for a 'busy Grade 1 listed residence of national importance' where hospitality and good service were required to be of the highest standard. It was clearly a grace-and-favour residence, and the gig came complete with a three-bed house attached. As ever, I was very tempted to apply myself. I told Ben that I've always thought that the real juice in the mag was in the back, and all the best stories, which is why I've launched a column in the mag called 'Small Ad, Big Story', which Vicky Murden, our letters and website coordinator, researches and writes.

'You're not wrong there,' he said. 'There's a whole bunch of them down in *GMTV* who when asked what their guilty pleasure was said it was reading *Lady* classifieds in the bath.'

12 May 2010

Have had two meetings with telly peeps following the doc. The first was with Simon Shaw, the editor of *Antiques Roadshow* (10 million viewers can't be wrong . . .) He came up from BBC Bristol to see me in the boudoir. Gillian made him a cup of tea.

His idea was – me going round advising regional papers how to survive the savage recession in publishing. I didn't think this inspiring. The last thing I want to be seen to be is some blonde bitch Trinnyishly telling people what to do. Then I went to see Optomen in their groovy, open-plan HQ in Camden complete with Gaggia machines for in-house macchiatos. I told them that BBC Bristol (i.e., Simon Shaw) had had one idea and that it hadn't grabbed me and I started to tell them what it was and I saw them look down, and then one of them – little blonde Becky – said, 'That was the first idea on our list too!' and merrily scored a line through it. They clearly want me to come up with something glittery . . . so sent them this.

From: Rachel Johnson
Sent: 12 May 2010 13:04
To: Becky Clarke
Cc: Pat Llewellyn
Subject: 3 and a half thoughts

Off top of head before I go to have lunch with Ben and discuss our collaboration with Mills & Boon and National Trust called The National Tryst (am not making this up):

1. a tongue-in-cheek series on couples who have second homes and who decamp between two places:
    'Two for the Price of . . . Sanity/Our Marriage'.

2. a weirdly compelling Exmoor piece springs to mind (if I can't buy the *Exmoor* mag) – have you heard of LIZ JONES of the *Daily Mail*??? If you have, call me, if you haven't, ask someone else to explain. And read this. She moved near me on Exmoor. She is sort of publicly committing hara-kiri in her *Mail on Sunday* column. She comes to me for a week. Then I go to her. You film us until . . . one of us dies.

3. also like the thought of me finding my old schoolmates (all nine of them) from Winsford First School in 1972 – that could be fascinating and tell the story of rural decline in nine vignettes.

13 May 2010

Have had an email from a couple who used to be pastry cooks for the Beckhams and the Queen Mother. Of course, everyone knows that the Mitfords' nickname for the late HRH Her Majesty The Queen Mother was 'Cake', so that bit made sense, but I couldn't imagine a crumb of scone or a spoonful of Sussex Pond Pudding ever crossing Posh's lips.

> We have in the past been offered to do various things for publications but with our Royal Household past, we believed we would be more suited to *The Lady*!

Well, the line 'with our Royal Household past' was the clincher. This was more like it. Posh and Becks, and the Queen Mum, encased in one package – like a sort of Royal Beef Wellington.

Have had to pull a massive spread on weddings by a writer who has been pitching a piece called 'Weddings: Then & Now' since I got here. The piece arrived, with three interviews with couples who got spliced in wartime. I thought this article about weddings of yore would go very well with a feature on the Lucy Mangan book about her own London wedding called *The Reluctant Bride*, in a something old, something new, sort of way.

Plus it's May – i.e., wedding season. Then the subs started subbing it and discovered that one of the main interviewees in the main part of the piece – a general – was dead. Not just a little bit dead, but very dead indeed. 1995 dead. Yet the author of the piece had conducted a long interview with the general about his wedding reception in Fleet, where he wore his khaki Marine uniform and bride Dorothy wore white. It's one for Derren Brown. We kept ringing the journalist, but she never rang back.

There are two possible solutions. 1. She did the interview more than fifteen years ago and has been sitting on the piece for that long. 2. She conducted the interview with the general from *beyond the grave*.

14 May 2010

Last night at dinner Peter Soros looked at me and said, 'You've had work. I can tell.' I couldn't have been more delighted. Have written crawly cards to the Osbornes and the Camerons and parcelled them up with commemorative *Lady* tea-towels and got Gillian to send them to atone for my Tits-Up tweet. I sent Clegg an email on his BlackBerry asking for his address so could do same for him and Miriam, but he never answered. How quickly doth power go to the head!

17 May 2010

I bumped into James Pembroke, the publisher of *The Oldie*, at cricket tea at Dragon School, Oxford, while Oliver was playing in the Third Eleven against Papplewick. I shoved scones laden with jam and cream into my mouth as Pembroke told me that Ben was very resistant to hearing pearls of wisdom from the old hands of magazine publishing, such as James Pembroke.

According to Pembroke, trying to sell copies at the newsstand is expensive and hit-and-miss, and what we should be focusing on is subs.

'Ben said on your Channel 4 documentary that he's been running media companies since he was a nipper,' said Pembroke. By this stage we were back on the green Dragon playing fields watching our sons play cricket in their whites, on a golden May Saturday, as students passed by languidly in punts on the Cherwell. 'But that's only if you count dealing in pornos from his dorm at Harrow as running a media business.'

In my view, we should give away copies of *The Lady* like the *Evening Standard* does, then advertisers might pay attention.

When I sent Ben a text challenging him to confirm that 'running media companies' since he was 'a nipper' meant renting out wankmags at Harrow, he responded immediately.

There have been many media ventures since Harrow, but whilst at Harrow at the tender age of fourteen I had a booze bootlegging business, a 'magazine', ahem, rental business and an illegal radio station pumping out vile sketches suggesting what we thought a lot of masters (beaks) did in their spare time. Of course since then a number of them have 'done bird' for just such 'indiscretions'.

18 May 2010

Matt Warren from the *Daily Mail* came in to have lunch with me and Ben at the Forge restaurant. Matt, should he come to work here, is nigh on perfect. He raises the testosterone level in Bedford

Street by about 100 per cent, he's an Old Shirburnian, he got a First from Edinburgh, he's an experienced motoring, travel and features hack . . . and he wants to work at *The Lady*!

Over lunch Ben admitted he feels outnumbered by the number of women in the building. 'One week in four I definitely feel tense and tearful,' he said. Then he and Matt snorted and gasped into their napkins.

The in tray:

- three more bottles of vinaigrette.
- a presentation box of teas in round tins rather like snuff/ rubbed tobacco, in strange flavours such as Pomme Prestige, Singapore Breakfast, Darjeeling Okayth.
- an anti-UVA product for Face and Neck called Symmetria.
- Her Ladyship's guide to the Queen's English, which helpfully tells me whether to say napkin or serviette, by the author of a book called *An Apple a Day*.

I do wish PRs would stop sending anti-ageing creams, endless speciality teas in pompous packaging, and salad dressing. What we want is CAKE.

Have had testy email from the journalist David Jenkins.

Dear Rachel,

I'm pretty appalled by this – see below. You've had my invoice for more than two months and I was always told that you had a twenty days after acceptance payment policy. I assume the Budworths are not cutting back on their lifestyles: it's just not on not to pay your writers. You've been a freelance, and you should know that it's an editor's prime duty to pay her/his contributors. I'd like to know what you're going to

do about it: in fact, I'd like to be paid tomorrow. Meantime I shall
phone other contributors and find out what's happening to them.

David

> Forwarded message
> **Date:** 17 May 2010 15:59
> **From:** Tracey Allsopp
> **To:** David Jenkins
> **Subject:** Payments
>
> Hi David
>
> Thank you for your email regarding payment of the invoice for
> the 30th March. At the moment we are doing our very best to pay
> what we can, when we can, from our outstanding invoices, and as
> the cash situation will allow us.
>
> I can only but apologize for any inconvenience that this is causing
> you.
>
> Tracey

This was bit of a shocker. Not only are we not paying contributors *again* but one of them is David Jenkins who *knows everyone*
and is Alexandra Shulman editor of *Vogue*'s boyfriend. I called him
and told him I was very sorry and would sort it out.

Oh God, we've just had another testy email from a contributor,
Drusilla Beyfus (Shulman's mother-in-law, aaagggh, so the word
is out). And Ben said that Hugh St Clair rings every day to complain he hasn't been paid.

If all this leaks out, it will be a very public death for us, and undo
all the PR that we've bought. I talked to Ben. He said 1. he wasn't
paying the PR companies either and 2. he was writing a business
plan to secure another loan facility. 'For how much?' I asked.

'Two-fifty,' he said.

'Two hundred and fifty thou?' I said. 'Is that all? Ivo and I have got a loan facility for half a million!' (This is sadly true.) 'Why didn't you borrow money from me?'

The upshot of all this is I've had to write a segment of the business plan. Which I did. Here goes:

Editorial

When I took the editor's chair at *The Lady* I faced a delicate challenge – updating the editorial so that it reflected the concerns of the modern woman aged forty-five upwards, while not mortally insulting the sensibilities of the readership (average age seventy-eight). I decided there was no point in hanging back, and by Christmas root and branch changes to the way the magazine both looked and read were in place. We redesigned the cover, editorial and classifieds and returned to a more classic, nineteenth-century rubric. On the editorial side, I brought in top writers throughout the magazine, so that the journalism contained therein is now as good as, if not better than, anything else available on a fast-paced weekly basis.

Eight months in, the new design has stood the test of time, the readers are happier with it, and new ones – assisted by a blizzard of *Lady*-related publicity – are coming on board. I now intend to consolidate after a period of frantic change and build up our readership subscription base (essential to the magazine's survival) while maintaining newsstand appeal with fresh covers that tell existing and potential readers that even in a crowded, lowest-common-denominator market where all other women's weeklies are offering the same diet of sex and celebrity and gossip, the full-colour *Lady* stands alone in having a more distinguished and upmarket product to offer.

Drring drring outside the boudoir.

'Yes she is. Who shall I say is calling? Oh yes.' Slightly breathless pause. 'Does she know what it's about? Er, Rachel. There's a call from Jeremy Pax—' – to her credit, Gillian knew who was on the line, and can barely get the name out – 'Paxman. Shall I put him through?'

I was in the middle of shifting all the reviews – from opera, which currently sits with 'News & Reviews', to books and film and radio – into a cluster at the back of the magazine, to make a new, all-singing and dancing Review Section, ending with Alexander Chancellor's TV page on the side back. 'OK then,' I said.

'Do you want a 4,000-word piece on cobnuts?' Jeremy asked. After the doc – in which it was revealed that I nicknamed random nature articles that used to run in *The Lady* 'cobnuts' – I get jokes like this quite a lot. Indeed, on April Fool's Day, I added 'Cobnuts Editor – Helena Handbasket' to the masthead.

Jeremy told me he'd received an email from a hack called Sonia Purnell who is writing a book called *Boris. The Man. The Myth*. An attention-all-shipping went out yesterday from the Mayoral Glass Gonad, i.e., City Hall, saying we were by no accounts to talk to her.

'Don't talk to her,' I said. 'The air-raid warning has sounded.'

I wasn't going to, just checking,' he said. After that I asked him for 5,000 words on the history of the horse chestnut and he hung up.

Kath Hanley from Classifieds came up all excited. 'Nutter alert,' she said, as she petted Coco. Apparently a woman had come in and said her husband had written a song called 'The Lady' and wanted to serenade me with it. 'We get that sort of thing all the time,' said Kath. 'They're usually harmless.'

The in tray:

• a Rococo cherry-studded choccy egg (rather unseasonal, but at least it's not another Simnel cake).

- a short story about a haunted drawing room and a soldier and a gramophone.
- an angry letter from a reader in Edgbaston complaining that the author Juliet Nicolson was wearing jeans in her picture and demanding, 'Has she no pride in herself?'

Lembit Opik – who has lost his seat – is now following me on Twitter. Well, I suppose he has nothing better to do.

19 May 2010

Marco Pierre White has demanded to know why he's not been on the cover of *The Lady* yet and is offering his services – *gratis* – as a columnist. When I told the subs/art teams everyone had hot flushes and started fanning themselves. I got Carolyn to agree he could write a column about seasonal English food, which will go nicely with our nifty new column 'Britstop', all about English oddities like lollipop ladies and Pimm's, football and Wimbledon, etc., which I have introduced on the 'Diary' page.

Amanda Holden wants to be friends on Facebook. Why?

21 May 2010

Went into Tesco on Portobello Road and looked at *The Lady* versus the competition. It was immediately obvious that we were too decorous. Too discreet. Too *ladylike*. We are up against *Chat* and *Take a Break* and *Bella* and *Women's Weekly*, not to mention the thundering juggernaut of *People's Friend*. We have to amp up our cover lines. Get away from the curly old-fashioned font. Go all shouty and neon. Think about *cover mounts*. I called Ben to tell him that we had to go down Via Vulgaris and plunge downmarket visually.

He sounded pleased with me for the first time in ages, as if I was finally on message.

I'm finding the whole HR side nightmarish. I've never managed anyone in my life – nannies always left, or I sacked them, while my parenting 'skills' merely seemed to encourage my own children to sit around issuing me with Caligula-like demands. It all makes me feel very uneasy. When you are editor, I now realize, you are responsible for taking decisions that change people's lives. It is buck-stoppingly hair-raising.

Meanwhile, more bad news. The bankers have ratted on Ben. I listened in silence as he told me of their perfidy. I hereby take it all back about Ben getting his priorities arse about face. It turns out that today Coutts have pulled the plug on the loan (great vote of confidence in the product . . . my editorship . . . and my contribution to the business plan). It's been decided at the highest level that even after making Ben jump through endless hoops, come up with the biz plan, etc., they are not, after all, now going to extend him another tranche of credit of £250k to keep the magazine going, a sum that would enable us to pay contributors like David Jenkins and Drusilla Beyfus, and staff payroll.

It's been agony. I had a long chat with him this morning. I reminded him that Ivo and I had taken out a loan facility of half a million quid that he could tap. He said, 'That's very kind. But it's OK. Last night, I had a Damascene conversion. I really believe in this business. I don't need a penthouse apartment in Battersea. I'm going to mortgage it if necessary.'

And Helen, the new head of display ads – the one who has splashed logos all over 'Coco's Corner' – has also offered to dip into her pocket too. We all, it turns out, love *The Lady* so much we are prepared to spend our own money to keep her seaworthy.

So, for the moment, the Ladyship is still afloat. But – to continue the metaphor for a moment – the forecast is for squally showers and choppy waters.

For how much longer she is going to sail, Lord only knows.
I hope a very long time.

25 May 2010

Diana Athill has turned me down as a columnist. She has moved
into a home, and written 'movingly' about it for the *Guardian*.

As soon as I saw this, I wrote to her asking for a regular column
called – what else? – 'At Home'.

I got a nice card back. 'It just so happens I have screwed myself
up starting (touch wood) a new book and I haven't the writing
energy to do anything else.'

Nor have I found a cleaning lady of literary ability who could
contribute a column called 'The Daily'.

Am waiting to hear if *Shire Hell* has sold in France. I hope so – it
could pay for the new (i.e., reconditioned) Aga I've just had to
install at Nethercote, as the old one, installed in the 1940s, has finally
crumbled.

I went into the boardroom, as it was a Tuesday and the numbers
come in by 10 a.m., but no Ben. Claire said, 'He's at home sweating
and puking apparently.'

Finally, the sort of email I've been waiting for since I arrived. Email
of the day!

> Dear Rachel, I have some great news! The Pudding Club is celebrat-
> ing 25 years this year & in recognition of this amazing achievement
> we are hosting a variety of events at The Home of The Pudding Club
> in the Cotswold village of Mickleton, & in addition we have just
> launched 3 new varieties of Pudding Club puddings into Waitrose
> to join the 3 classic flavours launched last autumn – Sticky Toffee,
> Treacle & Ginger Syrup Sponge Pudding.

A press release is attached, together with a couple of images to tempt you! If you would like to have some samples, please do let me know. If you could find a space to mention these delicious new puddings, I would be extremely grateful.

Jill of the Pudding Club – you got it.

Just bumped into Ben's PA Maureen in the ladies, where I was rinsing out my Her Ladyship mug prior to fresh infusion of a speciality tea.

She said Ben was poorly. She knew why.

'It got a bit hot in the boardroom yesterday. The chocolate biscuits were melting,' she said.

Then she said he hadn't had a proper holiday for eighteen months and it was getting to him. 'It's like my husband,' she said. 'He works in Aberdeen. I only see him when there's a Charlton football match.'

Nell Butler, of Granada, and an old chum, came in for peppermint tea and Extremely Chocolatey Chocolate Bites from M&S.

I introduced her to all and sundry as the inventor of *Come Dine With Me*, because she was the blinding genius who invented the format.

Everyone looked up from their screens (there is a bank hol. on Monday, so it's a pull-forward and we are losing a day from the production schedule) with beaming smiles. Finally, I'd got someone into the office they could all admire who had really done something!

Alain de Botton is following me on Twitter.

27 May 2010

Handed round copies of *The Lady* last night at a function with independent booksellers at Penguin. It was the latest issue, with

Mariella Frostrup on the cover, to time with the Hay-on-Wye litfest, at which she is much in evidence, as she presents daily programme called *Hay on Sky*.

To recap: in the interview, she generously said that the reason there was only one woman presenter on the *Today* programme was because BBC was run by 'a bunch of misogynists'. She went on to say that the search for a middle-aged female presenter wasn't exactly akin to looking for the Holy Grail as the 'streets of London were littered' with perfectly serviceable women past sell-by 'who'd been sacked by the BBC already'.

All this was gratifyingly picked up in *The Times* and *Daily Mail* this morning. '*Today* Programme run by Woman-Haters' was the half-pager in the *Mail*, crediting *The Lady*. She must have assumed that giving an interview to *The Lady* would be an essentially private experience limited to me and her, not knowing about the teams of PRs backstage. In the end, Mariella grovelled in a letter to BBC house mag *Ariel*, in which she took it all back. Quite unnecessarily, in my view.

Anyway, when I was handing round the magazine at Penguin, I noticed that everyone immediately turned to the back and started leafing through the classified and display ads, and started chuckling over the quarter-page ads for mare and foal sanctuaries, walk-in baths, and so on.

'Give your feet a treat,' tittered one top editor. 'Hand made by a small family firm in Somerset who specialize in comfortable footwear . . .' Eleo Gordon was reading out one of our in-house *Lady* offers.

Now, I knew our classifieds for valets and underbutlers and live-in couples were a weekly treat savoured by many, but I had no idea that the display ads and special offers were also so keenly studied for entertainment value.

Ben has returned from his sickbed with red-rimmed eyes, looking puffy and cross. Claire went into the boardroom, to show him photographic proof of the Ruby Wax cover, in which she was sitting against a brown leather banquette, resting her elbows on a table, looking at the camera quizzically.

'We can't have that shit,' he exclaimed, after giving it a quick look. Then he ripped it in half, and handed it back to Claire. 'She looks as if she's in a pub.'

I went to interview Amanda 'Most Powerful Woman in Publishing' Ross. She has adopted two little boys, the younger brother only six months old. After a long struggle with IVF. And has two terriers. Perfect material for pick-up in the *Daily Mail*, in other words.

We've had a spew of angry letters from readers after we ran a full-page display ad from an Italian company on page 42. It showed a pregnant nun in a habit spooning ice-cream into her waiting mouth, by the words, 'Immaculately Conceived'. Honestly, readers will complain about anything!

> I write to complain in the strongest terms about the ad . . . the depiction of a pregnant nun holding ice-cream with the side-bar 'Immaculate Conception' is highly offensive to Christians in general and Catholics in particular. I am surprised the magazine accepts this type of ad, which clearly contravenes the ASA guidelines. I have informed them of this advertisement. I will not be renewing my subscription.
>
> Dear Sirs
>
> [another one wrote from North Lancing:] The advert for ice-cream is irritating and offensive. Not suitable for *The Lady* even if it pays a higher fee for space.

Email sent in by Gillian marked 'Reader Call':

Mrs Ryan from Enfield, subscriber for many years, rang to complain about the advertisement of a pregnant nun in the 25 May issue. It's absolutely disgusting, and if anyone rings her up to talk about it she will be very rude. Likes the new look of the magazine otherwise.

The in tray:

- Church Commissioners Annual Report.
- a copy of *Wolf Print*, the magazine of the UK Wolf Conservation Trust.

28 May 2010

George Osborne has written a personal note, handwritten from Number 11, to thank me for my crawly card.

Dear Rachel,

Thank you for your kind card.
I can confirm that no one else sent me tea-towels.
Surely the big news from the election is the arrival of Jo Johnson MP?

Best wishes,
George

The Lady

A Journal for Gentlewomen

25 MAY 2010   £1.80

Wedding belles
STEPHANIE CALMAN &
Mr Incompatible

LUCY MANGAN
The reluctant bride

Lunch with
MARIELLA
small, blonde & very cross

NICK WELCH
Dad-dancing
in the mud

PHILIP MOULD
is the art detective

Dreamy
ENGLISH FASHION
by Katherine Hooker

FESTIVAL GUIDE

**JEFFREY ARCHER'S DIARY   GARDENING BOOKS   SPANISH COOKING COURSE
ROBIN HOOD**

JUNE

2 June 2010

I said to Ben, 'You're not going to see me much tomorrow . . .'
I didn't want to go to Covent Garden – Oliver was going back to
school, all the children were in a half-term tennis camp and all
have exams (Oliver Common Entrance, Milly GCSEs, Ludo A
levels in the next fortnight). I've seen them so little that when I do
I have to restrain myself from exclaiming how much they've grown,
as if they are lesser-spotted godchildren.

I also have to write 2,000 words for the *Mail on Sunday* by
9 a.m. tomorrow – to big up a Radio 4 documentary I have made
about posh girls who were sent by their aristocratic fathers to
Munich in the mid- to late-thirties, in order to thicken blood ties
with Royal Houses of Europe, and bring back the good news about
the Third Reich. The documentary is in turn bigging up my new
novel *Winter Games*, which I was writing this time last year when I
got the fateful call from one B. Budworth. Articles, radio, telly,
novels – we authors have to be multi-platform pluggers now.

Ben cut in before I could explain why I wasn't going to be present and correct in the office. 'And you won't see me unless you're
coming to the mid-Suffolk Show, a day out with something for
everyone, where I'm doing an udder inspection.'

'What?' I said weakly.

He said he was judging the dairy goats.

3 June 2010

Drove to Wales. On the way to Hay-on-Wye we stopped at Tre-tower, run by Cadw (i.e., that's Welsh for Welsh Heritage). I was walking around the shell keep on the motte when Ben rang on Ivo's mobile (I'd left my iPhone in the car).

'Good news,' he said. Then he gave me some good news about a possible hire.

It dimly crossed my mind that I have bullied Ben into hiring my own replacement, but what the hell. Then Ivo and Ben talked about the bombshell news that Ivo's nephew David, a brilliant Classics student who knows every word of *Withnail & I* off by heart, went out with office beauty, our Bedford bloom, Edwina. During the course of this Ben said something that makes Ivo roar with laughter. 'What were you and Ben laughing about?' I asked.

'Oh nothing,' he said. 'Ben was just saying if they've done their mock GCSEs they're already FAR too old.'

'Very funny,' I snapped.

Got to Hay. The sun was shining, everyone was wandering round with punnets of small English strawberries and licking ice-cream cones made of goat's milk, clutching cloth bags emblazoned with Hay logos. If I had to write the 'Social Stereotype' of the average Hay punter, it would be: someone in their mid-fifties, in Birkenstocks and mauve cropped trousers, with long grey hair and a sunhat, reading the *Guardian* Review section. Both male and female.

Inside the 'Artists Only' area, a big green room with drinks, crisps and sofas, I saw the radio DJ Chris Evans, who kissed me hello. 'I love your column in the *Telegraph*,' he says. 'And I love your programme on Sky.' I blushed, even though I haven't written for the *Tel* for three years and don't have a programme on Sky. I wonder who he thinks I am? I texted Ben the glad tidings that I am schmoozing the biggest star in radio. He texts back, 'Ask Chris

Evans about when he put his advert in *The Lady* offering his services as a private detective.'

Blez is here in force, doing about a hundred events. Haven't seen him since before his sacking. This is small cloud on horizon. John Walsh, Carolyn's ex, tells me that Blez was doing an event for a Burmese author in front of a mainly Burmese crowd of readers, and instead of introducing himself he told the bemused audience, 'You'll all remember me. I'm the guy who was fired on live TV from *The Lady* in that infamous documentary.'

Every time I glimpse his towering white-haired form and hear his booming voice emanate from within a tented stage I run for cover; meanwhile, he ignores me completely.

In the green room, Ivo introduced Ludo (now seventeen, doing politics A level) to Alastair Campbell, lounging on a sofa before his gig on the *Guardian* stage.

Naturally, I could not resist 'going in' (Ivo and Ludo cannot bear my beelines for celebrity, and term it 'waggling'.) 'Who's this?' said Alastair Campbell. 'The mother,' I said. 'Well, your son has just told me he wishes you'd sent him to a state school, not Marlborough.'

Ludo has always rejected suggestions that we save 30k a year and send him to our excellent state school down the road, Holland Park Comp, alma mater of many successful West London media creatives and Tony Benn's children.

'Did you, darling?' I said accusingly, whirling to face Ludo.

'Alastair's spinning you, you twit,' said Ivo, as Campbell grinned at me from the sofa. Apparently Ludo, when Alastair dutifully asked where my son was in education, had assured Campbell he was very happy there. When I tipped up, Campbell had flipped this conversation 180 degrees so that the new line was that I, against my firstborn's will and stated preference, was sending him to a posh private school rather than the local state school. Ivo was right – I was being spun like a roulette wheel. Course I was. It's what Alastair Campbell does.

5 June 2010

Went into Hay to hear, first, Max Hastings give a masterclass on Churchill, introduced by Tom Stoppard. It was very hot, and as he talked – and my God he talked well – Max wiped the sweat from his forehead with a New & Lingwood shirtsleeve.

I fell in love with him. He is tall and soldierly and prodigiously clever and productive. And he has thick, dark, glossy boot-polish hair. Love object number two: Tom Stoppard. Rosie Boycott nudged me. 'Don't you think Tom looks more and more like Germaine Greer?' she whispered. No! He looks like a Roman emperor.

The best bit: it was the London Library lecture, and in his pre-amble about how wonderful the Library was, how it was the only club one needs, and how a day in the Library was never a wasted one, Max got going on the resource that was the archives in the basement. 'You can look up back copies of *The Times*, the *Illustrated London News*, even *The Lady*,' Max said. I almost expired from heat and pleasure.

Then at 7 p.m. we poured back under canvas again to hear David Remnick, the feted editor of *The New Yorker*, talk about his top-selling Obama book, *The Bridge*. He arrived straight off the plane in spotless Dad jeans (I guess Gap), Persil-white trainers, black T-shirt and black jacket, *à la* Steve Jobs. He talked about how Obama didn't learn how to become properly black until the project-days as a community organizer in Chicago, and was fluent and funny, as one would expect. I sat next to loony adman Robin Wight, who was looking more crazed than usual in a parti-coloured suit, purple suede loafers and stripey socks, in the front row.

'Ask a question,' Wight hissed in my ear at the end. He gestured to one of the roving mics. The session came to an end, and I was still holding the mic. My heart started going like the clappers, and

Remnick said, 'There's a woman in the front who'll be very disappointed if she doesn't get the floor,' so I got the nod. I stood up in front of 1,200 people, and my flushed face filled the huge screen.

So I asked Remnick whether he had access to Obama, and whether he reckoned that when Obama did authorize a biographer, it would be a honky white boy ('I'm not white,' joked Remnick as I ploughed on sweatily) or someone of his own race.

Remnick totally spanked me with his answer, pointing out that there would be tons of books written about Obama, both authorized and unauthorized, now and for generations to come. As I sat down, I didn't spot that my chair seat had flipped up to the vertical, and I almost crashed to the ground.

I have been tormented by terrible *esprit d'escalier*. Instead of asking such a clinker, I wish I'd said, 'Speaking as the editor of a rival weekly publication . . .' (pause for laughter – *The Lady* v *The New Yorker*! ho ho) and gone on to ask him whether he thought that after a warrior leader, i.e., Bush/Blair, countries always went for a weed, i.e., Obama/Cameron-Clegg-Miliband.

Too late now, of course.

Dinner with Rob Albert and Revel Guest, the King and Queen of Hay, in their glorious crumbly Manderley-style house on a green hill. Sat next to Rob, who was all twinkly charm, my father's age, and Ed Victor, super-agent to the stars. He called me Rebecca throughout the evening as a tease, and we gossiped about Tina Brown until we proceeded in convoy to another afterparty in another mini-stately on another green hill, where there was a marquee and disco-dancing with Jamie Byng (co-founder of Canongate along with Ivo's cousin Stephanie Wolfe-Murray) on the decks.

The next day I was so tormented that I sent Remnick an email (address cadged from Ed Victor) making light of my awful question and sending him a little write-up of the Obama talk and the

Q&A from my POV. I get a slightly stiff response from him, telling me that, with respect, my 'entry was off'. I have displeased the editor of *The New Yorker*, the author of acclaimed tome on first black president, and probably the best journalist in the world.

Piercing agony!

6 *June 2010*

A perfect Hay weekend of walking and waggling in the Welsh sunshine was slightly spoilt at the end.

I felt terribly guilty whenever I saw the Blez – even though he is planning revenge novel *Saving Grace*. I do hope he gets a deal, then perhaps he'll cool down. Plus, when I did finally intersect with Peter Florence – who *is* Hay, and Paul's best friend for ever, he cold-shouldered me too. So my cunning plan to have a *Lady* tent here next year, with Lady Antonia Fraser interviewing David Walliams to the soundtrack of Lady Gaga's greatest hits, has already bitten the dust, I fear. Had to continuously dodge Blez in the green room aka the Hostility suite.

By the Sunday, I sensed it had been ten long, hot days on the Welsh borders and everyone – organizers, visitors, slebs, writers – seemed to be going on the turn, like a ripe Stilton sitting too long in the larder. Despite my idiocy with David Remnick, and getting the bum's rush from Peter Florence, it was still heavenly. The sun shone, the hills rolled, and there was that holiday mood that prevails whenever people who only ever see each other at London parties intersect in foreign lands, in this case, Wales. I've always noticed this. I think this explains the success of Hay much more than the embarrassment of choice when it comes to top speakers and gigs and crunchy debate.

Hay ho.

7 June 2010

Groaning in tray!

- three Yorkshire tea cakes from Betty's of Harrogate in three flavours: Moist and Tangy Marmalade, Moist & Rich Ginger & Treacle, and Moist & Fruity Tea Loaf. Most welcome! (Carolyn has also received the identical same three moist cakes so there are six cakes for tea today. It's getting like Test Match Special.)
- 4 x letters about the pregnant-nun advert from readers cancelling subs.
- a letter from Nottinghamshire from a woman who has been taking *The Lady* for fifteen years and not renewing because I have 'changed a perfectly agreeable magazine into one with a distinct air of being for a coterie of the rich well-connected from which I feel excluded' and ending, 'My real regret will be the loss of the Ladygram.'
- an invitation to Tea on the Lawn in Ashbourne, hosted by 'three passionate women supporting each other in their rural businesses', including a viewing of a 'scrumptious cut-flower collection in the edible water meadow.'
- two pairs of fold-up ballet pumps from CocoRose.
- an invitation to 'smile away the years' at a 3D natural face clinic run by a Finnish body-control teacher and a free massage to realign the overall balance between the facial muscles and head (a reminder that really not that much has changed since *The Lady* ran articles in the 1880s on how to preserve a youthful complexion, which was to 'avoid moving the face unduly').
- a press release from the Open Space Society, and their summer 2010 volume.
- a reader call, recorded by Gillian:

Mrs Rachel Hamilton from Coventry rang – been reading
The Lady since the Crimean War & thinks it's now absolutely
delightful! She doesn't subscribe because she loves the
fun of trying to buy it from Waitrose. Thinks we've had a really
difficult task to update it without losing its character, but
we've done it! She's 70 yrs old, and her London-based
daughter likes it too. Don't take any notice of the
complainers, she said!

Went off to the Royal Institution in Albemarle Street, to hear
John Sentamu, the Archbishop of York, give the memorial lecture
in the name of my great-grandfather Sir George Williams, who
was a hill farmer's son who left Ashwick farm on Exmoor, walked
to London and in due course founded the YMCA. At tea beforehand, I am introduced to the twinkling, buoyant Sentamu. 'Are
you related to the mayor?' he asked. 'You must be, because when
you smile your eyes recede' – the Archbish. squinched at me – 'just
like his do.'

8 June 2010

Went to Highgrove to a lunch thing to celebrate Waitrose taking
over Duchy Originals. The Prince of Wales/Waitrose had invited
lots of foodie writers to bear witness and sample the extended new
range of delicious things to eat and drink. There was to be a tour
of the garden followed by lunch. Dress was lounge suit, which
meant all the women wore florals.

There were endless stiffy white cards, and passes, and name tags
to be brought with us. We mustered at the platform at Paddington. It was drizzling. On the train I was reading a free copy of *The
Times* in First Class and I spotted an item that said the Prince

had a chest infection and was in bed somewhere called Birkhall. The train to Kemble started running slower and slower. It was now pouring with rain. Then I overheard a Waitrose PR say that 1. the Prince wasn't there and 2. there would be no garden tour. Great.

We decanted into taxis and drove in convoy to Highgrove. Tall estate walls. We gave our names to policewomen manning the gates at the back entrance, and drove in past signs painted a tastefully tubercular shade of palest green saying, 'You are now entering a GM-free zone.' We mingled in a clunky Tuscan new-build loggia called 'the Orchard Room', then formed up to go round the garden.

A handsome woman – a neighbour – called Amanda Hornby conducted the promised garden tour. Before we moved off, all the hacks were made to stand on lush Gloucestershire lawns under a bower created by dripping espaliered apple trees for her pre-amble (geddit?).

'The first question is, "How many gardeners does His Royal Highness have?"' (answer: eleven); 'the second is, "What does he do about slugs?"' she went on (answer: nothing) 'and the third is, "What was the Highgrove garden – about 20 acres, within a 1,000-acre estate – like before?"'

Then we went round the cottage and sundial gardens, the stumpery and kitchen garden at a gallop, taking care to keep on the right side of willow hoops placed in the ground to keep us from straying on to princely turf.

As HRH was in residence, we reptiles weren't allowed to sully the front of the house, where peons were raking gravel. Then we went back to the Orchard Room, where all the selected Duchy Original local producers, who trod lightly over their environment and loved their animals, stood smartly behind presentation tables laid out with tasting samples of their lines, wearing aprons.

And then lo, at the appointed hour, HRH/The Prince of Wales/ Prince Charles manifested and took endless trouble to meet and have a few words, and passed by every stall. He started with maple-cured ham and cheeses, proceeded past wine, apple juice, cakes, chocolates, scones, mueslis and granolas, lemon curds, preserves, ale, fizzy water; every item that had made the Duchy Original cut went into Royal mouth.

When he got to us – us being William Sitwell, editor of *Waitrose Kitchen* (who keeps telling me to have a 'Win a Stannah Stairlift' competition, not just once but every week), Lindsay Bareham, Allan Jenkins of *Observer Food Monthly* and Carolyn, i.e., a complete collection of reptiles – he beamed and said to me, 'Your brother's the only man I know who's made a speech in Latin. Do you speak Latin?'

Everyone looked at me expectantly. In fact, I had struggled with a Latin inscription carved on to a wooden sunhouse in the garden, by Horace, but wouldn't dream of admitting it.

'Yes, and Greek too of course,' I lied.

He was smaller than I expected. A slightly rumpled grey suit in a discreet Prince of Wales check hung off him. Despite his chest infection and weak voice – I could tell from his high colour he was running a fever – he made an expert speech in which he hailed the rain as a blessing from the gods without which none of the delicious foods we were eating could have been set before us, and thanked Waitrose for bailing out his Duchy Originals and setting it on a commercial footing. 'Thanks, Waitrose, for *showing such an interest*' were his exact words.

Only when I was leaving did I realize that I was so busy sampling all the blue cheese, ginger chocolate thins, etc., that I forgot to curtsey. I thought the Prince was bloody fantastic, took endless trouble to meet every single producer – in fact, every single person – in the Orchard Room, as well as chat to each and every hack. He does a jolly good oatcake too.

9 June 2010

The in tray:

- a care package from Tena Pants! I open it. 'TENA, the UK's leading bladder weakness brand, has launched two new products.' Which are without further ado 'TENA *Lady*' and 'TENA *Lady* with aloe vera'. There are samples – enclosed in a discreet rose-printed tin – plus other goodies. I am very grateful indeed for all this. Tena are big advertisers with us – without them, let's face it, the magazine would probably sink without trace, and we should retitle ourselves 'The TENA *Lady*' in honour of this lifesaving product.
- a letter from a reader in North Yorks asking me to advise her how many people read *The Lady* in Portugal.
- oooh this is nice. A bottle of Veuve Clicquot from JoJo Maman Bébé – the mumpreneur (bleugh) who brilliantly started this has won Veuve Clicqot Businesswoman of the Year.

I get a funny feeling in the building when I work late. Sometimes Janina appears at my door spectrally, but it's not that. I mentioned this to Claire – how jumpy I get – and we talked about the supposed *Lady* ghost. A previous editor called Jean Shepherd who'd been here ... actually, I know nothing about this. So I asked Edwina. And she said:

'An editor was halfway through an issue (two weeks before her retirement) when she tragically died of a stroke. Apparently, she haunts the building because she is desperate to finish the issue – some members of staff claim to have seen her. I remember Classified getting most cross with me when I went downstairs asking questions (so maybe not mention her name to anyone), but for your records, she was Editor from 1953 to 1971 (I think!).'

10 June 2010

Lunch with Marco Pierre White at Wheeler's in Jermyn Street. He was late, so I went to gents' hairdressers next door to stare at the shaving brushes and bottles. Barry Humphries was in there, buying cologne, wearing an ancient mac. I had a long chat with the manager of Truefitt & Hill about badger shaving brushes and the future of badger shaving brushes (he thinks they will soon, thanks to the cull, be banned; I wondered if that would make a good story for *The Lady* but decided it didn't as we are not called *The Gentleman*) then went back to see if Marco had arrived. He hadn't. I was shown to a corner booth, to await arrival.

When Marco did arrive, he was wearing a green faded polo; I was in jeans and trainers. He ordered for me – the egg mayonnaise, the crab, and the beetroot and goat's cheese and walnut salad; he had smoked salmon that had been cut very thin and spread out so it covered the whole plate like an oily orange lozenge. I took a photo of him sitting in front of the orange lozenge, staring moodily at me, on my iPhone and toyed with tweeting it, but managed to resist the urge.

I liked Marco a lot, even though he was the third person in a row that week who only appeared keen to chat to me (John Sentamu, Archbishop of York; Prince of Wales) because I was a blood-relation of Boris, which can be faintly pricking to the ego.

As we tucked in, he said the Tories had missed a trick by not grabbing 'working-class Tories' and using them as ambassadors for the party more, just as the Countryside Alliance had failed to see the PR value in the farriers and the whippers-in and the hunt followers, and focused on the toffs in the pink coats and black hats. 'But they didn't,' I pointed out (I seem to have read a million pieces about kennel keepers and stable lads in all publications). He is going to do a little column about dead-simple food such as we had been eating – no more than two ingredients – i.e., smoked salmon and lemon, quail's eggs and celery salt – and a bitty bit about his week in food.

He is mid-divorce and slightly crazed by it. Showed me a text from Mati, his wife. Said he was on the 'wealth diet'. Hates Blair, Labour – his line is that they are 'good for the working man but bad for the man who works'.

Not a bad line. Another Marcoism – 'Arrogance can breed success but only humility can breed greatness.' He puts his gift for the apophthegm down to early, undiagnosed dyspraxia. He worships the memory of his mother, who died when he was six, leaving a fourteen-day-old brother as well as his two older ones. He is the only one who has married. He went round all the tables after lunch, saying hello, and allowing diners to take pictures of him with them on their mobiles.

14 June 2010

Judy, our cosy production manager/den mother, who only wears M&S ('Marks'), was doing a key inventory. We realized that Janina still has the key to the Maiden Lane side entrance, as well as to the main entrance on Bedford Street. 'Why would she have that?' Judy asked Ben.

'Arline had it and presumably passed it down to her,' he said, in another terrible reminder of the *Wolf Hall* aspect of the Bedford Street HQ.

The in tray:

- a leaflet from Boots reminding me to stock up on flight socks and travel-sickness pills before I jet off on my 'exotic break abroad'.
- a letter from a reader decrying the Mary Killen and Penny Smith columns and saying the star of the magazine is, of course, Coco: 'and "Coco's Corner" is the first thing I turn to each week.'

- a letter from a man who wrote to Boris about the non-existence of a statue of Keats in London with a PS, 'I had an article published in *The Lady* a decade or so ago, "Pages of Pleasure".'
- one cancellation from Epsom, Surrey, from an 85-year-old reader who cites Mary Killen and Penny Smith, saying, 'I find so many empty articles, I read them and I wonder, "What was all that about?"'
- a cancellation (one of several) following Roger Lewis's review of the Jonathan King autobiography in which King says, 'Sex has been a huge and delightful part of my life.'
- a letter from a PR beginning, 'I rang to speak to you recently but you were not available and top marks to your PA for not letting me through.' (I offer up silent prayer of thanks to Gillian.) The letter wanted me to visit the Memorial Woodlands in Bristol. I read the whole letter. The PR invited me to come to see the Heirloom Tree. A family buys a tree, around which the entire family is buried over time, with relatives returning to visit, sit and picnic under their tree, and be with their loved ones, giving a whole new meaning to the phrase, 'family tree'.
- a letter from Mrs Budworth: 'Dear Rachel, Here we are, 5 June, and no answer from you to my letter of 29 May. Did it ever arrive? Julia Budworth.'

Email of the day:

> Good afternoon
>
> In view of the revamp of *The Lady*, I wondered if you would be interested in me writing an article on Cotswold sheep.

Feel like checking into the Memorial Woodlands, buying a *Lady* tree, and laying myself down underneath a spreading chestnut tree in the vestal glade, and waiting for the end to come quickly.

15 June 2010

Email of the day – received following yet another transmission of 'The Lady and the Revamp'.

> Hi Rachel,
>
> I have just watched the TV documentary on The Lady.
>
> It's obviously filmed some time ago, so no doubt you have had loads of HR people get in touch to offer assistance but if you or Ben ever need a lift with change management then give us a shout!

I must remember 'change management' for future ref. Change management is clearly central to editing. I henceforth intend to use the phrase all the time.

Runner-up email of the day from the oldest son of the Dowager Duchess of Bedford, who regularly advertises in The Lady.

> Good day to all at The Lady, the journal for gentlewomen read by Her Grace.
>
> Her Grace the Dowager Duchess of Bedford is celebrating her ninetieth birthday at her residence in Monte Carlo surrounded by all her children and grandchildren . . .

It is signed 'Didier, Her Grace's eldest son.' What does the family expect – a ten-gun salute?

Mrs Budworth has telephoned, in a bate about the fact that the word 'arsehole' appeared in the magazine. None of us can remember this and have been scratching our heads. It didn't appear in the Emin interview. Nor even in the Roger Lewis review of DJ Jonathan King's memoirs, in which he talks about his own penis and describes the appendage (a 'pink maggot') of a schoolboy he'd been intimate with (now a High Court judge). Jessica Lambert – a Cambridge undergrad, and our workie that week – was delegated to ring up Mrs B. in Suffolk.

'Well, I'm very glad indeed Ben is taking this seriously,' said Mrs B. 'I'm much too busy now in the garden of course to tell you which copy the word appeared in, but I definitely came across it. I thought, "Goodness gracious me! What is the dear girl Rachel doing?" Haven't we put our readers through enough already?'

So Jessica had to sit at a desk all morning, combing through the last few weeks' issues, but failed to spot the abhorrent item.

16 June 2010

Bad, bad news. The last two covers have tanked. Ben and I are trying to put brave face on. Ruby Wax only managed around 28,000 and then Mariella – I thought a slam dunk – not much better.

'Maybe the readers just didn't like the fifties-ish styling of the Ruby cover,' Ben mused. We chose a pic of Ruby lying in a bubble bath on the telephone. It was very Hollywood. 'Or maybe they just don't like Ruby.'

I pointed out that was unlikely, as our readers thought our cover star was not Ruby, anyway, but Gina Lollobrigida, born 1927, who was much more our speed (and demographic).

'How about a big fat sale to Condé Nast, or going down freebie alley?' I suggested to Ben. When I'm down, he props me up, and when he's down, I cheer him on. 'Why don't you sell to that chap from *The Dalesman*?' Apparently, Yorkshire-based *The Dalesman* is keen to walk up the aisle with *The Lady* of Covent Garden, and it does sound like a match made in heaven.

*

I heard from Judy that, last week, Janina insisted that the loo window in the Ladies was kept closed. According to Judy, Janina once heard shouts from the street calling 'Lesbian, lesbian,' when the window was left open.

As I lay in bed I remembered – the Mariella and Ruby covers were published over half-term – maybe that explains it.

Or maybe it doesn't.

The in tray:

- an adorable stiffy card from Sam Cam in sumptuous Smythson stationery – white, tissue-lined in bright orange, and laid with matching orange lettering – thanking me for lovely note and tea-towels. It is signed 'Love Sam x'. She must have written it while moving house. I am hers, for ever.
- a card from a writer called Christine Webber who has written a book called *Too Young to Get Old*. She boldly asks for a column about being an over-fifty and adds, 'You'd probably have to shut Ben in the cupboard permanently' if I wanted to publish it in *The Lady*.

17 June 2010

Gave dinner party in our communal garden for eight. It should have been ten, but Toby Young jacks at last minute and his wife Caroline is, he proudly told me, 'also unavailable as she is at a reunion for her year at Cheltenham Ladies' College', as if that was all right then, because his lady wife went to posh girls' boarding school.

The Bodens (the mail-order moleskin magnate and his wife, Sophie, whom Ivo finds v. attractive in a dark Mitteleuropean way), the Bazalgettes (of Endemol fame) and filmmaker Gaby Dellal were attending.

Nicky Haslam came late, wearing punk TV shirt and Liam Gallagher jacket with his hair rising in a quiff. He was sweet to come, as he'd done Stephen Fry dins to benefit the Terrence Higgins Trust. We sat around a table in the garden, surrounded by flares (i.e., oil lamps not wide-bottomed trousers). My favourite bit was when Ivo offered him some Duchy Originals wine (I should in the interests of full disclosure point out that Waitrose, who is now in charge of Duchy Originals, comped and cooked the whole dinner and also socked me the chef) and Nicky said, 'I never drink wine,' as if it was vulgar. Red wine is 'wine' and rosé is called 'pink wine', and only white wine can be called 'white wine' according to Nicky (because, as above, red wine is 'wine').

Then he said – apropos a tidbit about a mutual married friend parading about with his gay lover – 'Being gay is terribly common,' which made us all scream with laughter, not merely because he has described himself as a living link to 'post-war faggotry' but because he ritually describes everything as 'common', from loving one's parents to water and saying please.

21 June 2010

Roger Lewis did not win the Oxford Professorship of Poetry. In fact, he only got 167 votes. He emailed me in despair.

> Oh, what a weekend. The Oxon thing was a disaster – the dopey buggers wanted Geoffrey Hill from the start. But *where were my troops?* I polled so few votes (167!) – I felt like Antony at Alexandria, all alone in the field of battle. Even my sworn enemy Michael Horovitz got twice my votes, and he's a well-known twat. I was only a handful of votes better off than a *busker*! Boris evidently succeeded handsomely in making me into *toast*. Then I did a piece

in the *Mail on Sunday* that was cut by a half. I had a much funnier
para about 'The Johnsons At Home', these brilliant blond Turkish
brigands with scimitars. But worst of all – the online version was
sub-edited by a madman who made it look like I'd won! Thank God
for my insomnia – at 2.30 a.m. I was on the phone to the night
watchman/editor getting a rectification. Scandal only very narrowly
averted.

Is Rules your office canteen? Because you can take me there if yes.

Shall I stand again in 2045, when I am more Geoffrey Hill's age?

Merrily rolling along,
Roger

In the evening, I went to Paul Johnson and Marigold Johnson
summer party. Asked Princess Michael if she'd write a 'Diary'. She
agreed to immediately. Then I turned to Prince Michael and said
that any time he needed to advertise for a new valet or HRH
needed a new lady's maid, he just had to say the word, as if I would
pay them in kind. Then I winked.

22 June 2010

A Tuesday. Circulation figures up, but only up a bit. The problem
is, we pop two copies of *The Lady* in 11,000 newsagents, and we
either sell one or two (and then we don't have a presence on the
shelf) or none, and at £1.80, of that, 80p goes to the distributor.
The answer is to go fortnightly, but then that mucks up the reve-
nue stream that is the classified.

Lunch with Ben at Leon. He wants me to dream up things that
will make *The Lady* unmissable, something you just have to have
each week. Like *Country Life* has country houses, and *The Week* has

a digest of the week. The only thing that he regards as unmissable is 'Coco's Corner'. I wondered out loud whether to have a column by Nicky Haslam on what was common this week (Wimbledon, Glastonbury, glamping, barbecues, etc.) and what was not common (pink wine, sweet peas, chintz, etc.) and call it 'Common or Garden'.

On the money front, Ben has abandoned hope that Coutts will reverse their decision not to stump up the next tranche of money. He has announced he'll tap a different, even more exclusive private bank, which charges like the Light Brigade. I know this because I bank there myself – thanks to having high-born husband, I hasten to add.

'At least then I'll be able to boast that we've got Hoare's at *The Lady*,' he said.

I think the answer to all these intractable problems of identity, of circulation, unmissable columns, hooks, etc., is that there is probably no answer. We have to carry on producing a magazine people enjoy reading, and do it every week. Ben has a very difficult job, and I would not trade places with him for all the tea in China.

I asked about the board meeting on 4 July which Willy, Adam, Richard and Ben Budworth, plus of course Mrs Julia Budworth, will be attending in the boardroom.

Ben was non-committal as to what will be on the agenda.

'Is it my sacking?' I asked over Leon chicken superfood salad. Boiling-hot day on the Strand. Coco panting under the table.

'Well, I think it's safe to say that Mum's not your biggest fan,' he said.

'Well, tell Maureen to keep a note of what she says so you can tell me after,' I said.

'I will, but at the board meeting this time last year, Maureen appeared to take a careful note of every word and only admitted later that she hadn't heard a thing because they were drilling in Bedford Street,' Ben said.

23 June 2010

Lots to report! Apparently not only Blez is hawking a book about his time at *The Lady* around publishers, but Lindsay is too!

Mrs Budworth – who has been talking to Lindsay and Janina about their time here, which doesn't exactly make the heart sing with happiness – has submitted a six-page document of things to be discussed at the board meeting in July. I was allowed a quick look.

She has formally asked Ben, as chief executive ('What a pompous title,' she added), to supply the four other directors (i.e., his brothers and mother) a comprehensive dossier explaining who everyone is and how much they get paid relative to the Golden Age, i.e., Arline's editorship. There are suggestions from Mrs B. about having a country-life column, and using the Fromenti fashion drawings from the archive more (not a bad idea) and lots of pointed queries about the editorial process. For example, 'Who is reading the proofs?' one item demands to know. This is, presumably, so she knows who to dress down over further appearances of words like 'arsehole'. There is one item specifically concerning me. 'What do we think of the new editor?' The note goes on. 'I expect this meeting to take longer than usual and suggest we break for coffee and sandwiches at 1 p.m.'

24 June 2010

The comedienne and author Annabel Giles came in – to talk about doing a series of interviews – women and their dogs. She was beautiful. And single. And Ben is single.

Annabel gamely quizzed Ben in the boardroom. 'Are you enjoying it?' she asked.

'When I think I could be flying hairy-arsed, foul-mouthed Scots-men to oil rigs,' he sighed wistfully. He checked her out, before adding, 'Why don't we do something about biscuits? Everyone likes biscuits.'

We all agreed on that, then he told us a long anecdote about when he'd come back from flying helicopters in Florida to take over the old girl, and making desperate efforts to get rid of a tea cosy that kept appearing on the pot every time the tea service from Ros, who also multi-tasks as our dulcet-toned telephonist, came round.

He'd tried throwing it out of the window, burying it at the bottom of bins wrapped in plastic bags, but whatever he did, it would reappear the next day, laundered, over the pot, which Ros would bring in, pursed of lip. 'They still give me dirty looks if I try to make my own tea,' he finished.

'So, is it a bit like a girls' school here?' continued Annabel.

She'd just witnessed a scene in my office when Judy, the production manager, made me put cortisol cream on an insect bite on my ankle – an injury sustained during my father's seventieth birthday party in Regent's Park on Tuesday – while Gillian bustled about with TCP and cotton wool. It was a scene from Matron's landing in a prep school *circa* 1956.

'Yes it is, apart from the fact there's never lights out,' he said.

25 June 2010

So . . . speaking of lights out, it has come to my attention that I started this diary on 9 June 2009, I was announced editor in July, and I became editor at the beginning of September.

It's Friday, and am shirking from home. About to go to Nicky Haslam's in Hampshire for the weekend bearing a tray of figs (they surely can't be common?). I asked him for the dress code. 'A wisp of chiffon,' he replied.

Now, not wanting to be too pedantic about the subtitle, 'My first year as editor', and all that (Ben wearily knows, because I tell him all the time, I worked *pro bono* from the second I got the gig. I commissioned, for example, Charlie Glass's now-legendary article on humping the help exactly a year ago), it strikes me that this might be a good time to stop.

To date, I've commissioned and edited around forty-four editions of the magazine, and shifted around 1.3 million copies. That's about half as many as I was expected to sell. On the plus side, I've personally soiled around 323 tea-towels, and according to *Campaign*, '*The Lady* magazine has had more media attention in the past six months than in its entire 125-year existence. And it's all down to Rachel Johnson.'

(Their words, not mine. When I put the words 'Arline Usden' and '*The Lady*' into Google, it returned 323 results. When I put my own and '*The Lady*', it returned 995,000, and when Edwina did it, she got more than 3 million.)

Not that it matters much.

I fear that all the buzz in the world is not going to persuade new readers in their forties to pick up a magazine they last spotted in their great-grandmother's care home – not in a tearing hurry, anyway. The magazine has masses for them to read, but it's still an impossible gig, doubling the circulation. While my old readers are still being gathered (that's trendy vicar-speak for 'dying'), any new ones are still going online. The rats!

Another problem: the 'brand association' between *The Lady* with nannies, carers, holiday cottages and housekeepers for country piles – an association that keeps the business going – is not going to change quickly either.

But still. Whatever the old guard think, and I dread to imagine sometimes, I am proud of the magazine, and pleased with the quality of the writing contained within the curiously slimy, shiny covers (carry a bunch of copies, and they always slither out of your arms to the floor – we get Basildon Bond about it, as we do every-thing else).

I'm pleased I restored the subtitle, 'A Journal for Gentlewomen', in wiggly, toothpaste writing on the front cover, because I want to reassure everyone that I'm not going to turn the old girl into a fallen woman, *Lady*-to-Ladette-style, even if I did put Tracey Emin on the cover and have probably perpetrated many other sundry crimes against gentility.

So, I think this is the time to stop. Even though I don't know the outcome of the *Mail on Sunday* potato-growing contest; even though I haven't quite sat in the editor's chair a year; and even though the board meeting in which at least one director has called for my sacking hasn't yet taken place.

And even though I can't claim I've doubled circulation, or made *The Lady* cool, or pleased Mrs Budworth. But I don't rule either of those things out . . . oh, in the next 125 years or so.

Until that time, as Lady Thatcher once said, we fight on.

To be honest, I don't really want to return to my old life of strolling around the Portobello Road in yogawear, dipping into Gail's for their no-dairy, no-sugar bran muffin, and the Grocer on Elgin for a £4 packet of assorted, organic, hand-picked leaves. It was actually quite dull, even if I do miss those lunches in the raw bar at Daylesford, and those power naps after. To paraphrase that BP chap, I *don't* want my life back.

So, as I said, we fight on! We will fight them on the beaches, we will fight them on the landing grounds, we will fight them in WHSmith and John Menzies and in R. S. McColl, and in news-agents up and down the land, we will fight them in Martins with doilies and glass cloths and tea cosies. We fight on wearing Tena pants, and we fight to win.

And if we fail, I will always hold my head up high to have served my time as the ninth editor of the first and finest women's weekly in the land, the longest continuously published women's magazine in the world, the journal for gentlewomen, *The Lady*, 39/40 Bedford Street, The Strand, WC2 9ER, est. 1885.

It's been the best year of my life so far.

Postscript

Ten random things I have learnt about being an editor in one short year:

1. A full-colour, hand-tooled, weekly magazine containing 50 pages of glistening editorial must sell more than 35,000 copies at £1.80 at the newsstand to break even, and a weekly magazine must sell more than 45,000 copies before advertisers – I mean, real advertisers, i.e., those that do not advertise donkey sanctuaries in the Holy Land or surgery for poor, hare-lipped children, walk-in baths and pill dispensers – will even consider buying space. Remember – I couldn't even *give* away space to Burberry.

2. Never underestimate how difficult it is to get anyone to buy anything. I am now like a politician needing voters to stay in office – so this is what I say to my valued readers and subscribers and advertisers, past, present and future: *with my body, I thee worship.*

3. Even so, I feel like killing with my bare hands contributors who send me emails asking me when their piece entitled 'Amazing Mazes' or 'Scents & Sensibility', commissioned by the previous editor sometime in 2008, will run. When travel PRs call to ask me when a freelancer's piece on the cuisine of Tunisia following a three-week-long freebie in 2007 will be published, I want to order a massacre of the firstborns, followed by Gillian for putting them through. This is normal.

4. I have to restrain myself when journo friends email me directly complaining they haven't been paid. Invoicing is *so*

beneath my pay grade! Instead, I respond instantly with icy politeness, and call Tracey, in Accounts.

5. I have learnt that Ben, far from needing to 'grow a pair of balls', is a dynamic, kind, nay inspirational publisher and supreme commander, with rock-hard *cojones* you can see from space, who responds to my diva-ish strops with superhuman tolerance. I couldn't begin to control the operation that is *The Lady*, talk to distributors, advertisers – both display and classified – marketers, brand agents, PRs, printers, and so on. In fact, I barely know what the moving parts are, let alone have the ability to control them. I can barely keep myself in running order, get from A to B, etc.

6. Despite the fact that running a weekly magazine is like continuously standing on a beach in North Cornwall and feeling wave after wave hit you and then, just as you catch your breath, a really BIG wave (press day) smashes you and drags you under into the riptide, I quite like it, on the whole. This has been funner than anything else I've ever done, but is, it has to be admitted, quite ageing. I feel about 125 now, and no longer look in the mirror apart from to check for overnight apparition of rogue hairs on chin and inspect deepening of nasolabial lines, as if watching my face in time-lapse, speeded-up time.

7. It really matters what you put on the cover. Don't put Mark Thatcher (a mummy's boy of the first order) or Sharon Osbourne (a woman who has admitted to sending people excrement in the post) on the cover of a magazine called *The Lady* unless you want to offend virtually all your loyal readers of forty years' standing, who regard the magazine as the last remaining bastion of gentility in a thoroughly depraved universe.

8. Changes will offend most of your existing readers all the time, and new ones will clamber on board very slowly. Every time you replace a long-standing theatre critic or gardening column with someone dewier and fresher, your long-standing

readers will react as if you have taken a chainsaw to the Crown Jewels. You just have to be brave and take it on the chin because, after six months, they react even more furiously if you bin any of your own, initially unpopular, innovations. I got heaps of letters complaining about my column for chaps called 'The Gents'. And I got just as many after I canned it.

9. Online really matters. Online is our only hope. My children have never bought a newspaper. Magazines will not be around in twenty years. Nor will newspapers. This is what the doomsayers are saying, anyway, and it would be foolish to ignore them.

10. The magazine – especially a national institution, whose mere existence transmits 'something benign into the ether' (as the journalist from the *Khaleej Times* put it, as if the weekly magazine is like a Glade 'Sense and Spray'™ that spritzes the country, once a week, with deodorizing fragrance) – does not belong to me. It doesn't even belong to the Budworths. It belongs to the readers. All magazines do.

An editor forgets that at her peril. That's about it.

Ed's note:
Actually, that wasn't it. I couldn't resist carrying on keeping a diary because, as previously noted, three unbelievable things happen here every day before tea-time, and at least one of them is a Bedford Street Special (i.e. so utterly bonkers you couldn't make it up). So, after a hiatus . . .

The Lady

31 AUGUST 2010   £1.80

FLORA & FAUNA
gardens and women's writing

How not to
GET AHEAD IN TELEVISION

Sssshh...
SILENT FILMS IN PROGRESS

Why we still love
JANE AUSTEN

GUEST EDITOR
PENNY SMITH
takes on The Lady

LAURIE GRAHAM · ELIZABETH BUCHAN · SHELLEY VON STRUNCKEL · SALLY JONES
JOHN STAPLETON · HUNDREDS OF HOLIDAY & JOB ADVERTISEMENTS EACH WEEK

9 770023 716158

AUGUST

5 August 2010

Right. Picking up again after a diary-writing hiatus . . .

Claire the designer is off, so is poor Judy again, so copy is scattering everywhere and sometimes landing in the wrong places. Gillian is deep in invoices and sending calming emails to panicking freelancers who haven't been paid for months, and as it's August, all the children are on their ten-week summer holiday, so I am bobbing between Somerset and London. Ben is coming down to stay with us on Exmoor at the weekend. That would give Mrs B. plenty to chew on, bearing in mind she told Giles Wood she was sure Ben and I were having an affair. This was when Giles was embedded at her house Deerbolts Hall, creating an 'eyesore' (his word for painting) of the pale green drawing room. Apparently she wants him to do two paintings of the room – one as it is in summer, with sunlight pouring in from the garden through the French windows, and exactly the same scene in winter, only this one with a Christmas tree decked out in all its finery by the ladies of the village. When Giles told me what Mrs B. thought, I snapped, 'Well, I hope you told her we're not,' and Giles said, 'Oh no, I wouldn't do that. She who pays the piper calls the tune.'

Chrissie – whom Ben calls 'DR' for *dramatis regina*, or drama queen – is fighting off Ben's offensive to cut the number of subs from four to three and is chain-smoking in the street as she plots her counter-attack.

When I passed through the boardroom to heat up my EAT lunchtime cup-a-soup Ben was sitting there staring into space. I asked him what was wrong.

'Maureen's just asked if she could leave for her train to Eltham ten minutes earlier than usual at close of play. I said fine, any particular reason why? And she said, "My boxers have been poorly, they've had diarrhoea all weekend. And then she went on a bit,' he said.

11 August 2010

Ben's weekend on Exmoor went very well. A highlight (for me rather than Ben, I suspect) was my father taking him up vertical cleeves to the 'top of the farm' in one of the two antique and condemned Land Rovers he uses for 'wooding'. My father likes to do this to townies when he can, and makes a point of steering nonchalantly with one hand while failing to look at the terrain ahead, veering into muddy ruts, so the Land Rover bucks and growls while diesel fumes belch from the back, and his passenger hits his head on the ceiling struts. If you're not used to it, it's pretty terrifying. I am used to it and it's still terrifying.

Dada took him up Furze Ball (pronounced 'fuzzball'), a prehistoric stone track with sharply banked hedges on either side, low-hanging branches swiping the canvas roof, that leads up past bare ruined barns. They were gone a good hour. When he got back Ben joked, 'Just going to change my trousers.' He did look a bit pale, but Ivo gave him a stiffener and he soon recovered and sat by the fire telling us about his Exmoor safari. The weekend was delightful – Ben was a tremendous mucker-inner and accompanied us to the fête and the pub and even went on a walk. There was only a moment at dinner when he referred to girls as having 'grass on the wicket' or having 'no grass on the wicket' and I didn't know what he meant, but my children worked it out pretty quickly and choked with laughter. A model guest!

The Lady

7 SEPTEMBER 2010 · £1.80

TAMARA DREWE
We meet Posy Simmonds

ELIZABETH ARDEN
prize draw

GUEST EDITOR
COCO
gets her paws on The Lady

FAMILIES
on the radio

THE BAKE OFF
our TV critic's verdict

SARAH STANDING · CLEMMIE HAMBRO · NAOMI CLEAVER · KATE ATKINSON
THE MILROY · HUNDREDS OF HOLIDAY AND JOB ADVERTISEMENTS EACH WEEK

SEPTEMBER

1 September 2010

Coco is our cover girl this week. It was the only way I could prevent Ben from putting me on the cover. It's my first anniversary as editor today, and he was keen on making all the readers send in their comments, in a drive for more interactivity with our customer-base, and asking them to review my first year's performance.

'I don't want to have to print a *Shitschrift* about myself in the magazine I edit, or have me on the cover,' I explained. 'It's a grue-some hostage to fortune.' Penny Smith, the former GMTV presenter, our opera critic, guest-edited last week while I was in Scotland and so this week, as a cheeky nod to that, we have a shot of Coco posing in the communal garden and the cover line, 'Coco Gets Her Paws On *The Lady*'. We all think she looks lovely, but on the other hand, this could be because Bedford Street is a parallel universe, not a normal magazine at all, and we have gone completely nuts. The magazine is called *The Lady*. Not *The Bitch*. But I am confident. Every time there's a dog on the cover the issue does well.

8 September 2010

It's 'World Change Month', which reminds me: it's a whole year since our menopause special. How time flies when you're having fun and trying to think of ways to avoid using the words 'The Change' on the cover of a nationally distributed women's weekly. Right on cue, as if I am in mid-hot flush, I receive an email from a

PR drawing my attention to exciting news from a company that supplies 'Personal Cooling Systems'.

Edwina hasn't had a break all year so I am sending her to Malta to hear Elton John. She is very grateful. Also asked her to interview little Jenny Lord from Penguin who has a book out about knitting. Perfect for us. We are going to call it 'Purly Queen' or 'Reclaim the Knit'. I was very pleased with my cover lines till little Jenny sent me an attachment with all the knitting puns her friends had come up with – i.e., 'The Needle and the Damage Done', 'Tender is the Knit' – which were much funnier.

Every week, a woman wearing a hairnet and a housecoat hovers outside the boudoir. 'Can I clean your telephone?' she asks, waving some wipes.

'No. Can you clean my keyboard, though?' I said today, without looking up. My keyboard should be mailed to Centers for Disease Control in Georgia and is spattered with soup from EAT, and today's freebie offering – Battenberg cake from the Fifth Floor at Harvey Nicks. I started clearing the surface so she could come in with her wipe. But she didn't budge.

'No, I can't,' she said. 'We don't have the contract to do that. We used to, but Mr Budworth cut it two years ago. If you want me to clean your keyboard, you'll have to pay extra.'

Had coffee with Mr Bowles/Uncle Tom. He was standing outside the building examining the peeling paintwork in a proprietorial fashion, wearing sponge-bag trousers hoicked high at the waist and an ancient moleskin coat.

'I'm waiting for Steve from Chingford,' he told me.

I stood there, not sure what to say. I was about to get my morning latte from Caffè Nero. 'I'm going to get a coffee. Do you want one?' I asked him.

He looked startled. As if I'd suggested we went to the opera, and then perhaps had a little light supper somewhere in Covent Garden afterwards. He was already picturing the smoked salmon sandwiches under cling film at the interval. I realized . . . he thinks I am asking him for A DATE!

'Why not,' he said.

He started moving across the road in my wake. We stepped into Caffè Nero. He gazed around. He confronted the chill cabinet, full of smoothies and gluten-free brownies and muffins. He said with pride, 'I've lived here for forty years and I've never set foot in this building.'

He removed his hat inside the coffee shop and insisted on paying for the drinks. We took our paper cups and went to sit outside.

We chatted a bit about *The Lady*, which he still only refers to as 'your rotten magazine'. We spoke briefly about Mrs Budworth, and I let slip that his elder sister was perhaps not my greatest fan.

'If you disregard her rudeness,' said Tom Bowles, as he replaced the lid on his cappuccino (which he admitted he'd only got to keep me company, as he couldn't stand the stuff), 'and actually listen to what she says, she occasionally makes sense.'

Which is right – she was right about Debo, and right about us needing more countrywoman stuff in the mag, which is quite London-centric for our readership.

The in tray:

- pitch: 'I hope you are well. I have sent over my wedding feature to Carolyn to look at. In the meantime, I wondered if you would be interested in a feature about an Islington lady who turned a card-making hobby into a thirty-year career?'
- submission from a reader in St Leonards, Sussex. 'Enclosed is an article for you to consider about the history of tea drinking in Britain.'

I think that is the eighth pitch I've had about tea since I inherited what Rowan Pelling calls, 'the editor's silk crêpe bonnet'.

13 September 2010

Have sent Mrs B. a copy of my book, about my first year editing. But she sent it back, with a note saying that she thought it was better she didn't read it at all. At first I thought that this displayed not inconsiderable style and old-school reserve (she is of the generation where it was not done for gels to appear in newspapers other than within hatch, match and dispatch announcements on the Court and Social page). Then I found she'd left a bookmark about two-thirds of the way through, which was a slight worry.

Nonetheless, I decided to telephone her to alert her to the *Daily Mail* serialization that was about to appear in a week's time, as I've seen the extract, and my blood had run cold.

I thought they would take two or three big sequential chunks – but oh no, no, no. Someone at the *Mail* has read and filleted the whole damn thing, taking out every positive and humane and sympathetic nuance and leaving it pitiless, unsympathetic and critical. And they've totally majored on Mrs Budworth, Debo, Joan Collins, Lady Antonia, etc., and every time I bitch about a celebrity and name-drop. I had to warn her.

'Please read the whole book, not just the extracts,' I begged Mrs Budworth. But she sounded cheerful about the forthcoming serialization. And she is never cheerful on the telephone with me.

'I don't read the *Mail*,' she said, happily. 'It's a vile toe-rag! I only ever buy it if they've run out of *Telegraphs* in Stowmarket,' (or wherever Deerbolts is – I've never been, and after the bit about her asking me to jump out of the boudoir window on to Maiden Lane is in the *Daily Mail*, I recognize I am unlikely now ever to be invited).

But then she launched into one of her monologues. She lectured me that there was no need to 'wade into people' and that I should 'take a leaf out of cousin Debo's book'. She told me Debo manages to put the boot in very delicately using understatement. 'Cousin Debo would never be rude,' she said in Lady Bracknellish tones, 'but she manages to leave one in no doubt as to exactly what she thinks.'

Then she thanked me for sending her the book 'even though I have no intention of reading it'.

'Goodbye, Mrs B.,' I said.

'Goodbye, Miss J.,' she replied.

She has clearly read the book. And she has my measure exactly.

The in tray:

- letter from reader in Bury St Edmunds complaining about the Coco cover – or, as the reader insists on calling it, the 'front page':

Dear Editor,

I was very disappointed to see that horrible black dog on the front page. Why can't you bring a nice seasonal bunch of flowers, or a lovely picture from a little village, instead of all those soulless people on the front page? I'm not the only one who is very disappointed not having anymore that lovely, homey magazine I loved of yore, instead that modern magazine with artificial models on the front page.

- letter from a Miss Munro, Edinburgh, which makes it clear that Miss Jean Brodie is very much alive and kicking:

Dear Madam,

I am writing to advise you that there are two obvious errors in your magazine on pages 61 and 65. As an avid reader of the old *Lady*

magazine I must say I do not feel myself that it has in any way
IMPROVED in spite of being GLOSSY and having a distinct SMELL.'

(All caps are hers.)

I am amazed that for ONE WEEK ONLY you can allow a middle-
aged ex-newsreader to run this magazine (Ed's note: my reader is
referring to the fizzy Penny Smith) therefore there must be no talent
or experience required for this particular job.
To close, I have not been buying *The Lady* at £1.80. However, I feel
I will now buy the magazine as a source of amusement.

Eh? She hates the magazine but will buy it to laugh at it?

• a pitch about Scrabble, title 'Word Games', from a freelancer in
Wootton Bassett.

14 *September 2010*

Ding-dong with Ben about the Jilly Cooper extract from her new
blockbuster *Jump!* She chose the extract herself for us, is giving it
to us *gratis*, and the extract even name-checks *The Lady*. But all
Ben appears concerned about is that the extract contains the word
'erection', or, to be precise, the phrase 'huge erection steepling his
trousers', which is typically Jilly and rather jolly IMHO. I should
add that the extract also contains the words 'pubic hair'.

I was working away in the boudoir when I heard Gillian take a
call in my outer office.

'The Jilly Cooper piece?' she said. 'A print-off? OK, Ben, I'll
bring it through to the boardroom in a tick.' I heard the printer
crank into life by her desk.

'Don't show him the extract,' I howled, leaping to my feet. 'Just print off the Jilly Cooper interview with Laura James. OK?'

'OK, Rachel,' she said meekly.

After that, I felt a rather sinister silence had mantled the office. I get up, go past Gillian, past Judy, past Tamsin and Claire and Maria and Susie in the design room, and into the subs. 'Chrissie's in the boardroom going through the Jilly Cooper extract,' one of the subs said, when my gaze fell on Chrissie's empty chair.

I stormed through to the boardroom. I could see the A4 printed pages of the extract had been ripped up and scattered on the blue baize cloth.

'So what've you decided? Editing the magazine as well as choosing the cover this week?' I said in a nasty voice. I said this because earlier in the day, I'd been in a meeting with an outfit called Walford Wilkie. They do brands and marketing and are in league with us to flog something called the Alex computer (simple, bombproof laptops for oldies). We are running a part-work to promote it, written by Giles Wood, who has never sent an email, doesn't have a mobile or answer the telephone, let alone tweet or blog (he is too busy searching for flints in the Wiltshire Downs) and is therefore perfect for this assignment.

During the meeting – at which we were discussing the arrival of broadband in the Woods' grottage, and what each piece in the part-work should cover – Claire came in, as she does at this time of the week, holding up two cover choices. One had Jilly looking sad and pitching forwards in a man's oversized tweed jacket; the other had her roaring with gap-toothed laughter.

'Ooh, sorry, just coming to show the covers, I'll go away again,' she'd said, backing out.

'No, come in,' said Ben.

So she stood in the doorway and held them up.

'The one on the right,' said Ben, of the gloomy one.

'No, the left,' I said. 'Jilly is all about fun and laughter . . .' etc.

After the Walford Wilkie team had gone he started effing and blinding about how it wasn't my fucking magazine and how he was the fucking publisher and how I was not to contradict him in public and how the buck stopped with him and HOW could I even CONSIDER putting 'huge throbbing penises' into the magazine.

'It doesn't say "huge throbbing penises",' I pointed out, at which point he started piecing together the ripped-up pages littering the table, so we could read the offending passages.

'Here. It says "huge erection",' he said, pointing at the words.

So, instead of annoying Ben and risking another Tracey Emin episode/Budworth eruption with our readers, I thought what I would do is ring Jilly, and see if we could come up with acceptable synonyms for 'erection' and 'pubic hair'.

I called her in Stroud and got through to one of her two PAs, and she came to the phone. After we'd burbled to each other lovingly, I told her the extract was heaven and how much I'd been laughing over the names Throstledown and Pocock. Then I came to the point.

'The extract you chose . . .' I said, in more serious tones.

She understood immediately. 'Ah,' she said. 'You can't have erections in *The Lady*. Why don't you take one out?' (There are, to be precise, two erections in the extract – in another place 'something starts growing' in our hero Pocock's trousers.) 'I don't mind erections,' she said. 'I find them hysterical.'

We then both screeched hysterically for some time.

In the end, we decided to replace the word 'erection' with 'Everest', and I decided on 'lady garden' instead of 'pubic hair'.

Meanwhile, Ben is still insisting on the gloomy picture of Jilly sitting on a bench, hunched as if in pain, wearing a black ostrich cardigan, but the offending extract now reads: 'He discovered there was not a varicose vein in sight and her lady garden was the softest mouse brown. Scrambling down the ladder with an Everest steepling his dungarees . . .'

Ben just came in. 'We're not going to have another fight today,' he said.

I gave him a chill glare. 'That's a shame,' I said.

The in tray:

- a pitch from Wormley, Herts, of three short articles all entitled 'Lost and Found', true accounts of what can happen when things go missing and then, against all the odds, are eventually found.
- a letter from Raynes Park, London, complaining that there are too many photos in the magazine and asking me to commission a new book of Ladygrams because 'one a week is not enough'.
- an article about the childlike wonder that Christmas inspires, called 'Not Just a Load of Baubles', for consideration.

20 September 2010

No circulation figures last week because B-Cal is away and none of us can understand the net sales data or baffling spreadsheets. Well, I can't. The figures to come in are for the edition with the BBC's Katie Derham on the cover at the Albert Hall, our UK Proms and Travel special, celebrating the best of Britishness. It had a cover line 'Lands of Hope and Glory'. I hope it leapt off newsstands. That reader who banged on about soul has a point. Our covers which show idyllic country scenes, or grandchildren eating home-made ginger cake on gingham rugs, all hit the spot with our readers. Face-lifted, airbrushed hussies don't.

Went on BBC Radio Four's *Any Questions?* on the 17th. In Weston-super-Mare. Fellow panellists were Ben Bradshaw ... and I'm afraid I forget the others. On the way there tried to read the *Economist* and *FT* to prep myself – feeling sure Trident was coming up, as well as the Pope's visit – but kept nodding off. Felt it was a disaster. When asked about Trident, I said, 'Dump it, it's a willy-waving anachronism.'

Always feel I could do so much better when I do a radio or TV live programme, and am tormented for hours after by the things I should have said. There was a question about secularism – in light of the Pope's visit – that completely felled me. I spoke fluent gibberish for about ten minutes.

Found this on Twitter:

Listening to *Any Questions?* Not sure Rachel Johnson has formed one complete argument. Just a long cycle of randomly arranged sentences.

The *Mail* serialization is out. It's up on the website on the Friday night.

In the morning, receive furious tirade from Joan Collins following the serialization, via email from her husband, Percy Gibson. *Inter alia*, she calls me cheap, trashy, nasty and in need of inch-thick make-up.

Today in the *Mail* Peter McKay – an old friend of mine and Ivo's – calls for my sacking.

Text from Piers Morgan:

Saw the show (i.e., the Channel 4 doc) on flight back from LA yesterday, now reading the Diaries. HYSTERICAL. And for the first time, everyone is talking about *The Lady* for reasons other than nannies. Congrats Johnson, loving your work x

I sent him:

And that from master diarist! Only had virtual writ from Joan Collins and McKay calling for my sacking in *Mail* today.

Back from Piers:

Writs and sackings mean you're on fire. Keep stoking!

I've always rather loved Piers, I just have to hide it as people seem to hate him so much.

The in tray:

- some sparklers and burn cream from Nelsons' Years of Natural Healthcare 1960–2010.
- ticket, in the shape of a heavy metal oblong the colour of a beige trench coat, from Burberry to the Prorsum catwalk show.
- a pink pashmina and a how-to-tie-your-pashmina leaflet.
- a press release offering me books about how to make cloth dolls and 'mug hugs' – which look like little knitted condoms for tea and coffee cups.

26 September 2010

Am in Venice on a romantic marital city break with Ivo. Just five days. We haven't been away together for years, and never had a honeymoon (apart from one drunken night in Hartwell House). So there was a sense of occasion about this trip, in the planning stage, and when it came to lift-off, Ivo was very proud about how efficient it all was under his leadership (I was in charge of arranging the holiday, buying the tickets, arranging the accommodation, and he was in charge of passports and the E-ticket printout). We left our various places of work and met at Victoria, then went together on the Gatwick Express through a monsoon, gleeful that in only a few short hours, we would be touching down in La Serenissima, with a table in Harry's Dolci on Giudecca awaiting us. We even made it to the right desk in the right terminal with over an hour and a half to spare.

Ivo handed over the passports to the BA check-in lady with a flourish.

She glanced at them both, then at our faces, and then asked, 'So, which one of you two is Ludo?'

Ivo had brought our 17-year-old's passport instead, so he had to get back on the Gatwick Express, go to the house in Notting Hill, fetch passport, then fly to Bologna (there being no later flights to Venice) and stay the night in a hotel. I went to Venice on my own.

The following day we were about to settle down to a celebratory reunion late fish lunch *à deux* in San Polo, in a taverna only supposedly frequented by Venetians, by a bridge . . . and my mobile rang. Ivo groaned in disbelief. I took it outside while he tucked into the platter of *frutti di mare*.

It was hack Matthew Bell. He told me that Mrs B. has given an interview to the *Independent on Sunday*. With him. Which he had written up. 'Just wondered if you want to respond to the interview, for a news story?' Matthew asked.

'News story?' I squeaked, as a vaporetto slid past in the greasy water, and I wondered where I could buy some cigarettes without getting so lost that I'd never find the restaurant or Ivo again, which once happened to my father when he took a girl on a dirty weekend to Paris, installed her in a pavement café and went to find a hotel and never located the girl or the café again. I mention this now because, as chance would have it, this very same girl has turned into one of my lady columnists, Sarah Langton-Lockton, who writes a weekly, woman-of-the-soil account of her life on her allotment called 'Plotlines'. But back to Venice.

'Er,' Matthew said. Then he coughed. 'Well, the main charges are that you are mad, vain, a social climber, snobbish, and unsuitable

to edit *The Lady*, that you've caused the circulation of the magazine to crash . . .' he trailed off. And coughed again. 'Oh yes,'
he gave a light laugh, as if this was a joke, 'and that you are sex-
obsessed.'

In the *Mail* that Saturday (i.e., the day before), Quentin Letts
had done a phoner with Mrs B. in which he'd asked her for her
opinion of me and she'd told him she thought I was crackers and
that I was 'at my best when writing "Coco's Corner"', i.e., in the
voice of my dog. The Letts piece was very funny and referenced
Wodehouse and Wooster's terrifying Aunt Dahlia with her wig-
lifting voice, and christened the Budworth seat 'The Gorgon's
Lair' – which is going to stick, I fear, mainly because it's so accurate.
But Letts' column was only the tip, it turns out, of the iceberg my
editor-of-the-Ladyship was about to hit.

On Sunday the *Sindy* interview came out, and it was even worse
than Matthew Bell had told me. It was said I was 'completely
obsessed with penises' and that you 'couldn't keep me away from a
penis'. It was 'penis this, penis that', and the reason was that I was
brought up with all those boys and so was basically a boy.

Obviously all this went down a storm back in the UK. It seemed
to light up the weekend for the nation. I got emails from people
saying reading the Mrs B. interview was the most fun they'd had
all year, and that tears were streaming down their faces as they
read it.

The interview was raised on *The Andrew Marr Show* and even
raised a smile from the famously humourless Polly Toynbee. It has
gone viral. Meanwhile, Mrs B. now claims to be coming to the
book launch on Thursday and has even telephoned Matthew Bell
to congratulate him on his piece.

Apparently, she is thrilled with his article and only corrected
him on one point – she has no objection to our Trace (Emin) being
in *The Lady*. Only her being on the cover.

As a result of Mrs B.'s charges relating to the male member,

I suspect, my male followers on Twitter have doubled and include someone called @CumberlandSausage.

29 September 2010

Back from Venice.

Ben told me that Mrs B. is granting interviews to both the *Mail* and *Telegraph* tomorrow. And even worse, *The Lady* saga and the Mrs Budworth broadside were discussed on a programme called *Loose Women* today.

'We should go on *Loose Women*, tomorrow,' I said when I got back to base, after long lunch at Sotheby's, 'all three of us, you, your mum and me.'

'*Jerry Springer Show*, more like,' Ben said.

Could it be that Mrs B. has a severe case of late-onset celebrity addiction? In every interview she gives, she sounds happier and happier, more and more full of beans.

She is clearly having time of her life. I wish I was.

The in tray:

- a hessian sack containing chutney-making ingredients – sugar, onion, cooking apples, vinegar.
- pitch on a 765-word article on 'fashion etiquette post-World War Two' covering the variety of fashion from 1947 to the 21st century.
- a pitch to write a piece about the Paston family's connections since the Wars of the Roses with a church in Thorpe St Andrew from – yes, you guessed – a freelancer from Thorpe St Andrew called Paston.
- Jilly Cooper has sent me a silver letter opener from Highgrove with a lovely note.
- two letters to Coco, one sent from Quothquan, by Biggar.

30 September 2010

After work rushed to Mirror Mirror for a blow-dry and then rushed back to squeeze into blue sequinned dress for my launch party, which started in the office at 6.30 p.m. There was this in the *Standard* tonight on a *news page*:

> One of the most potentially explosive encounters on this year's social calendar takes place tonight.
>
> Rachel Johnson, editor of *The Lady*, will be in the same room as Julia Budworth for the first time since the title's publishing matriarch called for the Mayor's 'penis-obsessed' sister to be fired.
>
> Johnson, 44, is launching her book *A Diary of* The Lady at the 125-year-old magazine's Covent Garden offices.
>
> She vowed to be civil. But just hours before the gathering Mrs Budworth reopened hostilities by accusing her editor of blundering and lacking kindness.

At about 6.45 p.m. I was on the stoop, having a cigarette to calm my nerves before the predicted 'explosive encounter', and Mrs B. bowled up in a black cab. After paying, she got her things, her handbag and bundles, dismounted, and walked straight past me without a glance, through the Irish funeral parlour panelled entrance, and made for my launch party, pausing only to be photographed by assorted press photographers.

'Mrs Budworth, can I have one of you with Rachel?' one of them dared to ask. (He was definitely after the money shot.) I didn't think she would, but she did. After the indignity of posing with me – the hostess – she stomped into *The Lady*'s smoking room, which she has decorated at her own expense, with the mural of the dog and the Spy drawings and the rattan furniture, and held court to selective journalists, and, to their unconfined delight, told them how awful, mad, vain and penis-obsessed I was while the party roared on around me.

The *Evening Standard* account of the launch party, complete with errors:

NEVER A DULL MOMENT AT *THE LADY*

Unladylike fisticuffs were narrowly averted last night when editor Rachel Johnson, launching her new book *A Diary of* The Lady at the magazine's HQ in Covent Garden, got up to defend herself from attacks from her proprietor, Julia Budworth.

Brothers Boris and Jo were there to offer support, as brothers sometimes do, as well as father Stanley. 'It was the speech of her life,' said MP Jo. 'She has *cojones*.'

In the presence of Mrs Budworth, Rachel addressed Julia's charge that she is stupid, mad and obsessed with penises. 'I want to offer her a huge vote of thanks for so energetically addressing herself to the tiresome business of publicity,' said editor Johnson, pointing out that in her year in the job, sales have risen from 28,000 to 35,000. She then thanked her darling husband Ivo Dawnay for helping her manage her penis obsession.

After the editor's rallying speech in the crowded front room of *The Lady*'s elegant but eccentric premises, Mrs Budworth retired to a private room which she had decorated herself with *Vanity Fair* drawings, and a window painted with an English country scene.

Here she held court among admirers. 'What I object to is Rachel saying I have Dralon chair coverings,' said Mrs Budworth, a cousin of the Duchess of Devonshire. 'Please can you find Rachel so that I can show her I don't have any Dralon.'

Rachel declined a visit to the headmistress's study on the grounds that she had had enough confrontation for one day but a family member said she probably doesn't know what Dralon is.

When congratulated on the acres of publicity her outburst had caused, Mrs Budworth, who confessed that she wouldn't have minded being editor herself, said that wasn't the idea at all. 'I just want to kill Rachel for putting all sorts of unsuitable stuff in *The Lady*.'

The Lady

26 OCTOBER 2010 £1.80

MICHAEL CAINE MEETS
Justin Webb

BUTTERFLY MAGIC
in search of fritillaries

ROSE PRINCE
kitchen sisters

GIDDY WIDDY

Ann Widdecombe spins for the nation

LUCIAN FREUD
painted my portrait

GRAHAM GREENE · RAFFAELLA BARKER · ANTONIA FRASER · CHRISTINA FOYLE
MARY KILLEN · HUNDREDS OF HOLIDAY AND JOB ADVERTISEMENTS EACH WEEK

OCTOBER

5 October 2010

Ben called and asked me to go through to the boardroom.

'I called you in to say sorry,' he said. 'I've got something for you.' I toddled through, then he enveloped me in a spine-cracking bear hug. 'I shouldn't have done that,' he said. 'If I was going to shout at you it should have been in here with the door closed.'

Ben did shout at me – yesterday, I think. To be fair, he's had to put up with a lot. I forgave him instantly for shouting at me. I can't remember what I'd done. I can't remember why he shouted at me. It could have been any number of things. But as far as I was concerned, it was over.

'Don't worry in the slightest,' I said.

'And don't worry, you – this will pass,' he said (talking about the press cooking up the row between me and Mrs B.). 'These things are like a hot air mass meeting a cold front.' He always keeps a close eye on meteorological websites, just as he does air traffic control sites. 'It always creates a storm before it clears the air.'

6 October 2010

Up early to do *Daybreak* with Adrian Chiles and Christine Bleakley. Was airbrushed with brown paint beforehand, then went on set. It was freezing. 'I'm freezing but we have to keep the whole place this cold because he sweats,' grins Christine, showing a dazzling set of tombstone gnashers. I shield my eyes and regard Chiles, who looks at me, the autocue, and all his guests with a sort of questing sweetness, like a guinea pig who has lost his carrot. They sit clamped together so everyone else feels like a gooseberry. I have only agreed to go on because I have negotiated that I will be allowed to plug my book. I would never have gone on normally as 1. No one watches *Daybreak* and I hate getting up early, and 2. It was my least favourite subject under discussion – sibling rivalry – a topic I normally will not touch with a bargepole, but I knew I must promote my book.

They asked me a few questions about sibling rivalry. These I answered through gritted teeth. Then, that was it, they were saying thank you for coming. This wasn't the deal at all!

I fixed Chiles with a glare and mouthed, 'Book!' and he then segued into *The Lady* and the book and I got my plug in. But only at the personal cost to me of revealing to the world that darling Mama tried to get me to iron my brothers' shirts for 50p a pop but never asked them to do it themselves.

In other news, someone is now tweeting as @JuliaBudworth, mainly about penises.

7 October 2010

The in tray:

- letter from Mrs B. thanking me for inviting her to my 'book promotion party' in which she explains, 'I only went into the "cupboard" sitting room because of the noise, where I was very soon joined by Coco. So clever of her to find me among hundreds of people!' I like the implication that, given a choice, Coco would prefer to be with Mrs. B than me, her mistress.

She encloses a nice letter from 97-year-old Eva O'Reilly, who has written to me before. (Miss O'Reilly has very fond memories of roasting swans, etc. at Deerbolts Hall for Willie's twenty-first birthday party.) 'See you soon at the Lit Lunch,' she threatens. 'Renewed thanks for your invitation. Julia.' The PS reads, 'I am sorry not to have been invited to the contributors' party.'

Ed's note: what contributors' party?

8 October 2010

Went to a signing/reading thing in Heywood Hill, the Duke of Devonshire's wood-panelled and storied bookshop at 10 Curzon Street, where Nancy Mitford worked for years, in the heart of Mayfair. A woman called Bev came and to my delight told me she used to work at *The Lady*.

'I was the literary editor, and in charge of the annual short story competition,' she said, reminding me of another much-loved feature, such as 'Favourite Things', that I have killed stone dead since my arrival. 'We used to get hundreds of submissions from readers about wives who murdered their husbands. I used to regard the competition as a form of marital therapy.'

She also said that at Christmas, Uncle Tom Bowles would invite the staff up to his apartments. 'The floor show was always a lady with a banjo. She would strum the banjo and dance, and at the end she would raise her skirts and show us all her khaki bloomers,' said Bev. 'Tom Bowles would sit there entranced.'

Now I know why Chrissie, chief sub, called Mr Bowles 'Tombola'. He has a sort of fin de siècle, end of the pier, White Cliffs of Dover side to him I had never spotted up till now.

20 October 2010

Email from a reader in Nottingham who has attended something called a '*Lady* Research Group' (something I never knew was happening – Ben never tells me anything any more.)

Good Morning All,

I attended the above discussion group and would just like to say thank you for my 'goody bag' and the opportunity to join in something so positive.

I am currently reading Rachel's diary and am aware that the average age is perceived to be 78 . . . well, fear not . . . I am a 41-year-old single mum (a mere stripling), run my own mobile spray tan business and internet boutique, and love to party!

The Lady to me is a breath of fresh air and it is great to read about something other than sex . . . let's face it, there are only so many times you can rework that one!

I was introduced to the magazine by my neighbour who is 72 and a former Matron of Rugby School . . . two generations enjoying the same magazine is a job well done!

Looking forward to the next edition,

Kind regards,
Michele

PS More Kirstie Allsopp (Phil Spencer would be an added bonus but don't want to be greedy!), Cath Kidston-type things, please . . . will 'pass' on dormice!

The in tray:

* a letter from a reader in Esher:

Dear Rachel,

If you have finished collapsing with laughter about 'your' diary (as told to Craig Brown) you might care to turn your attention to other matters. If so, I may be able to help. With Christmas approaching, I have an ideal short story that you might care to fit in. Called *Stranger in the Night* (enc.), its theme is events centred on one Christmas Eve. And if that fails to attract you, I have a cheerful and amusing short story titled *A Slight Case of Sexual Discrimination* (also enc.).
Signed Dudley Paget-Brown

PS I was an editor much younger than you, Rachel; at 12 years of age. My first paid job (£1.10s) a week after leaving school was just round the corner from you in Southampton St.

Mr Paget-Brown attaches his CV. I read it. It reveals that in 1936 he was the founder editor of the world's first colour aviation magazine, *Flight Gazette*. Circulation was 11 copies. I totally HEART Mr Paget-Brown!

* a submission for a piece about women who have sheds, which begins: 'A woman's place is in the shed.'

22 October 2010

Suddenly got in a panic about Monday's literary lunch, at which Quentin Letts, Allison Pearson and Virginia McKenna are speaking – and myself. As I said a couple of days ago, it seems that people have completely stopped telling me what's going on. I've even stopped getting the round-robin about net sales and the circulation figures (not that I understand them). I had no idea what was going to happen at the lunch. Then I had a panic email from Quentin Letts, also wondering.

So I emailed the mag's Dorset-based events organizer, Mr Andrew Kaye, to ask what the order of service was on the day.

Mr Kaye replied that the timetable will be as follows:

11:45 Speakers and their publicists arrive for briefing and meeting each other as well as *The Lady*'s senior management.

12:00 Guests arrive to be handed a complimentary drink and buy the speakers' latest books from the Foyles Bookshop stand in the room. The speakers will be encouraged to sit at a special table signing those books – liquid sustenance provided as required!

13:00 Guests seated for lunch at rounds for 10. I shall guide our guest speakers to the 'top table' – which will also be a round for 10. The rounds work well as everyone can talk to each other.

13:05 Rachel Johnson, editor of *The Lady*, will welcome the assembled and the three-course lunch will begin. Rather than the speakers doing their thing one after the other during coffee, we have found that it works better if the speeches happen between the courses.

After the Starter, Rachel will introduce and invite Allison Pearson to speak (for 10 minutes). After the Main, it will be Quentin Letts' turn and after the Sweet, it will be Virginia McKenna and finally Rachel Johnson.

The speakers will have the benefit of a lectern (with microphones) close to the top table. A sound engineer at the back of the room will be adjusting for level and quality.

When all speeches are concluded there will be a quick draw for a cruise (courtesy of the sponsors) and I shall wish the assembled a fond farewell.

15:40 The event should be over. However, books will still be on sale courtesy of Foyles and some guests may still want their new purchases signed and so the final finishing time may be nearer **15:50**.

Much as I enjoyed it, I decided against sending it to Letts. I was sure he would enjoy the 'Main and Sweet' elements of the missive as much as I did, but I worried when he saw the extended timetable he would panic despite the lure of the 'complimentary drink' and decide to bail.

24 October 2010

Today I did *Pienaar's Politics*, a Radio Five Live show, which goes out live in the evening. I took Ludo to the BBC Millbank Studios with me (he hopes to read politics at university), having made him remove his stained yellow T-shirt saying 'sex and drugs and sausage rolls' on it and put on a nice, Jack Wills, pink striped number With Collar. Jonathan Powell – promoting his own book, a Machiavellian interpretation of power – was down the line from Plymouth. Also in the studio was the punchy Shadow Justice Secretary Sadiq Khan, who very disconcertingly kept saying as the programme progressed, 'I can't find a single word to disagree with what Rachel Johnson is saying.' At the end of the show the drummer from Blur came on and preambled his remarks to a large audience of Radio Bloke by saying, 'I asked my wife if she'd heard of RJ and so on and she said, "Yes, she's Boris's sister and edits *The Lady* and is the new Carol Thatcher."'

I heard Jonathan Powell snort with pleasure down the line as he delivered the blow to the head (sister of Boris) and then the punch to the stomach (new Carol Thatcher).

Anyway, turns out the drummer from Blur headlined Glasto last year and this year is training to be a solicitor.

'It's not very Keith Richards,' I observed.

Powell was quicker off the mark than me. 'You're just doing a Tony Blair in reverse,' he said. 'He only became a lawyer because he couldn't cut it as a rock star.'

25 October 2010

The Literary Lunch.

Just back from four-hour lunch at the Institute of Directors in the presence of Mrs Budworth, Ben, her four cousins, assorted jaded diary hacks, and about 180 Lady readers. To talk about my book in front of Mrs B., who has publicly announced via multiple media outlets that she'd rather slit her wrists than read it – and 'so would all her friends'.

So, a bit of a tough gig in the circs. Allison was superb and managed to be modest and funny about the fact that I Don't Know How She Does It is being turned into Hollywood blockbuster with Sarah Jessica Parker as harried juggling Mom. Then it was Letts' turn. He kicked things off by saying that I'd been causing trouble at The Lady, at which point Mrs B. nodded vigorously in assent. Then he went into a riff about how The Lady offices were at war and needed the services of Javier Perez de Cuellar as a peace negotiator – there was laughter. Then the laughter dried up because as he was speaking about Perez de Cuellar (and everyone was trying to remember who he was) a Lady luncheon guest keeled over. She fell backwards in her chair, hit the decks and lay flat on her back. I'm afraid to say it looked from Table A as if she had died. Edwina jumped to her feet and called an ambulance. Then the luncheon attendee seemed to come round, which was good news, but she started being sick, which was less good news. Someone had the presence of mind to pass the water jug from Table E (round of ten) to the Table J (round of ten). She filled the water jug and it was placed on the table with a napkin decorously covering the mouth of the jug.

Those of us on top table sat in silence, wondering what to do. Whether we should go on with the entertaining speeches, or whether we should abandon ship.

'That jug is like a chalice of chunder,' said Letts.

Some paramedics arrived, and the guest was stretchered off. Letts finished his speech as if nothing had happened, Virgina McKenna did her turn – which was a bit airy-fairy – then me. I gave it a bit of welly but had to go into the Mrs Budworth saga a bit, which was gruelling, as she was sitting in front of me, boot-faced. When I came back to my seat Allison Pearson patted me. 'Don't worry, it's all right. She's like the *Graf Spee*,' she said. 'Unsinkable.'

As the events had been so delayed by the *Lady* collapse, I made Andrew Kaye speed things up so McKenna talked over pudding and me ditto. It was all a bit hairy, and I didn't get many laughs (or so I felt).

On the way back to the office, as we walked though T. Square, Ben said, 'You're still not getting there, Rach. Have you had media training? I'm going to send you on a day's media training. Remind me to set some up, will you?'

The in tray:

- a box of biscuits from Biscuit Village offering me a 15 per cent discount on 'all biscuit products'.
- a letter from reader who heard me on *Saturday Live* and wrote to tell me that she used to buy *The Lady* in the local Bilsby Post Office & Village Shop run by a Gill Marsh but that Mrs Marsh no longer stocks it.

28 October 2010

Only just recovered from the Lit Lunch.

Allison Pearson emailed:

Dear Hostess with the Mostest,

What a swell party it was. I had a wonderful time. St Trinian's Goes to the Golan Heights. You must have such a hoot. No wonder you wrote a book about it.

And I am a little in love with Ben. Is that normal?

Please remind me of the Joan Collins anecdote. Who did the secretary put through instead?

Be nice to do a column item – lots of overlap twixt *Telegraph* and *Lady*.

Thank you again, I would not have missed it . . .

Allison x

There was a bit in 'Londoner's Diary' about the woman keeling over during Letts' speech. And Mrs B. is also quoted in 'Londoner's Diary' after my talk as saying, 'Rachel's so boring, isn't she? She only ever talks about herself.'

I slept for eleven straight hours Monday night, then stayed home all week with the children – it was half term, after all.

Re: Joy, the woman who keeled over (Gillian has already rung to find out how she is, and has offered her a free ticket to the next literary lunch – if there is one, that is), Ben said, 'I was all for covering the old dear with a tablecloth and carrying on.'

The Lady

16 NOVEMBER 2010   £1.80

...as read at
DOWNTON ABBEY

HEALTH
Eyesight special

The new
LADY ALMANAC

Samantha Bond
KISSING 007

WHO'S THE DADDY?
Ivana Lowell

SEX ON A STICK
LORD BATH IN HOT WATER

Candy canes &
Christmas trees
FESTIVE FOOD

FEAST AT FORTNUM'S • MAUREEN LIPMAN • CANDIA MCWILLIAM • PATSY SEDDON
KIKO ITASAKA • HUNDREDS OF HOLIDAY AND JOB ADVERTISEMENTS EACH WEEK

November

NOVELLER

1 November 2010

Matt Warren has arrived! So the Male from the *Mail* is in situ and tearing through copy, rewriting, dealing with freelancers, telling me that it's got to be more newsy . . . phew! Such a relief. Carolyn and I have been alone in Editorial since April and are worn out. Have 300 emails sitting in a folder called 'pitches' and feel a bit more in control. A bit.

Matt had a piece in *The Spectator* about how much he hated his cat so I have commissioned a companion column to 'Coco's Corner' for him to write – on the grounds that Coco's column is the only popular thing I've done with readers young and old, existing and new – about his cat, Eric. I have decided that the col will be the 'Matt on Cat' and they will tweet, both as @CatonMatt and @MattonCat, about each other.

Chrissie, the chief sub, came in this morning to resign as chief sub, though she'll soldier on two days a week. She has been carrying too heavy a burden for too long – and anyway, one sub has to go and she wants it to be her.

'I'm just sorry the cut has to be you,' I said. I like Chrissie very much. She has a very good ear for the marmalade-dropper and, for example, made us take out a joke about anal sex in the Joan Rivers copy for this issue (it was all about how Rivers was all in favour because you could get on with other stuff like answering emails, filing nails during anal). As the joke wasn't good, I was happy to take it out but I continue to think that if you interview Joan Rivers, you're going to have to accept a fair degree of smut because that's what she does.

Chrissie also held up a yellow card at Rivers' reference to Michael Jackson as a 'fucking pederast' in the same piece. Given that Mrs B. got our workie Jess Lambert to spend a whole morning looking for the word 'arsehole' that is probably very wise of Chrissie, and has saved us all earache (and some poor workie weeks of hassle).

The in tray:

- four cupcakes from a reader who wants to contribute a craft blog or 'How to' page that will show readers how to create 'easy yet elegant handmade crafty projects' and enclosing photos of examples, to wit: cupcakes to impress your friends during a pre-polo picnic; hand-beaded flower tiara to wear to a ball; simple sailor bag for Cowes; and a fascinator at Ascot.
- a sweet, shamefaced letter from Joy, the reader who fainted during Quentin Letts' speech: 'Dear Madam, I expect that you heard I was taken ill and fainted while attending the literary lunch?' The letter continued, saying she'd never fainted before and lamenting the fact that her friend, Mrs Glaister, had to miss the occasion as well as Joy. 'Will we be allowed to come again?' she asks. Of course – Gillian has sent free tickets for both Joy and Mrs Glaister.
- a reader from Louth, Lincs, asking me where he can buy type-writer ribbons, saying, 'I am positive they are still manufactured.' I'm on it!

2 November 2010

Feel gloomy. Could be the clocks going back.

'I took the credit this morning rather than Sunday,' said Ben smugly, as I crawled in on Monday morning, after the customary five-hour drive from Exmoor, which involved the M5, M4, M25 as per usual and this time the M3, then the M25, and M4 in that order as we were returning master Oliver to Wellington after his two-week (yes, that's right, TWO WEEK) half term.

The EPOS figures are not in yet but it looks like Audrey Hepburn is down on Sandra Howard, who was down on Coco Chanel. So is the direction of travel is BACKWARDS, and SOUTH, again?

Matt is here and we don't have anywhere for him to go. He's in the sulphurous 'cab's office' at the moment where, as he has pointed out, damp is creeping down the walls and it smells like rotten eggs. I want him to be near me, i.e., near Carolyn and Gillian and within shouting distance. But as Claire points out, if Ben takes down the wall between Carolyn/Gillian and Judy, there is a staircase in the way. 'And we lose the fashion cupboard,' I said, throwing open a door to reveal three four-way stretch nighties, some Slendcrella long johns and Judy's Puffa jacket on a wire hanger.

3 November 2010

Just sent a testy email to Ben because Helen Robinson, the stunning blonde glamazon head of sales who has become his Ladywife, wants to have an editorial sales special, i.e., travel, motoring, care homes, dental, bridal, packing for travel, retirement homes, etc., etc., EVERY WEEK while Ben wants us to cut our subbing strength by a third. These two positions are incompatible and poor Chrissie is chain-smoking Silkies on the Maiden Lane stoop as it is.

'I'd like to have a meeting tomorrow if poss to discuss the continuous extra workload Helen's ambition to have an editorial sales spesh every week will place on the team at a time when you're cutting down on subs. I think we have a potentially serious roadblock here. If we are to have so many editorial specials, presumably they will bring in enough dosh to pay for a fourth sub – at least, when required?' I said.

Ben has not answered.

The in tray:

- mince pies from Betty's of Harrogate.
- Christmas pudding from Betty's.
- three boxes chocs. YAY!!!
- offer from pet company to send Coco new hypo-allergenic dog bed and fur-wipes to keep her clean between baths, and meanwhile Matt has arranged for Coco to have a set of canine beauty treatments at Harrods.

4 November 2010

Ben and Hels disappeared yesterday to the Forge – the restaurant opposite the Garrick where he conducted the 'I have a bream' series of interviews – to be presented with the marketing results from the focus group I didn't know about.

I do not know if they all had a bream but this is, I think, significant.

5 November 2010

Meeting with Hels about these editorial sales specials – on dental, bridal, funerals, heart and stroke, etc. – that are driving Chrissie and now Matt into early graves. Why can't we have education, health and property, and rotate them like normal magazines? She wants us to do a cruising special and a long-haul special, which could mean going up eight pages every week while Ben wants to cut the subs.

It's not going to work, and I told her so. 'I'm not going to send freelancers on long-haul holidays or cruises and pay them,' I said.

Then I saw red mist. 'I know, why don't you and Ben go on a cruise together? Round the world. Go for at least six weeks!'

She laughed. She was wearing a clingy purple dress and high heels and a lot of paste jewellery, and a feather boa was hanging on the back of her door.

'Are you going to a party tonight?' I asked.

'No,' she said, 'lunch with Terry Wogan.'

We worked through the list till we came to an item in February called 'Pets on Holiday', to which she wanted to devote six pages of ads and six of editorial. I stopped and gasped. 'Pets on holiday!' I screeched. 'Twelve pages?'

She gave me a steady look. 'Lots of people take their pets abroad these days,' she said. 'My friend Denise always takes her red setter, Rafferty.'

Email from Howard Jacobson. I'd seen him at a talk I'd given at The Tabernacle in Notting Hill at the 5x15 series of events. I had to go first, and was followed by the authors Diana Athill and Howard Jacobson, both of whom had turned me down when I asked them to be columnists, and Jacobson had just won the Booker – so no pressure there, then. Afterwards I'd schmoozed Howard at the dinner and asked him again, and he'd sort of said yes. Well, he hadn't said a flat no anyway.

I dug out my original email to him. On 5 November 2010, at 15:46, Rachel Johnson wrote:

Dear Howard

Were you serious? Restaurant review?

What would your terms be?

Please say yes. I'm yours.
Rachel

Then I got this:

Rachel –

How very nice to hear from you. Fun the other night, I thought.

I was serious at the time, yes. I would have said then that I'd previously commanded £1,000 per review plus cost of meal for two and travel expenses, and wouldn't do it for less.

In fact, I couldn't do it now anyway – don't have a minute to call my own. When and if that will change I don't know. But were it to, at least you know where I'd be starting from.

Warmest
Howard

9 November 2010

Roger Lewis says he hasn't read my book but 'lots of people tell me I'm the best thing in it'. I've asked him to interview Dame Edna Everage about the hell of being a woman.

Message from Maureen:

Hi Everyone,

Our usual telephone cleaning lady is on holiday and we have a replacement for her who has not been here before. He is in the building now, starting in the Classified Department. I have instructed him to go up to Editorial, up again to the second floor across to Display and then down to Accounts, where I will see him and check what he has done.

If he looks a bit lost, can you guide him to the next office or floor?

If the replacement telephone cleaning man gets lost in this Bermuda Triangle of a building, you can be sure of one thing – he'll never be seen again.

10 *November* 2010

Adam is moving into Bedford Street, so we will be seeing a lot more of Madam (my name for Adam as he has luxuriant dark locks).

Chrissie has been told again by Ben to cut down our subbing strength to three subs, on the grounds that *The Oldie* has two. She has bought *The Oldie* and established that there are 46 pages of editorial that the subs have to work on, out of 90 in total. This is almost exactly the same ratio that pertains at *The Lady*: 44 pages of editorial out of a total of 90.

Only, *The Lady* comes out four times a month, and *The Oldie* only once. I think – well, I hope – this wins the argument.

When I told Ben, he knocked it down immediately. '*The Oldie* has one sub who works two weeks per month on the title, another week on admin and the final week on their books,' he told me.

So I told Chrissie Hels' (i.e., Helen Robinson's) line, which is that the subs have to be more efficient. When Chrissie shrieked in outrage, I also let slip that Helen had revealed that she wants Matt Warren (the Male from the *Mail*) to write all the pages and pages of advertorial on dental and bridal that she wants us to run every week. I told Matt immediately, of course, and he paled. 'And for this you left the *Daily Mail*,' I teased him. 'To write the twelve-page Death Supplement.' (That's what the care-home special has been called since the dawn of time.)

The in tray:

- offer of a piece explaining how to make a Christmas Crib with Sellotape, MDF, acrylic paint and a cardboard box with

upright figures of Jesus, Mary, Joseph, lambs and shepherds, etc.
- letter to Coco from a reader in Gorleston, Norfolk, saying, 'How delighted I was to see the lovely picture of you on the front cover of *The Lady*. I have been a reader for many years.'
- a letter from a woman called 'Anges' de Lumiere, and a paper-back book that 'revolutionizes the world of slimming by offering a true mind, body, spirit and integrated approach' and a plug for a book called *The Journey of the Slim Soul* which tells women that it is only through self-love they can ever attain any hope of being permanently slim.
- a letter marked 'Personal' from Deerbolts Hall from Mrs B. – who I'd graciously asked to contribute a Diary:

Dear Rachel,
The Lady Diary

On reflection, how would it be if I guest-edited the anniversary issue in mid-February, instead of a Diary in mid-January? If Coco can do it, so can I. Let me know what you think and what the procedure is. All this, of course, is assuming that *The Lady* is still afloat by mid-Feb!
   The last few issues (she ends conciliatorily) have been so (underlined three times) much better, especially the covers, which is encouraging.

I write back, thanking her for her generous offer of editing the magazine instead of me, but declining it.

11 November 2010

Stuart Rose the Silver Fox has emailed me to tell me he is chasing his people to have *The Lady* put inside M&S. Which is great (but very expensive for us, according to publisher Ben) as M&S is very selective. His email ends with an emoticon.

I notice that in our edition this week there is a full-page advertisement for a forthcoming Lady Taverners event at which I have been persuaded to speak by Hels, who is the event organizer for the Taverners. I notice there is also a photograph of Hels on p. 55, modelling a large black and violet scarf 'beautifully made in the heart of England from the finest crêpe de Chine' according to the advertorial.

'Doing your bit as publisher, I see,' I said to Ben. 'You know I've been roped in to a Taverners lunch?' I had been, months before, and had been staring bleakly at the date in the diary as it approached.

'Stop whingeing. You'll sell loads of books at the Chaveners,' he replied.

16 November 2010

Prince William has asked Kate Middleton to marry him. Therefore, tonight I am doing *Evening Standard* 1,000 London Influentials party followed by *Newsnight*, then tomorrow BBC Manchester followed by the *Daybreak* sofa. Even though I once told *Guardian* editor Alan Rusbridger earnestly when I was a BBC reporter that I used to hate rent-a-quotes who'd turn up to the studio and say anything to get on air or their mug on TV, I now accept far too many requests and therefore break my own rule ('don't go on unless you've got something to say') many times a week, in the interests of what the PRs call 'building the brand'.

Have been in touch with Sarah Sands, deputy editor, to ask her which dreaded category of *Standard* Influentials I'd been placed in this year. Last year it was Party Blondes or something, which made me sound like a hooker.

'Darling, you're in World Leader category,' she teased.

Keep trying to reach Ben to agree line on Middlebum. In interviews, I've been saying that we're thrilled (I start every sentence with that) about Royal Wedding but that Waity K hasn't done much of note so far except nail her Prince. And that from *The Lady* POV that's not enough. We are only interested in Women of Substance who have Done Something With Their Lives, not skinny Marlburians who waited eight long years for their Prince to come and propose. Having said that, I am very impressed. She played the long game. Mentally remind self to commission feature 'How to Marry a Prince' from my sister Julia, who is Kate's age and has just got married after eight-year courtship too. (Answer in Kate Middleton's case was, I think, eat pizza, put out, shut up.)

17 November 2010

OH MY GOD! Piers the IT guy has spotted something so ghastly, I can only hope and pray Mrs B. hasn't seen it. In our cover story on Lord Bath – he's on crutches, and Carolyn came up with the brilliant line 'Sex on a Stick' – there is a spread inside and the full-page opening photo is of the Loins of Longleat holding a paint-encrusted palette, wearing a Liberty-print waistcoat over a plaid shirt. It's such a busy image that neither Tammy, nor Claire, nor designer Maria, noticed that he is standing against a backdrop of one of his murals. On the mural Lord Bath has depicted his trademark scenes of carnivalesque depravity in hideous impasto. A black man is buggering a girl on all fours, who is sucking the cock of a man with orange hair and a beard and a blazing hearth of orange pubes. There are three other carnal scenes with exaggerated genitalia all too visible.

I used to be able to laugh off Mrs Budworth's charges that I am penis-obsessed as the ravings of a woman who lived on her own for far too long in a big house Suffolk. Now – after this pornographic spread that would make Bob Guccione himself blush – I have not a leg to stand on.

Am in such dilemma whether to put Kate Middleton on cover. I'd really prefer Carole Middleton. She's a former air hostess who's made millions out of a mail-order website, kept herself tidy and produced the next Queen. She's done something. It would be *The Lady*'s brave stand against snobbery – the BBC is openly using terms like 'self-made' and 'commoner' with reference to the Berkshire Middletons. On those grounds alone, Carole Middleton is more than cover-worthy.

When I went in to see Ben, ready to collapse in a heap over the appearance of the Loins in his mag and beg forgiveness for the slip, Piers our IT guy pushed open the door and flipped the magazine open before I'd opened my mouth in penitence. He laid the magazine open on the blue baize so we could all get an eyeful.

'If you look carefully we've got a spit roast, a woman rimming a black man, and buggery, all on one page of *The Lady*,' he said, pointing to the offending scenes. 'The best thing is the way the Lord Bath figure with the orange beard and pubes is high-fiving the girl who's giving him a blow job, as if to say, YEAH! YEAH!' Piers roared.

'We're *DOING* this.' We all laughed helplessly. What else could we do?

Have decided to stick with Amanda Foreman cover and not go for a Carole one. Rushed to somewhere called the Ministry of Waxing to have a tidy up in preparation for writing piece for *Vogue* about downstairs grooming protocols.

The in tray:

- a cushion from The Heraldry Society saying HEAD GIRL.
- a letter from a reader in Winchester asking me where she can find a winter trouser suit in a bright colour such as pink or blue.
- copy of *Rowan Knitting & Crochet Magazine*.

22 November 2010

Had to speak at the literary lunch, held at the Ivy, by *The Week*. Other guest was Matthew Parris, always a delight. We scoffed haddock and egg tartlets then hearty individual shepherd's pies that Parris complained were made of beef not lamb. At 2.45 p.m. I was almost falling off my chair, I was so sleepy. I got up and told the story about Lord Bath.

Then I got back to the office, watched the DVD that Sky ARTS sent me of *The Book Show*. They'd come in and shot a whole segment in Bedford Street. At the end of the package, Mariella's other guests – Judith Kerr, Jilly Cooper and Salman Rushdie – sat there looking rather stunned at the amount of time they'd had to sit and watch me prance about the boudoir and talk about Stella Gibbons, and so on. The package was about eight minutes long, and was very lovingly done.

Mariella picked up off the back of the package by asking her distinguished panel wasn't it odd *The Lady* still published, despite our classless society, etc.? They looked a bit flummoxed, then Salman managed, 'My favourite magazine is *Milady's Boudoir*,' (the fictional PGW title) and Jilly sweetly said I'd had a horrid press and was a very nice person.

The heater had been on all day and it was baking in my office where Matt Warren, Male from the *Mail*, is working as there's still nowhere else for him to sit. 'It's hot in here,' I complained, switching off my heater.

'Yes, it's freezing till about four and then even I start having hot flushes,' said Matt.

The in tray:

- lavender-filled doorstop.
- an unsolicited piece about the advantages of storage heaters

and the challenge of planting a northeast-facing garden, by a reader from Lewes.

24 November 2010

Off to the Portobello Rugby Fair on Westbourne Grove to flog copies of my book. All very festive with yummy mummies surging around with cheese straws and canapés, Veronica Faulks selling Christmas decorations, my columnists Clemmie Hambro and Sof McVeigh selling pot plants, and *le tout* Notting Hell mingling. I was up on the stage in the books and baubles zone. The other author was the Israeli cook Yotam Ottolenghi. Bookseller/agents Felicity Rubinstein and Sarah Lutyens were both in their Lutyens & Rubinstein aprons. When I got there Yotam Ottolenghi, in close-fitting V-neck and even nattier stubble, had been there for ages and was doing terribly well. It was hot cakes for him. Everyone kept coming up and drooling over his book with its mouthwatering spreads of chargrilled beef with chermoula scattered with jewel-like pomegranate seeds, etc.

'It's a lovely book,' they would say and buy several copies.

'So's Rachel's,' Felicity would say loyally.

Occasionally a Notting Hill matron with blow-dried hair and Georgina Von Etzdorf scarf would come up to inspect me, say something direct like, 'I voted for your brother,' as if they expected me to congratulate them, and walk off without buying my book.

25 November 2010

After checking in with Ben in the boardroom this morning I was heading back to the boudoir and he stopped me and asked me if I would be around later.

'Why?' I asked.

'Oh, only because my old headmaster from Cothill, Adrian Richardson, is coming in for lunch,' he said. 'Mum's sent him, to keep order.'

I was working quietly in the boudoir, writing 'Coco's Corner' – about going to an appointment at Harrods Pet Spa today (each canine slot is 2.5 hours – they must wash and dry each hair individually) – when I heard fruity, upper-class tones outside. Then a tall man with a Guards Officer bearing hove into sight. It turned out Ben's old headman had taught English at Ashdown House – where I'd been the first girl boarder – and knew everyone, so we got on like a house on fire.

29 November 2010

Sat next to the junior oligarch Evgeny Lebedev at a dinner for the *Evening Standard* Theatre Awards given by Louis Vuitton, held above the shop at 17–20 New Bond St in exquisite, black-lacquered apartment filled with white flowers and famous thesps: Imogen Stubbs, John Suchet, Roger Allam (the actor who played the slightly sleazy author in *Tamara Drewe*, a film which sent Ivo into a fury when we watched it, and had him leaving the cinema complaining audibly, 'I'm fat and old too, so why aren't I fucking Gemma Arterton?').

Loved Evgeny. Had two-hour chat about his love life. Then I told him about the business conundrum that is *The Lady*: one sister and her four sons co-own the title, the brother lives upstairs and still owns all the property, i.e., the collateral. We talked about circulation, covers, etc. I explained that the title was ancestral and that everyone loved *The Lady* because it was like *Downton Abbey*, a reminder of a universe where everyone knew their place and where people were looked after. He appeared to think about all this. Then he said, 'I can see only one solution to your liquidity problems,' and I said, 'Yes, yes,' waiting for a proper *Dragons' Den*-type answer. 'You must push that old uncle down the stairs,' he said.

At the end of dinner I went home with mischievous Emily Sheffield (the Sam Cam sis who works on *Vogue*) and husband Tom and left one of my new, expensive, green leather gloves in the taxi but am too shy to be a bore and call them to see if they picked it up.

Call from Ben, Saturday morning. 'There I was, stood in the shower, thinking it was all set fair, the credit line in place, the business plan for next year squared off, and my iPhone gives me a Google Alert . . .'

I'd already seen it.

His secret half-sister has given two pages to the *Mail* under the headline '*The Lady* and the Lovechild'. It is about his secret half-sister Kathy, who is the illegitimate daughter of his father and the district nurse. Everyone emerges with credit, apart from perhaps Mr Budworth *père*, who doesn't seem to have provided for Kathy terribly much after he died in a light aircraft accident. Kathy (and I am going by the *Mail* here) only found out her father had died when she came in and found her mother, the nurse, sobbing over the paper. Mrs B. tried to adopt Kathy (she had five boys) and sent her a cheque after the insurance money from the plane crash came through. I said that Mrs B. comes out of it best of all – as a cross between selfless materfamilias and living saint – and told Ben as much.

'Yes, Mum does come out of it very well,' agreed Ben, 'if you read the *Mail*. She's also knocked eight years off her age and has gained a title (indeed she has: as the Budworth eruption has progressed through newsprint, she has segued from Mrs B. to Lady Budworth and this morning was called Lady Julia, as if daughter of an earl) as well as being the driving force and proprietor of *The Lady*.'

I fluffed Ben for a bit and then we both hung up.

Later took train to Cambridge in sub-zero temperatures to

address the CUCA termly knees-up in Peterhouse Hall. Hadn't really – as usual – prepared a speech. King's Cross was spattered with sick and signs saying we are working to improve your station everywhere (I'm always working to improve my station too – ha ha – which is why I find myself on trains to Oxbridge colleges on Saturday nights). Was shown into panelled Fellow's guest room with dressing room and lovely bathroom to change. But it was so cold I sat in my coat and during dinner had to wear two more coats donated by gallants of the Cambridge University Conservative Association, and Milly's nylon Topshop tippet. Everyone was joking about Clegg. 'I wrote to him, offering to convert his CUCA membership into lifetime sub, but he never wrote back,' one handsome boy told me. According to Fergus McGhee, the charming white-tied chairman, he only joined because someone else paid for him, so he could vote for them. 'He's such a Tory,' he concluded.

In Hall, it was so cold I could see my nostril breath. We ate duck pâté, then I glanced at the menu and it said 'Quail FFS' for what Andrew Kaye would call 'the Main'. 'What does FFS stand for?' I asked. 'For fuck's sake,' said Fergus. 'That's what it's always called in the *Guardian* Diary when they write up this dinner.' After Quail For Fuck's Sake we had a suite of Sweets: panna cotta, devils on horseback, coffee, chocolates and port. At the appearance of the port, we all stood up and gave the Loyal Toast, which was my cue to get up on hind legs.

Whenever I said something remotely funny they all banged the tables, like Cameron said they did in Cabinet at the announcement of the Royal *fiançailles*. It was so cold in the guest rooms at Peterhouse that I decided to train it back to London that night. The next day, flowers and a card arrived from the Cantab Tories from outgoing CUCA chairman Fergus: 'I do hope there was enough warmth in our welcome to make up for the college's glaciality . . .' and admitting that he and his boyfriend Nicky 'had a wonderful time' in my Fellow's guest room in my absence.

Fergus will clearly go far.

30 November 2010

Email from Maureen:

To: All staff
Subject: [allstaff] Crackling phone line
Reply-To: Maureen Goodman

Hi,

I have not forgotten the crackling on the lines and I have already been in touch with BT this morning and told them off for leaving us struggling with the crackling line. They said I will definitely have a man today.

Maureen

To the Bad Sex Party, always held, for old times' sake, at the In & Out Club. As a previous title-holder (I won in 2008 for *Shire Hell*) I enjoy going. It brings back fond memories of winning jointly with John Updike and making a triumphal speech which I concluded by telling *The Wire*'s Dominic West, who handed me my prize of a heavy plaster foot, 'If you ever want Bad Sex, there's plenty of it at my house.'

However, it wasn't as jolly this year – my mood was lowered by Sebastian Shakespeare, my ex, who told me about some item in the *Bookseller*, sneering about how few copies my book had sold. So I told him – mainly to rally self – that there was a nice review in this week's *TLS*.

'*The Times Literary Supplement*?' he reeled back, as if could not hear me right, or I was making it up.

'Yes,' I affirmed. Though inside, I felt cast down. My book must have sold even fewer copies than Gordon Brown's last tome. I have to face it. Not even my mother bought a copy.

Came in today to find the cover crisis has been sorted by Carolyn. She's sourced a beautiful vintage image of a woman quaffing (no other word seems apt) a goblet of champagne to go with our feature about ladies who produce champagne. We were going with Inès de la Fressange, former Lagerfeld muse, current 'ambassador' for Roger Vivier shoes, epitome of Parisian chic, etc., but all the images were a bit 'soft', i.e., not crisp and punchy and high-res, or she was in black next to Karl wearing white gloves and a high-collared shirt.

'I'm not having that pomaded Kraut on the cover of my magazine,' said Ben.

TheLady

14 DECEMBER 2010 · £1.80

INTERNET DATING
worked for me…
…and me

HOSTESS WITH A HEADACHE
our guide to entertaining

Losing the Abbey habit: what's next for

MAGGIE SMITH

SISTER WENDY'S
Christmas message

DECEMBER

1 December 2010

One of Ben's many new wheezes for saving *The Lady*'s bacon is to hawk, off-page, a product called Steril-Aire. If the reader buys one (big IF), we get a cut.

Steril-Aire, as you might have guessed, removes the smell of urine out of old people's homes. I am depressed by this but Ben says that if I provide advertorial that suggests yummy mummies can buy it for their teenagers' bedrooms, and publicans for their beery front rooms, any association with wee will be eliminated.

A row between Claire and Chrissie. Claire wants a sub to provide a page of advertorial about this life-enhancing product, and Chrissie says the subs are too busy and that Claire shouldn't be giving Chrissie orders let alone a bollocking. When I got wind of this, I stepped in and asked Edwina to provide a few hundred words of soaring uplifting prose about the Steril-Aire. 'Think a thousand points of light, and Obama's speech on race,' I instructed her. We can't afford to pass up commercial opportunity. Not right now, anyway. If necessary, I will write the copy myself.

Ben came in looking a bit shook up. Told me he'd had a cig on the stoop (this wasn't the reason for his mood – he has about two packs a day so spends most of day in perishing chill). No. Apparently there was a man standing there looking up at the glorious cream Georgian façade. An hour later, when Ben descended to the street for his next fag, the man was still there, in the same position, staring up at *The Lady*.

Then he approached Ben and told him that voices in his head

had told him to get on the train from Leicestershire and come to *The Lady*, and tell Ben that Ben's father (who died in a plane crash when Ben was at Cothill Preparatory School) was with his uncle. 'Can you give me any more detail?' said Ben politely. The man then sloped off. 'He did seem reasonably sane, so he can't be a member of the Budworth family,' Ben concluded.

Meanwhile, in other nutty news, Ben was in a meeting with Hels and the man who had come in to sell Steril-Aire via our gracious pages. They were standing quietly in the boardroom discussing air-freshening technology when suddenly Maureen, Ben's PA, erupted through from the other side (Ben's office acts as a passage-way between editorial and accounts/Ros the telephonist, et al). She charged between the two doors of the boardroom with a large screwdriver in her hands, almost knocking them over.

'Hold on, Maureen,' said Ben. 'Where's the fire?'

'Tom Bowles has locked himself in the downstairs kitchen,' said Maureen. 'He called me and said the knob came off in his hand. I can't stop.'

When Ben told me this I remarked that if Tom Bowles stayed in the kitchen for ever, all our problems would be over.

'Oh, but that can never happen when we have Maureen, the fourth emergency service,' said Ben.

2 December 2010

Ben picked up a postcard Stephen Bayley had sent me, showing a detail of a woman's vulva on a Renaissance statue. 'Why have you got this flange picture?' he said, replacing it after careful study.

The in tray:

- many unsolicited submissions. Among them: 'Common Sense While Holiday Driving'; 'Everlasting Fame' about people like Mackintosh, Diesel and Plimsoll whose names will never fade; 'Astrology and Health' about astrology and health; 'The Day the Classics Died' about the decline in literature since Mary Shelley.

- a letter from a man in Lincoln, saying: 'I am enclosing a newspaper article about myself that appeared in the *Lincolnshire Echo*. Although it may not appear immediately relevant, I have had a long history in horticulture since 1967, I am currently unemployed and looking for a position as a Head Gardener on a country estate, and your clientele are the very kind of people I would like to present myself to.'

Email from an editor on the *Sunday Express* asking for Clemmie's address as they want her to write a piece (bound to be about being Di's bridesmaid, I fear).

3 December 2010

Email from Ben:

Please put 8 pages aside for the magazine's anniversary special.
These 8 pages can be edited by Mrs B. (Lady B!)

Thanks
Regards,
Ben

I assumed this was a joke, so I merely whizzed one back of only three words. They were: 'ha ha ha'.

6 *December* 2010

Attended the Lady Taverners Christmas Lunch, held in the basement banqueting hall, literally size of football pitch, of the Kensington Gardens Hotel, in front of 400 people. Hels – who is chairwoman of events committee and wearing a sequinned mini-dress – wanted me there at 10.30 a.m. to 'mingle' with the Lady Taverners, when I have to prepare for an interview, write book, edit magazine, etc. Lunch is at 1 p.m. That's two and a half hours of mingling. I instead arrive at 12.30 p.m. and sell a few copies of the book from a stand in a draughty hall near the lifts. We go into lunch, say grace, then we all have to sing 'The Twelve Days of Christmas' as a round. Each table is given a verse. My table's verse is 'geese a-laying' so every time this line comes round we have to leap to our feet and show festive cheer and sing out lustily. Rachael Heyhoe Flint, the president, introduces me to the raucous rowdy crowd wearing hats, fascinators, embalmed with make-up and dripping with bling (I feel so under-dressed I run out to the Christmas bazaar to buy a sparkly necklace between courses) as Boris's sister. I speak for fifteen minutes, ending with the Loins of Longleat and running not one but four penises on a page. It brings the house down, especially with Judith Chalmers and Baroness Heyhoe Flint.

Hels is very sweet to me all through lunch and I regret my snooty attitude about attending the 'Chaveners' gala Chrimble event.

Then I go to interview Rory Bremner in the Bluebird Café in Chelsea. He is very nervy and keeps pointing to my iPhone, which is recording him, and saying, 'This isn't for . . .' But it is BLISS when he lapses into voices. He does Matthew Parris, Gordon Brown, Tony Blair, Vince Cable. I feel blessed.

7 December 2010

A repeat performance, only today it is at the Lancaster London hotel and is the *Daily Mail* Literary Christmas Gala Lunch in front of 600 people. Who have paid to hear me. I sit in front of salmon and chicken and Sauvignon Blanc, not feeling hungry or able to drink anything.

Gyles Brandreth compères brilliantly. I sit next to the other speaker, Michael Winner, who is next to Ed Victor, super-agent to the stars. I lean in between Ed Victor and Winner and say to them, 'Laugh at my jokes.'

I talk for 15 mins, which is our allotted time, some jokes fall flat and I forget others. Michael talks for 40 mins. Afterwards lots of people come up to Winner at the signing table, grip him moistly and say, 'I could have listened to you for ever!'

8 December 2010

Two parties last night. First was a Feminista Fundraiser at Faber & Faber, full of female columnists and hacks and writers – Natasha Walter, the high priestess of Third Wave Feminism, Viv Groskop of this parish and others, Janice Turner of *The Times*, and Julie Burchill. I asked Janice where Julie was, and she said, 'Sitting in the corner by the drinks table, like an installation.' I fought my way over and Burchill flapped a hand lazily in greeting and introduced me to a young man called Jack. Or that's what I thought she said. 'Jack!' I cried over the chatter. 'So you're Julie's son by Cosmo Landesman!'

The young man smiled. 'It's Dan,' he said. 'Julie's husband.'

Julie and I then had a brief love-in – she recalled, to my delight, first meeting me at 19.

'But I remember you – it was like meeting the Pope,' I gushed. 'In the Groucho! With Toby Young . . .'

And then she said, 'And I remember how I described you afterwards.' (I hoped she was going to say 'Patsy Kensit with a library ticket', because it is the most flattering description anyone's ever made of me – the best I usually get is 'Boris in drag'.) 'Patsy Kensit with a library ticket,' she cheeped in her high-pitched Bristol voice.

I high-fived her, then I was dismissed, so made my way towards tables covered in chocolate and brownies. Nigella was there, looking curvy and pouty in black. She told me she hadn't made the brownies.

Then I zoomed on to the Mandarin Oriental for the Piers-Morgan-becoming-Larry-King party. Ri-DIC-ulous! Banks of paparrazi, mounted on bleachers, as if we were at Cannes, not Knightsbridge. Red carpet. Clipboard Nazis. Rivers of champagne, blizzards of canapés . . . ex-Prime Ministers, Naomi Campbell, Bruce Forsyth, daytime telly peeps like Adrian Chiles and Christine Bleakley, editors.

Gordon Brown entered the room just as the camera crews spotted Brucie. They surged after him, while Brown crossed the floor completely unnoticed, but looking (to my credulous eye) attractively brooding and Heathcliffy.

Piers made a nice speech in which he thanked everyone from his mum to his agent, but forgot to thank Celia. I stood in front of him making a big 'C' with thumb and forefinger but he didn't see me. Disaster! Poor Celia. No blow job for Piers tonight!

Email from Roger Lewis:

Dear Rachel

Barry Humphries CBE hasn't been answering my emails so do you want to try? I suggest you take his face off with a scaffolding pole.

In my *Daily Mail* piece I have said you are *modern royalty*. It gets worse after that, alas.

Now, *The Sunday Times* wants a 3,000-word seasonal suicide note from me – I am going to say that I clip out discount coupons for the Dignitas Clinic from *The Lady* to send to my mother. Whilst this is a joke, I suddenly thought: bloody good idea. Tell Rachel and the comical Budworth Family. Worth considering.

Was in Rules last week (I won't go anywhere else except Sheekey's) and spent a penny – actually £45.87 – through your letter box.

I should have heard about my New Year's Honours CBE by now. Nothing. Fuming.

Keep it oiled, girl

Love
Roger, Hon DLitt (from an ex-poly)

Email from attendee of *Mail* literary lunch:

Dear Rachel

Hello – I was at your table at the *Mail* thing the other day, but alas wasn't quite close enough to talk. So I thought I'd just write briefly to say that your speech was very lively and amusing – and I'm sorry if you were rattled! And I like what you've done with the magazine.

Very best wishes
Joseph

I knew this was too good to be true – and it was, as I realized when I got to the PS:

'I once was honoured to be seated next to Boris at one of the old *Speccie* luncheons.'

Lunch with Mark Thompson, director general of the BBC, and assorted hacks at RIBA. The only other female, Emma Duncan, deputy editor of the *Economist*, didn't turn up so I was the only woman present. Gave the DG a hard time about moving to Salford, no women over 50 on screen, and the underfunding of radio. I asked him how much he thought contributors like me were paid to write, record, research and present half an hour of Radio Four.

He said, 'You tell me.'

I said, 'No, you tell me. You're the DG. Take a wild guess.'

'Four thousand?' he ventured.

It was a Gotcha moment. 'Nine hundred quid.'

He should have said, 'That's quite right, value for the licence-payer,' and so on, but he just looked a bit shocked.

I liked him and made an unashamed pitch to be an on-screen presence as am now 45 and therefore invisible on street and our screens.

9 December 2010

Ivo's birthday.

Oh noooo! I just said to Claire, our chief designer, 'Now I've got Matt I can't help it, I lie in bed worrying about you or Maria leaving.' Maria Rodriguez is our brilliant designer. Claire looked at me with wide eyes, as if she'd seen a ghost. She scurried to her desk without speaking and a few minutes later I got an email catchlined 'Nightmare', saying that Maria has been offered another job! And IS leaving! This is a disaster of the first order. I sent one back saying, 'What do we do?' and hers came in reply, 'Head in Oven.'

The fact is, the designers and subs do the lion's share of the actual work.

Have to go in and meet an advertiser called Chris Nieper who does a lot of business with us. In the 7 December edition he is hawking sumptuous burgundy nighties and bed jackets under the banner headline 'Night-Time Luxury' in 'superb pure silk & fine pearl satin'.

10 December 2010

It's a Friday, working from home day, but it is also the The Day of the Office Party, so I trot in at noon. There is cava and peanuts laid out in Classified. Kath has her festive specs on, Joan has changed out of her slippers, and what Hels calls a 'Sloaney Pony' catering company are handing round salmon blini and foie gras on little roundels of pumpernickel. Everyone's glammed up and Joy from advertising is rocking out to 'It's Raining Men', which is blaring forth from Kath Hanley's Kermit-green iPod nano and it's only 12.15 p.m.

It's going to be a long afternoon.

Then my phone rings when I am talking to Adam Budworth and Carolyn about their respective domestic situations. It's the *Mail*. Can I write '400 jolly words' about whether women should show cleavage in the office? Anything for respite . . . I run upstairs and sit at my computer while eating red velvet cupcakes sent by a PR. I sent one version, in which I said that it was all very well getting your tits out for parties but on the whole I loathed seeing crêpey cleavage and baps should be kept under wraps. Then I got an email back, saying no, what we want you to say is that tits out is always a good thing, the bigger and more visible the better. So I served up a pro-bazookas piecette instead, like a short-order cook.

The in tray:

- an invitation from The Savoy in the shape of a silver card embossed with the Savoy hotel hallmark, giving me priority access to The Savoy and entitling me to entertain up to three guests 'with our compliments' in the River Restaurant, Beaufort Bar, American Bar. When I showed this off to Ben he told me that he was quite happy with his Covent Garden haunt, the Seven Dials Club. 'It's a pound a pint, they are proud to serve "freshly brewed Kenco coffee" and members are invited to piano singalongs,' he told me. Actually, I know he has joined Two Brydges and he and Adam – who has now moved into a room in Uncle Tom's modest suite of 22 rooms (I saw the bed going in) – go there quite a lot.
- letter from NW9: 'How many widows read *The Lady*? I recently came across an old copy in which Liz Hodgkinson wrote an article called "How to Survive Having a Husband at Home All Day". Many of us, who will never see our husbands again, would LOVE to have our husbands at home all day.' Heartbreaking . . .

Matt Warren said his mum and his mother-in-law were now regular readers. 'Good,' I said. 'Only 10,000 more to go.' Actually, only another 50,000 to go if we are to reach the glory days of pomp when we sold 80,000 without breaking sweat.

15 December 2010

Disaster! My *Mail* plops on the mat and there is a banner headline over the masthead shouting: 'CLEAVAGE. THE GREAT DEBATE. Pages 29–30!'

I open up my *Daily Heil* and, to my utter horror, there is a massive centrefold picture of me chatting to Dave at the *Speccie* party over two pages with speech bubbles – a pic I'd begged the *Mail* not to use mainly because 1. I look as if I have a deformed jaw and bingo wings in it and 2. It will not go down well with the party.

In the speech bubbles, I am asking Dave, 'So, can you show plunging cleavage in the office?' and he is going, 'Erm ...' as he stares down my front.

16 December 2010

Packed day. Came in, settled down, then chatted to Peter York (co-author of *The Official Sloane Ranger Handbook*, and style guru) who is doing the *Sunday Times* News Review front they asked me to do about domestic staff, upstairs downstairs, class – all the stuff that kicked off with *Downton Abbey*.

I did not, of course, mention that *The Sunday Times* had asked me first, and began by saying that the real juice of *The Lady* was in the back, in the classified ads, and that I had a mental picture of *Vanity Fair* editor Graydon Carter and his adorable wife Anna (who claim to love *The Lady*) lying in bed poring over them. 'I can't claim they're reading the glistening editorial,' I admitted. 'I imagine them drooling over our legendary classifieds. Each one is like opening up an Advent calendar – they offer a window to another world, a world where prestige marque cars are lovingly polished, where valets look after his Lordship's smalls, where little couples tend walled vegetable gardens ...'

I went on in this vein for some time. I talked about how *The Lady* is about people caring for other people and is therefore about LOVE. Then, more perilously, I spoke about the risks of palling up with your staff. 'The problem nowadays is there isn't enough demarcation between upstairs and downstairs,' I averred. 'The green baize door has been flapping for decades. Never sit in the kitchen chatting to your nanny, it'll end in tears before bedtime.'

Then I hotfooted it (in an AdLee taxi) to Henry Wyndham's Christmas lunch at Sotheby's. It was the second year running I'd been invited, so I felt very honoured. Also present: Richard Caring (tombstone teeth, leonine grey hair springing back from tanned forehead); Michael Winner and his 'fiancée' Geraldine; Tracey Emin (who showed me her tits again – they're marvellous, 'done by a man in New York'), the painter Maggi Hambling; Barry Humphries . . . I sat next to a man called Philip Hook who had also won the Bad Sex Award for describing the act of 69 as 'mutual mastication'. So we bonded over that. After Michael Winner had given the same speech as he'd given at the *Daily Mail* lit lunch, Ronnie Corbett read out a scatological Christmas poem to wild laughter – thanks not so much to the verses, but to his brilliant comic timing.

20 December 2010

Walked into work over a snowbound London. Didn't see tarmac till I got to the Mall. As I walked, I got colder and colder, despite North Face jacket and ski gloves. Coco bounded ahead joyfully.

The in tray:

- invite from Fuller's Brewery, suggesting we 'work together', i.e., I come along and address a meeting of their senior management team, or, alternatively, we could come along and meet the head brewer. This is puzzling. Why do other, well-established companies, assume I know anything about anything?
- several Christmas cards for Coco:
  card from *Vogue* signed from the features team I did nether regions waxing piece for, and Emily Sheffield who said 'have Evgeny gossip for you'. When I emailed Emily Sheffield she never emailed back. I knew she was naughty.

card from a man called David Griffiths suggesting we interview Sam Cam and Cliff Richard. He goes on: 'My wife is a subscriber and enjoys the Ladygram, but is not keen on the Penny Smith and Mary Killen columns, which she describes as boring! I only read 'Coco's Corner', which we both never miss . . . it is important that *The Lady* survives as an oasis of good taste in a sea of sleazy and sensational publications. Please keep up the good work.'

- a Magnum of Waitrose Champagne from Waitrose press office.
- a Guinness cake with cream-cheese icing, which I eat and which isn't as good as it sounds.

Had email from Tim de Lisle, the editor of *Intelligent Life*. I'd emailed him as I'd spotted somewhere online – or Google Alert had told me – that both our publications would make good subscriptions for mothers. The commendation had come in the *Telegraph* via a chap called Ed. 'Ha, well spotted. Ed is one of our ex-interns, so the compliment to you is worth rather more,' said Tim. I had made the mistake of not reading his CV properly until I was interviewing him. Got to interests – drama, Cambridge Footlights, blah blah, 'and can put own willy in mouth'. I uttered a strange yelp of astonishment and tried to pass it off as a sneeze. His career has flourished nonetheless. The *Telegraph* got him to write about the incident the other day, but then lost their nerve about using the word 'willy', so 'Disgusted, Tunbridge Wells' must have been mystified instead.

22 December 2010

My last day in the office, 2010. We're supposed to be driving up to just south of Edinburgh tomorrow. On my behalf, Ben is glued to Trafficmaster website, which shows we are unlikely to make it up to Scotland tomorrow as the M1 and M6 are at a crawl, and it's awful around Birmingham as per usual.

'Say "I'd like a kipper tie",' he said to me. He was sitting at his desk. A Steril-Aire was blasting away, and he was watching Alan Partridge on YouTube.

'I'd like a kipper tie,' I said.

'Milk and two sugars??' he burst out in a Brummie accent, sounding like Adrian Chiles with a hangover. He has had man flu all week and, to be fair, looks terrible.

Mrs Budworth has complained about the 'Princess Diaries' column I've launched, written by D. J. Taylor. In its raw form I agree it's all very *de haut en bas*, with Betjemanesque cracks about serviettes and fish knives but I have instructed Carolyn to tell DJT to tone it down. We must NOT be snobbish. It is a big mistake. And wrong, actually. We are very pro-Middleton here and I've heard Ben saying that if he hears anyone going Lord Snooty on us, he will personally cancel his or her subscription.

Ivo is calling me every ten minutes about the drive North, and I agree – I don't want to spend Christmas wedged between the children, a Stilton and Coco on the M6 either. But we should at least try to Shackleton our way to Scotland tomorrow if we can. I made the mistake of telling Ben Ivo was in a flat panic and he said happily, 'I'll call him and wind him up. I'll tell him that the safe decision is the right decision. That safety is no accident.'

The in tray:

- Christmas Pudding from Daylesford.
- a perfumed 'palet' (no, me neither) from Diptyque which I might hand on to Matt, who is still sharing my office, putting up with me shouting and flossing, etc.

26 December 2010

So Christmas is over and I come blearily down to breakfast where we're staying in Scotland with my in-laws Jamie and Sarah. Ed Glass (Charlie Glass's friend who is married to Olivia, Jamie's son) said, 'Have you seen this?' Then he handed me a special annual supplement devoted to the smuggest people in Britain. I am number 22 – after Nick Clegg, who is 21. There is a huge picture of me smugly carrying a copy of *The Lady*, and the copy reads:

Rachel Johnson
   Sister of Boris (as if that is MY JOB!)
   Putting the Y into *The Lady*, Boris-in-drag first set about sacking most of its staff and hiring posher ones, and then wrote a book on how she – not they – had transformed the magazine's fortunes. Apart from authoring the smug manuals *Notting Hell* and *Shire Hell*, nobody's quite sure what she's for.

I have a vision of the *Sindy* picture desk tasked with illustrating this list combing through all the pictures of me online and saying, 'She looks really slappable in that one,' and then another one saying, 'No, that one of her grinning is unbelievably smug, use that.' But they probably just used the first one they came across and the truth is, once you look at photos of people smiling under the headline 'The Smuggest People in Public Life', there's no getting away from it. They all do look, excruciatingly . . . *smug*.

29 December 2010

Two lovely letters awaited me at home in London on our return from Scotland. It was twice as long on the way down – seven hours on the M6 in freezing fog – plus pit stop for Burger King (even Ivo and Oliver are now sickened by the grease of the Whopper) and M&S for the rest of us.

It was good to be back, but all the grot I'd left behind stared me in the face: unfinished novel, filthy carpets, even a saucepan of pasta alive with blue mould, and a bowl of Cocoa Krispies just left to congeal.

Xmas cards, letters, children's reports (all wonderful – very pleasing).

The first letter was addressed to 'Rachel Johnson (Sister of Boris)' on the envelope and was from Giles Wood, Mary's husband, whom I adore and who has been executing the second of his seasonal commissions for none other than Mrs B. at Deerbolts Hall.

'Just finished another four days at Mrs Budworth's, painting her Christmas tree,' he wrote. 'Only the room was freezing on account of prolonging the life of the tree. Lots of talk about you, and I learnt lots of new things. Especially that the "insensitive" side of your personality is because you are of "German extraction". We had a lovely candlelit dinner, her "roasties" are to die for.'

Nice letter from Ann Widdecombe thanking me for the correction (I had repeated the libel that she is in favour of pregnant prisoners being shackled while they deliver – lazy of me, and wrong). It was posted to me from Widdecombe's Rest on Dartmoor, which made me pine for our valley. 'Hope all goes well for *The Lady* next year and I am keeping the one with me on the front cover, lying around the lounge ostentatiously, for visiting relatives to see at Christmas!'

The Lady

4 JANUARY 2011 £1.80

2011 HEALTH AND BEAUTY

The first **BIBA GIRL**

JANE FONDA
Fabulous, fit & 73

ENGAGEMENT MUGS

New **ANTIQUES COLUMN**

ROSE PRINCE
Anything with a pulse

BARBARA CARTLAND • CHARLES NEVIN • TOILE DE JOUY • JULIA STEPHENSON
PHILIP KERR • HUNDREDS OF HOLIDAY AND JOB ADVERTISEMENTS EACH WEEK

JANUARY

4 January 2011

First day back. Walked in with Coco, listening to first Vampire Weekend and then Van Morrison as Milly has uploaded her iTunes as well as mine on to my iPod.

All the Christmas decorations are still up in the office, the robins and tinsel over the desks. The edition with the Christmas cover – which shows Santa in the Blitz – is still arrayed in the display cases in the windows of Bedford Street. Looks VERY tired and 2010. Why did we put Father Christmas on a cover that would hang around until 4 January? Must remember not to make that mistake next year. If I'm still here next year, that is . . .

Went in to see Ben. First thing he said was the Christmas cover was out-of-date (which it was). Then we talked about staffing and hot-desking for ages. He wants to move Gillian out of my outer office to what he calls the 'lambing pen', i.e., where Judy Lamb (who is not in today as she has gastric flu) sits, and make an administrative 'super-hub'. He wants Matt to sit where Gillian is in the outer office with Carolyn, then move Beenie and Nicola Bourton and so on into the new, souped-up, recarpeted 'cab's office', where Janina and Lindsay used to sit. All fine by me.

Told Claire that Ben and I wanted to see the cover on Thursdays, i.e., just as one edition is going to press, I want to have first sight of the cover of the next. She didn't flinch too much. But like my plans to see picture selections, have regular features meetings, and so on, this New Year's Resolution will probably go by the board.

Speaking of New Year's Res – the *Daily Telegraph* emailed me and asked me for mine. So I said, 'To go to fewer parties, play more tennis, get up earlier, and stop smiling in photographs.'

When I got the paper on New Year's Day they didn't run mine but they did run Stanley Johnson's resolution to climb Kilimanjaro aged 70 in order to try to save gorillas, which is much worthier.

Ben is threatening to remove my loo and make it into 'tea and coffee spot'. When I protested, he asked in front of Matt and Carolyn and Gillian, 'Well, when was the last time you had a dump in there?'

I yelped. A lady should never be asked questions like that, let alone answer them. Then he stood there bullishly. 'And furthermore, do you have any idea who did the dump in the Ladies editorial?' he asked out of the blue. He was at Gillian's desk, looking into the boudoir. 'Ben, that happened before my time,' I reminded him crisply. Then he looked inquisitorially at Gillian.

'I never even saw it!' protested Gillian.

'Mmm. I remember that Judy had concussion,' he said, apropos nothing. Obviously Ben will not die happy unless he finds out who was responsible for the brown puppy.

Disaster! Mirror Mirror – motto: 'A better-looking you or your money back' – has closed! Where will I go for my lunchtime blow-dry now?

The in tray:

- a book called *Best After 40: New Body, New Life, New Love* from a woman called Anna Dun in Walton-on-the-Naze, and a personal letter to me about making the best of myself.
- the Winter 2011 edition of the magazine *Beating Bowel Cancer*.
- letter to Coco from border collie called Rapsie and her playmate Dancer (one-year-old chocolate Labrador), plus several cards for Coco from a lurcher, a black greyhound called Josie,

and a fawn lurcher called Bryn (all rescue dogs). Coco is now getting more correspondence than me and is so busy she will soon need her own PA.

5 January 2011

Had to leave the office early yesterday, and when I came in this morning the cover had been surreptitiously changed behind my back from Rory Bremner, whom I had interviewed, to Roger Moore. It isn't even a new picture of Roger Moore, but one of him as 007 pointing a gun that must be thirty years old. Went in to see Ben. Asked why, if he had such strenuous objections to Rory Bremner, we couldn't shoot Vanessa Feltz as an alternative. We have a good interview with her; she's over 50, and smart, etc.

'If we scrape off the make-up and put her in a nice blouse,' I wheedled. 'Show her as the Cambridge bluestocking rather than bottle-blonde shock jock.' Then I named, as other cover possibles, Riz Lateef, Konnie Huq, Emma Forbes (whom I mentioned because Ben is always banging on about her), June Whitfield. And he gave me endless reasons why he didn't like each one. 'And Emma Forbes needs bringing down a peg or two,' he said. 'She sounds very smug on *Loose Ends*.'

I tried not to lose my temper. 'That's Emma Freud,' I said, 'not Emma Forbes. Listen. We're not going to find a perfect woman 51 weeks a year,' I said patiently, thinking, as I do at these moments, even though I like him unreservedly and he makes me pee with laughter, NO WONDER BEN HAS NEVER GOT MARRIED.

Then he said that one week in six we could have a nice travel picture or a bloke so only needed to find 'a bird' two-thirds of the time. 'I don't always think with my cock, you know,' he said. 'I'm not an elephant trying to pluck a bun out of the park-keeper's pocket.'

I wasn't sure what he meant by that, but whenever he sees a cover image of a woman he can be guaranteed to find something wrong with her – the sight of most women on the cover seems to untap a slight trickle of somewhat look-ist misogyny, although Ben would deny this. He says he only assesses the appearance of middle-aged women on the cover on the basis, 'Will it sell?' Anyway, I laughed at the 'park-keeper's pocket' joke, went back in to Claire and got her to put Roger Moore against a hot pink background. And a love heart. Then I realized that this would look like a Valentine's Day issue and told her to drop the heart.

The website is being 'flipped' today, apparently. Now we have a website, an online edition for £1 a pop, and a hard-copy product, BUT we're still not making as much money as single-platform low-rent websites called things like 'Fifty & Fabulous'.

Aaaargh! Was just talking to Chrissie and Matt about the annual Death Supplement (aka the special on residential care homes) when Gillian buzzed: 'I've got Mrs Budworth on the line, wants to know what she has to do with regards to the anniversary issue.' I dimly remember in a recess of my brain that Ben had, last year, joked that 'Mum could edit the anniversary issue'. This was around the time I'd asked as a peace offering whether she wanted to file the Diary on 18 January. I had assumed he was joking.

AAAAGGGGHHH! Have just had flaming stand-up row with Ben. Went into boardroom and after a lot of chitchat about the website (he accused me of not knowing my way round it, which is fair enough) and sundry other topics, I said, 'Mrs Budworth rang for Judy, but Judy's ill again so she got put through to Gillian. She was saying that she'd been commissioned to edit and produce an eight-page supplement for what she called the "anniversary issue".' Then I paused significantly. 'Anniversary issue, Ben? EIGHT PAGES?'

He looked cross and evasive and told me I knew all about it.

'But I thought you were JOKING,' I said. 'We did all this twelve months ago for the 125th anniversary, which was a landmark worth celebrating. Are we going to publish a special every February?'

Then he wittered and flannelled for ages and every time I tried to make him see reason he shouted 'stop fucking interfuckingrupting' and 'you're interrupting yourself' and 'if I might just finish' and then I said, 'Another eight pages on the glorious history of *The Lady* magazine may be a Mum-pleaser but it's not a crowd-pleaser.' And I also questioned whether we'd sell any ads off the back and then Hels came in and was right behind Ben's plan to have Mum guest-edit and said that Bridget was 'already on it, ad-wise'.

I think it's barmy. Mrs B.'s already penned a book about *The Lady*, she did a piece for the anniversary last year . . . The big question is, will she come up from Deerbolts to oversee the special?

The in tray:

*   letter from a nurse suggesting a nursing column. The letters after her name go RGN RMN RNT MSc. I read her letter carefully, as midwifery and nursing memoirs of the 1950s are inexplicable bestsellers.

Dear Rachel Johnson,

We met briefly at *The Lady* Literary Lunch in October. I was the nurse who leapt forward to assist poor Joy who collapsed off her chair during the meal.
I was last seen disposing of the first two courses, caught deftly in a water jug! Experience counts, you see.

I still can't see it in the mag, but at least Nursey didn't bury her lead and wasn't slow in playing her ace about being the angel of mercy with the chalice of chunder.

6 January 2011

The row over Mrs B. curating eight whole pages in February's 'birthday' edition rumbles on. Ben insists it will placate our more trad readers and Mum at the same time. Matt thinks it's insane to have a birthday special every year. Mrs B. rang Wendy, who does our archive research, and asked her to go on a hunt for any of the artist Fromenti's illustrations. Ben reminds me that the reason he offered her the 126th 'birthday' edition was because she'd written to me asking me to guest-edit on the grounds that if Coco could, and Penny Smith could, she could. Then I reminded Ben that with his blessing I'd said no to that very tempting suggestion. Plus they haven't sold a single ad off the back of the 126th anniversary of *The Lady*. Or a Steril-Aire, for that matter.

Laurence Llewelyn-Bowen seems very keen to meet. His PA Donna keeps emailing. He's coming in next week. When I mentioned this to Matt, who's still hot-desking in the boudoir, Matt said that poor LLB had been named and shamed in the *Mail* to illustrate a why-oh-why on 'Why Are Men So Fat These Days?' alongside unflattering pic of his moobs.

OMG! On the subject of fat men, I was watching a doc about a mountain of flab called Paul last night and Ludo said that he was very proud that the fattest man in the world was English. I tweeted this. It was retweeted 80 times, including by Piers Morgan. Then I got a tweet from Nick Hewer from *The Apprentice*. Saying that he'd been astonished how vulgar my website was, especially the gallery of gruesome photos.

So then we started a Twitter flirt. It was a bit like Shane Warne and Liz Hurley. Hewer astutely detected that this was of more benefit to me than him (he has 20k followers, I have 3k) and said at one point, after I'd replied too fast to his last tweet, 'Just checking – do these "things" of yours pass quite quickly?'

*

Email from Hugh St Clair, our in-house 'home help', wishing me a Happy New Year and warning me to expect a letter from a lady who said she was a top fashion model in the 1950s but wants help in restoring a gateleg table.

7 January 2011

I can't believe it's come to this. On my way into work I called Matt and said, 'I want to have a meeting about meetings.' I want us to have a regular features, pictures, covers and production meeting. I feel I am losing my grip.

Matt called Mrs B. to discuss the dreaded issue of the eight-page 'birthday' special that Ben asked her to edit, even though we have a dental special that week to run as well and may have to go up 16 pages to accommodate both, despite poor circulation figures.

I have decided that I am being mean-spirited and am all in favour of *The Lady* anniversary special on one condition: that Mrs B. does manage, as she has hinted she might, to wring a piece out of Cousin Debo, preferably on the subject of the Dowager Duchess's recent distressing experience of being stalked by an ardent seventy-something admirer. I made Matt call her on Friday. I made him do it in front of me – he's still sharing my desk, i.e., Ben's old dining-room table – so I could be like GCHQ and monitor the exchange.

I am clearly the topic. Matt's face worked with amusement as Mrs B. talked. He coloured at one point. I could hear her barking all the way from Suffolk.

'Well, she certainly doesn't like you, does she?' he said when he put down the phone. 'She said that she would ask Debo to write only on the condition that she has no contact with you whatsoever. 'Apparently, Debo is very upset with you.'

I laughed uncontrollably. 'You were on the phone for ages. What else did she say?' I asked.

Then Matt said that Mrs B. had commented on how polite and gentlemanly Adam was, compared to Ben. 'He's a lovely boy really (i.e., Ben) but can be so rude sometimes.'

The in tray:

- card actually from TUNBRIDGE WELLS from a reader saying the 'Princess Diaries' column is 'unpleasant, unfunny, nasty and unfair' pandering to all the 'Hurray Henrys' who think 'trolley dolly' is witty.
- a 50-page proposal from a man who has just completed an MA in Furniture Conservation and wants me to publish in some form his dissertation entitled 'Great Furniture and Disputed Taste'.

12 *January 2011*

Tamsin Omond, the fizzy, lesbian, crop-haired eco-activist who organized the scaling of Big Ben, and runs two environmental pressure groups, came in on a mission. She was wearing a neon-yellow, long-sleeved T-shirt, a black sweater over the top, and tight black trousers and Converse. Eyes ringed with kohl. Bleached crew cut. Only in her early twenties. She wants me to front a campaign to save England's 1,000 forests which will be under threat from developers when the bonfire of the quangos goes through.

'Sure,' I said. I can't think of a better campaign. They've been protected since 1215 (or something) by a Forest Charter, but when the Forestry Commission is abolished, they will be up for grabs at once, and if charities and communities and the Big Society fail to come up with the millions they will need to muster from banks in only a few weeks to buy them, they will be flogged to the highest bidder. I haven't read the consultation document, but this seems like bad politics from every angle: foreign companies can buy

Savernake or Burnham Beeches and turn them into woodchip for boilers, rights of way will be lost, and the fire sale won't even save taxpayers' money.

So I have signed up to become the President of the Save England's Forests campaign, and to launch it in *The Lady*. Will soon start making people call me 'Lady President', much like our now-retired crime writer is now Dame Lady Antonia. We started drafting a letter to send to the great and the good that Omond hopes to detonate eventually in a Sunday newspaper.

Laurence Llewelyn-Bowen invited himself in to tea. When he arrived in a floor-sweeping black leather coat, and a Prince of Wales check three-piece suit, all the women in the office did a double-take. I took him through to Claire so he could pick between our two cover choices: Natalie Portman in *Black Swan*, either looking scary, with red eyes and black make-up round her eyes, or in a tutu with her eyes closed. He correctly divined that the one with red eyes was a bit avant-garde for where we are now, and picked the dull, demure one of Portman in a filmy white tutu.

Then I took him, trailing clouds of aftershave, past the subs and in to Ben, who blushed slightly when he saw him. 'I'm a dyed-in-the-wool *Lady* reader of many years' standing,' said Bowen in the boardroom. 'I have to say, I hit a bump with the rebranding but I'm back on board now.'

Ben twinkled at him. Then we came back into the boudoir for tea and talked nineteen to the dozen – how LLB hates Daylesford ('I go into beige rage') and how horrid it was being papped on a Barbadian beach wearing swimming trunks (he declined our tea offering of Victoria sponge, patting his tummy), and then he moved on to Prince Charles's obsession with his wife's breasts.

He was good on *Lady* branding. Basically said we had to be more OKA/Noa Noa, and less Country Casuals/Edinburgh Woollen Mill. I agree. Said we should do stuff with Classic FM. When I handed him my card and apologized for interlocking Ls on the back, he said he liked it. 'Very David Hicks,' he noted and said his card, with LLB initials, looked like a pattern of swastikas.

As he was leaving, Matt asked him what his aftershave was. The boudoir was very perfumed and very hot by this stage – it's always hammam temperature by teatime – especially with all of us (Matt, LLB, me, plus Coco and the tea) in it, and the sweat was standing out on LLB's forehead.

'It's not aftershave,' he disclosed. 'It's room spray, from Florian in Venice. It's called Chamber of the Important Gentleman.'

Typical travel feature pitch from unknown freelancer (1):

Hi Rachel,

Hope you are well.

Desert Ranch (part of the Al Sahra Desert Resort, around 30 minutes from the Dubai World Trade Centre) offers visitors something a little different from the usual spa and shopping experiences of Dubai. It offers various animal and outdoor experiences including Camel Cuddling – a two-hour session getting to know the herd, learning their language, helping out at bath time and feeding them . . .

The in tray:

- pitch from a woman in Nottinghamshire who thinks she might be able to secure for me an exclusive interview with the very elderly lady who is 'guardian to the 200-year-old original Bramley Apple Tree in Southwell'.
- letter from an Avon Lady called Faith who wants us to interview her and who was in the original 'Ding Dong, Avon Calling' ads in the 1960s.
- crazed, typed missive headlined 'Theological point of view about women and ambition' by a man who signs himself

'Oblivionist and Letter Writer' and with letterhead medallion with his face in the middle and the logo 'Peeved Off Of Pontypridd'.

13 January 2011

Mary Killen says Mrs B. is giving Giles gyp over the painting he has done of the drawing room at Deerbolts. The bone of contention is whether or not he should include a log basket in the picture. According to Giles, he and Mrs B. agreed at the outset that it would ruin the composition, and so he left it out. Then he laboriously completed the painting. And now she wants to come to Bedford Street and leave the painting for Mary Killen to take to Wiltshire so he can put the log basket in, *post eventum*. Mary Killen also told me she'd been on a train with Richard Ingrams and he'd said *The Lady* was on her deathbed, would never last the year, etc.

'Never mind Ingrams, did she mention the special edition she's curating in February to Giles?' I asked nosily. Giles has been spending time at Deerbolts and would be bound to know.

'I think she did,' Mary replied.

16 January 2011

Have had brainwave. The *London Review of Books* is inexplicably giving up publishing its famous literary personal ads: 'Sexually I'm More of a Switzerland. Woman, 46' and 'I am an animal in bed, probably a gnu. Man, 56'. I think we should hijack them and get the *LRB* formally to pass the torch to *The Lady*.

That would show Richard Ingrams. I hope.

17 January 2011

Raymond Blanc – pocket-sized dark heart-throb with rounded pot of tummy under grey cashmere – suddenly appeared in the boudoir. I had no idea he was coming in – Matt was interviewing him for a feature about the perfect Valentine's supper.

I was sitting with my feet up on my desk so all he could see of me was some purple tights and very off-trend slouchy boots. I jumped to my feet and greeted him in what I hoped was my best French. He congratulated me on my *succès* and so then I said *quel succès?* and said something about *circulation*. But in fact *circulation* in French means 'traffic', not copies sold, so we switched to English.

Later on, turbo-eco-activist Tamsin Omond is coming in again, this time with Jessie Brinton of *The Sunday Times* to talk about our forest campaign. Have got Tracey Emin on board. I called her on her mobile and said I was president of a campaign to save England's forests and she thought I'd said 'England's Boris' and so she signed up to that on the spot. I had to break the news that it wasn't our Mayor we were trying to protect but forests, and she said yes to that too. Waiting to hear back from Rory Bremner and many other luminaries but the signatories are coming in thick and fast. Told Ben that Tamsin was coming in and he had already Googled her and found out she was on the pink list of powerful gay and lesbian personages. 'It's only because she hasn't been on my conversion course yet,' he said. 'I once trained with a helicopter pilot called Tiffany who claimed to bat for the other team. We called her Tight Fanny.'

When Tamsin came in with Jessica Brinton I took them through to the boardroom to show Ben. When we go there, two ladies in tweed and headscarves were sitting at the blue baize, having tea. And Hels, of course. Hels is always in the boardroom nowadays – Ben and Hels have cosy picnic lunches *à deux* in there sometimes, despite his pathological fear of crumbs. 'Hello, meet these two

ladies who may be doing some flower arranging business with us,'
beamed Ben, as he moved a tea cup on to a coaster. I loved the
juxtaposition of gay eco-starlet Tamsin plus Jessie Brinton – who
was wearing a sort of man's coat as a dress with a bright yellow
lumberjack shirt, and writes a party column for the Style section –
with the doughty ladies from the Shires.

The first thing the editor of the *Flower Arranger* said to me was,
'I met your brother the other day when I was planting trees for
London,' looking me up and down. I hadn't really dressed up that
day and was wearing brown cords, in honour of the forests. '*He's*
gorgeous!' she said with emphasis.

Afterwards I Googled the mag:

> The *Flower Arranger* is the superb full-colour quarterly magazine of
> The National Association of Flower Arrangement Societies.
>
> Learn how to arrange flowers with step-by-step instructions and
> enhance your home with beautiful floral designs. Enjoy up-to-date
> news and views on ever-changing trends.

The truth is, they probably sell hundreds of thousands of copies
a year more than we do.

The in tray:

- a massive package from Laurence Llewellyn-Bowen containing: 8 DVDs of his show about moving to the Cotswolds on
  Living TV called *To The Manor Bowen*; a copy of his book
  A Pinch of Posh: A Beginner's Guide to Being Civilised; a letter
  on paisley-bordered paper from LLB himself, telling me 'only
  read the bits about Sex, Death and Anal Itch, the rest is rather
  overwritten' (I immediately turned to the index and was distressed to find there was no entry for 'anal itch' but there was
  one for 'wife-swapping parties' and 'codpieces'); LLB's designs
  for the Blackpool Illuminations.

18 January 2011

Have received posh letter with a Cyrillic head, from an outfit called The International Foundation For Socio-Economic And Political Studies open brackets The Gorbachev Foundation close brackets.

The letter invites me to the Gorby eightieth birthday celebrations at the Royal Albert Hall on 30 March, an evening to be hosted by Sharon Stone and Kevin Spacey. The letter goes on, 'You have been selected as a committee member alongside Gov Arnold Schwarzenegger, Rt Hon Sir John Major, Hugh Grant, Sir David Tang, Claudia Winkleman, Boris Johnson, Katherine Jenkins and Elizabeth Hurley to name but a few who have already pledged their support.'

In return all I have to do is buy a ticket and help with ticket sales. The letter ends, 'Please do join me on the Gorby 80 committee for what I know is going to be a magnificent event.' I showed it to Ben as I am not forking out for a ticket, to see if he would stump up.

'I cut him up on the A3 once,' he mused, avoiding the issue. 'I was in my Rangie and overtook and suddenly realized I was in a motorcade of Rangies, and I looked in my rear-view mirror and saw that red splodge.' Then he said, 'You had Rebecca Front in, didn't you? I'm her biggest fan,' and looked sad that I hadn't brought her through to meet him in the boardroom like we do most people – Raymond Blanc, Tamsin Omond (of whom he said, 'looks like she needs a good long shower'), etc.

'How did you know?' I asked.

'You put a picture of you both on Twitter,' he said. 'Fireman Fritter had a twitter stuck up his shitter.' I looked blank. 'That's copyright *Viz*,' he said.

I do hope Ben isn't following me on Twitter.

The in tray:

- a piece from a reader in Worthing about the piano accordion. 'I hope it will be of interest to readers of *The Lady*,' writes Mrs Verenne. On the back of the letter there was an ominous addendum: 'Accordions to follow.'
- a letter telling me that Dulverton Library is to close. This is very sad. And asking me to campaign to support the Library Services in West Somerset and elsewhere. Of course I will. But if I do Gorby, Forests, Libraries as well as my secret committee on WikiLeaks (of which more later) I am virtually turning into Jemima Khan.
- a letter from a woman who sends me quite a lot of letters from her 'mas' in the *Sud* of France telling me what a pleasure it was to see Jane Fonda on the front, 'a beautiful lady ageing without Botox'. (Ed's note: no comment.)

HURRAY!!! Apparently our figures are up to 32,000 the past two weeks. Over Christmas, I did not even dare write this, but for a couple of weeks we'd sagged to 27,000 plus. I am SO relieved. The Ladyship sails on.

Lunch with Sarah Baxter of *The Sunday Times*. Hugely good fun. She made me have a glass of wine. We had mega-gossip and decided we should try to replicate the success of the US chat show *The View* with Babs Walters and Whoopi Goldberg. I'm afraid I broke my New Year's Resolution (Not to Show Off) and told her about the stage play of *The Lady*.

Justin who works in production just said, 'Mrs B. in the building. She's with Kath.'

Carolyn observed, 'It's a pity you don't have a priest hole to escape to.'

Ben had asked me to potter through to meet the owner of the

Dalesman and *The Countryman* magazines after lunch. So at about three I knocked on the boardroom door and he said, 'Come in,' heartily. So I went in.

Shock! Instead of the proprietor of the *Dalesman*, Mrs B. was sitting there, and when she saw me she started shaking with rage and couldn't speak.

'Hello, Mrs Budworth,' I said, smiling.

'I've just this minute walked in,' she hissed. Then she started shaking.

'I'll leave you to it, then,' I said pleasantly, backing out in terror.

19 January 2011

Lots of people – from Joanna Trollope to Richard E. Grant – signing our Save England's Forests petition to – yes! – save England's forests. Only Al/Boris won't. Having agreed he would. 'Why shouldn't the government sell off the forests?' he flashed back when I sent him the open letter signed by Tom Stoppard, Rowan Williams, the Poet Laureate, etc.

I spoke to Giles about my awful shuddering confrontation with Mrs B. He told me that she's trying to gang up with two of the Budworth boys to make a caucus on the board to unseat me and wants to have my handwriting analysed by a graphologist to try to assess my character flaws and the scale of the problem I represent.

20 January 2011

Jonathan Guinness, aka Lord Moyne, Diana Mitford's son, in office to research his piece for Mrs B. for the anniversary spesh, so I trotted through to say what-ho to him.

'What's it about,' I said, after we'd greeted each other with beams in the boardroom (I am very charming to all the posh cousins of the Budworths, i.e., the Guinnesses and Mitfords of this world). 'It's about Tello,' he said, as if I would know who that was, and then went into a long anecdote about who Tello was (nanny to the founder's children and mistress to Thomas Gibson Bowles as well, and then had another family by him – and an early editor of the magazine).

Later, i.e., two days after the Mrs Budworth shock (I've told Giles to paint in the log basket if he values his sanity, and Craig Brown has even come up with an ingenious compromise solution which involves a removable log basket made of fuzzy felt), Ben called me into the boardroom.

'I just wanted to say I'm sorry, Rach,' he said, looking sorry. 'When Mum was like that with you . . . I saw how she was . . . well, I was very ashamed and you shouldn't have had to go through that.'

It was very sweet. I immediately felt very sorry for Mrs B. 'Don't worry, Ben,' I said. 'It must be difficult living on her own at Deerbolts, obsessively working out ways to try and have me sacked. So, of course, when she claps eyes on me, she's going to wig out.'

Good news! Mrs B. rang to speak to Matt about the 126th birthday edition and she HAS got Debo to write us a piece! She won't say what, and is only telling Matt that 'the commission has been secured on the basis that Debo has absolutely nothing to do with Rachel Johnson'.

I don't care. A piece by Debo on any subject – bloodhounds, plum pudding, hens – is a scoop and she can be a cover girl again.

Row is brewing about the website. Ben has got it into his head that he wants it to be a completely separate entity from the magazine, and hook in younger readers. Matt, Vicky Murden and I think it should be a site that reflects what the magazine is doing, has flashes of features, and completely reinforces the brand. Whatever, it's got to be a 'sticky' site that people find hard to leave once they've landed on it, like an adhesive mouse trap.

The in tray:

- a piece about lemons called 'Lemons Aren't the Only Fruit' of 1,700 words. It makes me almost nostalgic for cobnuts.
- six-page letter from a reader in Totnes on the importance of manners.
- letter from a retired headmistress who took on a failing school and turned it round, sympathizing with my challenge at *The Lady*.
- a long letter from a 78-year-old in Far Headingley, Leeds, criticizing my first novel, *Notting Hell*. 'It didn't have an ending,' my correspondent complained. 'Were we supposed to invent the ending ourselves, or had I misunderstood, and it has a perfectly clear ending?' She then changes tack, and says that even though she hardly goes out any more, being old, 'I might be glad to take advantage of your Introductions scheme.' (This is our Dateline Platinum service). She goes on. 'I'm obviously a bad bet in every way as, apart from my age, I have osteoporosis, so am shrinking all the time.'

Ken Wharfe (the late Princess Diana's former bodyguard) came in to see Ben. So Ben Wharfed him through to the boudoir. Wharfe looked a little flushed. 'Show him that nice card you got from the 92-year-old,' twinkled Ben.

So I went to my special box where I keep letters from George Osborne, Jilly, Debo, etc., and found it. Wharfe – a former policeman – spent ages examining the postmark and did indeed notice that on the back of the envelope, it was sealed with a kiss (an X). He withdrew it only to reel back when, after seeing the snoozing kitten and puppy on the cad, he opened it to read, 'You and your daughter are a pair of greedy cunts xx.' (I can only imagine this is because my daughter penned a review of a Lady Gaga concert for which, I might add, she has not at the time of writing been paid).

'Do you want me to send it off to forensics?' he asked.

21 January 2011

Walked to work door to door, Notting Hill to Covent Garden. Stopped at the newsagent in Chandos Place.

'How's *The Lady* doing?' Mr Patel asked me.

'You tell me,' I said.

'Well, we used to sell no copies, now we sell three a week,' he said.

'That's a 300 per cent increase,' I chirped.

Felt knackered after the walk in and had to lie down on the *chaise* shit and put my feet up on one of the chairs.

In deference to our readers who do not have an Interweb, I have reinstated something that I canned when I first arrived: a letter from a reader who doesn't have a computer and wants a question answered. I am pleased to report that the first reader's question is where can a mature lady buy a pair of capacious bloomers 'so useful in this colder weather'?

Our lovely workie Scarlett, 17 (we always have a workie/intern, and they work very hard); discovered that there was an online underwear retailer, The Big Bloomers Company, and has replied to the letter giving all the details, all of which we will print on the letters page in the next issue. 'A very intrepid first foray into journalism,' I commended her.

The mag looks great today (we get it in the office on Friday, subscribers get it on Saturday, and newsstands on Tuesday – it's very mysterious). It looks lovely, though I say so myself. There are glossy Sandals bridal ads ('At Sandals your wedding day is as unique as your love' – images of white-clad couples on coral strands, cupcakes, bouquets) which almost make it look like a women's magazine.

Gillian was on the telephone to a courier company (I think, kindly, on my behalf) and instead of using the accepted air traffic control words Alpha, Bravo, Charlie when she was spelling out something, she said, 'N for Noddy,' and for some reason – it was the day of Coulson's resignation, and the day after Alan Johnson resigned because his wife had affair with bodyguard, and the day Blair appeared before Iraq Enquiry for second time – I found that terribly funny.

I was lying on the *chaise* shit reading the *Indy*. Matt and I started imagining the other words Gillian uses over the phone when she wants to make sure the spelling's right. 'T for Teddy', 'B for Babar', 'P for Piglet'. I had tears of laughter running down my face. And so did Matt, who was also bright red as it was teatime, by which point the radiator's been on for hours and we're all passing out.

As this piece in this week's *Campaign* noted:

> Times are hard in publishing-land as *Campaign*'s trip to the premises
> of Britain's oldest women's weekly, *The Lady*, last week revealed.
>
> Even ensconcing Rachel Johnson, the sister of Boris, as editor
> hasn't heralded a modernization. The establishment seems not to
> have changed its office decor since before the Great Depression.
>
> The rooms are straight out of an Edwardian museum, including
> a ladies' smoking room (used for editorial meetings) and a looming
> oil painting of the founder, Thomas Gibson Bowles. There's no
> central-heating system, so the ladies potter about in fluffy slippers
> with electric heaters on high.

Hels came in during our giggling fit and asked if we could change the name of 'Husband's Corner' – a nod to the great P. G. Wodehouse (as 'Husband's Corner', of course, was in *Milady's Bou-*

doir, his fictional spoof of the mag). She explained. Chivas Regal might, she said, come on board to sponsor the column if it was more brand-reinforcing and called something like 'The Gentleman Sponsored by Chivas Regal'.

I then explained about PGW, etc. But she gazed at me as if I didn't get it. I then dumped the problem on Matt's lap and said we could have something gentlemanly and regal in the Almanac.

Mrs B. rang a couple of times. So far, the gala anniversary special comprises: Mrs B. on the illustrator Fromenti, Jonathan Guinness on Tello, the naughty *Lady* editor and founder's mistress, and Debo Duchess of Devonshire on her father, 'The Real Uncle Matthew'. Mrs B. has persuaded Debo to contribute to *The Lady*, a triumph that has so far eluded me, so credit where it is due.

23 January 2011

Slight shock to wake up at 9.30am, idly switch on my iPhone to read the Google Alert headline that said, '*Sunday Telegraph*, Rachel Johnson and Archbishop of Canterbury campaign to halt forest sell-off' and several emails from BBC and ITV asking for interviews. When I go to get the paper in Clarendon Road it turns out the Save England's Forests campaign is the splash in the *Sunday Telegraph* and, slightly problematically for me, Tamsin's name has been removed. So it looks like it's me against the Government. On page 2 there is a montage of me looking almost superhumanly smug, in front of a padlocked five-bar gate in front of a wood, presumably to suggest that all woods will be barred to the public if the sell-off proceeds and I alone am standing between this depressing development and the status quo.

I call Tamsin in alarm and she confirms this. 'The *Telegraph* thought it would catch fire if it was just you.' Presumably, I think, because I am Boris's sister and this is Bad For Dave. And Embarrassing for the Mayor.

So it's my campaign. I am, after all, the President. I refer all bids for press and TV to Tamsin and go for a long walk with Philippa Walker (Mrs Alan Yentob), who is very soothing at these moments.

My mobile keeps ringing. In the end I turn it off. Philippa tells me utterly blissful story about an eco-dinner Trudie and Sting are giving (£3,000 a head) and also about dinner in Charles and Nigella's new house (she served marrowbone and a hunk of beef) but I will be flung into outer darkness for ever if I repeat them here. Forests story is also in *Mail* and *Sunday Times*, with credit to the *Sunday Telegraph*, and on BBC News. Er – well done, Tamsin! Clearly, if you want something stopped – third runway, fare increases, whatever – she's the go-to gal.

24 January 2011

PC from Giles, who is still in total paralysis about whether or not to paint in the log basket, a dilemma that he says is blocking him from doing any other work. In the postcard he also warns 'Adam is third man in boardroom putsch' against me, but I'm sure he's teasing. Giles and Mary are always teasing me.

Hugh St Clair is in office looking very smart in wool pinstripe suit when I finally make it into the boudoir after a long lunch with Channel Four at the Café Anglais (wonderful *assortiment* of artichokes, steamed hake, and a chocolate tart of such exquisite viscosity I almost fainted).

'I had a call from Mrs Budworth,' he said to me when I tottered in, breathing white wine and chocolate fumes over the subs, and having forgotten I was seeing him. 'She wants me to send samples of stuff and wallpapers so she can redecorate *The Lady*'s smoking room.'

'But why,' I panted. 'She says she spent £25,000 of her own

money already on redecorating it and that's why she's so furious
with me for pointing out it's got nasty sofas and bamboo occasional tables, and the depressing trompe l'œil of the spaniel all the
time.'

'Actually, she says she spent £50,000,' said Hugh.

Jeez. Have had call from the Secretary of State for the Environment
Caroline Spelman, who wants me to discuss the Forests Campaign.
I immediately call Tamsin. 'I need briefing if I'm going to talk to
her. What do I do?' I gibbered.

'Well, that's funny because I had a call from Ed (Miliband –
Tamsin is very well connected) this morning also wanting to bend
my ear about the campaign, saying what a good thing we are doing,
and how he's right behind it,' she said. 'And I told him we couldn't
discuss it with him. It's not a party political issue.'

'Yes, Tams,' I agreed fervently. 'The forests are bigger than that.
We can't let either party hijack them.' Though I felt a bit wobbly –
there was very firm piece in *The Times* by Matt Ridley, the former
chairman of Northern Rock, saying that the Government should
sell off the forests, that the Forestry Commission was bleating like
turkeys protesting against Christmas, and selling all our woodlands to the highest bidder was the best of all possible outcomes. If
asked about this, I will say in the strongest terms that I will receive
no lectures about public ownership from Ridley as his bank went
bust, his shareholders (or should that be 'stakeholders'?) lost
money, and he had to go cap in hand to the taxpayer.

So we have agreed that I will not talk to C. Spelman and Tamsin
will not talk to E. Miliband and we will float above the fray.

Have just come back from boardroom in tears from meeting
with the very nice Christopher Nieper, who is one of our biggest
advertisers, whose nighties and velour bed jackets and sensible,
English clothes, made by Englishwomen for Englishwomen, sell

and sell. It wasn't Mr Nightie, who couldn't have been more charming. He is fiercely proud that his clothes are designed and made in England, and so he should be. I am sending Matt to write up the Derbyshire factory – which has an apprenticeship scheme, and so on – at the same time as he is chased by a pack of bloodhounds on the Chatsworth Estate (as the garment factory is one stop before Chesterfield and he can do two features for the price of one train ticket).

No, am in tears because Hels' dog – a big chocolate Lab – bit me in the face just under the eye during the meeting about nightwear. And drew blood, and thudded into my cheekbone with the force of a dumper truck.

I staggered back, clutching my bleeding face.

'He's never done that before,' said Helen. 'I wonder why he bit you?' As if, were I a nice, normal person, the dog would have greeted me with a sloppy lick.

I had to go through rest of meeting mopping cut below eye with kitchen towel that Ben always has to hand in case someone spills so much as a drop of tea on the boardroom table.

'Well done, Rach,' he said, as I got to the end of the meeting with Nieper's nighties, without dissolving into tears. Even so, I called my GP and she insisted I came by for antibiotics. Just before I left, Caroline Spelman called a third time.

At the surgery nice Dr Bloom said that she had to report Arthur to the police and get something called a 'Dogbo'.

25 January 2011

Was on the telephone to my chum Camilla Long, self-pityingly describing my bite, when this popped into my inbox:

From: A. A. Gill
To: Rachel Johnson
Sent: 25 January 2011 10:17
Subject: Re: Barking

How's the dog?

When I told him the dog was receiving counselling, he replied:

What breed?

Is nose intact or in mongrel?

Etc., etc., until we got bored.

First thing, Ben came into the boudoir. He doesn't usually. 'I'm on my morning round,' he said. He peered at my face, which has a slash across my cheekbone like duelling scar. 'That'll be gone by tomorrow,' he told me. I wouldn't expect Adrian Gill to be sympathetic, but no TLC from Ben Budworth either.

A man in Italy, whose olive farm the journalist Rosie Millard stayed at, has ordered 10,000 copies of the 9 January issue of the mag because he wants to distribute the three-page travel-puff piece with many colour photographs amongst his friends and family. So Ben asked B-Cal to find out how many returns there were and whether we could recuperate them to 'sell them on to the Eyetie' for £1 a pop.

B-Cal was in the boardroom when I went in. 'The edition of 9 Jan has just been pulped,' he said. 'Well, why don't we reprint it?' I said, thinking, *10,000 friends?* I don't know if I could round up a dozen.

B-Cal went off to get a quote. But then I had a better idea. While Ben was doing his rounds this morning I said, 'Look, why don't we just run the olive-picking feature again? It'll be much cheaper than reprinting the whole mag, even if the plates are still available.'

'That's a good idea,' said Ben, looking as if I was at last of some use to him. 'Cheaper' is always a good word to throw around with publishers, I've noticed.

Then I had to ruin it.

'Our readers are so old they won't notice. If they like something, give it to them again, is what I say,' I went on, deliberately trying to annoy him. He hates it when I say anything about the readers' ages. At this juncture, I thought I should say something about the dog incident, so I told him my GP had said she has to report dog bites to the police and if Arthur bit anyone again things would not be looking up for the old boy.

'But Arthur was only being friendly,' he said. 'It was like a boy's first kiss! Just a bit clumsy! He wasn't being aggressive.'

'Ben!' I snapped. 'Arthur bit me in the face.' I looked at Matt for support but he was gazing innocently into his screen.

'That's not what I saw,' Ben insisted, but his eyes were darting around. 'I just saw him being friendly. He did the same to Ros earlier and she agrees, he wasn't trying to bite her, he was just being friendly.'

'Ben, if Arthur's done it once he'll do it again,' I said.

Then he said threateningly that if I went on in this vein he would have to ban all dogs from the office (i.e., Coco) for reasons of elf and safety. So I shut up, feeling upset.

I tweeted a pic of Tamsin Omond sitting on the *chaise* shit last night. It was retweeted by one person – @maturedatinguk. I haven't told her as she's only about 25 and might be creeped out.

Finally, after the DEFRA website kept failing to put us through to each other, I spoke to Caroline Spelman. She told me that she was adding additional amendments to the Public Bodies Bill to protect all public forests, not just heritage ones we've heard of like Savernake and the Forest of Dean. She explained why the Forestry Commission couldn't and shouldn't continue in its current form: it is both the main seller and regulator of the timber market.

'That sounds very positive, Mrs Spelman,' I oiled. 'By the way, you did very well on *Question Time* (it was a head to head with George Galloway and Ali Campbell) and more importantly, you looked very nice too.'

26 January 2011

Lunch with Ed Victor at the new French Covent Garden brasserie called Les Deux Salons where had delicious ravioli made of meat, followed by citrus-infused, very fancy quinoa salad. Like everyone else except me, Ed hasn't been drinking all month and looked pink and healthy. Ed said that he'd been to one of Josephine Hart's poetry readings at the London Library. At which Antonia (Dame, Lady, etc., now known as Notre Dame by her friends, or merely Goddess) had told Charles Dance, the actor, that he should play Ed in the Victor biopic. 'I would be honoured to,' said Dance, politely. 'And who should play you, Antonia?'

Antonia beamed. 'Scarlett Johansson, of course.' I laughed so much I almost fell off my banquette on top of Sir Jeremy Green-stock, the top diplomat and ex-PUS, who was on next table being lunched by two men (who looked either like spooks or hedge funders – so hard to tell these days).

Yesterday Ben told me that he is terminating the contract of the cleaner who wanders round with a damp cloth once a week and gives our telephones a desultory wipe. 'I'm thinking of getting in an old-fashioned char for five hours, once a day, six to eleven p.m.,' he said.

'Good plan,' I said.

'How long do you think we've had a contract with the cleaning company BTW,' he said, flicking open a dog-eared folder.

'Dunno,' I said.

'Since 1948.'

27 January 2011

Email from Zebedee our delicious cartoonist asking me who is commissioning the cartoon that accompanies the ed's letter? 'Is it me, or is it Mrs B., as it is the epochal edition commemorating 126 years of publication.'

'Me!' I whizzed back.

Got this back from Zeb:

I'm a reasonably perceptive chap. Mrs B. told me with great pride that she was guest-editing and then, slightly more humbly, that maybe she wasn't exactly editing but would have some input on the 126th anniversary edition, about 8 pages she hoped. (I pointed out that the 126th birthday probably wouldn't be marked in quite such a pronounced fashion as the preceding one but she sounded so excited.) . . . She then sent me her handwritten article about Lady Diana and a rat and asked me to illustrate it. Not being completely sure of the editorial merit of the piece (I am no judge) I made sure that we (me and Mrs B.) came to an agreement that whether the piece made the mag or no, I would receive payment for my drawing as she would purchase the original.

As far as I see it, this is one of those win-win scenarios I am so fond of. I hope you think so too.

Zebedee.

We have the first black *Lady* cover girl, the scrumptious, smiley Lorraine Pascale, a supermodel turned telly chef.

'Can you come into the boardroom,' Ben called, as I was skimming Mrs B.'s piece about Lady Diana and the rat and the Taj

Mahal, which was as bonkers as it sounds. There is a board meeting tomorrow and he is preparing madly for it.

I went round and knocked ostentatiously and long on the boardroom door. The last two times I'd been in there I'd been given my marching orders to leave the room by Mrs Budworth and then mauled by Hels' dog. (Ivo is jokingly saying that in order to achieve the desired effect she must have been holding up photos of me to the dog, pointing, and saying to Arthur, 'Kill! Kill!')

'Come in,' sang out Ben in his cheeriest tones.

Richard was sitting at head of table. Graphs showing our wildly zigzagging circulation and soaring costs were littered on the blue baize alongside the remains of the coffee. Richard was staring at the toothsome cover image of Pascale in a tight sweater, holding up a lemon meringue pie covered with luscious red strawberries. 'I'm in shock,' he said.

'Yes,' I said stoutly. 'First black on cover. Am really proud.'

The brothers exchanged a glance. 'No, it's not,' said Ben. 'You had that township tyke on the cover when the Princes went off to South Africa.' They searched the magazine rack of past issues and pointed to the small African child in a beanie hat standing, indeed, between William and Harry on the cover (which did very badly).

Let's see how Lorraine does. I think it's another big leap forward, but our readers might not.

28 January 2011

Am member of a secret committee set up to defend the right to publish that is preparing a sharp open letter in support of WikiLeaks and Julian Assange. The first meeting I went to was at the Frontline Club in Paddington, and we were generously hosted by Vaughan Smith, the owner whose 'stately home in Suffolk' (actually an organic farm in Norfolk, but he can't be arsed to correct the press) is where Team Assange has been holed up for weeks. My only contribution to the meeting – which was attended by several of the world's leading intellectuals, including Anthony Barnett, founder of openDemocracy, who is so intelligent that when he looks at you it's as if you're being scoped by a laser beam – was to suggest Jemima Khan joined the committee. No one had suggested it, and yet Jemima ('please don't call me a socialite') is closely associated with the freedom to publish campaign, and has been at Assange's elbow at every twisty turn.

They did. So when I turned up to the committee meeting on Thursday, she was there, in Prada leggings and lovely, slouchy grey Burberry coat.

'I think we've already met, I'm a friend of your brother Jo's,' she said.

'We did yoga for pregnancy together, at the Life Centre in Notting Hill,' I simpered. 'You were nine months pregnant but were so slim I complained to the instructor that you were in the wrong class.'

We were in the members' function room and it was freezing as Vaughan was having the roof fixed. A waitress came round and took our orders for hot beverages.

'Tea, please,' I said. 'Do you have any herbal?' And Jemima and I carried on chattering. At which point, the writer Henry Porter exploded. 'Yoga!' he shouted. 'Peppermint tea! We're here to save freedom of speech, not have a Notting Hill coffee morning!' We giggled. She is – like her brother – sculpted out of caramel. I loved it when she said 'Hugh' because it meant HUGH GRANT! And Zac meant ZAC! Etc. When I got in the car afterwards, one of her long auburn hairs was sticking to the cover of my iPhone. I almost kept it as a holy relic.

The in tray:

- letter from a man in Blackpool telling me about his ulcer, which led to the amputation of his right foot. 'I died during surgery. I was rushed to intensive care and brought back to life,' the handwritten letter went on.

- a man from Grantham, Lincs, sending me examples of his puzzles, word searches and quizzes in hope of inclusion.

- invitations to speak at three events: Scottish Women of Achievement; Kensington and Chelsea Women's Club's celebration of International Women's Day; and at a breakfast for an outfit called Chartwell. I don't want to do any of them but in my new guise as a member of Great and Good my instinct is always to say yes. However, re the K&C one, the heart did sink even more than usual. 'We would like to extend a heartfelt invitation to be our Guest Speaker ... the members begin arriving at 9.30 a.m. (I blenched: 9.30 a.m.? It's an even longer day than *The Lady* literary lunch!) for coffee and fellowship (COFFEE AND FELLOWSHIP!!! Words fail me). The meeting proper is called to order at 10.30 a.m. Your 30- to 35-minute talk will be followed by a short Q&A. We are happy to offer you a small honorarium as a token of our appreciation . . .'

Victor Olliver – the blogger who writes as Madame Arcati and calls us the 'old cunties' weekly' – has been in touch. He has moved to Hove, and become an astrology student. So I have commissioned him to write our horror-scopes but told him they had to be *Lady*-appropriate, i.e., all about gardening, grandchildren, untidy husbands, tiresome aches and pains, and things that go bump in the night.

The Lady

15 FEBRUARY 2011   £1.80

My father
The Lady's man
by **Debo**

FRANKIE
HOWERD'S
WIG
*& the day
Peter Cook
got frisky*

Jojo Moyes
**WHY I
STOPPED
'TALKING
PROPER'**

**HOW TO
PAINT**
*Just add
water*

**DAISY
WAUGH**
*seduced by
Valentino*

ANNIVERSARY SPECIAL

DULWICH GALLERY · JONATHAN GUINNESS · DENTAL HEALTH · JANE SHILLING
JANE CLARKE · HUNDREDS OF HOLIDAY AND JOB ADVERTISEMENTS EACH WEEK

FEBRUARY

1 *February 2011*

Matt has just been offered a Valentine's-themed piece on testicular cancer, I've been asked by the *Mail on Sunday* to write about my Raynaud's Syndrome and I've just had a call from the *Mail* asking me to rewrite my vajacial piece for them! Apparently PAUL DACRE manifested in person at 'Femail' and demanded it.

I've emailed *Vogue* saying I can't bear to have my vagina in the *Mail* and begging them not to syndicate the piece.

To Downing Street for a reception for magazine editors. What a palaver! We all got an email during the day:

Please can we ask that you arrive at tonight's Reception as close to 5.30 p.m. as possible as it will take some time to get through security. It is imperative that you bring photo ID with you that matches the name on your invitation – please ensure that you let us know as soon as possible if your photo ID is in a different name.

Please remember that the event is off the record, no personal photography is permitted and the dress code is smart (no jeans or trainers). For security reasons guests are asked not to tweet about the event beforehand.

We look forward to seeing you later.

The policemen are very friendly, but inside it's really a bland cross between the Goring Hotel and a stage set, all plush carpet and stripey-wallpaper walls and long corridors. As everyone says, it is much bigger than it looks (just as movie stars are always smaller on screen, the interior of Downing Street seems to expand infinitely in an *Alice in Wonderland*-ish way as soon as you go through the glossy black door).

Chatted to *GQ* ed Dylan Jones, who said, as I pitched him a piece about playboys, 'I'm falling asleep.' Saw Dave, whose face was a curious bubblegum pink colour. Much speculation about his migrating bald patch. I was too shy to talk to him as I am being openly irritating on the forests and Al/Boris had just scrapped with George Osborne in Davos over the 10p tax rate.

Had a nice chat with the woman I'd met in the boardroom before – the editor of the *Flower Arranger* magazine, who always asks me if I can get her an interview with Boris. She asked me again in Number 10.

Then to the Royal Opera House with Penny Smith to see *Die Zauberflöte*. Quick snifter first, then into the stalls. Found it a bit slow. David Mellor, another opera critic, who was there with his wife (wife? Not sure – I think also called Penny) asked me for my view and I said it lacked propulsive energy. Then he told me the conductor was second to none. During the interval, we had sandwiches and more Chardonnay, and Penny (Smith) and I found ourselves on the same table as Dr Christian Jessen and his mandate. He was rather nice. And very ripped (i.e., super-fit).

Afterwards, the Mellors invited us to carry on drinking and chatting so we went to Tuttons, round the corner, and David Mellor (very sharp, very good fun) moaned about the Tories lacking a real sense of what it means to be a Tory.

In cab on way home got an email from Camilla Long warning me my piece for *Vogue* about the bikini wax was all over the *Mail* website. This puzzled me; we'd refused to syndicate it, and I'd refused to write a bespoke version. So what could they have?

Turns out they did a write-off. 'Boris's publicity-mad sister, her teenage daughter and a confession on the perils of bikini waxing' was the page 9 lead. It was in what Matt calls the 'bad family slot'.

2 February 2011

And then followed first a day and then a week of complete misery over which I will draw veil. Everyone is furious – family, friends, employers, random strangers who accost me in the street. I probably should never have written the *Vogue* 'intimate waxing' piece, and certainly never have made the cardinal error of writing about my own child in such a context. *Je regrette tout!*

But the show had to go on and after looking at the papers (beyond bitchy, the Glendas) I took a Valium and went to the House of Lords, where the Save England's Forests campaign, i.e., me and Tamsin, plus David Babbs (from the 38 Degrees campaign) were meeting with biddable peers. Even though the Public Bodies Bill which contains the forestry clauses is political suicide, the peers are going to have to vote on it. It looks at the moment as if the Government is wedded to selling off the forests on ideological grounds – it will cost more in grants and subsidies, etc., to sell them than to keep them on.

On the plus side of this torrid day, at least no wag has written a hilarious nib about the coincidence that I am saving England's forests while having my own bush removed. Yet.

Card from Alex Shulman with my voucher copy of *Vogue* with the offending piece, saying, 'Thank you – the most talked-about piece of the year!'

I was quite pleased – until I realized it was only 2 February.

3 February 2011

Typical travel feature pitch from unknown freelancer (2):

> Hi Rachel,
>
> I wondered if you'd be interested in The Womb Room in Gran Canaria? It's part of the Corallium Spa on Costa Meloneras. You enter through the neck to the uterus which is made out of pink carpet while the room itself has a pink carpet splashed with vermillion fabric revolving to simulate a giant umbilical cord and there are blood-coloured waterbeds representing the amniotic sac. Breathy music is played to recreate the noises heard within the womb.
>
> I've seen pics, and it doesn't look as gross as its sounds – and it is supposed to be very relaxing. The spa also offers all the usual things: sauna, steam, treatments, etc. I thought it might work on its own, or perhaps work as part of a round-up of other wacky spas and treatments?

The way I'm feeling, I might check in – and never descend the birth canal into the outside world again.

7 February 2011

Question of the week is proving a surprising hit, even if most of the queries are about pants. I've had letters about where to buy ladies' bloomers, and then this:

> Dear Madam,
>
> I'm writing in the anticipation that *The Lady* is able to pass on to me the address of a ladies' underwear firm that produces ladies' pants

made of nylon. Years and years ago it was easy to find pants made of this material, usually made by Walker Reid, now I only come across this material in nylon sheets coming by mail order from Bedford – a very smooth interlock nylon. Even to find pants that are comfortably loose-fitting is difficult, except in cotton. The nylon was easy to handwash and dry quickly.

My lady from Hankerton continues in her letter, written in pencil, 'Modern materials seem to be for garments that are skin tight and rather restricting.'

And this – written in capitals – from Windsor: 'Could you please kindly inform me where I could write to, to stop junk mail from coming through my letter box. I have presently been greatly distressed by a company offering me £25,000. I would be greatly pleased if you could tell me how to stop this. I am aged 78 years, with no nearby relatives.'

When I get letters like this, I realize we've got to keep publishing no matter what. *The Lady* is not merely a magazine; sometimes I think we are, for some readers, their last remaining point of contact with the frightening, modern outside world.

9 February 2011

Editorial meeting. Talked about doing travel more systematically, and beauty in-house, so we can all share in the serums and spa treatments, not to mention the press trips to Madeira and Malta, as they come in.

We are running Rosie Millard's piece about olive picking in Tuscany again because the Italian/Eyetie who owns the olive grove wants to buy 10,000 copies to distribute among his friends and family. The same week, the price is going up. So the readers will be paying an extra 20p . . . to read the same piece again!

At the editorial and production meeting we talked about covers going forward, and I mentioned Kay Burley, the Sky News presenter. Ben went into one of his rants about how our readers wouldn't like her. 'She's good-looking, all over the telly, and she's got a novel coming out,' I said. He denied all this and said that I only thought Kay was cover-worthy because I do Sky News and go to London parties. As he spoke he squashed his thumb on the desk meaningfully, as if to say, 'You're on thin ice and under my thumb. Do NOT contradict me.'

Had to leave early to go to the Frontline Club for meeting about WikiLeaks with new friend Jemima.

The in tray:

- two chocolate cakes.
- a Peggy Porschen Easter cake with buttercream icing (already??).
- a tray of Medjool dates that come in a smart dark box that people keep opening, seeing the dates instead of chocs, and closing again.

10 February 2011

Email from Gillian:

> A reader, 92 yrs, rang (didn't want to give her name). She loved the Xmas issue, but really doesn't like the 'Princess Diaries' column – feels it's misleading because it says 'by Kate Middleton' and she didn't realize it was a spoof at first. It's not in the best of taste. This reader's not a subscriber, but has been buying the magazine for 40 years.

11 *February 2011*

Walked in with Coco through driving rain, wrote two pieces, then looked at the notes that had been prepared for me by the nice men from Walford Wilkie for my speech today at the Institute of Directors to the eighty new '*Lady* Ambassadors'. This is a wheeze dreamed up by Walford Wilkie. In our case, *Lady* Ambos will get a name badge with their own unique number, discounts at selected companies like Pickett and Champneys, and, I think, commission on each subscription they flog plus a prize (luxury trip on Orient Express) for the *Lady* Ambo who does best over the year. They had all dressed up to the nines and came from all corners of the country: St Andrews, Aberdeen, Wales. They were all bushy-tailed and keen to get stuck in. I was terrified.

There were cakes and tea laid out on tables at the back, and serried ranks of chairs. Me, Hels, Ben and Susan Wade Weeks (who is going to run the Ambo programme) sat up front, alongside Nick Steyn from Walford Wilkie. Steyn opened proceedings by thanking everyone for coming, then Ben launched into a passionate address in which he windmilled his arms and howled, 'Praise *The Lady*,' as if we were all in a Southern Baptist Church, and gave a potted history of *The Lady* (quite a lot about Uncle Tom).

In between the Tony Robbins-style motivational stuff he made some soundly sincere points. Adam was there filming it all from the back – not sure what for – so Ben kept saying things like, 'If you get caught drink-driving on the way home, Adam's your man.' He mentioned the beauty contest to win *The Lady* editorship, and then how he had known he had to get Helen Robinson on board too. He stopped, and looked across at Hels in her tight purple dress, colour coded with our signature *Lady* shade, and said, 'Maybe I just like blonde hair,' and went a bit red and lost the thread.

I then gave an impassioned speech in which I said things like, 'You are all *Ladies*,' and then Helen walked them through the brief of being a *Lady* Ambo. I sensed they were there not because they were after commission on sales, but because they wanted to be part of something, and to help. They were not after small change, in fact, but Big Society. They also wanted a chance to vent about *The Lady*. A couple from Norfolk bearded me about Tracey Emin and about the fact she used the word 'fuck'. 'I've been reading *The Lady* for forty years and I've never read the word "fuck" until you put it in,' one said. 'Fuck! What were you thinking of!' she banged on, as if she had Tourette's.

I felt there was much more of this to come so when we broke for tea and cakes I made Walford Wilkie reconvene so we could continue the Q&A. This went on till 4.45 p.m. so I was there for almost four hours.

Raced back to the office where Tamsin Omond, my dad, and the Woodland Trust were waiting for me to join strategy meeting on forests. They had cups of tea provided by Gillian. When I burst in, the boudoir was boiling hot and Coco was hiding under my desk. All the shelves that Viktor the Bolivian housekeeper had put up under the Hugh St Clair plan had collapsed on top of her and piles of books littered the floor.

The in tray:

- a box of Devonshire tea.
- box of Prestat chocs to celebrate the Royal Wedding – 'finest truffles' in red, white, blue and gold Union Jack box.

Well, they were in my in tray when I left for Pall Mall, in a carrier bag addressed to ME but when I returned from rallying the *Lady* Ambos they had already been consumed. 'Is that all that came today?' I wailed, not having had lunch.

'There were some fishcakes in yesterday, Rachel,' replied Gillian, 'But Judy and I ate them. They were very average, I'm afraid.'

Email from Maureen, Ben's PA:

Hi Everyone,

The Maiden Lane doors may be blocked off today due to the work outside.

They do not want anyone to come out of the door and fall down a hole.

Maureen

Kind regards
Maureen Goodman
PA to Publisher

15 *February* 2011

A team from a blog/website called the Weekly Wrinkle came in to see if there was anything we could do together. I hate meetings but I liked this lot. Just as I like Walford Wilkie. One is so grateful that anyone shows an interest. And the tide is going out so fast for print magazines that we have to consider any port in a storm: we will have to do more events, more lit lunches, even conferences. Soon I will, I predict, be living in Travelodges and giving after-dinner motivational speeches to Avon Ladies or those roving teams from Colour Me Beautiful.

The problem is we are trying to make our own website a destination place of loveliness and utility too, and we have many more unique users than Weekly Wrinkle do. So even though what they do is personal, and tasteful, and has character, I can't really see how they can help us.

Piece in 'Londoner's Diary' this evening:

Look out, Rachel Johnson. Today's special 126th anniversary issue of *The Lady* is co-edited by Julia Budworth, the proprietor who claims Johnson is obsessed with penises.

Mrs Budworth, granddaughter of the founder, has already scored a notable coup by recruiting her first cousin, Deborah, Dowager Duchess of Devonshire, to write for the mag.

When Johnson asked the Duchess to be *The Lady*'s agony aunt a year ago during the Channel 4 *Cutting Edge* documentary, The Lady *and the Revamp*, she declined, saying, 'Do ask me again next year, if I'm still alive.' But now, with one telephone call, Mrs Budworth has persuaded Debo to write about her father David Mitford, who was once general manager of *The Lady* and used his pet mongoose to catch rats in the basement.

She has also signed up Debo's nephew, Jonathan Guinness, Lord Moyne, to write a piece about the 'Naughty' *Lady* editor. But it's not Rachel this time. Mrs Budworth has written two articles herself, one about *The Lady*'s founder Thomas Gibson Bowles and another about Marcel Fromenti, a *Lady* contributor who designed for Dior. The days when *The Lady* was largely populated by Johnsons are well and truly over.

To the Royal Opera House for the Orion annual author party. Arrived at same time as Antonia Fraser. 'Hello, Dame Lady Goddess,' I greeted her. It was a scrum but at least the champagne was cold. At one point I was talking to the historian Antony Beevor and Julian, now Lord Fellowes, came up. We were introduced. 'You've forgotten me,' he cried. 'No, I haven't,' I assured him. Then I tried to suss him out on the forests – we need to get some Tories to vote against the Public Bodies Bill, most cross-benchers (I had already turned Lord Browne of BP at the same party) and all the bishops.

He seemed quite amenable and started saying the legislation did seem puzzling, and there seemed little point to lose so much political capital for so little gain.

'Yes,' I agreed. 'Not even Margaret Thatcher thought selling the forests was a good idea.'

'Don't mention Lady Thatcher,' he snapped. 'How dare you bring her name into it!' Then he turned on his heel and barrelled through the party away from me as fast as his legs could carry him.

It was all very dramatic, and odd. Is one not allowed to say 'Thatcher', as in Harry Potter the word 'Voldemort' is *verboten*?

Then to Ruby Wax's opening night of her two-woman show, *Losing It*, in which she – a Notting Hill celebrity – talks about the shallowness of the Notting Hill celebrity lifestyle, how attention is an addiction and how getting old sucks. It was brilliant, but I felt like slitting my wrists afterwards.

17 February 2011

The Government has yew-turned on forests. They've canned the consultation. I am rather embarrassed.

'Rachel Johnson has duffed up the Government,' it says on the *Spectator* website. On *PM*, Eddie Mair cued in the story with the words, 'Rachel Johnson has defeated Caroline Spelman.'

This is all nonsense, of course. It just makes the story better if the media can say that Boris's sis has created so much noise that there's been a U-turn. In reality, it's been the thousands of emails clogging MPs' inboxes that have seen the sell-off wither on the vine. Tomorrow they are likely to announce the withdrawal of the forestry clauses from the Public Bodies Bill – in other words, a total success.

Also, all I can think about is the dream I had, just before dawn. I was with Al. He could fly, and I couldn't. So he put me on his shoulders, and he flew up into the air, with me riding piggyback. We flew up and up over London till the city was spread beneath us. I was worried we were flying too high and we wouldn't be able to land. We were over Trafalgar Square and I said, 'I want to go down,' and we both just plummeted to earth, and I was about to be impaled by Nelson's Column, and then I woke up. It was just a dream. But so painfully obvious in meaning we do not have, this time, to page Dr Jung to reception to interpret it, I fear.

Despite the horrors of the *Vogue* piece, and my warning from Ben, it's not been a bad week.

1. The forests sell-off has been halted, in a tiny way thanks to Save England's Forests (Pres: Rachel Johnson) but, in a much larger way, thanks to the irritation of backbenchers that thousands of emails from tree-hugging constituents are clogging their inboxes.
2. Much more importantly, when it comes to the key issue of the future of the mag (i.e., where are we going and is the conveyance a handbasket or not?), the audited ABC figures for the past six months have come in. And they're not bad at all. The context is, the women's weekly market is down 8.4 per cent. Eight out of the 25 titles in the sector recorded double-digit falls in sales. Only two titles have posted increases – something called *Real People* (me neither, but I can't wait to get my hands on a copy), which is up 1 per cent. But at the super-soar-away *Lady*, we are up 4.9 per cent year on year. *OK!* and *Heat* are down more than 20 per cent. Against the downwards trend, we are up more than 13 per cent. Edwina and B-Cal had put together a press release under the heading '*The Lady* Bucks the Trend', which I thought was a bit bland so I dictated a quote

for Ben to put under his name: 'These fabulous figures reassure us there will always be a healthy appetite for an intelligent, quality offering in the crowded weekly marketplace.' Well, you have to sound confident.

3. We have our first personal ad! It's a corker. 'Deaf, Asthmatic Grandma,' it begins.

4. Mrs B. just called to speak to Matt and complain that we used a black and white photograph of the founder Thomas Gibson Bowles with a quill pen in one hand, a cigarette in the other, instead of a 'lovely colour image of the Chartran portrait'. Usually he passes on choice nuggets that Mrs B. says about me but this time she was docile. It may be that peace has broken out. 'Did she say anything unpleasant?' I checked. 'No, she was quite restrained this time,' he said. I have to say, I felt almost disappointed.

5. The telephone rang outside my office, and Gillian just answered pleasantly. 'Hello. Editorial,' she said. 'No, I'm her PA. Can I help?' Pause. 'It's about thirty inches long,' she is saying. 'You can rest your hand on it if you get tired.' I have no idea what she's talking about, but it doesn't matter.

Item in Richard Kay, *Daily Mail*:

They are both expert practitioners of the mot juste, but when newly ennobled writer Julian Fellowes and Rachel Johnson, editor of *The Lady* magazine, clashed over Lady Thatcher, it led to an unsophisticated verbal spat.

The two were discussing Government cuts at the champagne-fuelled Orion authors' party at the Royal Opera House when Lord Fellowes, a great admirer of the former PM, snapped and stalked off. 'I know I've made a fool of myself, but you have to stand up for what you believe in,' he said later. 'Rachel made a very rude comment about Margaret Thatcher, and there is no need for it. I am fed up with the disrespect shown to Margaret by media people like her.'

What prompted such anger? Rachel, who is campaigning against the sale of woodlands, had observed: 'Not even Mrs Thatcher thought it a good idea to privatize the forests.' Impudent pup!

I keep trying to finish this diary, or this section of it, so Penguin can get cracking on it. But every day, something happens that I simply can't leave out.

I was getting ready to leave the house – i.e., taking Coco round the garden a few times – when a new number popped on my screen. 'Rach, it's Hels.'

'Oh hi, Hels,' I said. I wondered why she was ringing.

'Ben's been in a terrible accident,' she said, sounding choked. 'On his bike.'

Then she told me: he'd been going past Buckingham Palace and a woman did a U-turn on the Mall and he 'T-boned' her. As Hels said the word 'T-boned' I heard Ben saying it, and I had a vision of him on his massive bike, ploughing into the flank of a woman driver. He's in the high dependency unit of St Thomas': broken sternum, cuts to leg, bruising to face, and the danger is there's blood loss and it's collected around his heart, so he's on a monitor.

'I was in Cheshire and I got on the first train,' said Hels.

I was so glad that Ben had Hels. She is very, very nice, even if her dog bit me. And she has all the right maternal/nursey instincts. 'I left my twelve-year-old in Cheshire with my parents, and just came,' she said.

On the way in, I called Gillian. 'Mrs Budworth rang to speak to you,' she said. 'She said that Ben must be left in total peace and quiet, and can you call her.'

A return to form – so Mrs B. had already rung to tell me not to go in to see Ben in hospital. As if the mere sight of me might induce cardiac arrest!

I called Mrs B. in 'The Gorgon's Lair'.

'Rachel,' she said, as soon as she picked up the phone. It was as if she knew it would be me. Then, far from telling me not to venture near the bedside, we had a lovely chat. She sounded more cheerful than I'd ever heard her sound, despite her son, in her words, 'being plastered all over the road'. Gales of laughter pealed forth from Deerbolts Hall, and echoed round the boudoir in Bedford Street. I thought that peace really had broken out, but then we started talking about how Ben would get up and down the stairs as a hobbling invalid, and she raised the notion of installing something called a 'bosun's chair' on the Maiden Lane staircase.

'Is that like a Stannah stairlift?' I said. 'Those stairs are awfully steep.' Then she said that she'd often thought about putting a piece of string across those stairs. 'To stop people falling down them?' I asked innocently. She roared with laughter, even louder.

'No, dear girl,' she said. 'You really have no idea of the murderous instincts of *Lady* staff, do you?'

Then I got it – the string would be to send her brother, Uncle Tom, tumbling to his death. 'Ah, a trip wire,' I said.

'Oh, one day, there'll be a nice piece of string for you too,' she sang out gaily, her voice bubbling with joy and mischief. 'You'd better watch it,' she said, affectionately almost.

After eighteen months of Bedford Street, nothing would surprise me.

As I left to go to Tesco Metro at lunchtime, there was a man at the Irish funeral parlour entrance, with a linen sack over his shoulder, just standing there. 'The laundered tea-towels,' he told me.

Joan came to the front, with her fluffy slippers on. 'Hold on, I'll just get the soileds,' she said, and disappeared.

Speaking of soileds, this just in from Maureen, Ben's PA:

Hi Everyone,

Viktor will be coming round tomorrow morning with samples of
toilet paper and kitchen rolls. He will give each department a kitchen
roll to use, and he will place a toilet roll in the toilets. I would like your
opinion on them. You will see the difference as the sample toilet roll
is smooth not patterned and the kitchen roll has a diamond pattern.

Look forward to your comments.

Maureen

The in tray:

- an invitation from Beatrix, an Old English Sheepdog, to Coco
  to her eighth birthday party at the West Meadow at Kenwood
  House.
- a bottle of Mateus Rosé with a label round its neck saying
  'Quench your thirst for a Eurocamp holiday this year'.

22 February 2011

Ben still in hospital. Will go and visit him this afternoon with his
get-well card signed by all staff. I put, 'Enjoy your break from Bedford Street.' Piers is going around showing Ben's enormous shiner
to everyone on his iPhone and saying that Ben organized the smash
as another way of getting out of dealing with payroll this month.
The in tray:

- invite from English Speaking Union, from a kind-sounding
  former women's page editor from the *Yorkshire Evening Post*,

asking me to speak at the annual Thanksgiving Luncheon on Sunday 6th November. I look at this date and feel blank. I have no idea what I'll be doing in November this year. I don't know what I'm doing in the summer or Easter holidays, let alone November. I take the letter through to Gillian. I've decided I'll reply with a variant of what Debo said to me when I asked her to be agony aunt and she didn't want to say yes but didn't want to say no either. 'Tell Jacqueline Millington' – I peer at the name after the sign-off, which is 'Happy Days and Cosy Nights, Yours Sincerely, Jacqueline Millington' – 'to ask me again next year, if I'm still editing *The Lady*. And still alive, of course,' I added.

I must stop now and pass the edition of 1 March (Hermione Norris from *Spooks* on the cover) and go and see Ben in hospital.

It's not so much Happy Days and Cosy Nights at the moment, more a cross between a French farce and *Holby City*.

The inevitable piece in the *Standard*:

BIKE CRASH BRINGS PEACE TO
THE LADY

The war between Rachel Johnson, editor of *The Lady*, and her proprietor Julia Budworth is over, at least for the time being. It's thought the outbreak of peace may have something to do with Julia's son Ben, publisher and chief exec of the mag, falling off his motorbike near Buckingham Palace and breaking his sternum.

'I was knocked off my 650cc Suzuki outside the Queen's Gallery in Buckingham Palace Road,' Ben tells me from St Thomas' Hospital, where he is now out of intensive care. 'A dear lady driver did a U-turn in a people carrier right in front of me. There were six police witnesses. This may be why her insurance company was on the telephone immediately accepting the blame. Maybe the Queen was watching.'

Julia Budworth recently co-edited an issue of *The Lady* featuring her cousin the Duchess of Devonshire.

'Julia has been a pussycat,' says Rachel. 'It's either the duchess or Ben who has brought us together.'

Ben is delighted Rachel and his mum stopped bickering. 'I have no intention of having to go to intensive care every time I want a bit of peace and quiet.'

23 February 2011

I've had a letter framed for the boudoir.

I've propped it next to the picture of me beaming at David Cameron in my tight blue Tory dress while he replies to my tits. When I read it, it reminds me that I've had more nice letters than nasty ones in a year and a half, more good times than bad, and that even at the worst of times, there's no job I'd rather be doing. It's the one letter out of the Santa-sackloads I get that I turn to in times of trouble. Here it is (in slopey, spidery black-ink handwriting):

Dear Editor,

I am 96 years old and I first read *The Lady* in 1936.

To say that you are performing a revolution is mild. The joy it gives me is immense.

Yours faithfully,
Mary Channell de Chanel MBE (Mrs)

I don't believe it! Another email from Maureen!

Hi Everyone,

I have not had a lot of response on the new toilet rolls and kitchen rolls. You all must have used the toilet by now and used some paper!

Awaiting your responses.

Maureen

Right, instead of writing a proper ending for this diary of *The Lady*, a magazine that has, together with its owners, staff and readers, given me untold but not unalloyed joy for a year and a half, I will now have to lay down my pen to prepare a detailed, *Which?*-style dossier on the various toilet-tissue options that have been placed for my sampling in my own private Ladies, with its avocado WC and peach washbasin.

As ever, there is an issue to pass – and the serious and important work of *The Lady* editor must go on.

RACHEL JOHNSON

THE MUMMY DIARIES

Rachel Johnson lives in Notting Hill with her three children, husband and her dog, Coco. This, she sometimes needs to remind herself, is a good thing.

For if the endless succession of school runs, birthday parties (including one for Coco), meal times, shopping trips, skirmishes over undone homework, second-home trials and au pair tribulations doesn't get her, then deciding to keep a diary of her social, school and holiday year probably will. What follows is a hilarious and heartwarming rendition of a year with a not-so-ordinary Notting Hill family trying desperately to live an ordinary life.

'Wonderful! Such joy, such giggles…Johnson writes beautifully and I thank her for cheering me up' Jilly Cooper

'Deliciously complicit…a sprightly footnote to the official history of our strange times' *Sunday Telegraph*

'Johnson's self-deprecating style makes this an irresistible read' *Babyworld*

'Very, very funny…you get the distinct impression Johnson is making up this whole wife/mother thing as she goes along' *Heat*

He just wanted a decent book to read ...

Not too much to ask, is it? It was in 1935 when Allen Lane, Managing Director of Bodley Head Publishers, stood on a platform at Exeter railway station looking for something good to read on his journey back to London. His choice was limited to popular magazines and poor-quality paperbacks – the same choice faced every day by the vast majority of readers, few of whom could afford hardbacks. Lane's disappointment and subsequent anger at the range of books generally available led him to found a company – and change the world.

'We believed in the existence in this country of a vast reading public for intelligent books at a low price, and staked everything on it'
Sir Allen Lane, 1902–1970, founder of Penguin Books

The quality paperback had arrived – and not just in bookshops. Lane was adamant that his Penguins should appear in chain stores and tobacconists, and should cost no more than a packet of cigarettes.

Reading habits (and cigarette prices) have changed since 1935, but Penguin still believes in publishing the best books for everybody to enjoy. We still believe that good design costs no more than bad design, and we still believe that quality books published passionately and responsibly make the world a better place.

So wherever you see the little bird – whether it's on a piece of prize-winning literary fiction or a celebrity autobiography, political tour de force or historical masterpiece, a serial-killer thriller, reference book, world classic or a piece of pure escapism – you can bet that it represents the very best that the genre has to offer.

Whatever you like to read – trust Penguin.